A WYATT
BOOK for
W
ST.
MARTIN'S
PRESS

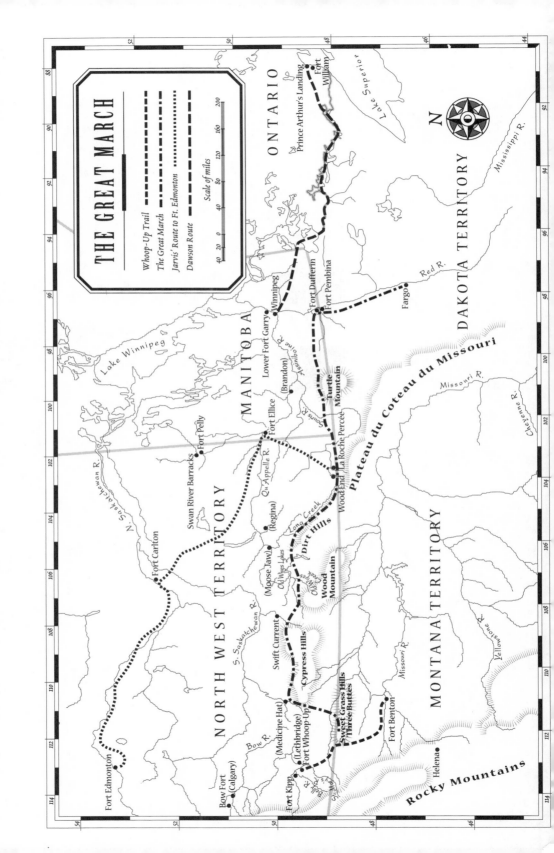

The GREAT ADVENTURE

HOW THE MOUNTIES CONQUERED THE WEST

David Cruise and Alison Griffiths

A Wyatt Book *for* St. Martin's Press ❦ New York

Maps by Molly Brass

Library of Congress Cataloging-in-Publication Data

Cruise, David.
   The great adventure : how the Mounties conquered the West / David
Cruise & Alison Griffiths.
       p.   cm.
   ISBN 0-312-15538-7
   1. West (U.S.)—History—1860–1890.   2. Royal Canadian Mounted
Police—History—19th century.   3. Whiskey industry—West (U.S.)
—History—19th century.   4. Indians of North America—Alcohol use—
West (U.S.)—History—19th century.   I. Griffiths, Alison.
II. Title.
F594.C88   1997
978'.02—dc21   97-5813
                                                                        CIP

First published in Canada by Viking, a division of the Penguin Group

First U.S. Edition: May 1997

10   9   8   7   6   5   4   3   2   1

To our good friends
George and Marguerite Duck

Contents

Photo Credits

Preface

This book has had several incarnations. We intended to write
a complete history of the Royal Canadian Mounted Police,
that venerable institution which has played such an integral
role in our history since 1874. The red-coated Mountie, next
to the flag itself, is the most recognized symbol of Canada.
But, as we delved into the records of the North West Mounted
Police, as the RCMP was first called, a fascinating story
emerged. Then as we researched the early days of the Force,
we became enamoured of the Great March, the largely
unknown nine-hundred-mile, epic trek from Fort Dufferin to
Fort Whoop Up.

The Great Adventure was just that; a swashbuckling, glorious, near-tragic, humorous and often poignant adventure. Its
improbable cast of characters—tenderfeet, remittance men,
teachers, doctors, clerks, ne'er-do-wells and the odd profes-
sional soldier—embarked on an almost impossible mission
122 years ago. With little training and less experience they

signed up to march into the wild frontier and pacify the Indians, stop the whiskey trade, police the Canadian border and bring law to a lawless land. Even Hannibal with his elephants might have quaked at the prospect.

The story of the march west by the North West Mounted Police has largely been dictated by the Force's first commissioner, George A. French, through his diary, reports and dispatches, which were widely circulated at the time. But his version is far from complete. As readers will discover, French had his own agenda and his own reasons for including or omitting certain information. Over time many more diaries have come to light revealing the intensely personal experiences of the young men who wrote them so eloquently. What emerges from their words is an entirely different interpretation of an extraordinary event. We see through their eyes the harsh beauty of the plains. In just a decade everything would change; the buffalo would be gone, the Indians corsetted by treaties and reservations and the country girded by the steel rails of the CPR.

The thirteen diaries and first-hand accounts which form the spine of our story are written by men from vastly different backgrounds. They wrote on horseback, in ox carts and sometimes by candlelight after sixteen hours on the trail. In many cases spelling and punctuation are creative—at best. We have left in errors and other peculiarities except when they hinder comprehension. Many of the guides' and scouts' names are spelled differently, even by the same diarist, so we have tried to eliminate the confusion by standardizing the spelling in our narrative. Additionally, the spelling of many tribes and place names differs widely, and in the text, if not the quotations, we have simply chosen one spelling and stuck to it.

Since the troopers were spread out over many miles during the march and frequently did not camp together, there are often slight disagreements in their accounts. In a few cases we have had to choose one version over another. By and large, however, it is remarkable how closely their stories match.

The dialogue and scenes sprinkled throughout the narrative come from many different sources. Most are direct quotes from diaries or later first-hand accounts. Occasionally we have taken several accounts and amalgamated them into a single story with dialogue. Sometimes diarists have put conversations into their own words and we have rendered them as dialogue. In all cases the characters and events are based on historical fact or impressions from individuals who were there. Historians and researchers will be able to determine the sources from our endnotes.

Working with these diaries and memoirs has been a wonderful experience for us. The difference between secondary and primary sources is a little like the difference between canned and fresh-squeezed orange juice. Through these young men we saw and felt our country's history come to life. After living with these first Mounties for nearly two years, we also began to understand the emerging character of our nation, a few years after Confederation.

And, through the eyes of Jerry Potts, a half-white, half-Indian warrior chief, we were introduced to the soul of another great nation, the Blackfoot Confederacy. Potts was a remarkable character who would have been every bit as famous as Kit Carson or Wild Bill Hickok—if he had been white. Brave, ferocious and unforgiving, yet diplomatic, funny and full of lust for all life offered, there isn't another to match Jerry Potts in the Wild West of either lore or reality.

To many of us, native people are either tragic or cardboard figures. History *is* written by the victors. Certainly the last 200 years of white occupation has produced a simplistic picture of the Plains Indians, which often ignores their individual character and homogenizes a civilization as subtle, sophisticated and contentious as any on earth. That any of them survived the last 200 years is an astonishing accomplishment. The Indians of the Great Plains—the Sioux, Cree, Crow, Blackfoot and Assiniboine among them—have a glorious history which, thanks to their own enduring strength, is re-emerging.

We have attempted to show Indians, half-breeds and Métis as they were then; neither all good, nor all bad—but unique with heroes and villains, like any other population. We have also adhered to the terms of the day—half-breed, squaw, Negro, etc.—though they are now considered offensive by many. Rarely was a distinction made between French and English half-breeds, and the term Métis, though known, was not in common usage.

Similarly, we have attempted to depict the early Mounties as they really were—some weak, some strong, some cowardly and others imbued with the spirit of bravado and heroism that sowed the seeds for their modern-day legend.

Let the adventure begin.

The GREAT ADVENTURE

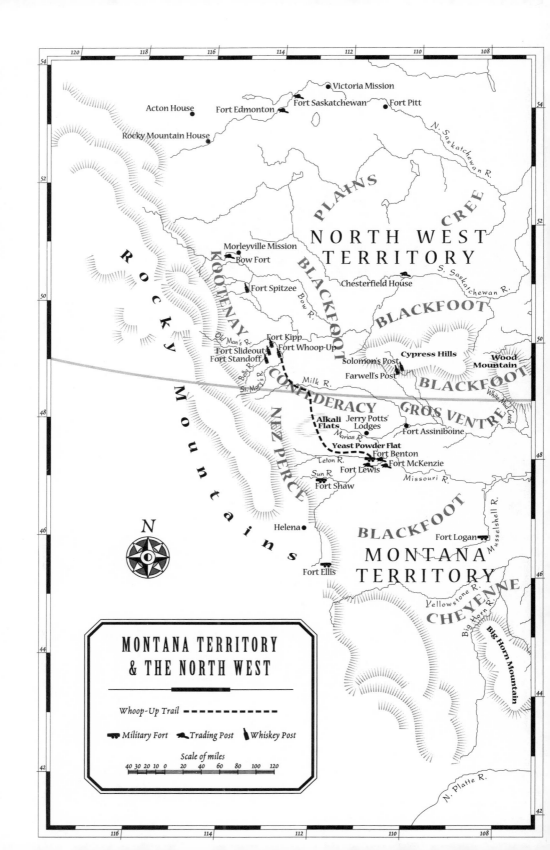

120　118　116　114　112　110　108

54

Victoria Mission

Acton House　Fort Edmonton　Fort Saskatchewan　Fort Pitt

Rocky Mountain House

N. Saskatchewan R.

PLAINS

52

NORTH WEST
TERRITORY

CREE

KOOTENAY

Morleyville Mission
Bow Fort

Chesterfield House

S. Saskatchewan R.

50

BLACKFOOT

Fort Spitzee

Bow R.

BLACKFOOT

ROCKY

Old Man's R.

Fort Kipp
Fort Whoop-Up
Fort Slideout
Fort Standoff

Bull R.

St. Mary's R.

Solomon's Post

Cypress Hills

Wood
Mountain

48

Milk R.

CONFEDERACY

Farwell's Post

BLACKFOOT

White Mud Creek

NEZ PERCE

**Alkali
Flats**　Jerry Potts'
Lodges

GROS VENTRE

Fort Assiniboine

Marias R.

Yeast Powder Flat　Fort Benton
Fort McKenzie

Teton R.　Fort Lewis

Sun R.
Fort Shaw

Missouri R.

M　o　u　n　t　a　i　n　s

46

Helena

BLACKFOOT

Fort Logan

Musselshell R.

MONTANA
TERRITORY

N

Fort Ellis

44

Yellowstone R.

CHEYENNE

Big Horn R.

Big Horn Mountain

MONTANA TERRITORY
& THE NORTH WEST

Whoop-Up Trail - - - - - -

🚚 *Military Fort*　🏠 *Trading Post*　🚩 *Whiskey Post*

Scale of miles
40 30 20 10 0　20　40　60　80　100　120

42

N. Platte R.

116　114　112　110　108

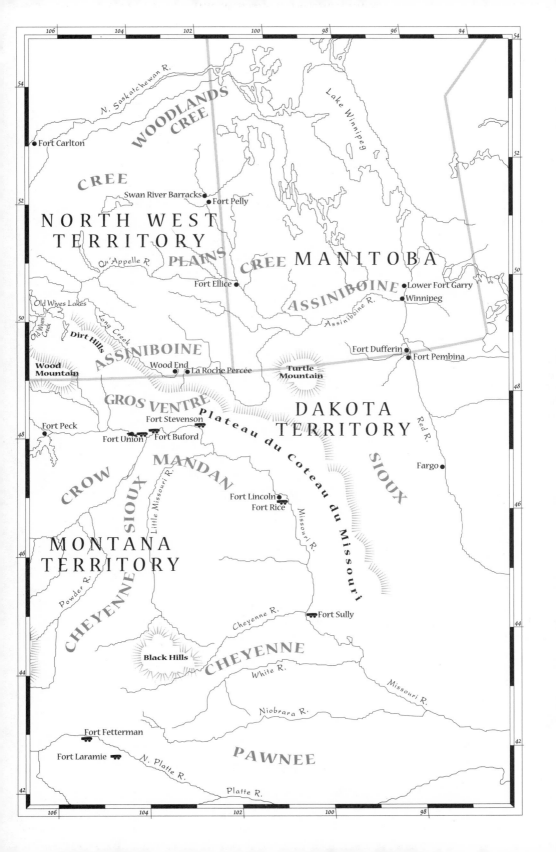

PART ONE

The Adventure Begins

CHAPTER 1

The Adventurers

JEAN D'ARTIGUE, 22, SCHOOLTEACHER

In April, 1874, I was in Montreal, and, one morning opening the [*Daily*]*Witness*, my attention was directed to an advertisement, the substance of which ran as follows:

The Dominion government requires 150 volunteers for the North-West Mounted Police. The knowledge of English or French is obligatory. Moreover, the candidate must have good antecedents, and be a good horseman. For further particulars, apply to Colonel Bacon.

[George] A. French,
Commissioner

Monsieur Jean D'Artigue, of Basses, France, believed he fit the description perfectly. The advertisement said nothing about skill with arms but it stood to reason that if one was joining a police force, one would eventually need to shoot something, or someone. Jean D'Artigue humbly felt that few could hit a *canard* on the wing with his precision. And when it came to horses, his seat was as good as the next man's.

Not only did he speak French and English fluently but, as a schoolteacher, he felt his written work was beyond reproach. As for antecedents, the D'Artigues were a respected old family of the French Pyrénées, somewhat provincial the Parisians might say, but certainly of sufficient standing here in the New World. In short, Jean D'Artigue was a civilized man, precisely the sort needed by a police force charged with conquering an uncivilized land.

Having made the decision to enlist in the North West Mounted Police, the only difficulty D'Artigue faced was determining exactly where in the Dominion of Canada the North West was located.* He vaguely knew of Manitoba and the Red River, where Louis Riel's Métis had created such a fuss in 1869. D'Artigue had never seen a Métis but thought it would be an interesting thing to do.

Beyond those scraps of salon gossip, D'Artigue knew little. Fortunately, one of his Montreal friends who fancied himself an expert on the subject agreed to repair the deficiencies in his knowledge. Though a well-educated Frenchman, impressed only with such refinements as literature, wine and music, D'Artigue couldn't help but be a little awed by the vastness of the North West, as described by his friend. Apparently it stretched from the western edge of the Great Lakes all the way to the Rocky Mountains, which his friend claimed made the Pyrénées look like so many bumps, then south to the American border and north to the mysteries of the polar seas. *Incroyable!*

His friend expounded on the rich bounty of this territory, farmland that surpassed anything known in the civilized world; rivers, lakes and streams bursting with huge, succulent fish, game roaming in unbelievable numbers. And the only people to take advantage of it were a handful of savages who didn't know a good thing when it lay right at their feet.

D'Artigue's friend predicted the land would change dramatically once a ribbon of steel linked the Atlantic and the Pacific and brought in a flood of hardworking immigrants to till and plant and prosper. It was unlikely, he opined, that a single homeless person in the entire world need remain that way once the North West had been tamed. Of course, taming was the problem.

"If everyone knew as much as I do," he advanced modestly on the topic of the new police force, "I doubt that the government would be able to find enough people to fill the positions. No indeed, the government would be forced to recruit from the ignorant in places like the Gold Coast or British Guiana or," he added, "France."

---

* In diaries and historical documents the North West is variously spelled North-West, Northwest, NorthWest and even Norwest. We've chosen to use North West throughout.

"Why is that?" queried D'Artigue indignantly.

His friend rolled his eyes heavenward, then leaned forward conspiratorially.

"Scalps!"

"Scalps?" repeated D'Artigue stupidly.

"Indians will lift them as soon as look at you. Civilized hair is like an aphrodisiac to those poor brutes. They can't help themselves."

Undeterred by the gruesome warning, D'Artigue pumped a little more information out of his friend. Amid lurid details of Indian atrocities, he learned that three divisions, about 150 men, had been recruited the previous fall. They had spent the winter at Lower Fort Garry, a Hudson's Bay Company post twenty miles north of the village of Winnipeg. Three new divisions, another 150 men, would be recruited from the Dominion and trained in Toronto before joining the rest of the Force for the Great Adventure, a nine-hundred-mile march into the heart of the frontier, a whiskey trading post called Fort Whoop Up. Their mission: penetrate Indian territory, stamp out the nefarious liquor traffic and bring law to a lawless land.

> On my way back to my lodgings, I began to ponder on the last words of my friend, the word "scalp" rousing in my mind scenes that I had quite forgotten. In my younger days, the works of Fenimore Cooper, and other novel writers had impressed me with a desire to visit those countries, whose inhabitants could perform such wonderful feats, and I rejoiced that now it was in my power to satisfy my curiosity; all I had to do was enlist in the North-West Mounted Police Force.*

---

* Punctuation in many of these first-hand reports is often erratic. To make comprehension easier we have occasionally added or deleted it. James Fenimore Cooper was an American author who wrote the Leatherstocking Tales—*The Pioneers*, 1823; *The Last of the Mohicans*, 1826; *The Prairie*, 1827; *The Pathfinder*, 1840; and *The Deerslayer*, 1841. These scintillating tales, starring his hero Natty Bumppo and featuring authentic Indian and frontier lore, virtually singlehandedly created the Western novel.

D'Artigue hurried to locate the Colonel Bacon referred to in the *Daily Witness*. Happily, he found him in quarters and offered certificates detailing his age, nationality, character and education. Bacon encouraged him to present himself at the nearby military barracks for examination. D'Artigue dashed to the barracks, where he found a distressingly long line-up of men, every one of them a physical paragon, clutching glowing references from men in the highest reaches of business, politics and the church. Each man D'Artigue tentatively engaged in conversation seemed to be related to a bishop or minor royalty.

His dream evaporated. A Frenchman with credentials written in a foreign language by people thousands of miles away would have little chance. He was gloomily cursing fate when he heard his name called out. His heart thumped, his palms sweated. Would he make it past the next test? To his surprise, it was over quickly. A short-arm inspection from a chilly-handed doctor, a few cursory questions from an officer, *et voilà*, Jean D'Artigue, schoolteacher, became a policeman. He stumbled out the door, a little dazed by his good fortune, barely remembering the instructions to report to the Grand Trunk Railway station in Montreal in a week's time for the trip to Toronto.

> I fancied I saw myself, with some of my comrades riding days and nights together, over the vast plains of the North-West, fighting the Indians and the whiskey traders. I saw settlements destroyed by the red man, the ladies carried away to worse than slavery; husbands and fathers calling upon us to rescue their wives and daughters; ourselves rushing immediately to horse, and over the plains *pêle mêle*, in hot pursuit; and, after a long day's ride, coming upon the Indians at night, when a brief but fierce struggle would ensue and we would rescue the captives, and carry them back in triumph to their desolated homes.

Just before he left, Sub-Constable Jean D'Artigue dropped in on his friend.

"Well, Mr. C., I start the day after tomorrow for Toronto."

"For Toronto?"

"Yes," D'Artigue said smugly. "I have enlisted in the North-West Mounted Police force."

His friend laughed long and hard.

"Tell that to those that don't know you! One doesn't give up an advantageous career like yours, to embrace an adventurous one."

"You don't believe me," sniffed D'Artigue, "come to the railway station tomorrow night, and you will see."

> Seeing that I was in earnest, he then tried to dissuade me from following up my projects; stating, in eloquent and earnest language, the folly of giving up teaching for a life of adventure. I let him talk for an hour without interruption, and I am sure his reasons and arguments were good. But with my Quixotic ideas, and my young imagination of twenty years, I could only see fights, sieges, and victories.

WILLIAM PARKER, 21, FARM LABOURER

> Sarnia, April 5th, 1874
>
> My Dearest Mother
>
> ...And now I have got some news to tell you, your dear old son Willie is a North West Mounted Policeman. I joined the force or was rather examined and selected with twelve others, out of about a hundred & fifty at London, Ont yesterday. Directly I got back from Woodstock I saw the advertisement in the paper & I wrote for information and was told to meet Col French at London yesterday, so I went down Good Friday and stayed all night because there was not an early train Saturday morning.

The sun was barely up when Parker walked into Tecumseh House, the hotel where Colonel George A. French was staying.*

---

* George A. French was the commissioner of the North West Mounted Police and his official title was Commissioner French. However, colonel was his rank in the British Army and the men and officers under him usually referred to him as the Colonel.

He buttonholed a waiter and asked how he could get a few minutes of the Colonel's time. The waiter parked him on a chair outside the dining room with a good vantage point. When French came down for breakfast, Parker's supplicating look caught the Colonel's attention. The waiter sidled up and told him the lad was a potential recruit.

"Did he say he could ride?" demanded French.

"Oh yes sir, I understand that young boy can ride anything with hair on it."

"Send him to the recruiting room."

Parker leapt from his chair and all but ran to the recruiting room, where he stopped short. One hundred and fifty men, with thighs like sides of beef and arms the size of trees, milled about, towering above him. No chance for a slightly built youngster who looked as if a mild breeze might topple him over. But when his turn came, Parker easily answered all the Colonel's questions and was beginning to feel quite optimistic.

"Let me see your character, young man."

Parker's hand flew to his pocket. His face blanched.

"Oh sir, I've forgotten it!" he stammered. "I have one, sir. A very good one, from the Bishop of Dover! But I've left it in Sarnia."

"Who is your nearest relative in this country?"

"My cousin, sir. Alfred, sir...Alfred Barber in Sarnia."

The Colonel thoughtfully twisted the carefully waxed ends of his luxuriant moustache.

"I'm looking for good men. So far you appear to have what I want but I absolutely must have your character," he emphasized, pulling out his pocket watch and staring pointedly at it. "I'll give you two hours to get one from this cousin."

A lucky break: Tecumseh House had a telegraph office where Parker wired his cousin, then fretted for an hour and three-quarters waiting for the answer. When the telegram arrived, the operator scanned it with considerable amusement, carefully sealed it and then informed Parker it could be read only by the addressee, Colonel French.

Parker raced to the recruiting room, telegram in hand. No pugilist could have been more aggressive than Willie Parker in the next few seconds. As he struggled through the crowd of hopefuls, his toes were stomped on, his ribs elbowed and all the buttons of his pea coat ripped off.

Colonel French checked his watch and opened the telegram. His impassive features relaxed slightly and a trace of a smile crept across his face. "I have known William Parker ever since he was a kid. He has been well brought up, and he is a beggar on the fight, and a good judge of whiskey." French glanced at Parker, back to the telegram, and then to Parker again, this time with his sternness recaptured.

"I will give you a note to the doctor, and if you pass I will accept you."

Unaware of the telegram's contents, Parker bounced out of the room and flagged a hansom, urging the cabbie to drive as if the devil were nipping at his heels. After eighteen years of living quietly in the village of New Romney, Kent, and three years of farming in Woodstock, Ontario, Willie Parker was ready for a change. He fancied becoming a gentleman farmer one day, but for now he hungered for excitement.

Arrived at the Doctors, he told me to peel off and he examined me thoroughly measured my calves & chest, arms and your dear old boy turned out to be perfectly sound after knocking about Canada for three years. I go to Toronto to join on the 9th of this month, that is next Thursday. I am not sure when we shall go up to Manitoba, I rather think that we shall remain in Toronto some little time first.

Everybody around here thinks it is a splendid thing for a young man to go into, the pay is very good for constables a dollar a day & Sub-Constables seventy five cents a day and everything found, travelling expenses paid, a bully good horse to ride upon, and if I serve three years I shall get a grant of one hundred & sixty acres of land, but this is where the tug of war comes in.

I thought to have been home this coming autumn and see all you dear ones but Providence has willed it otherwise, so we shall have to bear it the best way we can. It is most probably that we shall not be wanted three years and if we are not we shall get the grant all the same. I shall also be able to save a good pile of money, and now if you come to look over the thing, it is a very good opening for me.

Give my best love to Dear Father and I hope he will approve of it, there is only a hundred & fifty of us & they are all you might say the picked young men of Canada as the Colonel was very strict, a hundred & fifty applied at Hamilton and he only took fifteen out of that large number. The Col is a very nice man and if I behave myself properly I daresay he will push me on.

So you see it is all for the best Dear Mother....

Believe me

Ever your affectionate son

W. Parker

FREDERICK AUGUSTUS BAGLEY, 15, ADVENTURER

Fred Bagley dreamed of roaming the vast, unknowable territory west of the Great Lakes. There he'd find none of the suffocating fustiness of Upper Canadian society, no rigid conventions, just life as it was meant to be lived, by wits and guile. It was, Fred Bagley knew, the life he was meant to live.

In April 1874 his heart soared when he spotted a few lines in a local newspaper announcing a second recruiting drive for the North West Mounted Police. Enlistment became his obsession.

I had always been a close student of the works of James Fenimore Cooper, and imagined that life in the N.W.M.P. would be one grand round of riding wild mustangs (I was always an expert horseman), chasing whisky traders and horse thieves, potting hostile savages, and hobnobbing with haughty Indian Princes and lovely unsophisticated Princesses.

Bagley knew his father would forbid enlistment. As for his mother, he didn't even want to think about her reaction. But he couldn't contain himself.

...I, imbued with the romance and enthusiasm of callow youth, hied me to the "New" Fort in Toronto where the newly raised troops were gathered preparatory to leaving for the Great West, my object being to enlist for service in that wild and woolly section of Canada.

But before becoming a member of that Force...my father had to be reckoned with. He and Colonel French, the Commissioner of the Force, had been old comrades in the Imperial Army, and so my Dad was promptly informed of my criminal intent.

Then followed a serious confab between the two the result of which was that my father, in view of my determination (stupid stubbornness he called it), consented to let me go as Trumpeter for not more than six months.

Before enlistment, a complete medical was necessary. A doctor briefly peered, poked, probed and eyed Bagley's thin, underage frame with scepticism.

"How old are ye, son?"

"Eighteen, sir."

"Ay. And I'm the Queen of England. Off with you then." The doctor turned to his medical log and wrote, "Very youthful but may develope."

Back home, Bagley packed his kitbag and prepared to leave for Toronto and several weeks of training. His father imparted some titbits of knowledge gleaned from his years in the Imperial Army. He'd seen men in the dark countries lured into indiscretions by the savages. The frontier, he cautioned, was unlikely to be different. Bagley Sr. impressed upon his son what happened to a man's personal equipment when he succumbed to temptation; the volcanic sores, the immense swelling, not to mention the excruciating agony of trying to pass urine when pus and infection plugged the channel.

"You don't want to have to carry yourself around with a wheelbarrow," emphasized his father. No matter how tempting and available the "squaw," he warned, keep it in your pants.

HENRI JULIEN, 21, ILLUSTRATOR

In early June 1874, a letter arrived at the Montreal offices of the *Canadian Illustrated News*. Addressed to the manager, the letter, penned by Colonel French, invited a reporter/artist to accompany the Mounted Police expedition, which would travel through some of the wildest terrain known to mankind to the foot of the Rocky Mountains.

The terms were appealing to a struggling publication trying to establish itself; free passage by boat and rail from Toronto to Duluth and then to Fargo, North Dakota, on the Red River, where the police would mount up and ride north to join the men recruited in 1873 for the great march west. The government would also provide a good horse, full kit and all the benefits and comforts of an officer—a personal servant, private tent and special rations. Aside from the adventure there would be unlimited opportunity for sketching, exploring and hunting. In other words, complete freedom to do as one wished.

Opportunities like that didn't pop up very often. The manager liked the idea immediately and showed the letter to his editor, who also salivated at the prospect. He wanted to go himself, but family responsibilities made it impossible on such short notice. Who to send? The best choice would be a young, unmarried man with a little adventure in his soul.

Henri Julien, perched on his stool in front of a window, was finishing a sketch of a recent lacrosse match.

I had just been giving the finishing touches to the figure of a tall, gawkish fellow, running across the field in hot pursuit of the ball. His weapon was brandished aloft, one leg high in the air and—

"Well."

"Well, sir."

"Want to go to the North West?"

"To the North West?"

"With the Mounted Police. Here's a letter from Col. French. Asks an artist to go. Not a bad idea. Think it'll do. What do *you* say?"

As I did not understand what it all meant, I did not say anything. But probably looks betrayed no unwillingness, for the manager immediately subjoined:

"Will you go?"

"I don't care if I do."

"You'll have to ride hundreds of miles bareback."

"Yes."

"You'll have to eat pemmican for months."

"Yes."

"You'll perish of thirst in the desert sometimes."

"Yes."

"You may get scalped."

"Yes."

"You may get lost and devoured by bears."

"Yes."

If the manager thought to frighten me by these pictures, he was mistaken. The stronger he put it, the more I liked it, and by the time he got through, whatever little misgivings I may have had entirely disappeared, and the expedition spread before me as glorious fun. So when the manager repeated his question:

"Will you go?"—I jumped from my seat, gave my trousers a good shake and answered promptly:

"Yes."

I made instant preparations for the journey. I left my studio... My running lacrosseman gave me a suppliant look, as if he asked me to let down that lifted leg of his. But I did not mind him. He must balance on the other leg for the next six months. If he doesn't, he will fall and break his nose.

The NWMP Goes to School

No person shall be appointed to the Police Force unless he be of sound constitution, active and able bodied, able to ride, of good character, able to read and write either the English or French language, and between the ages of 18 and 40 years.

North West Mounted Police Act, passed May 20, 1873

That was the theory. Reality, however, was different—with eight weeks to recruit, assemble and train 150 men, much had to be taken on faith. There was no time to check a recruit's

references to find out if they even knew the person they so lav-
ishly praised, or to confirm claims of military experience and
expertise with gun and horse—all rather crucial to the success
of the enterprise. "According to the Act, all men should have
been able to ride; but when put to the test, it was evident that
a good many rated their abilities in this line too highly,"
Colonel French later complained to the minister of justice.

"Too highly" didn't begin to tell the story. Barely 25 percent
of the former clerks, schoolteachers, farmers and coopers rode
with anything remotely approaching authority. A good half of
the men had never sat on a horse, much less ridden one. In the
saddle the newly mounted sat like sacks of flour from the buttocks up, but as rigid as rail ties from the buttocks down.
They handled the reins as gingerly as one might shake the
hand of a lady. The delighted horses promptly took the bit
between their teeth and did whatever they wanted, their masters impotently shouting whoa, giddy up or whatever phrase
they had learned from five-penny Westerns.

When Jean D'Artigue arrived at the New Fort barracks in
Toronto, thirty men were already there and training was under
way.

"Make yourselves comfortable," said one of the sub-constables, showing the new arrivals into a cavernous room.

"And how would we do that?" D'Artigue asked, staring
around the bleak room. "There's no furniture here."

"There's a table. What more do you want?"

"A bed would be nice. And perhaps a chair."

The sub-constable, superior to D'Artigue by virtue of his
additional few days in the Force, took pleasure in jolting him
into his new life.

"Your bed is coming. In fact, you'll get it yourself," he said,
pointing to the store-room.

D'Artigue claimed his mattress, which turned out to be a
bag, inadequately filled with straw, two blankets rough
enough to make an elephant itch, and no pillow. At that
moment he had a tiny niggling doubt. Had he made a mistake? Despite the official notice posted on the door of their
quarters reminding them that they were civilians, not soldiers,
this alarmingly resembled military life.

It wasn't the first time D'Artigue had wondered how well

he'd fit in—doubts had assailed him on the train from Montreal to Toronto.

In the car, sitting opposite me, was a traveller, apparently about thirty years of age, whose dress would indicate the clergyman: long black coat, waistcoat buttoned to the chin, straight collar, and broad brimmed hat; and yet, his piercing eye, his moustache à l'impériale, and his martial appearance, told me that I was facing a soldier.

Feeling somewhat lonely, and in order to make the time pass quickly, I entered into conversation with my neighbour by asking him in a true Yankee style: "Where are you going sir?"

"To Toronto," said he, "to join the North-West Mounted Police,—a military corps, organised for the purpose of putting an end to the liquor traffic in that country. I am an apostle of temperance, sir, my whole life is consecrated to that cause."

If all the members of the force are like this one, thought I, the whiskey traders will do well to decamp before our arrival. For my part, being accustomed to, and fond of, good wine, I did not share the opinions of my fellow traveller, who went on discussing the injurious effects of alcohol, and condemning even our best French wines.

This was too much for D'Artigue. It was one thing to advocate temperance, but another to cast aspersions on French wine. D'Artigue was on the verge of an indignant retort when three rough-looking men barged into the compartment.

"I don't think there is anyone here for the Mounted Police," one said dismissively after looking around.

"Here is one," the Apostle announced. "And one that will count."

He immediately launched into a sermon denouncing alcohol, emphasizing his intent to make the West a dry and moral place to live. The three men stood mutely through the lecture. When the Apostle ran out of steam, one of them pulled out a bottle.

"Hold on, old fellow. Here is the kind of beverage that would be of service to us in the coming expedition. Have a swig—you must be dry after so long a speech."

The Apostle recoiled. "Is it possible that you expect with vice to correct vice?"

The men nodded eagerly. This was exactly what they thought. Disgusted, the Apostle returned quickly to his seat opposite D'Artigue, who tried to convey, with a sharp look, that he wouldn't stand for any more attacks on French wine. He was relieved to see that at least three of his fellow recruits had a healthy regard for drink but, if the Apostle was more representative of the kind of man attracted to the Mounted Police, the three years of service he'd signed up for would seem like eternity.

D'Artigue needn't have worried. Rather than a haven for the temperance movement, the Mounted Police proved to be an enclave of two-fisted drinkers who frowned upon over-eager whiskey hunting and became positively ill at the idea of pouring confiscated whiskey onto the ground.

D'Artigue soon discovered that the Apostle of Temperance was far from being the only peculiar individual attracted to the Force. A few weeks later, en route by train to Fargo, North Dakota, with the rest of the police, he noticed a melancholy and taciturn young man sitting by himself. D'Artigue never let an opportunity slip by to learn more about his fellow recruits.

> ...and wishing to know the reasons that induced such a man to enlist in the Mounted Police corps, I went over to him and addressed him in the following and familiar style; "comrade, what do you think of this beautiful country? I never saw anything like it."
>
> "Do you really think so?" said he, staring at me in surprise.
>
> "Why," said I, "look at these beautiful gardens and parterres, really it is an Eden!"
>
> "What you wonder at and admire, I detest," said he, "I would not for worlds live in this country that you seem to think without an equal; for under the appearance of rich fields and beautiful houses, are hidden vices which undermine every society. The country I cherish, is one that would show no vestige of civilisation."
>
> "Such a land," I replied, "you will find in the North-

West Territories, and yet, if we succeed in restoring peace and order in that part of the world, civilisation will soon reach it."

"I hope not," said he, "but to avoid it reaching *me*, I intend, as soon as we reach Manitoba, to ask for my discharge, when I will marry an Indian woman, and settle down in a region entirely savage."

"I see you are not only a countryman of the Swiss philosopher, Jean Jacques Rousseau," said I, "but also his disciple. As he did, you think the uncivilised man is, in many respects, superior to the civilised, and admitting for argument's sake that it is, don't you see that in a few years those wild North-West Territories will be settled by colonists?"

"If that should happen," said he, "I will shift my quarters farther, even to the midst of the Rocky Mountains, if necessary; and now that you know my projects, keep them to yourself."

Once settled into their spartan quarters in the New Fort barracks, the recruits faced drills, drills and more drills. D'Artigue got through the initial foot exercises without stumbling too often, acquiring a crop of blisters or otherwise drawing attention to himself as a tenderfoot. But then to horse.

First came manège, a drill where the men rode without stirrups, and often without reins, to improve their balance and efficiency in directing the horses using only their legs. The sergeant-major called out, "Trot on!" and within minutes the drill ring rained bodies.* "Who the hell told you to dismount,

---

* The Act creating the Mounted Police stipulated an equivalent military title to assigned mounted police ranks: commissioner = lieutenant-colonel, superintendent/inspector = captain, superintendent/sub-inspector = lieutenant, paymaster = captain, veterinary surgeon = lieutenant. But the officers often preferred the more imposing-sounding military titles, creating considerable confusion about rank. To complicate matters, some officers, Major James Walsh for example, retained their militia rank, even though it was higher than they were entitled to in the Mountie hierarchy. On the other hand, James Macleod, even though he was assistant commissioner, was usually referred to as Major, a lower rank than he was entitled to.

sir?" bellowed the RRSM (rough-riding sergeant-major) at one unfortunate who left his horse by vaulting over the animal's head. The men clung frantically to their mounts, sideways, upside down, legs and arms scrabbling for purchase. The drill instructor waited just long enough for the victims to heave themselves upright, then cracked his whip. He smiled as the horses bucked themselves free of their troublesome loads and galloped off to the stables. The recruits, covered in sawdust, dragged themselves to their feet and limped after them.

Fred Bagley chafed at riding lessons, being one of the few who hadn't overstated his skill. But when he could escape from his various duties, he sneaked back to the drill ring to watch the other troopers being put through their paces. As high entertainment it had no equal.

"Blimey! Look at 'im a-flapping of 'is wings!" one of the regular audience observed, marvelling at the energy one recruit put into staying upright. "Hi there!" the onlooker called out. "Open the bloomin' windows, and let the blighter fly out!"

The most laughter was reserved for the Professor, as he was quickly dubbed. Jean D'Artigue was one of those guilty of inflating his riding ability. His seat might have been fine for a gentle ramble about the countryside, but hopelessly inadequate for military-style drilling. He spent most of his time draped octopus-like over his horse. "That's right, young fellow me lad!" roared the sergeant-major as the Professor attempted to post with the trot and ended up nose deep in mane. "Kiss 'im and 'e'll be good to you!"

D'Artigue took consolation from the fact that his superiors were hardly superior, at least when it came to horses. "Even the officers were most of them as bad as ourselves at riding, but managed by some means, unknown to us, to get out of the manège drill, and went only to the field drill, where stirrups were allowed to be used."

Bareback riding, romantic in novels, proved even more

Similarly, the non-commissioned officers preferred military nomenclature. The seven chief constables were all known as sergeant-majors, while the fifty-odd acting and full constables were called sergeants. Sub-constables, equivalent to privates, were about the only ones who referred to themselves by their proper NWMP rank.

painful than manège. The men argued that they had no intention of charging around bareback, so why add more bruises to their tender parts in the unavoidable clash of their anatomy with the amazingly sharp backbones of their mounts?

North West Mounted Police
New Fort
Toronto
April 15/74

My Dear Father

I expect you were surprised when Mama received my letter from Sarnia, informing you how I came to join the Mounted Police. I arrived here last Friday evening, and like the life very well so far, all the men & horses have not arrived yet, but will do so in a few days, there are about hundred & twelve men and seventy horses here now.

I was out for my first ride to day and got on very well, the saddles have not all arrived yet so we had to ride bare back, some of the fellows are sent spinning over the horses heads, they are a splendid lot of horses & very frisky the stables are also very good.

We have splendid rooms to sleep in, the size of rooms 40 x 30, twelve men in each, there are quite a lot of decent young fellows joined and a good many of them are from England, two are from Kent. I am very fond of drilling in fact I was told that I had got on capitally for one that had never been drilled before.

At half past six we have to fall in ·& are marched to the stables, clean & feed the horses & finish them up, fall in again, marched back in front of our rooms & dismissed for breakfast at eight o'clock. At nine there is a general parade to drill, dismissed at half past ten, parade again at eleven for riding exercise, dinner at one & fall in for drill at two, & again at five for the stables, tea at six and can go down town from six to ten so you see we have not bad times at all....

Believe me
Ever your affectionate son
W. Parker

Willie Parker's enthusiasm was the exception among the drill-weary recruits in Toronto, who had no idea how lucky they really were. The weather was warm, the sawdust soft and the food plentiful. The men also had civilized horses, purchased by Colonel French from stables in Ontario.

The first contingent of 150 recruits, now in Manitoba, had endured an eight-month nightmare. They had been even more hastily assembled than the second group, with a scant five weeks from swearing in the first nine officers on September 25, 1873, to the recruitment of men and their arrival at Lower Fort Garry. Only nine of them had any military experience; the rest were a motley collection of students, gardeners and thrill seekers such as James T. Fullerton. "My friends who wanted me in the cricket club tried to dissuade me from joining, but the great adventure was too big an attraction to miss."

The trip from Toronto to Manitoba was nothing short of awful. The men were violently sick during the crossing of Lake Superior and when they disembarked at Prince Arthur's Landing (near Thunder Bay), the officers in charge were horrified to discover that the Dawson Route, the primitive water and land track to Winnipeg, "more suitable for aquatic animals than for human beings," was in such vile condition most supplies had been removed, tugs and steamboats abandoned and many of the stations and shelters along the way shut down.

Because everything had been done in such a hurry, the provisions thrown together for the men were meagre at best.

JAMES T. FULLERTON

We did have one good feed. The officers had several boxes of beef for their personal use. One dark night we reached a portage and, in unloading the canoe, by some "accident" those boxes were broken. Bivouac fires that night gave off delightful aroma of roasting beefsteaks....

Another very serious mishap came about that no one could understand. The officers had a 20-gallon keg of fine whiskey, presumably for use as medicine. Somehow that whiskey turned to water in the keg.

It was an unseasonably cold October. The men arrived at Lower Fort Garry minus most of their equipment and provisions, which, after a heavy rain, had frozen so solidly into the ground that no amount of hacking and pulling could dislodge them. During their last few nights one group of men slept in the open during a snowstorm because they couldn't unfold their frozen tents. All looked forward to some warmth and comfort after their ordeal but that was not to be. An appallingly cold winter settled in at the end of November and the mercury barely nudged above -30°F for months on end.

Since their winter clothing had been left on the Dawson Route, the men scrounged a ragtag assortment of cast-offs from the militia, the Hudson's Bay Company and the Boundary Commission.* Saddles were cracked, stirrups bent, guns rusty and blankets mouldy. For beds, the men made do with wooden pallets set on the frosty floor and piled themselves with buffalo robes in a failed attempt to keep warm. The stove in the barracks smoked so badly, the scant heat it gave off was hardly worth the bother.

> To the Editor
> Toronto Globe
> I'd as soon be in a penitentiary as in this corps. Our clothes are too large for us and they are made of very inferior cloth...thus far we have been treated more like brutes than men. We have to run like fury in an inclosure with horses that have never had a bridle on them before, some of them just taken off the prairies and lassooed before they could be captured. I'd give six months' salary to be home once more. We rise at 6 a.m. and go to bed at 9:30 p.m. We get dry bread and bad coffee for breakfast,

---

* The International Boundary Commission, a joint venture of British, Canadian and American surveyors, geographers and engineers, mapped out and marked the 49th parallel from Lake of the Woods to the Pacific between 1872 and 1876. The Canadian contingent was headquartered at Fort Dufferin, south of Winnipeg.

boiled meat and worse potatoes for dinner and real bad
tea and dry bread for supper—such grub!

Anonymous

Every morning sergeants roused the shivering recruits.
"Show a leg, boys! On the jump!" Standing orders were to
drill the men daily, except Sunday, unless the thermometer fell
below -36° F. Temperature became an obsession. Every micro-
scopic movement of the mercury was hailed with cheers if it
fell below -36 and kept them in quarters, or jeers if it crept
above and forced them into the frozen drill ring.

Sam Steele was in charge of breaking the horses and instructing the non-commissioned officers and recruits in riding drill.
Though Steele was only twenty-two, the new commissioner,
Colonel French, desperate for a man who knew horses and had
real military training, had made him a sergeant-major, ahead of
many older men. At nineteen, Steele had been a member of
Colonel Garnet Wolseley's 1870 expedition to the Red River to
squash the Riel insurgents. By 1873, he had become a sergeant
in the Kingston artillery under Colonel French.

Samuel Benfield Steele also had the right "antecedents."
Born in Simcoe County, Ontario, he came from a long line of
British sailors and soldiers, all of them officers and gentlemen.
His ancestors specialized in extricating themselves from spectacular scrapes and turning blunders into honour-laden victo-
ries. His father, Elmes Steele, capped his distinguished service
in the Royal Navy with an escapade that would have cost
most men their careers. In the early 1790s, while Steele Sr. was
the master's mate of H.M.S. *Caroline*, they captured the
French vessel *La Bonne Mère*.

Elmes Steele was put on board as prize captain. His poor
supervision allowed the crew to break into the brandy stores
and while they were happily occupied, the French retook the
ship. When they were forced to call on Steele to help them
navigate the unfamiliar waters, he gave them false bearings. In
the resulting confusion, Steele released the now sober crew
and recaptured the ship.

On the surface, Sam Steele was a Herculean man with large
appetites and extraordinary strength. Tales of his prowess
always included statements such as "he did the work of two

men" and "strong as an ox." But there was a pensive, intellectual side to him that few ever saw. Alone among the officers and men at Lower Fort Garry that miserable winter, Steele took time to consult French and English half-breeds about the conditions they would find out west and made copious notes to share with his superiors. And in his rare moments of leisure he sketched wild flowers and animals.

Nor did Steele's adventuring, man's man reputation fit his looks. Though broad-shouldered, his body was slender, almost delicate, and his vaguely effeminate face and round, dark eyes, pulled down at the corners, spoke of a softer nature inside than outside. The recruits whispered that Steele wore a sash wrapped around his waist to thicken his torso and make him appear more physically intimidating. Steele put an end to such talk by pole-axing the largest man in the troop with his carbine.

Sam Steele wore his manhood like a badge of honour but pushed himself as if it were on loan and might be revoked at any time. He would drink heartily and kick up his heels with the best of them but be up the next morning long before dawn to break a string of unruly mustangs, drill an entire division, shoot enough game to feed them, discipline the ne'er-do-wells and finish off with a lengthy report of the day's activities.

But even Sergeant-Major Sam Steele admitted that the winter of 1873–74 took hardship to new levels. "Our work was unceasing from 6 a.m. until after dark. I drilled five rides per day the whole of the winter in an open *manège*... With very few exceptions the horses were broncos which had never been handled, and none but the most powerful and skilful dared attempt to deal with them. Even when we had them 'gentled' so as to let recruits mount, the men were repeatedly thrown with great violence to the frozen ground..."

Smoothbore Sam, as the men dubbed him, never talked when he could bellow and never stroked when he could kick. "Drill, drill, drill," grumbled one recruit. "Foot drill, rifle practice, guard mount, horseback, all the fatigues. Breaking in my new mount isn't my idea of fun. Especially with Steele drilling. The man has no feelings."

Whether it was the first contingent in Lower Fort Garry or the second in Toronto, grousing became a favourite pastime. But there was one recruit blessed with a sunny disposition who could always be counted on to see the silver lining, no matter what the circumstance.

New Fort
Toronto
June 3rd/74

My Dearest Father

Last Monday I went down town & had my photograph taken in my uniform, and am afraid they will not be done in time for me to send one in this letter, but will send one in my next which I expect will be from Manitoba. I rather expect we shall have a pretty good time at Red River, we shall camp out in tents on the prairies all summer & back to Fort Garry in the winter. There is most splendid shooting up there and I am taking my gun up with me, which I hope will do good execution amongst the prairie chickens, and from what I hear there is magnificent fishing so we ought to live well.

I still like the life very much, we live very well. I am very fat & strong [&] have played in two cricket matches since we have been here. I will enclose the score of the first match, the second we did not finish. We are going to take up a lot of cricketing things with us so that we can still keep up the old game although we shall be a good way from our friends....

Believe me
Ever your affectionate son
Willie Parker

The Colonel

Colonel George A. French had been appointed commissioner of the North West Mounted Police on October 18, 1873. His first few weeks on the job were among the worst of his life. The officers and men of the first contingent had already left for Lower Fort Garry, leaving him nothing to command. In

Ottawa he had no headquarters, no staff, no office, no administrative structure, no policies or guidelines—he didn't even have an orderly to write his letters.

Trying to accomplish anything in Ottawa in October 1873 was like wading through custard. The entire city was alternately paralysed and frenetic with the government crisis, brought about by allegations that railway tycoon Sir Hugh Allan had corrupted Sir John A Macdonald's successful 1872 re-election campaign with $365,000 in bribes, in return for the charter to build a transcontinental railway. Ottawa crackled and heaved as political alliances were broken and formed anew. The King was toppling; no one was interested in the picayune problems of the freshly minted commissioner of the North West Mounted Police.

French had trouble finding the decision makers within the government, let alone convincing them to make a decision. Sir John A. Macdonald, both prime minister and minister of justice, had simply disappeared—assumed drunk. His heavy drinking during times of stress was legendary in the capital—those close to him worried that the fall of 1873 might be a repeat of 1867, when his binges had delayed, and at times threatened, Confederation negotiations. Hewitt Bernard,

deputy minister of justice, was directly responsible for the new mounted police force. While sympathetic to French's urgent concerns, he was desperately trying to put out political fires all over Ottawa and shore up support for his brother-in-law, the prime minister. In any case, Bernard basically operated the Mounted Police out of a desk drawer—just a small problem among the many responsibilities of the justice ministry.

What French had been able to discover about the Force's

Colonel George A. French

readiness was dismaying. Basic supplies such as clothing, guns and ammunition hadn't been ordered, nor had tenders been put out for food, cattle, horses, wagons, harnesses and tents. He didn't personally know the officers already chosen and he feared that Sir John A. Macdonald's proclivity to slip family, friends and Conservative Party members into any job remotely connected to the government might have infected the Force as well.* It was one thing to be cursed with the ineffectual in the comfortable and safe confines of Ottawa—quite another to depend on such people 1,500 miles from civilization.

On November 5, 1873, Sir John A. Macdonald, grey and shaking with the after-effects of a long drinking bout, rose in the House of Commons to resign. Hewitt Bernard, feeling the new prime minister, Alexander Mackenzie, would soon replace him, was reluctant to make further decisions about the Force. French couldn't bear the inaction any longer. He left Ottawa for Lower Fort Garry on December 1. At least there he would be among his command and away from the political mire.

George Arthur French had coveted the job of commissioner of the North West Mounted Police. It represented an excellent career move, exactly what he needed to vault him into the upper echelons of the British military. To date his service record was exemplary but dull. He had attained the rank of lieutenant-colonel from his command of the artillery battery in Kingston, Ontario, and held the title of Inspector of Artillery and Warlike Stores for the Canadian Militia—impressive-sounding appointments, but basically desk jobs. French had high aspirations for the future but it was hard for an officer, no matter how well connected, to advance without a war record or a battlefield command.

Born in 1841 in Roscommon, Ireland, French had excellent ancestral military credentials and the right familial political

---

* It is impossible to know the full extent of patronage appointments in the recruiting of the first contingent but there are signs that Colonel French had good reason to be concerned. Of the nine officers appointed on September 25, 1873, three had direct ties to Macdonald. Dalrymple Clark, the quartermaster and paymaster, was Sir John's young nephew. William Drummer Jarvis, an inspector, was Hewitt Bernard's nephew; and Charles F. Young was connected with the Conservative Party.

connections to move him swiftly through Her Majesty's service. He attended Sandhurst and Woolwich military colleges and joined the Royal Artillery as a lieutenant, distinguishing himself as a marksman and horseman. He came to Canada with the Royal Artillery detachment posted at Kingston, Ontario. In 1871, when the British Army withdrew from Canada, French was seconded to the Canadian Militia as a lieutenant-colonel and assigned to organize the School of Gunnery. Commanding the North West Mounted Police was the perfect next step.

Sir John A. Macdonald envisioned a mounted police force in 1869 to secure Rupert's Land, the territory he was negotiating to purchase from the Hudson Bay Company.* According to the explorer John Palliser, who surveyed the area in 1857, much of it comprised a massive desert populated by, among others, the ferociously territorial Blackfoot. The rest, approximately thirty thousand Indians of many different tribes, French, Métis half-breeds and a scattering of whites, were constantly squabbling—if the reports from missionaries and fur traders were to be believed.

The United States had gobbled up Texas from the Spanish, Louisiana from the French and Washington and Oregon from the British. And Sir John feared they had an appetite for more. "I would be quite willing, personally, to leave the whole country a wilderness for the next half-century, but I fear that if Englishmen do not go there Yankees will." In 1869 U.S. Congressman Ignatius Donnelly, the so-called "Voice of Minnesota," advocated a Texas-style absorption of the Red River lands in British territory using the Métis. "If the revolutionists of Red River are encouraged and sustained by the avowed sympathy of the American people," he orated, "we may within a few years, perhaps months, see the Stars and Stripes wave from Fort Garry."

The Mounted Police were conceived in Sir John's fertile mind but, true to his nickname "Old Tomorrow," he procrastinated. Consequently, late in 1869 when the first Red River uprising

---

* The agreement was signed in March 1869. Rupert's Land, part of which became the province of Manitoba a year later, was purchased for £300,000.

flared, there was no force stationed in the West to deal with it. Macdonald hurriedly flung together a 1,200-man expeditionary force drawn from the Imperial Army and two newly created Canadian rifle battalions. They went west in the summer of 1870 under the command of Colonel Garnet Wolseley.

The United States formally acknowledged Canada's existence as a nation in the 1871 Treaty of Washington, allaying fears of Yankee expansionism, but pressure was building on Macdonald from another front. That year he enticed British Columbia into Confederation with the promise of a railway spanning the continent. But a railroad meant settlers and if the American experience was anything to go by, settlers meant conflict with the "wild people," as Sir John quaintly called them. An Indian war wouldn't go down well in England, where Macdonald was hoping to find not only settlers but investors to make the railway scheme a reality.

Sir John cared little, and knew less, about his new acquisition, beyond the fact that it linked the rest of Canada with British Columbia. His original plan for a mounted force was an egalitarian mix of "Pure whites & British & French Half-Breeds" but since all three groups hated one another with varying degrees of intensity, as the Red River uprising so abundantly demonstrated, he shelved the idea.

Macdonald thought of the mounted force as a small, mobile squad of fifty men that could be quickly and easily sent into hot spots at a moment's notice. An ardent reader of five-penny Westerns, Sir John loved to lie in bed, drinking port and following the exploits of highly fictional and romantic heroes of the wild frontier. In those stories it was nothing for a single white man to subdue dozens of Indians, often with little more than a steely look. But in the real world, relying on a fifty-man force to police the entire North West, a territory as big as Europe, was a little like going on a bear hunt with a switch.

While Old Tomorrow procrastinated, reports of impending catastrophe piled up. In 1870 Adams Archibald, then lieutenant-governor of the newly created province of Manitoba and the North West, commissioned a remarkable man with the gift of observation to report on conditions west of Winnipeg. Captain William Francis Butler, travelling three thousand miles in 119 days, most of it during the dead of winter, brought back an appalling tale of Indians decimated by smallpox and victimized by whiskey traders. "Terrible deeds have been wrought out in that western land, terrible heart-sickening deeds of cruelty and rapacious infamy—have been, I say? no, are to this day...." Butler recommended that 150 trained men be stationed immediately at several garrisons in the North West.

Wesleyan John McDougall, one of a handful of missionaries in the North West competing for the red man's soul, sent barrages of letters to Macdonald warning of "the wholesale poisoning" of Indians by American whiskey traders. Throughout 1872 Alexander Morris, the new lieutenant-governor of Manitoba, peppered Macdonald with warnings about the "frightful disasters" waiting to happen. Though a decade had passed since nearly eight hundred settlers and Sioux had been slaughtered, raped or wounded in the Minnesota massacre of 1862, Morris was convinced the same thing could happen in Canada.

Still delaying, in August 1872 Macdonald sent west another military officer, Colonel Patrick Robertson-Ross, adjutant-general of the Canadian Militia, to report on how best to police the territory. His conclusions, delivered personally to Sir John in December 1872, largely agreed with Butler's, except he recommended a force of 550 men.

By this time, Butler's colourful views had received wide circulation. His book *The Great Lone Land*, based on his trip, became a best-seller in Canada and England. Butler's depictions of the danger and savagery of the Canadian North West presented problems for Sir John's campaign to promote the frontier. Who would want to live or invest in a part of the country where butchery and the threat of war were everyday occurrences?

The Hudson's Bay Company belatedly joined the clamour for police protection. In the past the HBC had deliberately discouraged interest in the North West, disparaging the quality of the land to deflate the interest of troublesome settlers and possible competitors. But in 1872, faced with increasing competition for furs from American whiskey traders, the company suddenly became keenly interested in having its trading posts protected as tension between traders and Indians threatened to disrupt business.

During the early months of 1873, with pressure mounting on Macdonald to produce his police force, the prime minister became mired in a boozy rearguard defence of his office over the bribery scandal. With British Columbia threatening to leave Confederation unless Macdonald kicked some life into the still moribund railway project, the prime minister pulled himself together sufficiently to draw up the legislation needed to make the police force a reality.

The bill to form the Mounted Police received royal assent on May 23, 1873. Overnight Macdonald was deluged by applications, all from good Conservatives, for the head position. He wanted an Imperial Army officer to command the troops and refused to consider domestic candidates, no matter how well qualified. He also insisted the man be a gentleman, which disqualified the eminently qualified and very eager Captain William Butler.*

All through the summer of 1873 Sir John drank, dithered and fretted about the corruption allegations. No commander of the police was appointed. He considered offering the job to thirty-seven-year-old Captain Donald Cameron of the Royal Artillery, who had a distinguished service record in India. It was the kind of appointment Macdonald adored. In Cameron he would get a competent officer with the right background, while at the same time doing a favour for a political colleague—Conservative Sir Charles Tupper was Cameron's father-in-law. But Macdonald couldn't make up his mind and by the summer of that year, Cameron had given up waiting and accepted the job of commanding the Boundary Commission survey corps.

Then, in August 1873, all the dire predictions were fulfilled. Horrible reports began filtering east describing the slaughter of as many as two hundred helpless Indians by Americans in the Cypress Hills area, about 600 miles west of Winnipeg. Manitoba officials feared it might be the beginning of an Indian

---

* Though William Butler was one of the most interesting and competent officers of his time, he had neither wealth nor the right birth. His inability to purchase a commission hampered his career, forcing him to advance on the basis of sheer merit alone—not a principle firmly entrenched in the British military at the time.

war of retaliation. "What have you done as to the Police force their absence may lead to grave disaster," Alexander Morris telegraphed frantically to Macdonald on September 20.

Delay and procrastination had put Sir John in an untenable position. The "frightful disaster" that he'd been warned about so many times had already occurred and worse might soon follow. "It would not be well for us to take the responsibility of slighting Morris's repeated and urgent entreaties," he wrote on September 24 to Lord Dufferin, governor-general of Canada. "If anything went wrong the blame would lie at our door." The next day hiring began with the appointment of nine officers and a temporary commissioner, Lieutenant-Colonel W. Osborne-Smith, the deputy adjutant general of the Manitoba Militia District.

The officers fanned out across Upper and Lower Canada, grabbing able bodies everywhere they could. Within two weeks the hastily recruited and ill-equipped men of the first contingent were on their way west to Lower Fort Garry.

When Colonel George French arrived in Ottawa in October 1873, he found that every scrap of political energy available for the Mounted Police had been used up. Leaving detailed memos for Hewitt Bernard or his successor, the minister of justice (Sir John), or his successor, the minister of the interior (Alexander Campbell), or his successor, French shook off the stultifying dust of Ottawa and headed west.

On December 1 Colonel French departed by train for Lower Fort Garry, via Fargo, North Dakota. He took a dog team to Fort Dufferin and rode the last stretch to the fort, arriving on December 16.

COLONEL FRENCH

I regret to have to state that a large number of men sent here are quite unfit for the work. The doctor thinks that about 20 will have to be rejected on medical grounds, and I fear as many more will have to be dismissed for misconduct. The fact is the men were enlisted in too great a hurry, and they fancy themselves to be more militiamen than policemen. If when in the Old Country,

I had authority to obtain 15 or 20 men from the Royal
Irish Constabulary, I could pick out the very best men,
and they would make a splendid leaven for the present
unleavened mass.

French spotted a man with one eye and another who looked
like Quasimodo, his shoulder was so badly dislocated. French
called in David Young, a local doctor, to head a medical
board. Nineteen men were quickly discharged for conditions
ranging from syphilis and heart disease to haemorrhoids.

The Colonel set about fixing the faults with characteristic
fervour, devoting as much emphasis to the correct format of
memoranda as he did to discipline and training. He found the
riding drill haphazard and immediately ordered a strict daily
regime, rotating officers and men in the riding ring.

Isolated by weather and location throughout the winter,
many of the men whiled away their off-duty time drinking. As
was the way with such things, the whiling spilled over into
duty hours. With the drinking came gambling, and several
bankers among the corps established a brisk money-lending
business. The Defaulters Book bulged with long lists of drunk
and disorderly charges. Typically the punishment was
"admonishment," occasionally a fine and once in a while dismissal, but only if the drunkard struck a superior.

Colonel French changed all that on January 8, 1874, insti-
tuting a schedule of fines for drinking infractions; first
offence—four days' pay, three dollars to a sub-constable. Fines
were doubled on subsequent infractions, tripled if the drinking
took place during normal duty and quadrupled if it occurred
on guard duty. Eleven days later French outlawed gambling
and fraternization between sub-constables and constables.

Daily Order Book
January 19, 1874

Constables who are in the habit of drinking or Card
Playing with Sub Constables or having money transac-
tions with them, or who by their general conduct do not
endeavour to inspire the Sub Constables with proper
respect for the position of constable, will be unfit for
the rank they hold.

Osborne-Smith had divided the recruits into three divisions, A, B and C, attempting to spread trade skills evenly among them. But the rapid recruiting left many important jobs vacant. There was an abundance of clerks but no farriers, saddlers or hospital aides. There were also no uniforms as most of the supplies were still frozen solid along the Dawson Route. It pained French to see his men on parade looking more like misfits than troopers dressed in their rag picker's array of second- and third-hand items.

COLONEL FRENCH

Fur caps, mitts and moccasins, sent by the Militia Department via Chicago and St. Paul by rail six weeks ago, have not yet arrived, and Heaven knows where they are. The officers generally are a good lot of fellows, the men are also, but 15 or 20 of them should never have been sent here, being altogether too weak.

Thirty-eight horses have been purchased, but the animals are scarcely fit for our work. As far as I can see, we will require from 200 to 300 horses by next June, and all these *must* be brought from Canada or the States, as they are not to be had here....

The bureaucrats in Ottawa had little idea of the enormous task they had set for Colonel French. The new government's indifference towards the Force frustrated him but he knew that one way to keep key politicians in his corner was to out pennypinch the most thrifty of them. The Americans were spending twenty million dollars annually on their "Indian problem"—roughly the annual Canadian federal budget for the time. He would make sure the North West Mounted Police did a better job for a tiny fraction of the cost.

French concluded that the cost of getting heavy equipment to the West by freighting it to Fort Benton in the Montana Territory via U.S. railroads and steamboats was prohibitive, so he decided the Force would haul all their supplies themselves, including mowing machines, forges, stoves and anything else they needed to set up and equip several posts in the West. French confidently predicted this one decision alone would save the government between sixty and seventy thousand dollars. But it also meant dozens of additional wagons and carts, not to mention the extra horses, oxen and manpower necessary to do the hauling, more iron for shoes, coal for the forges, harnesses and on and on.

Another major decision facing Colonel French was how to provision three hundred men on the nine-hundred-mile six-week trek from Fort Dufferin to Fort Whoop Up. Conventional wisdom recommended pemmican, the frontier staple. Traders and travellers, from the *coureurs de bois* to the International Boundary Commission, had relied on it for over two hundred years, but French decided instead to purchase a herd of cattle to take with them as a walking larder.

COLONEL FRENCH

January 17, 1874

I send you today a full report on the requirements of the N.W.M.P. and on the programme which I believe to be necessary for the present year. You will doubtless be somewhat astonished at all that is required, but to take a considerable force into an almost unknown country, and with but little chance of obtaining supplies, is emphatically big business. It is absolutely necessary that the Force should start by the middle of June, and there is little use in my going over the grounds for my conclusions—I am well aware of the objection to reading weekly reports, but I must really ask that mine receive *immediate* consideration.

Sir John A. Macdonald had emphasized to French that the NWMP must be promoted as a civil force, not a military one. This was essential to distinguish the police from the American soldiers and cavalry, who were loathed by the Indians and detested by whites west of the Mississippi. "There is nothing so little thought of in this part of the country as a soldier," a long-time resident of Montana wrote to the New York *Herald*.

"There are only two creatures who look upon a soldier here without scorn and contempt, and they are little children and dogs."

In the West, Americans used cavalry and infantry like a bludgeon, driving the Indians onto reservations and solving any number of problems from horse stealing and whiskey trading to murder. Out of the heavy-handed strategy came massacres, corruption and retaliation, not only from the Indians, but also from traders and settlers.

Colonel French often repeated the *civil not military, police not soldiers* maxims in his letters, memos and addresses to the men but the fact remained, George French was military from his starched collar to the spit shine of his boots. He commanded the NWMP first, last and always as if it were an Imperial Army battalion—he knew no other way. Conceived as a corps of small, quick-acting units, French trained the men in elaborate large-scale troop movements both on foot and horse, even though there wasn't much call on the frontier for the kind of battle manoeuvres that helped the Duke of Wellington win the day at Waterloo.

Colonel French relentlessly trained troopers with the mortars and two nine-pound artillery guns he intended to take west.* By the time he finished, the artillery troop could load at a reasonable speed and shoot with a fair degree of accuracy. But it was hard to imagine where they would use the guns, except for show. With the exception of the whiskey traders' stockades—most of them hastily thrown together—there were no fortifications to besiege, no walled cities to shell, and any Indians they might fight were unlikely to line themselves up in an orderly way and charge into battle, line upon line, like an infantry unit.

The Force's *raison d'être* was to police, monitor and enforce laws, and much of that work would be accomplished by small groups of men, sometimes only one or two. The small groups would be required to spend days travelling from point to point, yet their training was bereft of the basics of wilderness survival. And though troopers would be called upon to act as

---

* The shells weighed nine pounds, but the guns themselves were a hefty 2,200 pounds each.

magistrates and customs officials, there wasn't even an attempt to educate them for those roles.

While he was whipping the first contingent into some semblance of a fighting unit in Manitoba, Colonel French became convinced that 150 men weren't enough. They would need the full three hundred men the Mounted Police Act provided for.

COLONEL FRENCH

There will be hot work for us next summer. The governor has reliable information that there are five forts between Milk River and Edmonton, one of them containing 100 outlaws and desperadoes, and mounting several guns.

The manner in which they got the guns will give you some idea of the ruffians we will have to deal with; it was simply this: they assaulted an army train which the U.S. Government was sending to one of their western forts, captured the guns, and ran them across the line.

They boldly give out that they will fight it out with any force that goes to disturb them, and as most of them have been outlawed in Montana, I think it is possible they mean what they say. I hope so.

While in Lower Fort Garry, Colonel French consulted closely with Lieutenant-Governor Morris, Captain Cameron, head of the Boundary Commission, and Captain Anderson, its chief astronomer. But he didn't bother with William Hallet, chief scout for the Commission, then living in Winnipeg. It proved to be an omission with many repercussions as Hallet had much more first-hand experience in the West than the others.

In early February 1874, French hurried back to Toronto. He was pleasantly surprised to find that Alexander Mackenzie, the new prime minister and an ardent prohibitionist, had already started the process of bringing the Force up to strength. Colonel French decided to recruit two hundred men, fifty more than the act allowed, in order to make up for the anticipated desertions, medical discharges and dismissals in Manitoba. He threw himself into a frenzy of organizing, ordering, recruiting and purchasing—only five months remained before the Force would march west.

Colonel French set June 6 as the second contingent's departure date from Toronto. This was the latest he felt they could leave and still rendezvous with the first contingent before heading west. Any later and they'd risk getting caught in early snowstorms. Just before departure, he ordered all three divisions to prepare themselves for a field exercise. This would be the first drill involving the entire second contingent—an opportunity to assess the men's progress and build a little pride and respect in the uniform.

On the parade ground French barked out the general command to his troops. Nothing happened. The officers looked at each other, then looked at their boots. The troops looked at each other, then at the officers, wondering what they were supposed to do. French repeated the order, only louder. The inspectors and sub-inspectors, in charge of relaying the general command to their divisions, went into action, yelling out a series of incoherent and conflicting orders. Within seconds, the parade had dissolved into a free-for-all.

Before an apoplectic French could explode, the sergeant-majors who, by nature, are blessed with the loudest voices, the evilest tempers and the most fervent need to be obeyed of all military types, shouldered the officers aside and took matters into their own hands. Swearing, whipping and whacking, they bullied the troops into position, screamed out their orders and led them into the field. The officers followed.

On June 6, 1874, Divisions D, E and F of the second contingent of the North West Mounted Police assembled for departure at Union Station, Toronto. They would avoid the tortuous Dawson Route and travel by train to Fort Dufferin via Chicago, St. Paul and Fargo, North Dakota. The troopers were fine-looking specimens. Spit-polished, hair trimmed, moustaches groomed, clothes cleaned and mended, tack shining dark mahogany, horses' coats burnished—the sight was splendid enough to encourage dozens of young women to decide right then and there that the frontier life and a mounted policeman for a husband would be an excellent choice.

The men were also in excellent spirits, many having fortified themselves well the night before in preparation for the long dry days ahead. The smell of whiskey, wine, ale and pomade mingled, not unpleasantly, with the aroma of saddle soap and horse sweat.

Toronto loved an event and thousands gathered to say good-bye and good luck. Gentlemen and ladies, servants and labourers pressed against each other vying to shake a police-man's hand. Several military bands played enthusiastically, as if the NWMP were off to bring Genghis Khan to his knees. The faces of wives, mothers and girlfriends were etched with worry that the Wild West would be too fearsome a place for their husbands, sons and boyfriends. Even fathers with mili-tary experience had no real idea what their sons would be fac-ing, beyond a very long ride.

"Mind your back, my boy. The red man is treacherous."

"Don't let those godless whiskey traders talk you into trying any. It's the edge of ruin. Be good, my son."

"You will write," wept a mother, "will you not?"

"Don't forget your Mary with all your adventurin'!"

"My son, remember your life belongs to your country. I would rather hear of your death than of your dishonour."

"Be a good boy," murmured Fred Bagley's mother, pressing a new diary, key winding watch and chain into her son's hands. "Say your prayers regularly, and come back soon!"

"Don't forget your dearest Angelica when you are among the Indians!"

The train began to move. The bands struck up "Vive la Canadienne." The men sang "The Girl I Left Behind Me." The Mounted Police were off.

CHAPTER 2

Revenge

SPRING 1872

Jerry Potts squatted low beside the river bank, drinking from cupped hands. Beside him, a string of horses whickered and snorted as they drank their fill. Mid-swallow, Potts froze. A hoof clicked faintly on a rock above. He knew he wasn't visible from the trail that passed by, which was why he had chosen the spot. Even so, he rose slowly, drew his revolver and lay it across his horse's back, pointed towards the sound. For long seconds he listened hard, then relaxed. Unshod hooves clattered distinctly—two Indian ponies, both with riders, heading to Fort Kipp. This close to the fort they were unlikely to be hostile. But such were the times that he didn't holster his gun.

As the riders came briefly into view, Potts caught a good look. They were Blood Indians—his own people.* First rode

---

* Jerry Potts was born a Blood Indian; however, in later years he married two Peigan sisters and came to spend all his time among that tribe of the Blackfoot Confederacy. Today his family thinks of him as a Peigan.

Morning Writing, then behind him—Potts' heart lurched painfully. Instinctively, his finger took up the trigger slack. He had a good, clear shot—a killing shot. But with jerky, laboured motions, he willed himself to lower his gun.

Good Young Man owed a blood debt and he ought to know who collected it.

That day, in the spring of 1872, Jerry Potts was about thirty-five years old. He'd never cared to keep count, but he'd killed a man for every year of his life—at least.

Several months earlier Potts' mother, Crooked Back, and his half-brother, No Chief, had been living among the Many Children band of Blood Indians, led by Chief Heavy Shield. Among Heavy Shield's people was Not-Afraid-of-the-Gros-Ventre, a formidable warrior who had fathered more than sixty children with his ten wives. The Not-Afraid clan formed a powerful faction within the Many Children band.

The band was camped just outside the gates of Fort Kipp, one of the two main whiskey trading forts in British territory, just north of the Montana border. They had arrived a few days earlier after sending two messengers—really diplomatic emissaries—to announce them. The messengers served two purposes; they warned the traders to get their supplies ready for business and they let any enemy tribes in the vicinity know that it was time to pack up and leave.

First the Blood exchanged furs and horses for guns, powder, blankets, utensils, tobacco and food. Then the real trading began—firewater. The white men were anxious to get this part over with as soon as possible, then shoot the log bolt across the gate and settle in to wait out the inevitable drunken revelry.

Not everyone celebrated. Chief Heavy Shield, an old man, remembered a time when his people's pride could not be bought. He had long counselled against contact with traders and their fatal brew, but inexorably his people had become dependent on the white man's goods and their thirst lodged an insistent demon in their souls.

A Blood chief had no legislative authority; he advised, counselled and made speeches. His position depended on three things; his own ability as a warrior, the quality of the advice he gave and his ability to create consensus within the tribe on important issues. He didn't have the power to forbid whiskey to his braves. He could try, but if the tribe ignored his advice, Heavy Shield's influence would dissolve forever.

Whatever vile concoction the traders doled out this day quickly transformed the usual high-spirited dancing, singing and wrestling into random shooting and venomous argument. Normally, when the braves went to trade for whiskey, the women hid knives, tomahawks and guns. But so many women had died during a smallpox outbreak in 1869, there weren't enough of them to commandeer all the weapons before the firewater took effect.

Heavy Shield, tired of the escalating cacophony and worried that a child might be shot accidentally, moved his family out of earshot and bullet range. With him went Crooked Back, her son No Chief and his wife.

The Not-Afraid clan was incensed at the slight. They talked and railed, magnifying the rebuke into a great affront. But

who should they challenge to avenge the insult? Not Heavy Shield. He was a popular chief and, though old, his reputation as a warrior still carried potent medicine. Crooked Back and her son, on the other hand, were appealing scapegoats. To dwell in the proximity of the chief was an honour. What right did they have to this special treatment when the valorous Not-Afraids were being rebuffed? Crooked Back didn't even belong to the Many Children band, let alone Heavy Shield's own family. What's more, No Chief had married a daughter of Not-Afraid-of-the-Gros-Ventre. His place was rightfully with his wife's people, not at Heavy Shield's side.

The Not-Afraid's anger ignited

Jerry Potts, Bear Child

into action. Braves enticed No Chief to their camp with the promise of a gallon of whiskey. Once No Chief arrived they set upon him, badgering, taunting and pushing him back and forth among them. Buoyed by the drunken crowd, Hairy Face, No Chief's brother-in-law, pounced on him. As they fought to the ground, No Chief managed to draw his gun and kill Hairy Face.

Howling with rage, Not-Afraid-of-the-Gros-Ventre flung himself at No Chief, whose knife sliced into his father-in-law, sending his spirit to join his son's. No Chief managed to wound a third brave before another brother-in-law, Good Young Man, shot him down. Contemptuously, the Not-Afraid left No Chief's body in the middle of camp for the dogs to tear apart.

Potts understood these skirmishes—drunken brawls really— he'd taken part in more than his share of them. It was the sickness of the time. Bands turning inward, gnawing their own hearts out. Family against family, blurring the once clear lines between enemy and ally—the trust in and respect for chiefs and medicine men enduring only until the scent of whiskey was in the air.

No Chief had died as a warrior, taking two lives before he lost his own. The disrespectful treatment of his body was shameful, but Potts could have let that pass. Before dying No Chief had exacted his own price, and that would ease his way into the spirit world. But what followed burned inside him like the foulest of the traders' potions—it could not be forgiven or forgotten.

When Potts' mother heard of her son's death, she rushed to the Not-Afraid camp to save his body from the dogs. It was honourable but foolish. Better to have waited until the whiskey sent all the men into a paralysed slumber. But Crooked Back rode into the camp and defiantly began loading her son's mangled corpse onto a travois for a warrior's burial.*

Good Young Man, still drunk, mocked her, ordering her to

---

* Blackfoot typically put their dead high in the branches of trees, where they might be closer to the spirits. When the flesh disappeared and the bones fell to the ground, the skeletons were buried in groups, sometimes with the skulls placed in a circle, faces pointed towards the centre. Such an arrangement is called a Village of the Dead. Prominent men and women who died were placed in their tents on hilltops. The tents were sealed by weighing down the edges with rocks.

leave the body where it lay. When she refused, he shot her. Crooked Back lay sprawled at her son's feet until the camp dogs, yipping with delight, set upon her as well. Sour grief clawed at Potts when he thought of his mother's ignominious death. This he could not ignore.

Potts had been back at his lodges (teepees) on the Marias River in Montana when he learned of the killings two weeks later. He grabbed his horse and galloped, like a man possessed, towards the Canadian border, covering many miles before he fought down his lust for revenge. The Blood roamed a huge territory and Good Young Man would try to make himself scarce. But whiskey forts, coupled with the Indians' thirst, had effectively shrunk the great plains by their presence. Potts worked as a hunter at Fort Kipp, a whiskey post just north of the international boundary on the Bow River which carved through the heart of Blackfoot territory. Fort Whoop Up, the biggest whiskey fort in the North West, was less than half a day's ride away. He knew from his own thirst that the lure of whiskey eventually eroded any man's caution. Potts cleaned his guns and waited. One day soon Good Young Man would come to him.

And here he was, bold as a coyote, riding towards Fort Kipp. Potts methodically corralled his horses inside the fort and provisioned himself with biscuits, pemmican and bullets. Then he slipped away on his best horse, taking a position on a bluff overlooking the trail.

Sure enough, a couple of hours later, Good Young Man rode away from the fort with Morning Writing, now both on the same horse, having traded the other for whiskey. Potts could track a ghost on a week-old trail and identify animals by the smell of their urine; following two whiskeyed braves on a single horse would be so simple he'd have plenty of time to toy with them.

Potts watched them pass, then pulled onto the trail about two hundred yards behind, following steadily at the same pace. The braves had been drinking, but they were still alert enough to notice a lone man dogging their wake. After several furtive backward glances they upped their pace. Potts matched it. The braves drove their heels into the horse again but Potts stayed glued behind.

At a lope, even an Indian pony would soon tire with two men on its back; then they'd be at Potts' mercy.* He wanted to enjoy their terror and draw out the agony as long as possible. But he had to be careful. If he waited too long, he'd follow them right into their camp. Then he'd be the rabbit with the foxes chasing him. He closed the gap a little. Their horse was blowing hard and shedding lather with every step. Now he was close enough to savour the recognition and fear in their faces. As they neared a coulee by the river, Potts caught a whiff of smoke. Realizing he'd almost left it too late, he kicked his horse to a gallop and snapped off two quick shots without aiming.

Panicked, Morning Writing tumbled from the exhausted horse and fled towards camp. Potts now had a clear shot at the man he wanted. He didn't waste it. The bullet knew the way and smashed into Good Young Man's spine. He pitched forward off the horse, rolling over the edge of the coulee, and careened down into the camp.

Ignoring the tumult erupting from the lodges below, Potts coolly shifted his aim to Morning Writing. The Blood, sensing his destiny, halted his flight and turned to face Potts. After a moment, staring into the brave's resigned eyes, Potts holstered his revolver. This man had killed no one.

The sudden arrival of Good Young Man's body galvanized the camp. Women and children wailed and the men milled uncertainly about, not knowing whether to go for their guns or wait and see what this madman intended. Potts looked down at them, his hand now resting lightly on his Henry rifle. The band members nervously watched him.

All could see that this was not Jerry Potts' day to die. Any who tried to change that fate would surely die themselves. Potts' anger and sorrow over his mother's death dissolved in the sweet rush of revenge satisfied. He felt cleansed. Emitting disdain from every pore, he turned his horse around and slowly rode away.

---

* Indian horses, renowned for their strength and endurance, were descendants of the Spanish horses introduced into Mexico and Florida in the sixteenth century. They were typically smaller than the English stock, hence the term used by whites—pony.

The Confederacy

Jerry Potts was born into violence, cocooned in it, nurtured on it. He wasn't yet walking when a Peigan Indian with a grudge blew his father's face off. It was a case of mistaken identity, but such things were common in the mid-1800s across the northern Great Plains where the hand of civilization poked tenuous fingers into the last Indian stronghold on the frontier—the land of the Blackfoot Confederacy.

For 150 years various fur companies had tried to forge links with these aggravatingly independent Indians who occupied a vast, rich territory, tantalizingly just out of the white man's reach. By 1830 sixteen thousand of them were spread out over a land that stretched from the south branch of the Missouri to the Rockies and from the upper Missouri plains to the North Saskatchewan River. They were not one people, but many. The chief tribes of the Confederacy, the Blood, Peigan and Blackfoot, shared the same language while their sometime allies, the Sarcee and Gros Ventre, were linguistically different but equally warlike.*

The Blackfoot were the last of the Plains Indians to submit to the temptations of the white man, either the goods of the trader or the gods of the missionaries. The Blackfoot were also the last to be displaced by the white man. Most of the Plains Indians, like the Cree, Assiniboine and Sioux, had their roots in the woodlands of the Great Lakes and the valleys of the Red River and the Mississippi. They were pushed west by fur traders, settlers and tribal warfare, transforming themselves from trappers, fishermen and farmers into people of the buffalo. Early explorers believed that the Blackfoot originated in the woodlands of central and eastern Saskatchewan but when Crowfoot, the powerful Blackfoot chief from the late 1860s to 1890, was asked about it he scorned the idea. The Blackfoot

* The Gros Ventre split from the Confederacy in 1861 and drifted into northern Montana. The Sarcee remained loose allies in trade and war but retained a stronger individual identity than the three main tribes. The population given is for all five tribes. The Sarcee and Gros Ventre made up only about three thousand people within the Confederacy in 1830.

were the warriors of the plains, he proclaimed, always had been and always would be.

To the north and east of the Confederacy ranged the Plains Cree, their territory extending all the way to Hudson Bay. Initially a woodlands people, their early contact with the Hudson's Bay Company had made them a wealthy and well-armed nation that migrated west in the late 1700s, searching out more furs for the insatiable traders and becoming middle-men between the HBC and other tribes. In the process they pushed up against the Blackfoot, shoving them south across the North Saskatchewan River and farther west towards the Rockies, but they could never successfully penetrate the heart-land of the Confederacy, the western plains of the South Saskatchewan River and the north-western plains of the Missouri. With their southern allies, the Assiniboine, the Cree fought the Blackfoot for control of the central plains, and they raided the Sioux and Mandan as far south as the Missouri. With the best horses and guns of all Plains Indians, the Cree were feared warriors. But being the first to acquire white man's goods came with a price, white man's disease. Smallpox, diph-theria and measles attacked them again and again from the mid-1700s until the mid-1800s, almost halving their numbers.

The Blackfoot rejoiced in their enemies, and they had more of them than any among the Plains tribes. The Blackfoot's hatred of the Cree and Assiniboine became legendary but they loathed with equal fervour their enemies to the south—the Nez Percé near the Continental Divide, and to the east of them the Crow, the Cheyenne, the Mandan and, most particularly, the Sioux.

No other tribe had been displaced so much by civilization or changed so utterly in a short period of time as the Sioux. The first thrust of white men past the Great Lakes in the late seventeenth and early eighteenth centuries pushed the Ojibwa or Chippewa into the Minnesota River woodlands, territory of the Sioux. The Chippewa drove them west and south and into the land of the Sauk and Fox Indians in Iowa. After 150 years of war, the Sioux nation was split into three main groups: the Santees, who managed to retain a precarious toehold along the Minnesota River; the Yankton who migrated as far east as the south branch of the Missouri; and the Lakota or Teton

Sioux—the people of famed war chiefs Red Cloud, Sitting Bull and Crazy Horse. They changed themselves from foot nomads to mounted hunters in just fifty years. By 1830 there were between fifteen and twenty thousand of them spread out from the upper Missouri to the Platte River and from the southeastern branch of the Missouri to the Big Horn Mountains in Montana. But they never dominated along the upper Missouri because everywhere they went the combative Blackfoot repulsed them.

War had refined the Sioux fighting machine, but in the first half of the nineteenth century the Sioux had none of the sophisticated weaponry of the Blackfoot. Like the Confederacy, the Sioux had been hesitant to trade with whites, but they were less resourceful at acquiring guns from raids and wars. The Sioux were intensely contemptuous of the easy capitulation by other Plains Indians to the white man. Sitting Bull expressed a century-old scorn in 1867. "I have killed, robbed, and injured too many white men to believe in a good peace. They are medicine [*wakan*], and I would eventually die a lingering death. I had rather die on the field of battle," he told a trader at Fort Union, near the confluence of the Yellowstone and Missouri. And he taunted some listening Assiniboine, "The whites may get me at last, as you say, but I will have good times till then. You are fools to make yourselves slaves to a piece of fat bacon, some hard-tack, and a little sugar and coffee."

God's white hand had been attempting to bring the Sioux to the Bible in the mid-19th century, and though American missionaries had some success with the eastern Yankton tribe, they had almost none with the Sioux who had moved west. Part of the reason lay in the fact that American missionaries stuck to the handful of fur trading posts along the Missouri, rather than venture out and establish missions on their own. One of the few who went into the Sioux camps was Black Robe, Father Pierre-Jean De Smet. He spent many years among the Sioux and by the 1860s had become one of the few whites the Lakota Sioux would even talk to, let alone trust. Canadian missionaries were bolder than their U.S. counterparts, setting up a string of missions in the British North West after 1840—many away from fur trading posts—but they were as unsuccessful converting the Blackfoot as the Americans were the Sioux.

Competition for the savage's soul in the North West was fierce after 1840 when Reverend Robert Rundle, a Methodist, built a mission at Fort Edmonton, a Hudson's Bay Company post. A score of Anglicans, Methodists, Jesuits and Roman Catholics stampeded after him. By the mid-1850s the contest had settled down to two main contenders, the Methodists and the Catholics. "But there is a Papal power there in wakeful exercise," warned a Methodist voice from the North West in 1854, "only less pestiferous and godless than Paganism itself, which must be enervated and annihilated, with all the inane superstitions, and corruptions, and savagism of every debased tribe of the frigid North."

Catholic missionary Father Albert Lacombe infuriated the Methodists in 1859 when he brought three Grey Nuns from Montreal to establish a school forty-five miles north-west of Fort Edmonton. The exotic allure of oddly dressed white women attracted hundreds of Indians and half-breeds who normally would have given the Bible a wide berth. It was, fumed Wesleyan Methodist George McDougall, a despicable way to take advantage of the innocent pagans.

There are five priests to one Protestant missionary; they are anti-British in their national sympathies; and if we may judge the tree by its fruits, anti-Christian in their teachings.... By them the Sabbath is desecrated, polygamy tolerated, and the Bible ignored....

One of the tricks of these gentlemen is, when a child is born in a Protestant family,

Blackfoot warrior in 1830s
by Karl Bodmer

a female agent enters the tent, fondles the infant, and then, professing to show it to their friends, carries it to the priest, who baptizes the babe.

The policy of the Protestant missionaries has been to avoid controversy and simply to preach Christ. The very opposite has been the practice of the Priest. And if trouble should arise between the tribes of this country and the whites, the cause, in a large degree, will lie at the door of the Papacy.

Even though they generated enough fervour to power a crusade, there weren't more than two dozen competing missionaries west of Manitoba in the 1860s. Like the fur traders of the past century, they stuck to the waterways of the wooded northern prairies and the more welcoming and "civilized" Indians who lived there. They had great success converting the Cree, Assiniboine and Stoney Indians, but the Blackfoot eluded them.

The Blackfoot were different from any Indians the explorers, fur traders or missionaries had encountered. Adaptable, intelligent, curious and dangerous, they dealt with the white men only on their own terms. Once small, disparate bands of hunters who travelled by foot and hauled their possessions on dog travois, their lives revolved around the buffalo. A Blackfoot's most valued possession was his buffalo-skin teepee, which required between twelve and twenty-four hides to construct—impossible for a single hunter to accumulate in the time before the horse and gun, so they became the first among the Plains Indians to develop sophisticated communal hunting techniques using pounds and buffalo jumps, where they drove thousands of the animals into disguised pens or over the edge of a precipice to their deaths.

From isolated, shy nomads in the late seventeenth century, the Blackfoot, in little more than a generation, evolved into a strong confederacy of ferocious warriors. They developed a complex system of secret military-style societies, a powerful hierarchy of chiefs and medicine men and intricate traditions and spiritual beliefs. Many of the Plains Indians, like the Sarcee, came to emulate the Blackfoot's social structure.

Although feuds and intertribal warfare were frequent, intermarriage—particularly among the Blood, Peigan and

Blackfoot—ensured that when an enemy appeared, the Confederacy presented a united front. Because they were so spread out, yet connected, retaliation against an atrocity on the Missouri Plains might be avenged as far away as the North Saskatchewan.

In 1690, the Hudson's Bay Company, eager to tap into the fur potential of the western prairies, sent Henry Kelsey, from York Factory on Hudson Bay's south-west shore, deep into Blackfoot country. He became the first white man to see the northern plains buffalo and likely the first to lay eyes on the Indians who would later become part of the Confederacy. Because the Blackfoot were curious and hospitable—though wary—Kelsey was confident his mission would be successful. But when he broached the subject of establishing formal trade links, he was politely but firmly refused. They would starve or be killed by Cree, the Blackfoot explained, if they had to make the long journey to York Factory with their furs. It would be a senseless way to die when they already had everything they needed.

Sixty-five years later, rumours of the Blackfoot's wondrous furs and extraordinary skill in trapping and hunting tempted the HBC again. But Anthony Henday, a company employee, was no more successful in persuading them to travel to the nearest fort. The Blackfoot heaped gifts upon him and offered up feasts in his honour but when he tried to negotiate a trade compact, they met his suggestion with disinterest. The only route to York Factory was by canoe, the Blackfoot pointed out, and they had no intention of using the boats of their enemies the Cree—"white man's dog"—and the Métis—"white man's slave." Nor did the Blackfoot encourage the traders to come to them. Why should they? The buffalo provided everything they wanted or needed.

In ensuing years the HBC, still lusting after their furs, sent Matthew Cocking, David Thompson and Peter Fidler to the Blackfoot. They all returned empty-handed but with a healthy fear of the Confederacy.

While the Blackfoot weren't infatuated with the white man and his trade goods, they were intensely interested in his horses and guns. "We were anxious to see a horse of which we had heard so much," a Peigan elder told HBC explorer David Thompson in 1787. "[W]e heard that one was killed by an arrow shot into his belly, but the Snake (Shoshone) Indian that rode him got away; numbers of us went to see him, and we all admired him, he put us in mind of a Stag that had lost his horns: and we did not know the name to give him. But as he was a slave to Man, like the dog which carried our things; he was named Big Dog."

Big Dog had come to North America in the early to mid-sixteenth century with Hernán Cortés, conqueror of the Aztecs, and Hernando de Soto, explorer of Florida. Some of the Arabian type horses they brought to Mexico and Florida escaped, were lost or were left behind in the New World. But it wasn't until Juan de Oñate established a settlement at Santa Fe in 1609 that Big Dog began to transform first the southern, then the northern Plains Indians. By 1730 the Shoshone Indians were staging mounted raids into Blackfoot territory, sometimes as far north as the Saskatchewan plains. At about the same time, the Blackfoot were acquiring arrow points and Hudson's Bay Company muskets from trade and war with other tribes. They began to fight back. Stealing a horse from another tribe soon became almost as prestigious as counting coup, the striking of a slain enemy with a stick. By the time Henday travelled west in 1854, the Blackfoot were masterful horsemen and had fully converted to a military society with an elaborate system of camp sentries, perimeter guards and reconnaissance scouts, designed to protect their most valuable assets, their horses.

As it did with every Plains tribe, the horse transformed Blackfoot culture, changing hunting techniques and barter systems. Conflict, once avoided unless absolutely necessary, became both sport and ritual. By 1830 nearly every Plains tribe from the Mississippi and the Red River to the Rocky Mountains was on a permanent war footing.

"The Indian has the gift of being everywhere without being anywhere," marvelled Father Pierre-Jean De Smet, who'd often watched the Blackfoot fight.

> These savages assemble at the moment of battle, and
> scatter whenever the fortune of war is contrary to them.
> The Indian puts his wife and children in shelter in some
> retired place, far from the scene of hostilities. He has

neither towns, forts, nor magazines to defend, nor line of retreat to cover. He is embarrassed with neither baggage trains nor pack-horses.

He goes into action when a favourable occasion is presented, and never risks himself without having the advantage of numbers and position on his side. The science of strategy is consequently of little use in operating against such a people. There is on earth no nation more ambitious of military renown, nor that holds in higher estimation the conduct of a valiant warrior. No Indian could ever occupy a place in the councils of his tribe until he had met the enemy on the field of battle. He who reckons the most scalps is highly considered among his people.

Until the arrival of the gun and the horse, buffalo from the upper Missouri to the North Saskatchewan had belonged primarily to the Blackfoot.* But within a single generation killing buffalo became relatively easy for all Plains Indians. Tribes who rarely encountered the Blackfoot, like the Sioux and Assiniboine, began poaching on their doorstep. The Blackfoot responded by pushing hard against the pressures of white men and Indian enemies. They raided as far east as Fort Garry, an HBC post, worried at the Kootenay and Salish in the mountains, terrorized the Cree in the north and east and harassed the Crow, Mandan, Sioux, Cheyenne and Nez Percé in the south.

As pressure grew on the Confederacy from other tribes and fur-hungry companies in the late eighteenth century, the Blackfoot might have entered into a trade relationship to protect their territory and give them easier access to weapons. But some matchless bungling by two famous explorers slammed shut the door of opportunity. In 1804, a year after Thomas Jefferson's Louisiana Purchase—the "wildest chimera of a moonstruck brain"—the U.S. president sent two former army captains, Meriwether Lewis and William Clark, to explore the Missouri and evaluate its commercial potential.

---

* The Assiniboine came closest to emulating the Blackfoot's hunting techniques with pounds and buffalo jumps but no other tribes achieved the skill of the Confederacy.

They separated in Montana, each to search for the best route across the Continental Divide. In his journals, Captain Lewis congratulates himself on avoiding the Blackfoot, which he did successfully until July 26, 1806, when he and three others came upon eight Peigan. There was no diplomatic way to avoid sharing a campsite with them. The evening progressed well enough with the Indians providing valuable information about the unexplored northern plains. Lewis presented the requisite gifts, medals and greetings and "plyed" the Blackfoot with the "pipe" until late at night.

Inexplicably, considering his fear of the Blackfoot, Lewis failed to mount a guard. He woke up to find the Indians making off with four rifles and eight horses. Clark shot one Indian in the belly, and one of his men, Reuben Fields, stabbed another.

It was a relatively minor incident, as such skirmishes went, but the Blackfoot reaction to it was not. The Confederacy closed its border to whites for the next twenty-five years and made life miserable for any foolish enough to ignore the warning. In 1809, two former Lewis and Clark men, John Colter, discoverer of the Yellowstone geysers, and John Potts, were trapping on the Jefferson Fork in Montana when the Blackfoot surprised them. They "made a riddle of" Potts with arrows but planned a more torturous fate for Colter. Colter was already high on the Blackfoot enemy list after killing several of them a year earlier in a battle near the Big Horn Mountains.

The Blackfoot loved to combine sport with death. After a brief council they decided to "run" Colter. Stripping him naked, they gave him a four-hundred-yard head start, then charged. Colter, with his life in his feet, ran like none before or since. He outdistanced everyone, but the worst was ahead. "He was completely naked, under a burning sun; the soles of his feet were entirely filled with the thorns of the prickly pear; he was hungry, and had no means of killing game, although he saw abundance around him…"

Hobbling, running, crawling and gnawing on breadroot to keep himself alive, a shattered Colter arrived seven days later at the Fort Raymond post of St. Louis entrepreneur Manuel Lisa on the Yellowstone River. Colter was never the same. A year later, after several more brushes with the Confederacy, he told Lisa that the Blackfoot territory along the Yellowstone River was "bad medicine" and retired to a sedentary life in St. Louis.

Manuel Lisa had nothing but problems with the Blackfoot. Racing John Jacob Astor's newly formed, but already powerful, American Fur Company for control of the Missouri high plains, he built a fort on the Three Forks River—twenty men were killed before it was abandoned.

More traders followed and more of them died until they began to think the wretched high plains country patrolled by the bloodthirsty Blackfoot wasn't worth the bother. Most of them turned to the south or Pacific trade, leaving the Confederacy to slug it out with the Crow, Sioux and Cree.

While the Blackfoot shut the door completely on the American traders, the British were eventually able to build posts on the edge of the Confederacy's territory, but at tremendous cost. The two main Canadian competitors, the Hudson's Bay Company and the North West Company, established posts at Rocky Mountain House and Acton House on the North Saskatchewan in 1799. The forts were remote, surrounded by muskeg, expensive to maintain and difficult to provision. But the Blackfoot had dictated their placement. They refused to travel to the companies' other posts and wouldn't allow them to build in more amenable and convenient places. In 1821 the Hudson's Bay Company, uninvited by the Confederacy, established Chesterfield House and Peigan Post on the South Saskatchewan River. The Blackfoot promptly burned them out.

For years the Blackfoot successfully pitted the two companies against each other and, when they amalgamated in 1821, pitted the HBC against the American traders. "We have this season permanently established Rocky Mountain House for the accommodation of the Peigan," chief trader John Rowand crowed in 1827, "which will have the effect of drawing them during the winter from the Flathead lands and thereby keep them out of the way of the American Trappers."

The post was closed, opened and closed again many times as the Blackfoot granted or withdrew trade at their whim. When the American traders finally and successfully invaded the upper Missouri in the 1830s, the Blackfoot used them as a lever to cut better deals with the HBC. "One Rascal, the chief of the band, had the impudence to ask [for] a Chief cloathing for himself and a suit of each for his children, seven in number," grumbled trader Henry Fisher at Rocky Mountain House, "...and was very much displeased on being refused."

If the HBC upset them, the Blackfoot withheld their furs or, worse, meat. The traders relied on the Indians to trade them enough meat to get through the winter. When the Blackfoot didn't appear, the traders stretched their supplies, limiting themselves to a small daily meal. Just when the traders were ready to eat their boots, the Blackfoot would show up with a meagre supply of meat. Facing starvation, the desperate traders happily parted with whatever the Blackfoot asked for.

The worst sin, from the Blackfoot's point of view, was to trade with the Cree. Several times the Blackfoot punished the HBC by establishing their own links with the Kootenay Indians to the west. The Kootenay traded with the Americans along the Columbia River for clothing, blankets, liquor and guns, and the Blackfoot traded their buffalo skins and meat to the Kootenay for the American goods, thus cutting the HBC out completely.

When new HBC regulations in 1861 forbade the sale of liquor to the Indians, the Blackfoot virtually abandoned the post. "Two men arrived this afternoon coming ahead of Mr. Brazeau and Party from the Rocky Mountain House who have from starvation been compelled to abandon that establishment," reported an Edmonton House clerk. "Mr. Brazeau reports the Blackfeet who have always come in large numbers to the Fort armed, brought no provisions or anything else, came apparently only to beg Rum and threaten to kill the people.... The Blackfeet have been un-bearable for the last 3 years or more, always getting worse and worse, destroying our crops, stealing our Horses & doing everything they could to annoy us, in order to provide a quarrel so as to kill us." Severe Blackfoot harassment coupled with meagre profits forced the HBC to abandon Rocky Mountain House from 1861 to 1866.

Americans considered the French-Canadian voyageurs, *coureurs de bois* and their Métis cousins to be nothing short of invincible demi-gods of the wilderness. "I believe an American could not be brought to support with patience the fatiguing labours and submission which these men endure," marvelled adventurer Henry Brackenridge. "At this season, when the water is exceedingly cold, they leap in without a moment's hesitation. Their food consists of corn hominy for breakfast, a slice of fat pork and biscuit for dinner, and a pot of mush, with a pound of tallow in it, for supper."

But these same hardy yeomen balked on the doorstep of Blackfoot country even after half a century of on-again, off-again trade. The French and English half-breeds, who annually trekked from Fort Garry to the Cypress Hills buffalo hunt and were formidable warriors in their own right, quaked at the thought of encountering the tribes of the Confederacy. In 1859, explorer John Palliser nearly had a mutiny on his hands when he tried to force his Métis into Blackfoot country.

> Old Paul came to me and declared off, saying he was exceedingly sorry to leave me, pleading the commands of his "mother-in-law" as an excuse but, in fact, terrified at the prospects of travelling through the heart of the Blackfoot country.
>
> I remonstrated in vain, and at last had nothing for it but to give him leave to go; no sooner was that the case than all the other French half-breeds, commenced to signify their intentions of turning back also.
>
> I replied that I granted leave to Paul on account of his family, and on account of his long previous services to the expedition; also to his nephew Moise to accompany him, because he could not well get on without him; but I would not allow anyone else to leave the camp: a slight murmur of disapprobation then arose concerning this decision, and before they had time to get together or combine, I exclaimed, "Who is the first man who will say that he will turn back? Upon which, one bolder than the rest stood up and exclaimed, "I will go back."
>
> I rushed right at him, and seized him by the throat, and shook him, and then catching him by the collar, kicked him out of the camp. I called out then to know if any other wished also to go back but, fortunately, the retrograde movement extended no further.

Even in 1870, after smallpox had decimated the Blackfoot twice in five years, the mere mention of their name clamped cold fingers of fear around the hearts of frontiersmen. William

Butler, sent west by Alexander Morris, governor of Manitoba, tried to find a guide to take him from Rocky Mountain House to Montana. He approached one half-breed who had married a Blackfoot woman and spoke the language with fluency.

"It is a work of peril to pass the Blackfoot country at this season of the year," the man avowed, "their camps are now all 'pitching' along the foot of the mountains; they will see our trail in the snow, follow it, and steal our horses, or perhaps worse still." The man's fear intrigued Butler. "Who and what," he mused, "are these wild dusky men who have held their own against all comers, sweeping like a whirlwind over the arid deserts of the central continent?"

Butler was fascinated by the Blackfoot's legendary "wickedness," which had swelled into "a proverb among men." His first view of Rocky Mountain House quickly told him how fervently this particular proverb was believed. "The Mountain House is perhaps the most singular specimen of an Indian trading post to be found in the wide territory of the Hudson Bay Company. Every precaution known to the traders has been put in force to prevent the possibility of a surprise during a 'trade'. Bars and bolts and places to fire down at the Indians who are trading abound in every direction; so dreaded is the name borne by the Blackfeet, that it is thus their trading post has been constructed."

Destroyed from Within

In the 1860s the Blackfoot seemed invincible. For 150 years the Confederacy had stood off the white man. It had absorbed the revolutionary effect of the horse and gun on its culture, thrived on tribal warfare, survived three smallpox epidemics and kept the aggressive fur companies at bay, or at least under control. But however invincible the Blackfoot seemed on the outside, the seeds of their eventual destruction were sown forty-one years before Jerry Potts avenged the death of his mother and half-brother.

It was Kenneth McKenzie who turned the very foundation of the Blackfoot's strength into a weapon that burrowed its way into the Confederacy's heart, corrupting, compromising and dividing. Marriage. The Blackfoot had always intermarried freely, forging strong bonds among allied tribes. Within the Confederacy blood and marriage determined loyalties. Since both were out of the white man's grasp and since he couldn't coerce the Blackfoot with trade goods, he had no tools to build a relationship.

Kenneth McKenzie, one of the legion of Scots who formed the backbone of the Hudson's Bay Company, had been lured away from the Red River by the American Fur Company in 1827. McKenzie's job was to break the Confederacy's blockade by establishing a beach-head in Blackfoot territory. He had already absorbed the essentials of assimilation from the HBC and quickly took a Peigan princess as his wife, purchasing her with a dazzling array of high-quality goods. He then recruited men who could speak Blackfoot, rewarding those willing to take Blackfoot "country wives." He also instructed his people on important Blackfoot traditions, taboos and ceremonies.

Even so, in 1831 the Blackfoot burned him out of his first post, Fort Floyd, which he had built three years earlier at the mouth of the Yellowstone. Before erecting Fort Union on the same spot, he negotiated a trade treaty with the Blackfoot, relying heavily on the connections between his traders' native wives and their families. The fur company threw such a lavish celebration it drew thousands of Blackfoot from all along the Missouri. The blockade was over, though the agreement was fragile at best.

British and American traders were slow to understand the value of a country wife. The French-Canadian voyageurs and *coureurs de bois* had pioneered the strategy of living *à la façon du pays* a century earlier. An Indian woman in your bed did much more than provide scalp insurance and relieve the appalling boredom and loneliness of a trader's life. Free trader Andrew Garcia thought of his Indian wife as "a sleeping dictionary," claiming that having one was "about the only way you could learn the grunts and twists that go with most Indian talk."

Indian wives guided, interpreted, sewed, made boats, mended equipment, tanned hides, cured meats and generally kept the fur traders alive. "I have not a single one in my fort that can make Rackets [snowshoes]," bemoaned Alexander Mackenzie, a trader with the North West Company at Fort Chipewyan in 1786. "I do not know what to do without these articles, see what it is to have no wives."

Missionaries frowned on cohabitation, but their condemnation carried little weight with the fur traders, who realized that nothing oiled the commercial machinery as well as a country wife. "Connubial alliances are the best security we can have of the good will of the natives," instructed Sir George Simpson, the HBC's long-time Canadian governor in 1821. "I have therefore recommended the Gentlemen to form connections with the principal families immediately on their arrival, which is no difficult matter, as the offer of their Wives and Daughters is the first token of their friendship and hospitality."

Some liked the country wife set-up so much, they took more than one. "[Norton is] one of the most debauched wretches under the sun, who wished to engross every woman in the country to himself," complained Samuel Hearne of his boss, Moses Norton, governor of the HBC's Prince of Wales Fort. "He kept for his own use five or six of the finest Indian girls, took every means in his power to prevent any European from having intercourse with the women of the country, even owned a box of poison to be administered to anyone who refused him his wife or daughter."

Regular sex, economic value and scalp insurance spelled longevity and profits for the fur traders. But the mating between whites and Indian women wasn't totally one-sided. The relationship provided Indians with access to the goods and comforts available only inside the stockaded walls of a trading post. Some forts also provided discounts on goods for the wives' relatives, enhancing their status.

To the traders, the best feature of country wives was their disposability—one who wished to "turn off" his country wife simply left on a supply boat without a word. Those with a slightly larger dose of conscience made arrangements for the "object's" care after they emerged from the wilds.

[A] girl of about fourteen years of age, was offered to me; and after mature consideration, concerning the step which I ought to take, I have finally concluded to accept of her, as it is customary for all gentlemen who remain, for any length of time, in this part of the world.

[M]y intention now is, to keep her as long as I remain in the uncivilized part of the world, and when I return to my native land, I shall endeavour to place her under the protection of some honest man, with whom she can pass the remainder of her days in this country much more agreeably than it would be possible for her to do, were she to be taken down into the civilized world, to the manners, customs and language of which, she would be an entire stranger.

But when it came time to pass on his "object" to a new protector, Daniel Harmon, devout, guilt-ridden and socially rigid, preferred to weather the frown of society at bringing a savage into its midst, rather than pass her on.

We have wept together over the early departure of several children, and especially, over the death of a beloved son. We have children still living, who are equally dear to us both. How could I spend my days in the civilized world, and leave my beloved children in the wilderness? The thought has in it the bitterness of death. How could I tear them from a mother's love, and leave her to mourn over their absence, to the day of her death?

Kenneth McKenzie suffered from none of Harmon's soft-heartedness. Bringing his Cree wife with him to the territory of her hereditary enemies, the Blackfoot, would be a bad business decision and likely a fatal one too. So when McKenzie left the HBC, he abandoned his Cree wife and two daughters. Since she was without a white protector, the traders threw the woman out of the fort, ignoring her pleas for food and shelter. She couldn't even depend on her daughters to help her stay alive since McKenzie had enrolled them in the Red River Academy, operated by the prune-faced champion of Protestant rectitude, John Macallum. His school was designed to civilize half-breed children, "make them more English." But basically, it operated like a jail. "The ladies of this

Academy are as strictly guarded...as the inmates of a Turkish Seraglio," observed a visitor. Students were forbidden to see their Indian mothers, who were tainted by the sin of unconsecrated marriage.

In 1836 McKenzie hired a young Scot named Andrew R. Potts to work at Fort Union as a clerk. Potts quickly saw the lay of the land and acquired Crooked Back from the Black Elks band of Blood Indians. Sometime around 1840, they produced Jerry Potts. In 1841, Andrew Potts was on night duty at the fort when a Peigan looking to settle a grudge showed up. Little could be seen through the narrow slit in the fort's walls so the Peigan, mistaking Potts for his target, shoved his rifle through the opening and pulled the trigger.

At the time Potts died, Alexander "I never forgive or forget" Harvey had just taken charge of Fort Union. At six feet tall, 160 pounds, with a darkly handsome face and a Satanic aura, Harvey would have been a fearsome specimen even if milk had run through his veins rather than a barely controlled psychopathic anger. At a time when death and destruction were common currency on the frontier, Alexander Harvey was something special. Once, after shooting and wounding an Indian who was stealing a cow, Harvey ambled over to the fallen man, plunked himself down, pulled out a pipe and enjoyed a smoke while the man howled in agony and begged for mercy. At one point Harvey companionably offered the man a puff. After a couple of pipes, Harvey tired of the sport and fired a bullet into the brave's head.

The frontier was a magnet for the desperate, the dangerous and the pathologically independent—hardly an ideal pool of employees for fur trade companies. Harvey took the frontier character to new depths, but he was valuable. He could make even the toughest men tremble and that, coupled with a nimble entrepreneurial mind, made him a priceless commodity to a company operating on the doorstep of the Confederacy. A murder here, an atrocity there—small prices to pay for a man who got the job done.

When Andrew Potts was killed, Harvey took on his woman, Crooked Back, and one-year-old Jerry Potts. Shortly after that, he assumed control of Fort McKenzie on the upper Missouri. In 1844 a group of Indians stole a pig from the fort and during their getaway killed a "Negro" known only as Reese. No one knew which Indians had done it or even which tribe they came from. Alexander Harvey didn't care. On the frontier, a Negro's hide normally didn't rank much above that of a redskin. But as far as Harvey was concerned, any excuse for retaliation would do.

A band of Blackfoot arrived at the fort shortly after Reese had been roughly planted in the ground. Unaware of the pig incident, they congregated as usual outside the gate, waiting for trading to begin. Without a word of warning, Harvey fired the fort's cannon, primed with grape-shot, point-blank into the throng. When the acrid smoke cleared, thirteen lay dead and nine wounded. Yipping like a coyote, Harvey ran outside, dispatched the living and scalped the lot of them. Crazed with his bloody coup, he brandished his grisly trophies and performed a manic scalp dance into the wee hours of the morning.*

The Blackfoot returned, this time in force. They besieged the fort, trapping the two dozen traders inside. The Indians intended to starve them out but the Missouri ice broke up early that year, freeing the traders' boats. The desperate men slipped out of the fort, paddling madly to safety. The Blackfoot weren't entirely cheated of revenge: they burned Fort McKenzie to the ground.

A little mayhem was acceptable to the American Fur Company, but Harvey had gone too far. Forts cost money and as much as one hundred thousand dollars would be lost with the disruption of a season's business. If the delicate understanding that Kenneth McKenzie had pieced together with the Blackfoot collapsed, the potential loss would run into the millions. When the escaped traders fingered Harvey as the trouble-maker, the company promptly sacked him. McKenzie was rebuilt but named Fort Brulé, lest any taint remain.

Alexander Harvey, taking his dog and rifle, walked and paddled seven hundred miles to St. Louis to demand reinstatement—but the American Fur Company was adamant. An

---

* Despite popular misconception, scalping was practised by both whites and Indians on the frontier. In fact, some believe that the Spanish, demanding a scalp as proof of a kill before paying a bounty on Indians, introduced the practice to North America.

angry Harvey returned to the territory and set up a rival trading post near one just built by Alexander Culbertson, first called Fort Lewis, later Fort Benton. Harvey spent his spare time tracking down the traders who'd betrayed him. Vengeance was calculated precisely to the scale of the offence. Ring-leaders got a death sentence, those who'd merely gone along received a savage stomping. When the last man had been punished, Harvey moved to St. Louis, where his character must have mellowed as his wealth increased. When he died at the age of forty-five, reportedly a rich man, his epitaph read, "Here lies a brave, honest and kindhearted man."

When Harvey hurried off to St. Louis, he abandoned Jerry, then about five years old, and Crooked Back. Once again Potts was "adopted" by a trader who took over Harvey's claim on Crooked Back. This time he fared better as his new "father," Andrew Dawson, another Scot, had more honey than daggers in his soul. A skilful trader, Dawson taught Potts English and introduced him to the fur trade. Crooked Back stayed four years with Dawson but she longed for her own people. When Jerry was nine she said goodbye to the white man and returned with him to her Black Elk band. Her son joyously exchanged trousers and a buckskin shirt for breech clout and paint as he prepared to enter the world of the Blackfoot warrior.

Blackfoot warriors

Jerry Potts and his generation of warriors were blissfully unaware that they represented the last hurrah of Blackfoot invincibility. Outwardly, the Confederacy had survived everything the white man threw at it—the gun, the horse, intermarriage with the fur traders and all that followed: smallpox, whiskey and the buffalo's decline. But each assault on their culture insidiously nibbled away at the Blackfoot's will and cohesion.

Kenneth McKenzie's successful establishment of Fort Union in 1831 had been the beginning of the end. Slowly and surely, more posts were established, pushing deeper and deeper into the heart of Blackfoot territory. As time passed, the Blackfoot became more and more addicted to the white man's products—most particularly his whiskey. In the 1860s, though still invincible on the outside, the Blackfoot Confederacy was rotting on the inside.

PART TWO

The Great Lone Land

CHAPTER 3

My Horse Is My Bride

MY HORSE IS MY BRIDE

I'm away, I'm away, o'er the prairies so wide,
The prairie is my home, and my horse is my bride.
On, On good steed, we have got our release,
For your master is one of the Mounted Police.

In this wild Indian land, with the sun for my guide,
Revolver in hand, and a sword by my side,
And those who don't sign our treaty of peace,
Shall feel the cold steel of the Mounted Police.

We'll fight the rude savage, and cheer for our homes,
And ride o'er the prairie where the buffalo roams.
The proud desperado his robbin' shall cease,
We'll learn them to dread the bold Mounted Police.

When on guard on the prairie with carbine in hand,
My mind often roams to my native land
And the dear friends at home as I quicken my pace
But I am far from them now in the Mounted Police.

Then hurrah boys hurrah, for our wild life is free,
The care of a province our pastime shall be,
Our steeds feel the impulse their paces increase,
Make way there in front for the Mounted Police.

Here's a health to Paris, long may it reign
If God will protect me, I'll see it again,
When my time has expired, I will take my release,
And then bid "Adieu" to the Mounted Police.

There were really only two absolute necessities for a Mounted Policeman—fortitude and a good horse. The first thirty-eight horses had been purchased from the American military in Dakota and Iowa. They were small, powerful animals, largely unbroken, but accustomed to life on the frontier. These were the beasts that broke in the soft backsides of the first contingent.

Colonel French found plenty that displeased him during his first inspection of his command at Lower Fort Garry, but nothing more so than the horses. "Scarcely fit for our work," he declared after a cursory once-over. In truth, they weren't much to look at, a scruffy hodgepodge seemingly more suited to carts than saddles. Indifferent in colour with no breeding to speak of, they defied categorization, save the all-purpose prairie catch-all—mustang. Colonel French's years in the military had indelibly imprinted on him the importance of appearance. How could his command impress the savages and outlaws in the West if they were mounted on such creatures?

Sergeant Sam Steele, who had been breaking the horses, agreed they weren't pretty but, he pointed out, once gentled, they could box the compass as well as any he'd ever seen and, though small, were remarkably tough. Steele respectfully pointed out there was another issue: the half-breeds had told him that, unlike the mustangs, horses brought from the East needed a year's acclimatization before they could handle the harsher prairie conditions.

Colonel French would have none of it. He decided that he would supervise the selection of proper horses in Toronto and bring them to Manitoba when he returned.

The Irish love of good horseflesh was rooted deep inside George French. He was an excellent horseman. His own personal mount, Silver Blaze, stood out among the best thoroughbreds. A graceful chestnut, his face blaze and white socks shone like beacons in contrast to his rich, burnished coat. Silver Blaze epitomized the military horse, and riding him, Colonel French looked every inch the commander of men. He had purchased Silver Blaze in the 1860s at the annual County Monoghan horse fair when he was a young officer with the Royal Irish Constabulary. When the Colonel came to Canada, he brought Silver Blaze along because he couldn't bear to part with him.

Colonel French wasn't an officer who possessed an easy familiarity with his men. His stony countenance rarely changed and some of his men swore they'd never seen him smile. French rarely complimented or encouraged but was quick to criticize and chastise. In contrast, he lavished attention on Silver Blaze. Heaven help his batman if the horse wasn't perfectly turned out, mane and tail correctly braided, hooves trimmed, muzzle whiskers cut and coat brushed to a high gloss. This single observable passion didn't escape the men. Sub-Constable Joseph Carscadden, witty and perpetually sour, came to loathe the horse. "[T]he only thing the Colonel cares about—man, woman or beast—is his big chestnut," he grouched. "An unkind comment but one I'm sorry to say more than a few of the men agree with."

On returning to Toronto in early 1874, Colonel French chose the remainder of the horses. They were handsome specimens, tall thoroughbreds (none less than fifteen and a half hands), stable-raised and fed on the best grain and hay—these were suitable horses for his command.

On June 6, 1874, the second contingent of the North West Mounted Police left Toronto in two special trains containing 244 horses, 16 officers and 201 constables and sub-constables plus one civilian, Henri Julien, quickly dubbed the Artist by the men. At Sarnia nine cars containing disassembled wagons and hay mowers were added, and a further two cars with thirty-four horses joined on in Detroit.

On June 12, 1874, after an uneventful six-day, 1,300-mile trip, the new recruits of the Force disembarked in Fargo, North Dakota.

COLONEL FRENCH

> The train being shunted on a siding about noon, and the horses disembarked and attended to, we began getting the wagons out and putting them together. This was a very tedious business, as the persons who furnished the wagons had bundled them into the cars in detached parts; and instead of getting so many wagons complete in each car, one had to hunt right through to get all the parts required.
>
> Finally we had to empty all the cars together, place the parts on the ground, and in this manner more rapid progress was made. The saddlery from England was all in pieces, but each box was complete in itself, and consequently the saddlers, working under the saddler-major

got them together pretty quickly.

When one looked around, on this evening, and saw acres of ground covered with wagons and stores of all sorts, it did not look as if we would get away under several days. The Fargo people quite enjoyed the sight; they considered that it would be at least a week before we got off; but they had little idea of what can be done with properly organized reliefs of men.

At 4 o'clock a.m. of the 13th, the saddlers were at work on the harness and saddlery, the wheelers putting the wagons together, and an officer and thirty men getting out stores and loading them. This party was relieved at 8 o'clock a.m., again at noon and again at 4 o'clock p.m.

At 5 o'clock p.m. D Division drove out with twenty-nine loaded wagons; at 7 p.m. E Division following, and by the afternoon of the 14th F Division cleared up everything, (with the exception of heavy stores, going down by steamer), and came to where the other divisions were camped, about six miles from Fargo.

Though worn out by two days of four-hours-on, four-hours-off shifts, the troopers left Fargo in high spirits. They'd worked together like seasoned veterans, efficient and fast. As they pulled out of Fargo, the cheers of impressed residents rang in their ears—it was a good omen for the march west. The only blot on their departure was the mysterious disappearance of four horses. Rumours sped up and down the ranks. Had the officer in charge sold them? Had the Sioux crept into camp and stolen them? Or had some lazy lout not tethered them properly?

JEAN D'ARTIGUE

We proceeded about six miles when we pitched our tents and prepared our evening meal for the first time in the open prairie. With the exception of a few who took part in the Red River expedition of 1870, we knew nothing about prairie life, so the greatest tumult I ever witnessed reigned for a time among us.

Constables were shouting for night sentries, cooks were calling for wood and water, while at the same time, just by them, was flowing the river, whose banks were covered with fuel. Everything in fact was in confusion that evening. After many ups and downs order was at last restored.

The weather was glorious and the terrain beautiful, rich with the fertile bounty of the Red River in spring. The horses appeared fit and healthy, only one having died on the train. The thirty-four horses picked up in Detroit proved to be trail-ready western mustangs—in spite of Colonel French's dislike of the breed. Though many of the troopers never developed an affinity for their mounts, for others it was love at first sight.

HENRI JULIEN

My horse was a thorough bred mustang, with all the virtues and vices of his race. He was docile enough, affectionate after a fashion, at times dull as a post, at other times intelligent, vivacious and proud. He knew me well, as we had been constant companions.... But like all old acquaintances, he was sometimes inclined to be too familiar.

I had christened him "Old Rooster." And I have since fancied that he did not feel complimented by the appellation.

In the first place, he may have objected to being called old, when he was probably not more than fifteen, and in the next place, he may not have liked being compared to the type of ridiculous vain-glorious birds. "Old Rooster" was not much to look at, but for the jog of the prairie, you could not ask for a better horse. I kept him to the end.

Though free with their complaints, the second contingent had experienced little real hardship. Training had been rigorous but they had always had a roof over their heads, good horses, clean clothes, moderate weather and plentiful food. Then came the trail.

JEAN D'ARTIGUE

A repast on the prairies of the North-West had for us, at least, the charm of novelty. Let the reader represent to himself men seated in groups around several fires, each having a large cup of tea and a tin plate holding a slice of bacon and two or three biscuits, and he will have an idea of the food on which we had to live on our journey.

Such a plain and frugal meal aroused murmurs among the more fastidious. Some were complaining of the quality of the food, and some of the scant quantity.

"Does the government take us for slaves by giving us such victuals?" says one of the former.

"They must think we are babies by giving us such scanty meals," says one of the latter.

The grumbling was increasing when a constable [Sergeant-Major Joe Francis], an old veteran of the Six Hundred Light Brigade, interposed and asked what was the matter. One of them said he would die before he would try to live on bacon.

"Oh no," said he, "you spoiled child of your mother, before many days are over, a slice of bacon will be as welcome as a piece of chicken." Then turning to those who were complaining of the small quantity of food, he said: "If you are dissatisfied now, what will your feeling be when you have nothing to eat."

The first night, despite half-full stomachs, the men quickly fell asleep. When dawn broke, the trumpeter crawled out of his tent and, yawning hugely, blew reveille. Virtually no one moved. The only signs of life were foraging horses and a handful of officers scurrying about preparing for the day. That all changed abruptly when the sergeants unlimbered their vocal cords, offering a variety of unpalatable ultimatums to the laggards. After a quick breakfast, the three divisions moved off for their first real day's march.

FRED BAGLEY

June 15, 1874

Sounded Reveille at 4 a.m. Marched at 5 a.m. 8 miles, and halt for dinner of Biscuit and bread only. Helmets issued. Started again at 2 p.m. I had a lovely ride of 16 miles on a bareback horse with a backbone as sharp (so it seemed) as a cross cut saw, at the same time leading a string of several other horses. Was not at all displeased when I saw Fred Brown, the Troop cook halt his waggon and prepare to cook supper.

Only an excited fifteen-year-old would consider riding bareback when a perfectly good saddle was available. For the rest, chaffed thighs and blistered hands were the rule as Colonel French pushed hard to cover the 160 miles from Fargo to Fort Dufferin as quickly as possible.

JEAN D'ARTIGUE

That day we travelled thirty miles. Rather a long march for horses that had just ended a long journey by railroad, and after leaving Fargo, living on grass too tender yet to be substantial. Furthermore, most of them were not broken to harness. The same speed was kept up the following days; the result being that the horses failed rapidly in flesh and in strength.

On the morning of the 18th we found many of them disabled, and two of them went down to rise no more.

The reasons the Commissioner had for ordering such marches are still a mystery to me....

The capacity of Col. French, as commander of the expedition, was already being questioned among the men. We began to discuss what would become of us if, when once on the vast prairies, several hundred miles from human help, we would attempt to make marches such as we were then experiencing.

The disabled horses being unable to go as fast as the rest, were left to follow behind in charge of a small party of men, and it fell to my lot to be one of them. As for the main body, they went on as fast as before, and reached Dufferin on the evening of the 19th of June. The next day we arrived with our sick horses.

Major James Macleod had brought the first contingent from Lower Fort Garry to Fort Dufferin to prepare a departure camp for the whole Force. The rendezvous on June 19 of over three hundred men, A, B and C Divisions with the newer recruits in D, E and F, turned into a joyous celebration. Dufferin was a typical outpost of the day, with a couple of wooden buildings, a tent city, traders' shacks, and a handful of dirt streets. But after their long trip it seemed as welcoming and exciting as New York City. They were a colourful crew with their acres of tents, wagons, a herd of cows and calves brought from Lower Fort Garry, half-breed guides and scouts and Red River carts. The beginning of their great adventure was less than three weeks away. For the first time they began to feel like Mounted Policemen, a force, a community of daring souls bound to right wrongs and avenge the downtrodden—all of this in the face of untold dangers from the savages.

French was delighted at the thirty-mile-a-day clip from Fargo "without any particular mishap or accident to speak of"—other than the trifling death of three horses on the trail. "The conduct of the men had been exemplary," he noted with satisfaction, "their general appearance and conduct invariably attracting the favourable notice of the railroad officials and others en route."

But the half-breeds and handful of other locals who showed up for the arrival of the new troopers didn't trouble to hide their laughter when they saw the pretty horses the police had brought from the East. One trader, who claimed specific knowledge of the country, ventured a prediction. "Well, if you have luck you may get back by Christmas with 40% of your horses," he told an indignant Colonel French.

If the rough-looking welcoming party were contemptuous of the Force's animals, Colonel French's officers were deeply disturbed at their condition. Three were dead and dozens played out after a paltry six-day, 160-mile march over one of the best-travelled roads west of Chicago—thousands of settlers poured into the Red River Valley every year using the very same route. The weather had been excellent and water readily available. What's more, they had nothing much to pull since most of the heavy equipment had been sent along the river by steamboat. And because they were bringing extra horses for the second contingent, there were plenty available as remounts. What's going to happen, the officers wondered, when we're marching hundreds of miles into the frontier with heavily laden wagons and no spare horses?

That night French summoned his officers to receive reports on the Force's readiness for the march. A furious argument broke out. Inspectors Young and Richer were vehement in urging that the "horse killers," the nine-pound guns and mowing machines, be left behind. Richer, an experienced horseman, loudly disparaged the Toronto animals. Major Macleod, afraid that Colonel French would place the inspector under arrest, escorted him from the meeting.

Later Macleod privately suggested to the Colonel that it wasn't too late to lighten the horses' loads by sending some of their supplies via rail to St. Louis, then by river boat up the Missouri to Fort Benton. French responded tersely that the Mounted Police had the best horses ever taken out of Toronto.

While the officers argued, most of the camp was still; half the men were unconscious with exhaustion after the long ride from Fargo to Fort Dufferin. And, judging by the smell in the tents, their sleep had been aided by a good nip or two to help ease the ache from their bones. It was only 9:30 p.m. but seemed much later. Clouds rolling in from the west darkened the sky and drew down the night early.

Bagley's stomach growled, matching a faint rumble outside. To call the second contingent's first supper in Fort Dufferin lean was an overstatement. The cook wagons lagged far behind the troops, and they arrived to find the first contingent's supplies had run low. The weary troops had to be satisfied with a piece of fat bacon, an oatmeal cake and "23."*

---

* There were a number of Cockneys in the Troop, and many of the Canadians enjoyed emulating their slang, none more so than Fred Bagley. "Entries in my diary such as: Supper of 23, or 'Breakfast of wet and dry' (the former phrase meaning in the language of the funny men 'tea only', and the latter 'tea—or water and hard tack') were frequent," he recalled later.

Still, it all tasted exquisite to the famished fifteen-year-old. But many of the men dozed off during their tiny evening meal.

Bagley fell onto his hard bedroll, his arms and legs trembling with the effort of staying upright. But it was fatigue born of honest, physical labour. At fifteen the body has no memory. Aches and pains are sucked into sleep's cleansing machine. Each day on the march from Fargo, Bagley woke fresh, having forgotten the saddle's hardness, the sharpness of grit kicked up by hundreds of hooves and even the irritation of the loathsome mosquitoes, which obviously knew a good thing in two hundred-plus soft-fleshed young men.

As Bagley lit his candle, preparing to settle into *The Last of the Mohicans*, a vision of his mother's face prodded him. At home he would still be hours from bed, instead of reading by candle-light among a dozen heavily snoring men. Perhaps he would be finishing off the long summer evening playing cards with his mother, or listening to his father fulminate about the politics of the day before turning in for an hour's immersion in the Wild West. That world seemed awfully far away.

His book set aside, Bagley drifted into sleep, dream fragments flitting in and out of his mind: Chingachgook, Indian maidens, the crack of gunfire in battle. As he slipped deeper he imagined the stink of cordite and the ground shaking....

It was a massed Indian attack, unlike any Fred Bagley, veteran of a hundred Indian battles, had ever experienced before. The blast from the latest volley rolled across the plains, stunning his ears. The Indians had a lot of guns, the firing rose and fell in waves, yet never ceased. They had cannon too. Their deep boom swelled and died, swelled and died.

Where, he wondered, would Indians get cannon? The men on either side of him jostled and pushed as they scrambled to fall back. The opposition was too great. He grabbed his hat and rifle and looked for better cover. Crack! A gun exploded right in front of him. His side! Sudden, hot pain. He'd been shot. Bagley moaned in agony.

"Get up, goddamn it!" The sergeant-major laid another sharp kick at Bagley's ribs. "Sound alarm! Quick, boy. Blow your bloody bugle, like you've never blown it before!"

The Bride's Revolt

"Indians!" screamed one of the men, unable to control the frightened quaver in his voice. Still woozy from his brief sleep and rude awakening, Bagley vaguely heard a Scottish voice chanting a Gaelic prayer. Blind in the inky dark, he scrambled on hands and knees searching for his trumpet. All around the men flung themselves about, fumbling for weapons and clothes. A large boot crushed Bagley's arm as he swept it in a semi-circle desperately feeling for his trumpet.

There! His trumpet bell! In addition to the cacophony of the men and the terrible noise outside, he heard a rhythmic thud on the canvas. Arrows, Bagley guessed. He dimly made out the forms of men; some had charged outside, others, wearing only boots and undershirts in the hot night, were milling around uncertainly in the tent. Was it better to go out and fight or stay in and defend?

An acid flush surged in Bagley's throat. He had no gun. This was supposedly friendly territory. Only sentries, officers and a handful of men in the first contingent had been issued carbines. Their side-arms, personally ordered by Colonel French from England, hadn't arrived yet. Sergeant Steele had provoked a good laugh at supper a few hours ago, when one of the troopers asked about guns and ammunition. Steele told them that if the second contingent didn't shoot any better than the first, they might as well be issued slingshots. The Militia at Lower Fort Garry, hardly a steely-eyed band of sharpshooters, had trounced the Mounties in a recent shooting contest.

Bagley made his decision. Damn the arrows! He'd sound the alarm, rally the troops and save the day. But as Bagley bolted for the tent flap, the whole thing collapsed, flattening him. The heavy canvas nearly suffocated him as it lay like a foul dead thing pressing on his back and head. He thrashed wildly, crawling towards where he thought he'd last seen the opening. Muffled howls and curses filtered through to him. He fought down his panic. Bagley didn't care if a thousand Indians were waiting to strip his hide from stem to stern. He had to get out of there. The opening. Where? Where? He drove his fist against the canvas again and again. Suddenly he popped free.

Bagley erupted from the tent's clutches. Astonishingly, there were no Indians waiting, only pandemonium. It was night, but it wasn't. Every few seconds lightning bolts clawed through the sky, followed by sheet lightning that lit everything in an eerie glow. Then the black descended, the thunder bludgeoned. Back and forth it went, dizzying in the speed of change.

JEAN D'ARTIGUE

At that moment we were spectators of a scene which will be never forgotten by those who witnessed it. A dazzling and continuous glare of lightning, which seemed like one sheet of fire above our heads; crashes of thunder which appeared to shake the earth to its very centre, and a hurricane, which in spite of our utmost efforts blew down our tents, formed an imposing sight capable of frightening men less resolute than ourselves.

A wall of water smacked Bagley in the face, pummelling him with raindrops and hail bullets. Thunder almost knocked him down with its intensity. He filled his lungs and blew his trumpet until his ribs hurt. Again and again he blew until he gasped for breath. No one heard—a boy could hardly be expected to compete with Zeus.

Men struggled from tents and gasped as the storm lashed them. The noise was so loud it was impossible to make yourself understood to a man next to you. But by a freak of aerodynamics the storm threw words from the distant corral. "The horses! My god, the horses!"

A sheet of lightning spotlighted the corral, and Bagley saw horses rearing, bucking and kicking at the wagons and rope that penned them. Barefoot, he dove back into the tent, burrowing for his boots. Every square inch of canvas seemed to weigh a hundred pounds. He got lucky and his fingers closed on leather. He dragged his boots free and stuffed his feet into them but the rain instantly filled them to the brim. He hauled the boots off and threw them aside. His ears rang with the claps and crashes overhead and, as he ran barefoot towards the corral, he heard the groan of tent poles and the gun-like report as they snapped all over camp.

Tents were collapsing everywhere. Bagley dodged quickly as the wind suddenly gusted, picked up several hundred pounds of wet canvas and flung it across the compound, knocking over two men. Despite the rain he could smell the sharp tangy odour of lightning in the air. Bagley's mind flashed to recognition— this must have been the smell of gunpowder from his dream.

The high squeal of panicked horses punctuated the din. He could just make out a dark surging mass, taller than any one horse ought to be.

WILLIE PARKER

I was sleeping in a square tent with twelve men when I felt the ground trembling. As I jumped outside, it was like day with the continuous lightning. Then I saw a ter- rifying sight. The two hundred and fifty horses, with their eyes like fire, tails straight up in the air, and what looked like steam coming from their nostrils, were charging down on top of us at breakneck speed. In an instant they struck the heavy wagons and big rope,

Stampede. This and all subsequent drawings by Henri Julien. He prettied up the look of the Force for public consumption.

knocking over several of the former and breaking the latter. I know my hair stood on end as I stood at the corner of the tent. As the horses flew by me I hit two or three with my fists.

The tent was torn down but none of us were hurt. Our herd of cows and calves were about one hundred yards in the rear of our tents and as the horses struck them we heard them bellow. Then there was a human scream and we could also hear a tin pail being carried along by the horses' hooves.

Sam Steele had been riding near the corral when the storm hit. His first thought was to marvel at the ferocity of a wind that could whip the breath from a man's body. Constable John Coleman, driving a wagon and team, had just passed the gate and was heading to the corral when a ball of lightning struck in the horses' midst and exploded upwards like a firecracker.

Already jittery, the horses, tied by their halters to cables in the corral, rose up in a single mass of hysteria. Steele could hardly believe it as the horses not only bolted, but climbed over each other, two and three deep, to get out of the corral.

SAM STEELE

I shall never forget that night. I had full view of the stampede, being not more than 50 yards from the horses as they rushed at the gate and attempted to pass it, scrambling and rolling over one another in one huge mass. This and the unceasing flashes of lightning, the rolling of the thunder, and the loud shouts of the troopers as they vainly attempted to stop the horses and the mad gallop of Colman's team, gave it a weird and romantic complexion, typically suggestive of the wild west.

Steele's horse plunged and bucked. Reins in one fist, saddle horn in another, he clamped his legs hard and held on. The corral posts fell like twigs as the horses fought their way over wagons and ropes. Suddenly nothing stood between John Coleman and the seething mass of horseflesh except a handful of guards.

The horses quickly dispensed with the guards, trampling and driving them into the soup of mud. Sub-Constable Bill Latimer, vainly trying to grab a passing halter, fell against the onslaught and lay still, blood bubbling out of a gash stretching across his forehead from ear to ear. The drumming of a thousand hooves shook the ground as the stampede gathered force. The shouts of the men disappeared into the mêlée. Steele bellowed at Coleman, "Turn your horses! Turn them, man! Turn them!" Coleman had no more control than a baby and his team shot off at an angle, the wagon careening behind.

A stampede has its own life, reacting as a mass, shifting and weaving from the pressure of some unseen force. After careering through the camp like a tidal wave, knocking over wagons, trampling stores and buffeting men, the horses turned to the river, ears back, necks flattened and legs pumping full speed.

John Coleman, one of the few with any teamstering experience, bit back his terror and clung to his reins. The river meant death. If the initial somersault over the steep bank onto the rocks didn't finish him, the wagon and horses landing on him would. Through some lucky quirk the bit, clenched and useless between the teeth of his lead horse, suddenly slipped and took. He gained a little control, then more. Once their heads were turned, his horses calmed quickly, suddenly uninterested in the pounding herd just a few hundred yards away.

The camp looked like a massacre site. Constable Edward Maunsell, a hard-nosed Irishman, hobbled aimlessly, his clothes in shreds. "You all right, Constable?" Steele yelled, bending almost double from his saddle in order to be heard. Maunsell stared at the source of the words. His sleeve had been ripped from his shirt, the sole of his boot dangled, the other foot was bare and mud smeared his face. "Feel queer," he muttered over and over. Steele couldn't understand a word but figured that if the man was walking he couldn't be too badly hurt. Steele charged off and Maunsell sank to the ground.

The storm eased, allowing the men enough time to haul a couple of the leaden tents out of their mud lakes and erect one for the sick and injured, another for some men to crowd into for a few hours' sleep. Bagley, giddy with fatigue, rolled himself in a water-soaked blanket. His rest didn't last very long. The storm regained its strength and flung itself at them again. The men in the tent grabbed the flapping canvas and spent the night holding it down against the howling wind. Another group of about fifty men stood all night, shivering in the rain, holding the horses that hadn't bolted "over the hills and far away."

When dawn eased over the battered horizon, Bagley hauled himself up and gazed at the carnage. He didn't have much time for contemplation. Steele rode up, mud colouring him and his horse a uniform colour. "Saddle up, Fred!" he barked. "You're with Major Walsh."

Though by far the youngest, Fred Bagley was also one of the four or five best horsemen in the force. Energized, he ran to what was left of the corral and struggled with the muddy tack to cinch the girth, fingers fumbling in his excitement. He found James Walsh, who tossed him a biscuit. "Let's go!"

Sub-Inspector "Irish" Jack French, the Commissioner's brother, took William Parker and two others to scout the river bank, hoping to find some stragglers. Instead they found a half-breed, lying flat on his back.

"Is he dead, sir?" asked Parker, trying not to show his horror at the filthy body. French dismounted and walked over to the man. He shook him gently with his hand, placed his palm over his heart, searching for a pulse, and bent down to see if he was breathing. French stiffened, jumped up and laid a solid kick on the unconscious form. "Drunk, by God!" he exclaimed disgustedly.

Walsh's ragged group of a half-dozen men made for the border and rode miles into U.S. territory, knowing that they'd be a laughing stock if they lost their horses before they even began. The officers didn't mention it, but in the back of their minds was the thought that the stampede might have been caused by Sioux as a cover to steal their horses. The storm was merely a serendipitous addition to their plan. If that were the case, they might be riding straight into a Sioux ambush. They passed the U.S. military post at Fort Pembina. Still no sign. Adrenalin pumped them up at first, but hours went by without a trace of the horses. Bagley began to think they'd have to return empty-handed. Then they saw them—first one small group and nearby another, eighty horses in all.

Fortunately the horses were all so winded that rounding them up was easy. At midnight, Walsh's posse rode back into camp, driving the runaways in front of them. Many of the horses were on the verge of collapse and simply sank to the ground; some of them hardly moved for several days. Bagley's horse lagged behind. Walsh, thinking the boy was lost, rode back to find him. He spotted the animal, apparently riderless. In the darkness Walsh could just make out a lump draped across the saddle, arms hanging down. Sub-Constable Fred Bagley—sound asleep.

Walsh gingerly dismounted, easing his aching feet and legs back to solid ground. He lifted the boy off his horse and carried him to his tent, where he pulled off the boy's filthy boots and stuffed him into his still sodden bedroll. There wasn't a flicker of movement. Reveille would be late next morning.

"Not much Fenimore Cooper romance about this, but rather strenuous for a slip of a boy as I am," Fred Bagley wrote in his diary.

At dawn the following morning, Sub-Inspector James Walker herded his thirty-five trembling refugees into camp. He had tracked them during glimpses in the illumination of lightning flashes. Walker rode five horses into the ground, covered 120 miles, and got soaked and dried out three times. Steele pulled in not long after, bringing another fifty. He'd ridden 112 miles on one horse. His mustang's head hung to its knees, its legs, battered by bush and rock, were like raw meat and lather lay so thick on its coat it looked ready for a shave.

They Hang Horse Thieves, Don't They?

The number one lesson Fred Bagley had learned during his three-month career in the North West Mounted Police was how to make himself invisible. If you didn't get noticed, you didn't get put to work, which in a military organization never went away. As soon as one job was done, another always lurked just around the corner.

Bagley quickly came to the conclusion that invisibility was essential—particularly because, as the youngest sub-constable among some three hundred men, he was at the bottom of the pecking order. Everyone called him boy or lad, and everyone felt comfortable giving him orders; even the half-breeds had more status.

Bagley was so good at becoming invisible that the only officer who consistently noticed him was Colonel French himself. The Colonel had a knack of appearing at inconvenient moments—just when Bagley was settling down for a good read or heading over to hang around the half-breeds— demanding to know where he was going, what he was doing and who had told him to do it. Bagley took special pains to avoid the Colonel, but somehow the energetic commander always found him, as if magnetically attracted to idleness. Colonel French invariably had an inventory of important jobs, all of which had to be done yesterday.

The Colonel pushed Bagley to new heights of inventiveness; now he always took care to be in the midst of fulfilling a bogus order whenever he encountered him. Early one morning, for instance, while everyone else was sorting supplies for the march west, Bagley was prowling the camp. He'd snapped the buckle off his belt playing tug of war with a stray dog and he was looking for a replacement. If he could find one of the troopers not yet fully dressed and looking the other way, he might discover that another buckle had been "dropped."

Colonel French materialized from behind a wagon. Bagley stepped up his pace, snapped off a brisk salute and a hearty, "Morning, sir! Carrying a message for Inspector Walsh, sir. Wants it delivered soonest, sir." French paused for a moment. Bagley, heart sinking, thought his ruse had failed. French returned his salute. "Very good, carry on." Bagley hurried away.

Fred Bagley with dog in the early 1880s

Fred Bagley was no shirker. He was happy—or perhaps willing would be more accurate—to do his own work, but unwilling to do extra, particularly when that extra was someone else's. When he'd first enlisted, some of his fellow sub-constables in Toronto had sized him up as easy prey and shunted him on to the dreary job of room orderly, normally a position rotated through the men. Bagley soon realized his fellow troopers thought that "permanent orderly" was just the position for a boy.

In a way, being an orderly wasn't a bad assignment. He had to draw supplies for the cooks at ration call and, while they were cooking, set the barrack-room tables for the men. During dinner he fetched, carried and served, occasionally dodging kicks from men who thought their portion meagre or all fat and no lean. Afterward came clean-up: scrubbing the tables and benches and returning unused food to the supply stores.

It was hard work while it lasted, but orderlies were always well-fed and the work allowed plenty of unsupervised time for high jinks and daydreaming. But there was no getting around it, orderly duty was the lowest of the low. Frederick Augustus Bagley, hero of *The Last of the Mohicans*, hadn't joined the North West Mounted Police to become anyone's dogsbody.

Fred Bagley was small and skinny but he was fierce. He'd discovered that a savage counter-attack—or pre-emptive strike—with every iota of energy thrown into a vicious flurry of blows and kicks, usually discouraged any further annoyance. So, the next time Bagley found himself marshalled firmly towards the orderly room, after the sergeant had clearly assigned the job to someone else, he acted, with a head butt to one of his escorts, an elbow to another, then a sprint to the stables, which was where he had been assigned in the first place. By the time they arrived at Dufferin, no one went out of his way to bother Fred Bagley and he worked as orderly only when it was his turn.

There was one thing missing from Fred Bagley's complete satisfaction as a member of the North West Mounted Police— a decent horse. The one he'd been issued just after he arrived at Dufferin was a plug, a nag, a plodder—barely fit for an elderly lady, let alone an official member of the Mounted Police. He could hardly rescue an Indian maiden on an animal that actually groaned when you spurred it from trot to canter.

What he wanted was a buffalo pony, a mount suitable for Kit Carson, Wild Bill Hickok or Fred Bagley. To find his steed he would have to be creative. Fortunately, the horses had been issued to the men but not yet officially recorded.

After careful scouting, he found a nimble, spirited black whose owner was appropriately inattentive. He planned his move carefully, but just as he was ready to strike, Colonel French ordered that the horses be arranged among the divisions by colour, so as to present a more impressive spectacle on the march. A Division, which had the wagons, was assigned the dark bays, B was mounted on dark browns, C, which hauled the heavy guns, offered a splash of colour with bright chestnuts. D, Bagley's troop, drew the greys and mustangs, while behind them came E with black horses and F with light bays.

The organization by colour put paid to Bagley's black, but he didn't give up, especially when the daily rumours of Sioux atrocities were suddenly elevated from story to reality. Several reports from the U.S. military fort at Pembina told of raids up and down the Red River. The dispatches hardened Bagley's resolve; he must have a good horse if he was to go into battle with the Sioux. Others in the Force, more vivid in imagination or weaker in spirit, responded differently to the threat.

JEAN D'ARTIGUE

July 6, 1874

From my position in Division B, to which I had been transferred, I heard one morning a great uproar in Division A camping near by. Wishing to know the cause, I went out, and meeting a comrade of that division, who was splitting his sides with laughter, I enquired what it was all about. He replied:

It is a long story. You have brought us from Toronto an original character. Since his transfer to our division, he does nothing but preach temperance, and remind us of the noble duties which we are called upon to perform. Some compare him to Don Quixote, but others of more reflective minds, say that before judging him we must see him at work.

I was on duty last night when, about midnight, I suddenly saw issuing from our tent an individual clothed in white, who, after glancing rapidly on every side, made a dash through the sentry line, and out on the prairie. I thought to myself, here is one who has soon forgotten the regulations; he will doubtlessly return, and I shall know who he is. Without suspecting him of having any complicity with the Indians, I watched him closely.

Returning at last I arrested him at the entrance to the Camp, with the usual challenge, "Who comes there?" The fellow appeared disconcerted; but finding himself threatened with being marched off to the guardhouse, he declared himself a member of the Mounted Police.

"Give me the password," said I, but this he was unable to do. I was going to call the guard, when seeing him shivering with cold, I took pity on him and allowed him to pass, laughing to myself at the thought of the merriment which would be produced by relating the story of his spending the night on the prairie in his night-shirt.

Everything turned out as I expected and my story was received with the uproarious laughter that brought you from your quarters.

"Zounds!" said one, "I understand now why this fellow wears a night-shirt; it is to scare the Indians. See how cunning he is. If the Indians attack us, and are repelled, very well; but if it happens to the contrary, I would not give much for our scalps,—but he, on account of his night-shirt, will be looked upon as the Great Manitou of the whites and will remain unmolested."

The trooper, wiping his eyes after relating the story, gestured towards the gate. "Look over there! Don Quixote is on sentry."

Looking in the direction indicated, I saw a sub-constable of military appearance, walking along the sentry line, watching the surroundings of the camp, and glancing once in a while with a wistful look at his carbine and revolver, which indicated a longing to use them.

"What!" said I to myself, "can this man be the

Apostle of Temperance?" It was, indeed, but what a metamorphosis since our first meeting! The clergyman was no more, and there remained but the soldier. I was going to congratulate him on his martial appearance, when an Inspector intervened.

"Sub-constable L.," said he, "what are you thinking about to mount guard with your carbine full cocked?"

"Sir," replied our templar, "In circumstances such as these, in which we find ourselves at present in danger of being attacked at any time by Indians, one cannot be too well prepared to fire."

The inspector's face reddened, his eyes narrowed and he looked ready to hit the man, kick him, or both. "If you don't uncock your weapon," he bellowed, inches from the Apostle's face, "I'll have you arrested!"

Other recruits treated the stories of Sioux scalpings and mutilations as if they were mere trifles. Willie Parker became obsessed with the prairie's spring flowers, particularly the wild roses that coloured every nook and cranny, no matter how dry or poor the soil. Letters to his family in England bulged as he crammed in as many petals and sprigs as possible.

Fred Bagley had no time for posy-gathering. Only a few days remained before the start of the great adventure—and he had to find the right horse.

FRED BAGLEY

July 2, 1874

Reveille at 5 a.m. Breakfast at 8 of "wet and dry." General muster parade of horses 9:30 a.m. On parade until 12:45 p.m. During the parade (I am not on it) noticed a man in B Troop, very much under the "weather," holding a—yes, a real buckskin coloured mustang. As buckskin mustangs were a picturesque adjunct of the Fenimore Cooper brand of life in the wild and woolly west, and the man holding this one was in evident need of additional spiritous support, I, acting the good Samaritan, "loaned" him enough money to replenish his supply at the nearest grog shop, and offered to hold the mustang until his return.

"Shanks," slurred the soon-to-be-unhorsed. "Damn horsheeves 'r everywhere." Bagley waited until he was sure the man would not be returning precipitously, then scooted off with the mustang in tow.

As Bagley hurried back to his troop, he briefly felt sorry for his fellow sub-constable. The man was royally knackered. If he didn't complain, he'd lose an excellent horse, and god knows what kind of plug he'd get in its stead, but if he raised a ruckus, he'd be even worse off. He would have to explain how he lost him in the first place, and that would mean an admission of drunkenness and leaving camp without permission. If his record was poor, he might even be dismissed from the Force—at least ten troopers had been sent packing for drunkenness and insubordination in the past fortnight. Just that morning there'd been no tea, and only day-old biscuits for breakfast, because all the cooks were on a bender. That same day Sergeant-Major Tommie Lake was demoted to junior constable because of drunkenness.

Colonel French forbade the consumption of liquor both in camp and in town. But nobody paid much attention—it was easy to get whiskey from the many obliging traders and it was easy to hide. There were plenty of grog shops in Dufferin, and some traders had thoughtfully set up tents on the edge of the Force's camp where they did a landslide business. Barkeeps served the whiskey straight from open barrels, ladling it into cups. They'd boast about how fast they could take a full barrel "down to the wood" with nothing but the fragrant staves left.

Many of the officers, themselves prodigious drinkers, avoided punishing tipplers as long as they didn't fall down during drill or pass out on sentry duty. Colonel French grew more and more frustrated with the men's imbibing. After the incidents of the drunken cooks and Tommie Lake's demotion, the Colonel gave a long, admonishing speech during morning parade, berating the men about their consumption of alcohol. He reminded them of their duty and exhorted them to be temperate in order to set an example for the benighted savages, who couldn't be expected to know any better. He called upon them to cast the bottle aside in favour of their service to Queen and country. Fortunately, there was a strong wind that morning and he couldn't hear the quiet coughing and snickering.

Fred Bagley unsaddled his new steed, replacing the tack with his own equipment. He arrived back at his tent in time to see Major Walsh hauling one of the sub-constables, kicking, protesting and stark naked, out of his tent and cursing him with a brilliant stream of invective. Walsh liked to have his orders obeyed with alacrity; cajoling played no part in his motivational technique. This man, succumbing to the lure of a few too many "last" ones, had failed to rise for reveille and missed parade.

The commander of D Division was one of the original nine officers enlisted on September 25, 1873—a group often referred to as "The Nine"—and that alone gave James Morrow Walsh status in the Force. He had been a champion lacrosse player, and he exuded physicality in his flamboyant gestures and bravado, which always went one step further than necessary.

Adventurous and daring, Walsh was a perfect choice to lead men into the unknown. But he aggravated Colonel French constantly with his blithe refusal to attend to administrative details. He wasn't a smooth man or an easy one with his quick-tempered impatience and judgemental attitudes. But he was also humorous, loyal and steadfast, a perfect emotional foil to the glacial and distant Colonel French.

Some men thought Walsh too harsh, too quick to dish out a cuff or a kick followed by a startling string of curses. But Walsh's men almost never went on report, and even more rarely were they hauled before the Colonel, who fined troopers or confined them to barracks for even minor transgressions. Walsh's men also knew he would fight for them. On the hellish trip from Toronto to Lower Fort Garry via the Great Lakes and the Dawson Route, the troops of the first contingent had battled everything the weather and terrain could throw at them. Walsh unleashed his fury at an engineer who kept the troops waiting for twenty minutes on an open barge in the middle of a snowstorm. "He called me a murderer," George Dixon recalled ruefully, "a Goddamn blackhearted villain and told his men to kick me out and do as they liked with me. He continued abusing me for a full half hour in a very vile manner."

Walsh, well-known as one of the Force's "experienced"

drinkers, could hardly complain if his men imbibed. What he did complain about, most vociferously, was men who couldn't hold their alcohol and most importantly failed to fulfil their duties the next day.

"What's that you've got there, young rascal!" barked Walsh, turning to Bagley.

"Found him, sir. Wandering on the prairie he was, sir," Bagley responded with feudal submission.

"Wandering on the prairie? With your bridle, your blanket and your saddle on him?" Walsh queried sharply. He stood looking at Bagley for a long moment, then ambled over to the horse and gave it a quick, but thorough inspection, muttering approvingly.

"They hang horse thieves where we're heading," Walsh said loudly, then lower so only Bagley could hear, "There going to be trouble over this?"

"No sir!" Bagley snapped to attention.

"Right then. Book him in. He's yours."

Bagley landed a bonus with the horse—a full set of shoes, relatively new by the looks of them. There must have been some kind of Indian fever running through the blacksmiths because all but one of the farriers had deserted. With more than three hundred horses needing attention, an entrée to the lone remaining smith was worth a month's supply of tobacco or ready access to any of the camp's many private whiskey stores. It was well that the feet of Bagley's new horse wouldn't need attention for a long while yet.

When the sub-constable from B Division sobered up enough to realize his horse was gone, he sputtered impotently, "That boy Bagley is a natural born damned horse thief, and the vigilantes will get him some day."

With his frontier-worthy, buckskin mustang, Fred Bagley felt ready to tackle anything. He quickly got his chance. Gossip circulated around camp that the Sioux had attacked a Métis settlement in North Dakota and were massing at the border. Bagley prayed they'd cross and give him a chance to test his pony's mettle.

Telegram: July 6, 1874, Fort Pembina, North Dakota, to Winnipeg, Manitoba

"Sioux Massacre. Indian Massacre at St. Joe, or Walhalla, 20 miles West of Pembina, 2 half-breed families butchered. U.S. Troops and Canadian Mounted Police move west in pursuit of the murderers. Supposed attack on the B[oundary] Commission!"

FRED BAGLEY

July 6, 1874

Reveille at 5 a.m. Stables 5:30. Breakfast at 8 of "wet and dry."

Rumours in camp to the effect that a few days ago Sioux Indians perpetrated the massacre of the inhabitants of the village of St. Joe, U.S.A. not far from our camp, and carried off a white woman alive.

Pursuant to an offer (so it was said), by Colonel French to the O.C. [Officer in Charge] American Troops of the service of our Force in rounding up the Sioux marauders the whole Force paraded to day, in marching order, and marched to a point on the International boundary not far from where the massacre took place. "C" Troop, with the two 9 pounder guns occupied the middle of the column as we marched off.

Everyone (allegedly) overjoyed at the prospect of having some real active service when least expected, but warlike spirits dashed when despatch received from the O.C. U.S. Troops declining Colonel French's offer with thanks.

Military evolutions, with D Troop thrown forward in skirmishing order, were performed while on our return to camp across the prairie. Reached camp about 9 p.m., and although we had nothing to eat since morning, found only the familiar "wet and dry" for supper.

Jean D'Artigue, like Fred Bagley a devotee of Fenimore Cooper, set off on the Sioux adventure with high hopes.

JEAN D'ARTIGUE

July 6, 1874

As we were going along, some field manoeuvres were attempted; not very successfully, I might say, but how could it be otherwise,—men and horses cannot be well trained in three months' time for military service. Notwithstanding some defects, we did very well, and at all events we were soldiers at heart, which is the best proficiency for men in warfare. We expected to have to fight, and were ready to do it to the best of our ability.

"Did you take any part in the Franco-German war?" said a constable at my side.

"No, indeed," I replied, "this is my first experience in warfare."

"So it is with me," said he, "I long to see if the Indians have as good hands and eyes for warfare as the Canadians. It is going to be hot work, I fancy, for I hear the Sioux are well equipped and are good horsemen."

Being by this time two or three miles from the camp, in the open prairie, the command to deploy was given. I expected, at any moment to see Indians, as I had read of them in the novels, springing from the grass with their war-whoops, and charging us with their tomahawks; but I was disappointed in my expectations. We hunted the plain for miles around until sun-set, without the appearance of Indians, when, to the great dissatisfaction of all, the order was given to return to camp.

This turning out was only a sham; the Commissioner, thinking that there were still a few cowards in our ranks, and wishing to get rid of them, spread the news himself that the Sioux were in the neighbourhood, and in a state of hostility.

Sham or not, Fred Bagley didn't care. It was his first taste of the action he'd yearned for. He wasn't even upset when the troop returned tired and hungry after twelve hours to find the same "wet and dry" that they'd eaten at breakfast. The Force had marched out, looking very much the Mounted Policemen, and prepared to battle the dreaded Sioux.

In two days, July 8, the real Great Adventure would begin; the nine-hundred-mile trek to Fort Whoop Up, where they'd subdue the American outlaws and bring the wild Indians to heel. Sub-Constable Frederick Augustus Bagley, assistant trumpeter, North West Mounted Policeman #231, was going west in the footsteps of John Palliser, William Butler and Natty Bumppo.

Chapter 4

The Territory

Summer 1873

Jerry Potts squinted along his nose through the crease of two
low hills rising out of the shallow valley. Like a child's buttocks they sloped away from each other, dimpled, bald and
uneven.

Nothing. But something. A crickle at the back of his neck.
Potts sniffed the air—a long, chest-filling inhalation, then out
slowly. Nothing. He cocked his head to the side and listened.
Still nothing.

Potts sat for several minutes, immobile on his horse, staring
into the valley. Flies buzzed around his bushy moustache. Still
nothing. But something. The horse nickered, its feet scuffling
the hardpan. Five more minutes passed. Nothing moved
except Potts' hand, gently, almost imperceptibly, stroking the
cat-skin talisman hanging under his shirt. There! A wisp. A
puff, curling up through the calm afternoon air, melting away
as quickly as it appeared. Something coming.

A few years back, Potts wouldn't have been so cautious. But

a few years ago, times weren't so crazy. Nothing seemed right any more.

When Potts was a boy and living with the Black Elk band of his mother, there'd been a balance of sorts. Only a handful of whites lived in the area nurtured by the upper Missouri River and up across the Medicine Line in the land they called the British Territory. They were mostly fur traders, cautiously travelling through and occasionally living on the edge of the Blackfoot stronghold. They were rough men who depended on the Indian for furs and safe passage through the territory, as much as the Indian had come to depend on them for guns, blankets, ammunition and whiskey. It was hardly a peaceful time; there were plenty of deaths on either side, but the uneasy relationships, when broken, were always patched up again. Now the balance had shifted.

White men didn't care much about Montana until July 14, 1864, when gold showed up in Last Chance Gulch.* And they really started caring on August 29, 1866, when a small mule train guarded by fourteen heavily armed men pulled into Fort Benton, then little more than a trading stockade, a few shabby buildings and a smattering of tents. Pandemonium erupted when word leaked out that the wagons carried two and a half tons of gold dust valued at $1.25 million. Hordes followed the strike like a pack of dogs trailing a bitch in heat. Ten thousand people poured through the little trading post in the four years after the strike and Fort Benton became a boom town overnight—with all the problems that entailed.

Gold seekers came packed on river boats up the Missouri and travelled overland in a cockamamie collection of wagons, buggies and carts. They even used an animal the Indians believed

---

* Montana became a state in 1889. Between 1864 and 1889, it was usually referred to as the Montana Territory, or simply the Territory. Gold finds were recorded in the Montana Territory as early as 1852. The first sizeable strike was in July 1862, when John White and William Eades found coarse gold in the Grasshopper Gulch area of southern Montana. The Last Chance Gulch strike of 1864 was the first to have a direct effect on Fort Benton. Though hardly lucrative in the class of the California and Klondike rushes, between $100 and $200 million in gold was taken out of the Benton area in four years.

was a horse crossed with a buffalo. The result was a beast so tall it had to be beaten to its knees so a man could pack it for travel. The strange animal's huge shoulder hump was located right in the middle of its back, making it useless for riding. The white men soon gave up on these camels, as they called them, and a few eventually drifted into the upper Missouri. One drowned not far from Fort Benton and another was shot and eaten by the Gros Ventre. They stank worse than a maggoty carcass but the Indians claimed the meat was a fine treat.*

With the miners came the military. The army built Camp Cooke in 1866, south-east of Fort Benton on the Missouri, followed quickly by Fort Ellis, Fort Shaw, Fort Logan and Fort Smith, with a small contingent of infantry coming to Fort Benton in 1869. The troops were supposed to protect the steamboats, miners and the mail and telegraph service but they spent most of their time fending off attacks by the Sioux and the Blackfoot and thundering up to plundered, burned-out wagon trains—long after the Indians had left with their prizes.

Aside from the buffalo and war, the Plains Indians shared one thing—their hatred of the military forts. The U.S. Army provocatively placed forts at key points along the Missouri, the Yellowstone and farther south on the Red River in order to cause the most severe disruption possible to the Indians' travel, trade and hunting patterns—often locating them right in the middle of traditional camping sites. Tribes detoured many miles to avoid the forts—sometimes abandoning hunting grounds entirely. Before 1865 there were only three military forts and camps on the northern American plains; by 1873 there were thirty-three.

When Fort Benton was just a fur trading post the Indians arrived, did their trading and retreated to their camp. If a chief was powerful and respected enough, he might persuade his people to quickly leave the post's temptations. In those days

* The camels were shipped to Texas in 1856 and '57 in an experiment by the U.S. Army to move supplies from Camp Verde to California. Congress was cool to the idea, which it considered un-American, and denied further funding. The camels ended up in circuses, on ranches, on the Missouri Plains and even with a road-building crew in British Columbia.

the traders treated the Indians, especially the Blackfoot, with a leery respect born of fear. They knew if they pushed Indians too far, or cheated them too often, they'd go somewhere else to trade—or burn them out. But the new whites who flooded in during the gold rush had little stake in maintaining the fragile relationship with the Indian. They came to make as much money as possible in as short a time as possible, then leave. The upper Missouri suddenly became *their* territory.

As the number of newcomers rose, the whites' opinion of the red man fell. "I never saw an Indian of any tribe in northern Montana who wasn't a thief both by instinct and choice, and who didn't itch to kill a white man, if he thought he could do it and not be found out and caught," observed an early Benton trader and settler, Winfield Stocking, voicing a common opinion along the Missouri. "It is true that the mind of an uncivilised Indian was the mind of a child in many respects, but it is also true that he had a grown man's mind in the matter of selfishness, meanness, and wickedness."

It wasn't only the hard-bitten miners, settlers and traders who believed that the Indian embodied all the vices of humankind. William Blackmore was a British lawyer, entrepreneur and promoter who loved to go adventuring and hunting on the frontier, well-buttressed by damson preserves, pickles, bacon, canned olives, sherry and cognac. The Plains Indians were his hobby. When he wasn't being entertained by his wide circle of American politicians, scientists and businessmen, he was purchasing vast quantities of Indian artifacts to stock a museum in his home town of Salisbury, England. His hobby both fascinated and repelled Blackmore.

In a paper read before the Ethnological Society, he carefully toned down the more gory details of "savage life," later explaining his censorship in the published version.

> I abstained from giving any account of the atrocities committed by the Indians against the whites. The recital of these barbarities is so horrible, and the facts which have come to my knowledge are so much worse than anything I have ever seen written, that for the sake of humanity I should rejoice if they could be suppressed and ignored. In the cause of truth, however, it is necessary to

present the Indian as he really is—a degraded, brutal savage, devoid of either pity, feeling or mercy.

More whites meant more pressure on the Indian. The more that Indians pressed back, the more the whites felt justified in annihilating them. Before long it was open season on Indians in Montana.

Aside from fortune seekers, the Montana Territory attracted another kind of man—lawless adventurers on the dodge, keeping one step ahead of "civilization" with its bothersome rules and regulations. A lot of them came from Texas. When the Texas Rangers were formed in the 1820s, their first job was to take care of the Indian problem. During Texas's decade as a republic, its second president, Mirabeau Buonoparte Lamar, vowed to launch "an exterminating war upon their warriors; which will admit of no compromise and have no termination except in their total extinction or total expulsion." The sentiment didn't change much after 1845, when Texas became a state. Twenty years later, having finally solved their Indian problem by killing the Comanche almost to the last man, the Rangers turned their attention to white trash of all descriptions. By 1873 the state had become so tame that carrying concealed weapons was outlawed.

Montana became a favourite destination for anyone run out of Texas, people like "Farmer Brown," as he called himself.

The Farmer was not the simple settler his name implied. Oxford-educated, army-trained and an utter sociopath, he spent his initial years in America fighting as a mercenary for the Spanish in their raids on the borders of the new state of Texas. Though he'd killed his share of Texans, he preferred to boast of the many Mexican and Indian "Greasers" he had "wiped out." One day, wishing to field-test a new rifle,

Mule train in Fort Benton, 1870s.

the Farmer took a long-range bead on the head of an Indian woman while she was getting water from a creek, killing her instantly—a little too much, even for the pugilistic Texans. Numerous such episodes gave Farmer Brown's face a permanent place on "wanted" posters in five states.

By the late 1860s, the Montana territory bulged with Farmer Browns—hard cases, ready to explode at the slightest provocation. In Montana, you could be anything or anyone you wanted; no one asked for pedigrees or letters of reference. A killer in one town could be the law in the next.

Bill Hinson (a.k.a. Henson, Hynson, Hensel) drifted into Benton early in 1868, a few months after he'd slipped out from under a murder charge in Helena. In Benton, Hinson fast-talked himself into the position of night marshal—something the town sorely needed. The nightly clash of well-liquored traders, settlers, gold seekers and Indians created a volatile stew that erupted regularly out of the saloons and whiskey tents and on to the streets. One missionary declared the town was so vile with drunkards, prostitutes, gamblers and thieves that even the inhabitants of Sodom would be uncomfortable there.

Hinson topped up his salary by rolling the drunks he arrested; but he got greedy. Too many complained of finding empty pockets after sobering up. Before suspicion turned towards him, Hinson loudly denounced the thievery, proclaiming he would personally hang the varmint if he caught him. The local vigilante committee thought Hinson protested too much. One of its members laid a trap by ostentatiously flashing a roll in the saloon and pretending to be drunk. Hinson couldn't resist.

"We've caught the fella who's been doing these robberies, and in half an hour we're gonna hang him," one vigilante told Hinson the next evening. "You got a rope?"

"No," responded Hinson, adding helpfully, "but I can get one mighty quick."

Hinson hurried over to T.C. Power's trading store and bought a stout piece of manila hemp.

"Where's the son of a bitch? Show him to me!" he demanded, brandishing the rope.

"Here he is, right here!" shouted a large man, grabbing Hinson.

In short order, the body of the night marshal was dangling

from a chestnut tree.

There were a lot of lethal combinations rattling around the Montana Territory, but the most dangerous, so Potts believed, were the walking dead—veterans of the American Civil War. Dead Eyes, he called them. These boys were trained to kill. Some of them quite liked it and didn't hesitate to fire at anything even vaguely Indian, for sport. A lot of them were Confederate Civil War prisoners sprung by General Alfred Sully for his campaign to cleanse the Missouri of the Sioux. They had nothing to lose, it was either that or die in jail.

In the spring of 1873, three Peigan women and four children who had been bringing firewood to their lodges on the south bank of the Teton River west of Benton were found shot full of holes. The senior cavalry officer stationed at Fort Shaw dismissed the incident as a retaliatory strike by the Crow. But Potts knew for a fact there were no Crow in the vicinity at that time—only a mule train operated by a pair of free traders, Civil War vets.

With so many stray bullets flying around, Potts had taken to wearing a white man's hat and coat whenever he left his lodges. Dying in a fight was one thing, but having his head blown off by a trigger-happy white would be no way for Bear Child, warrior chief, to die.

As if the criminals, miners, settlers, traders and ex-soldiers didn't create an incendiary enough mix, there were the Sioux to top things off. When the American Civil War ended in 1865, the military was infused with new energy to make the Sioux strongholds along the south-eastern Missouri, Yellowstone, Big Horn and Elk Rivers "safe for human habitation." Defeats at the hands of the army in the mid-1860s had taught the Sioux a hard lesson. Their ancient muskets made any battle against the whites a hopeless cause. Sitting Bull dedicated himself to re-arming his people and together with other warrior chiefs targeted wagon trains, posts, forts—anything that might have a store of weapons. In the process the Sioux clashed, not only with soldiers, traders and miners, but also with any other tribes that got in their way as the skirmishes pushed them west and north, into territory once exclusively occupied by the Blackfoot.

They also began crossing over the Medicine Line in increasing numbers. To the Sioux the *chanku wakan*, the sacred road or holy trail separating Canada and the United States, held special significance. "[T]hings are different when you cross from one side to another," emphasized Sioux Robert Higheagle. "You are altogether different. On one side you are perfectly free to do as you please. On the other you are in danger." Crossing the border became their primary escape route.

If the constant movement of the Sioux weren't enough to add tinder to the smouldering fire in Montana there were the buffalo—or lack of them. Sizeable herds were becoming as scarce as firewood on the Alkali Flats. As recently as 1868 herds of thousands populated the upper Missouri and across the boundary line into the valley of the Bow and Saskatchewan rivers and east into the Cypress Hills. There were so many of them that the widely scattered farms in the Dakota and Montana territories were often threatened by their stampedes. A single herd passing through could destroy an entire field of crops, trample corrals and churn water holes into a muddy wallow.

Shirley Ashby, a trader at Fort Benton, had been heading east along the Missouri in the summer of 1868 with a large wagon train loaded with Indian goods when buffalo overwhelmed his party. "From the time we pulled up from the Marias, until we located, we were never out of sight of hundreds of thousands, and I believe millions of buffalo. Old Man, Louis Rivet, and I would frequently have to ride ahead and shoot into a bunch of buffalo, so that the ox team could keep the wagons rolling."

But that was before William F. "Buffalo Bill" Cody came along, followed by an army of hide hunters. Cody got the contract to supply the Kansas Pacific Railroad construction crew with meat in 1868 and he boasted of killing nearly 4,300 buffalo himself in just eighteen months. There were dozens more like him, eager to cash in on the eastern appetite for buffalo robes used for clothing, carriage robes and, increasingly, for industrial conveyor belts. More than 3.7 million buffalo were slaughtered between 1872 and 1874; fewer than 150,000 of them died by Indian hands. Bleached bones and rotting carcasses, minus the saleable tongues, skins and hindquarters, created a sickening stench across the northern and southern plains. For six years Dodge City was redolent of rotting meat throughout hunting season as Cody and the rest shipped out their kill on the railroad.*

"Let them kill, skin, and sell until the buffalo is exterminated," urged General Philip Sheridan, "as it is the only way to bring lasting peace and allow civilization to advance." Just in case the buffalo hunters didn't work quickly enough to starve out the Indians, the Army unofficially endorsed a campaign to set fire to the prairies, wiping out the buffaloes' forage.

As was the custom with powerful Plains warriors, Jerry Potts had more than one wife. A few years earlier, he had acquired Panther Woman and Spotted Killer, South Peigan sisters. They and their extended family spread themselves over seven lodges in Potts' camp. Every year he had to go farther afield looking for buffalo to feed them. His favourite meal, boss ribs, had become all too rare. The odd bones supporting the buffalo hump were partly smoked, then plunged very briefly into a kettle of boiling water. Eaten well-salted, the ribs oozed succulent, still-raw juices and fat. The Plains Indians all had their own ways to cook these ribs, but Potts knew none could better his Peigan wives.

Not long ago Potts had come across a small group of Sarcee so desperate for meat they were scouting the lakes and river bends for drowned buffalo. He rode along with them for two days, mainly to avoid a band of Cree scouring the territory looking to avenge the loss of two women and four horses to a Blackfoot raiding party. The Cree had set out under an egg moon and the pale oval had swelled, died and begun to form again but still no vengeance had been exacted. Potts knew that meant a dirty mood and any scalp would do. Even the scavenging Sarcee were better allies than nothing.

SUMMER 1873

That summer of 1873, Jerry Potts was thirty-five years old, or thereabouts, record keeping not being a priority in the frontier.

---

* Buffalo still numbered in the millions in the early 1870s, but by 1887 naturalist William T. Hornaday estimated only 1,091 were left in all of North America. Though there were some good years in the '70s when huge herds, particularly in Canada, showed up, the days of the buffalo were finished.

With all the turmoil in the upper Missouri plains, his longevity was a feat in itself. Living as an Indian but working for whites as a hunter, guide and scout created many conflicts. Potts had discovered early on that a cool head saw him through the worst of them. He could hold his own with a gun, a knife or his fists, but the key to coming out best in a fight was keeping your wits and hitting what you shot at. From experience Potts knew that at least half the men in battle didn't even fire their guns, and many of the rest shot hurriedly and missed. In the old days of the muzzle loaders, a man who didn't hit his target died four times in the thirty seconds it took to reload. The reward for patience was life.

These days, no one had patience. The new breech-loading rifles held many bullets and were quick to reload, so shooters fired recklessly, seldom hitting their mark. But if you waited for your enemy to position himself perfectly and beg for the bullet, the coup would be yours.

Right now, Potts preferred to lie low rather than fight, which was why he sat quietly waiting on his mule until the puff of dust turned into something.

The dust plumed into a cloud. Potts gazed at it thoughtfully. His head told him not to bother with it. Another hard four hours of riding would put him back in his lodges with his two wives, a good meal, a long pipe and an evening to satisfy his urges. On the other hand, the cloud of dust could be traders heading north from Fort Benton along the Whoop Up trail with a load of provisions—that meant whiskey.

Whiskey

SUMMER 1873

As the cloud of dust swelled, Potts knew for certain it was traders. Sioux, Cree and even the dog-hearted Crow were far more stealthy. The cloud was moving too quickly for a bull train, so it had to be mules. Potts felt a familiar burning in his throat, and a warmth in his stomach. Bull trains were slow but hauled huge loads. Mule trains were speedy but the loads had to be smaller, so no mule skinner bothered to carry more than a token amount of other trade goods; pound for pound, whiskey delivered by far the greatest profit.

Potts reached for a well-worn bladder from the back of his saddle. Being too anxious could kill a man. He dipped two fingers in and scooped out a mouthful of marrow fat. He had relieved a Crow of the cured antelope bladder some years ago. As it happened, he'd also relieved the Crow and three of his friends of their scalps. Marrow fat was a precious commodity. Tedious to make from buffalo bones chopped, then boiled, its oily silkiness was both delicious and sustaining.

A long drink was a pleasant thought, damn pleasant. Potts had sworn off working for the whiskey traders in 1872 after his mother was killed by her own people in a drunken mêlée. But that didn't mean *he* couldn't take a drink. Jerry Potts could, and did, drink just about anything. More than once, he had worn the badge of the frontier drinker, a moustache stained bright red with ink—an additive used to give particularly low-rent concoctions the requisite colour. Potts had also taken part in his share of Bacchanalian romps around the trading forts, so crazed with "Injun whiskey" he didn't know who he was or what he was doing.

Jerry Potts was a warrior, as dangerous as they came; but he wasn't a wanton killer, randomly dishing out death like so many in the West. He always had a reason or provocation—except when he had a belly full of bug juice. In his cups, he'd sometimes shot at acquaintances, mistaking them for old enemies. Man Fighting a Battle, a Blood Indian, nearly lost the war when he foolishly allowed himself to be drawn into an argument with a sauced Potts. Man Fighting was found alive, but well-ventilated with two stab wounds in his arm, two more in his chest and three in his back. Those who knew Potts were careful to tie him up before he reached critical mass in his drinking sprees.

There were pockets of whiskey trading all over the north and south plains of the American West throughout the 1850s and

'60s. Though the sale of liquor to Indians in American territory was outlawed, nobody paid much attention west of the Mississippi. Wherever the U.S. Army was thin on the ground—or could be bribed to look the other way—traders operated out of tents and wagons, dispersing their load, then hightailing it for the nearest settlement. You could make a good living at it, if you were quick on your feet, but real fortunes were to be made on the Whoop Up trail. Once across the border into the British Territory, there was no one to enforce the laws forbidding the traffic of liquor to Indians. The only whites in the North West were the increasingly fort-bound Hudson's Bay Company men and a handful of temperance-minded, but impotent, missionaries.

Traders plying the Whoop Up trail picked up their whiskey in kegs or drums from Fort Benton merchants, primarily the two big ones, T.C. Power and I.G. Baker. Both outfits stoutly denied supplying alcohol for the degrading whiskey trade, claiming any liquor sold was for spiritual or medicinal purposes. Judging by the huge quantity of Mass wine and medicinal brandy that came up the Missouri on river boats, an observer might conclude the Territory was brimming with ailing church-goers.

Traders carried as much high-proof alcohol as they could lay their hands on and took along as many as fifty empty kegs to use for the mixing. When the whiskey arrived at its destination north of the border, the mixing began. Typically the ratio was three or four gallons of water, plus additives, to one of whiskey. The additives were vital to give trade hooch the harsh bite the Indians liked and the flammability essential to prove it was truly firewater. Burnt sugar and oil added nicely to the colour and the fire power. Bourbon, which was cheaper, often took the place of whiskey. Paint, Jamaican ginger, molasses, red pepper and patent medicines all found their way into Injun juice.

The whiskey traders were the culmination of a long tradition in Indian country. The Hudson's Bay Company had perfected the art of doctoring booze and, as the fur trade competition in the seventeenth and eighteenth centuries grew, the Baymen developed a wondrous variety of drink. They created English "Brandy" as an alternative to the Indians' favourite, the fiery French brandy sold by their competitors. The traders mixed London gin coloured, according to the HBC manual, with four or five drops of iodine per pint to achieve the right hue. Later they substituted molasses, which sweetened as well as coloured the gin. The process for HBC "spruce beer" was a marvel of frontier ingenuity.

> To brew this beer, the kettle being near full of water, cram the kettle with small pine; from one experiment you will judge the quantity of pine that will bear a proportion to your water. Let the tops of the pine be boiled in water until the pine turns yellow, and the bark peels, or the sprigs strip off readily on being pulled; then take off your kettle, and the pine out of the water, and to about two gallons of liquor put a quarter of a pint of molasses. Hang your kettle on, giving the liquor off, put it into a cask in which you have before put cold water, the quantity of about two gallons. Then take a gun with a small quantity of powder, and no wad; fire into the bunghole. It will set the liquor a working; in about twenty-four hours stop the cask down, and the liquor will be ready to drink.

There was a delicate rhythm to whiskey trading. No matter how insistent the Indians, traders had to be careful not to run dry. It would be disastrous to be cleaned out by one band with another just around the corner. On either side of the Medicine Line, burned-out wagon trains and scalpless bodies were testament to the Indians' anger if they were refused.

In 1831, James Kipp, one of Kenneth McKenzie's traders, built Fort Piegan* at the mouth of the Marias River. One day, after a thirsty delegation had emptied Kipp's stores, a thousand Blackfoot unexpectedly crested the opposite river bank, declaring their intention to trade. He had a single thirty-five-gallon barrel of whiskey left. Frantically improvising, Kipp fortified that one barrel with all the patent medicine he had on hand, including Perry's Painkiller and Hostetters Bitters. The latter was a particularly nasty-tasting treatment for stomach upsets—of which there were a large number on the frontier.

---

* Americans spell it Piegan, Canadians Peigan.

Then Kipp added boiled red peppers, blackstrap tobacco and threw in every drop of red ink in the fort. Finally he diluted it all with copious amounts of water. By the time he finished he had 350 gallons of "whiskey" to appease the Blackfoot. The party lasted an entire week, and Kipp took in 2,500 prime beaver furs worth $46,000. Fort Piegan lasted only a year before it was burned out.

Smart whiskey traders supplemented their load of hooch with "Indian goods"—life insurance—just in case a man got stuck with empty kegs. They picked up tattered chimney-pot hats, stained lace collars, moth-eaten feather boas and any bits of military paraphernalia, especially gold braid. The whiskey traders weren't the only ones guilty of peddling worthless junk. "Legitimate" fur trading posts were bursting with sheet-iron steel spades, pasteboard shoes, rotten clothing, spoiled flour, diseased cattle and elastic garters for tribes that had no stockings.

But north of the Medicine Line the drawing card was whiskey. Potts noticed the concoctions had become fiercer and more diluted recently as the traders tried to dredge the last robe out of the Indian before the trade died. In a pinch, he'd still drink anything—and all there was of it, red moustache or not—but he much preferred what the white man saved for himself.

If there was one thing whites agreed upon, it was that the redskin couldn't handle his "likker," which, to Potts, was a little like blaming a dog for vomiting up a poisoned rat. Considering what went into trade whiskey in the first place, the wonder wasn't that the Indian couldn't handle his liquor, it was how he got it down in the first place.

Potts figured that if the white man drank what he served up to the Indian and the Indian drank from the white's personal preserve, there'd be a lot more understanding in the Territory. Frontier artist Charlie Russell, a man who liked to see how the other side lived, was never the same after he sampled trade hooch.

I never knowed what made an Injun so crazy when he drunk till I tried this booze.... With a few drinks of this trade whiskey the Missouri looked like a creek and we spur off in it with no fear.

It sure was a brave-maker, and if a man had enough of this booze you couldn't drown him. You could even shoot a man through the brain or heart and he wouldn't die till he sobered up.

When Injuns got their hides full of this they were bad and dangerous. I used to think this was because an Injun was a wild man, but at this place [on the Missouri] where we crossed the herds there's about ten lodges of Assiniboines, and we all get drunk together.

The squaws, when we started, got mighty busy caching guns and knives. In an hour we're all, Injuns and whites, so disagreeable that a shepherd dog couldn't have got along with us. Some wise cowpuncher had persuaded all the cowpunchers to leave their guns in camp.... Without guns either cowpunchers or Injuns are harmless—they can't do nothing but pull hair. Of course the Injun, wearing his locks long, gets the worst of it. We were so disagreeable that the Injuns had to move camp.

In 1872, Alexander Morris, lieutenant-governor of Manitoba, sent his brother William to the province's North West Angle to report on the incidence of smallpox and investigate rumours of whiskey traders in the vicinity. One night his Indian "constable" disappeared.

I heard the missing man was at an Indian encampment about a mile off, and acting strangely. Sending for him he soon appeared, and on my asking what was the matter, he suddenly drew the large hunting knife he carried and made a lunge at me, but was fortunately knocked down by the other man, in time to save me, and then went into a fit, foaming at the mouth and convulsed.

Powassan, a Lake of the Woods Indian, medicine man and chief, gravely explained to Morris that the poor man was in the grip of a Windigo, a devil. He and several other men appeared, "armed with their rattle and drums, and began the most awful row, accompanied by yells and shrieks" to drive out the evil spirit. Morris also blamed the devil but wondered if this particular one didn't come disguised as a whiskey trader. He decided to visit the Windigo itself when he heard that a group of traders had set up shop near a boundary marker a few miles away. Canada was stamped on one side of the iron post, U.S. on the other, and the traders, forewarned of Morris's assignment and nationality, had carefully located themselves just inches inside the American line.

"I suppose you know you can't trade that stuff on the Canadian side," Morris warned.

"We'd never do such a thing," the traders responded piously.

"Well, good," said Morris uncertainly, surprised at meeting such agreeable men. His information about the whiskey traders painted them as profane blackguards. "Well, then, I'll be off."

"Say, since you're here, why not come across and have a sip or two with us?"one of the traders asked genially.

"I suppose I could," said Morris, rationalizing that it was dry, dusty and hot and that no law existed against a white man having a drink in the middle of the woods. He walked from Canada into the United States and accepted a tin cup full of liquid from one of the smiling traders.

"Aaah! My God!" Morris shrieked, as a drop of the stuff hit his throat. Tears rolled down his cheeks. "What in God's name is it?" he croaked, scrubbing his fingers across his burning lips.

The traders, howling with laughter, revealed their recipe. First they boiled tobacco and lake water into a foul-smelling, dark brown soup, then they added high-proof alcohol and several pounds of blue vitriol or sulphuric salts. Blue vit, they explained, was the secret ingredient that gave the "whiskey" a powerful afterburn—few white men could even get it past their lips, they confided.

Sometimes, the trickiest part of whiskey trading on the plains of the upper Missouri was just getting out of Montana and into Canada. As the traders' routes were well-known they ran the risk of bumping into the U.S. Army en route to the border. All they needed was a zealous officer who took it into his head to enforce the existing liquor laws. While enforcement was sporadic in Montana, confiscation and a couple of nights in the Fort Benton jail or the lock-up at one of the military forts in the Montana Territory—Shaw, Logan or Ellis—

could put a big dent in profits. Traders always carried a quantity of high-quality hooch just in case they had to pay a "travel fee" to an officer who needed to be persuaded to let them get to the boundary line.

The whiskey trade compromised what little law existed in the West. It threw off so much cash that eventually virtually everybody was on the payroll, one way or the other. You couldn't exactly call it corruption—that implied some kind of honest regime had ruled at some time. It was more a matter of convenience, driven by the perfectly understandable need to earn a day's wage.

By 1873 the bent tradition of law enforcement in Montana had a brief, but well-entrenched history. Henry Plummer, stagecoach robber and murderer, became sheriff of Beaverhead County, the first county in the Montana Territory. Sheriffs weren't paid much, so he moonlighted as the leader of a notorious gang called the Innocents, identified by a special sailor's knot in their kerchiefs.

Plummer ran an efficient business. Being the sheriff, he knew where and when gold shipments were taking place and which wagon trains were carrying cash. He made a big fuss over train bosses and gold miners who passed through the territory, often giving them a gift of a distinctively coloured scarf to wear as they left town. So marked, his targets were easy to spot. Plummer then sent a deputy to mobilize his gang and, after they'd plundered their victim, joined the outcry condemning the robbers and calling for harsh penalties. Between 1862 and 1864, the hundred-member gang murdered dozens and pocketed over a million dollars in loot.

Plummer got tired of hearing about the fun second-hand and decided to participate in a few bust-ups, just to keep his hand in. During one pillaging spree, he was recognized by a man who managed to escape. Over a six-week period in early 1864, vigilante committees in mining towns all over southern Montana had a fine time arresting and stringing up twenty-two of the Innocents, including Henry Plummer.

Of course, not all the lawmen in Montana were such obvious criminals; most were simply moonlighting. On February 4, 1872, saloon keeper L.W. Marshall gunned down Dennis Hinchey in his Fort Benton bar. Sheriff Fred Kanouse, along with the constable, the coroner and the justice of the peace, missed the event because they were "presently out at Whoop Up, trading with the Indians." Shortly afterward, Sheriff Kanouse killed Jim "The Bluffer" Nabors while arguing about a horse, then fled to Canada where he went full-time into the whiskey trade. "There is no encouragement whatever for me to do work where there is no prospect of pay," Kanouse said, explaining his abrupt retirement.

Trouble followed Fred Kanouse around. In March 1873 he and a group of traders were enjoying a jar of good stuff in Sol Abbott's Whoop Up Saloon, located in a small cabin near the fort. A group of Blackfoot showed up demanding whiskey and got their answer in bullets. At the end of it, three Indians were dead and three whites wounded; one of them was Fred Kanouse, his shoulder severely mangled. Undeterred, he and a few others built a small whiskey post near Whoop Up the next spring. The walls were hardly erected before a band of Kootenay attacked. After driving them off, the traders celebrated their bravery with a good old frontier "stink-up," which always involved a lot of whiskey and random gunfire. One of the bullets ignited a keg of gunpowder, ending the post's brief existence.

Half a dozen other Fort Benton sheriffs plumped up their earnings in the whiskey trade between 1869 and 1874. Occasionally a lawman came along who thought he could clean up the territory. But for these lone individuals, the attempt was as futile as stomping on mosquitoes in a swamp. In 1871, U.S. Marshall Charles D. Hard was in hot pursuit of some whiskey traders led by Joseph Kipp. The traders stopped to make their stand at the confluence of the Belly and Waterton rivers. Hard faced a ticklish situation, his Henry rifle against a dozen guns.

"Well, Joe, I've got you at last!" snarled Hard. "Just turn around and head for Fort Benton."

"Hard, you're twenty minutes late," countered Kipp. "You should have overtaken us on the far side of the creek back there."

"Oh come! No joking!" barked Hard. "This is serious business. Turn your team."

"Hard, right here you ain't no more a Marshal of the United

States than I am. Right here's Canada; the north fork of the Milk river is the line."

The clicks of a dozen rifle bullets being chambered settled the matter of jurisdiction. Hard decided that he must be in Canada after all, and he turned and rode back to Fort Benton. Kipp built a new post near the spot on the Canadian side and christened it Fort Standoff.

The main means of transport between Benton and Fort Whoop Up was the bull train, which carried by far the most goods, particularly whiskey, at the cheapest price. Typically, teams of between six and twelve yoke of oxen pulled three wide-gauged wagons. A single team could haul up to ten tons of goods on the two-to-three-week trip to Whoop Up. But breakdowns and overturned wagons were common, often stretching the trip to four weeks, especially if heavy rains had turned the trail into a bog.

The heavy traffic of traders rutted the trail several feet deep and, in places, stretched it fifty yards across. Burned-down camp-fires, heaps of garbage and piles of "dead soldiers"— empty whiskey bottles opened by smashing the tops against the wagon wheels—marked the 210-mile route. Even a tenderfoot couldn't get lost.

For safety, the bull trains often joined into convoys of eight to ten teams that stretched as much as half a mile from the first nose to the last tail. Each team had a train boss, a whacker, a night herder and a boy to chop wood. Whackers usually walked beside the teams, whip in one hand, bottle in the other, and passed the time refining their verbal skills. At night the whackers took turns cooking the standard fare—hard tack, biscuits and beans. Whackers got fifty dollars a month and sometimes a bonus on a particularly rich trip.

Along the trail, the only thing

Bull train on the Whoop Up trail, 1870s.

louder than the squeak and groan of the wagons was the cursing of the men, proudly capable of more unbroken profanity
than anyone else on the frontier.

> The fully developed bull-whacker never pauses or stut-
> ters when he is once roused by surrounding influences
> to a full display of his powers, but launches forth in a
> torrent of the fanciest expletives, dressed in colours
> wonderfully gorgeous and eloquent, incandescent and
> irresistible. The principal portion of the existence of the
> bull-whacker is occupied in composing profanity of
> startling originality into which never iteration nor pla-
> giarism ever creeps.

Not everyone was impressed by the bull whacker's oration.
"Godless wretches," condemned one horrified clergyman,
"with whom, for very ignorance, oaths stand in the stead of
adjectives."

Whiskey traders carried death across the border. Sixty
Indians died in the vicinity of Fort Whoop Up in 1872 alone,
hundreds more—Potts' mother and brother-in law among
them—around the other forty-five posts crammed into the
southern prairies of Canada's North West. Still, it was hard
not to be impressed when a bull train, with its distinctive symphony of rattling, grunting and hollering, hove into sight like
an armada of the plains.

> We were approaching Fort Whoop-Up from the east
> and it was toward evening as we topped a small rise and
> looked down upon the plain beneath us. Some distance
> away, it must have been at least five miles, we could
> hear the sound of voices, ever and anon raised in hoarse
> shout.
>
> At first we could see nothing. Then, from a large cop-
> pice or clump of trees we saw emerge some toiling, plod-
> ding oxen. We could see them plainly through our field
> glasses, swinging along in that peculiar gait of the bovine.
>
> As they walked, the dust drifted from their plodding
> hoofs in little clouds. Team after team came into view,
> until there was nearly half a mile of them stretched out.

A man on horseback rode up and down the line. The sun was nearing the horizon and we stood and watched them until the plodding, swaying oxen, dragging their wagons behind them were lost in the haze of the autumn sun.

Mule trains, six or eight pairs arranged like the oxen, were a step up in speed. Mule skinners rode on the animal directly in front of the left wheel, controlling the team with a jerk line running to the lead mule. Hard yank for left, continuous pull for right. The mule skinners put whiskey in large flat cans that they could strap to the mules' sides as well as load in the wagons. They carried little but whiskey and guns, which made them a prize hit for raiding Indians.

Mules cost three times as much as oxen; they couldn't pull as much but they were much faster, often making it from Benton to Whoop Up in ten days. Greater speed allowed mule drivers to squeeze in an extra three or four trips per season. Small-time traders operated with mule strings, packing the whiskey directly on the animals. Their mobility allowed them to get off the main trail and head for known Indian camps. It was more dangerous than setting up at a post and waiting for the Indians to come, but a mobile trader could sell out his cargo, load up with furs and be back across the border before an oncoming bull-train boss realized he'd been scooped.

SUMMER 1873

Pleasant anticipation coursed through his body as Potts waited for the mule train to get closer. He knew that mule skinners and bull whackers, like all whites, avoided Indian whiskey like a poxed blanket. You could be sure they'd have a store of "good stuff."

Potts heeled his horse up the side of the hill to get a good look at the wagon train before he revealed himself. He wanted whiskey, but he'd rather stay thirsty than run into some of the men who worked the Whoop Up trail. The nervous ones would shoot first and worry about what they'd hit later. The mean-as-a-snake types would shoot first and not care. Either way you were dead.

The mule train stopped. Potts could see a stocky, dusty figure striding back and forth slashing at the ground with his whip and swearing ferociously.

"Blind-eyed, no-account bastard!" the driver railed.

Potts pulled his horse around and approached the train from the far side. By the time the driver spotted him, Potts was almost on top of him.

"Jesus!" shrieked the man, jumping almost a foot in the air. "Jesus! Why in hell d'you sneak up on me like a damn Injun."

"I am an Injun," observed Potts.

"You know what I mean!" the Trader snapped, mopping the sweat of fright from his brow.

Potts let the man's temper run down. The Trader, still muttering, marched to the last wagon and dragged out his snoring helper, letting him fall heavily to the ground.

"Look at him! I'm bustin' my ass with the mules and here he is, all nice and comfortable drinking my whiskey. I oughta leave him for the coyotes."

The Traders

Summer 1873

"Thought you maybe Kamouse," said Potts, "owes me a bottle."

"Pah! Squaw stealer?" snorted the now-calm Trader, hawking a copious brown bundle onto the ground. "Not likely. That old boy's probably still runnin'." He cackled. "He'll lose his carrot if the Chief ever catches him!" The Trader made a vigorous chopping motion in his groin area to illustrate the point.

Potts nodded. Gelding was indeed the likely fate for Harry "Kamouse" Taylor if he ever ran into the Blackfoot chief whose daughter he had stolen. And, knowing the Blackfoot, it was more likely to be burned off with a hot brand than neatly sliced off with a knife. Daughters became wives for a price. That was the honoured practice. But stealing one, especially from a chief—that took a special kind of lunacy. Still, you couldn't help but admire a white man who pulled it off and kept his scalp.

"Bugger's got sand," grunted Potts.

"Less'd be healthier," laughed the Trader, puzzling over the common sense of a man who actually called himself Kamouse, Blackfoot for squaw stealer and boasted about how he got the name.

Potts had heard that Kamouse came West as a Bible man, before he discovered that whiskey paid better than God. Potts sometimes wondered if wife stealing was one of those things the mysterious Bible allowed. Judging by the fuss the missionaries made about Potts having two wives, stolen or not, he doubted it.

After ditching his Bible for the bottle, Taylor went looking for scalp insurance. He offered the chief of a Blackfoot tribe everything he could spare—one horse, two blankets and a good portion of tobacco—in exchange for the chief's daughter. The chief politely refused and escorted Kamouse out of his camp. Unable to up his offer, Kamouse slipped back later that night and snatched the girl from her bed.

"Kamouse owes me a bottle," Potts repeated, making as if to get back on his horse.

"Forget that old thief, I got plenty. Good stuff too!" the Trader said hastily, figuring that keeping Potts around would improve his own chances of survival. The Blackfoot wouldn't bother him and, if any Cree or Sioux raiding parties were skulking around, Potts' gun would be useful. "Got a couple of buffalo steaks," he added.

Potts considered a moment. A hard ride could still get him to his lodges by sundown. He threw his reins over the nearest wagon wheel and walked back to where the Trader was carefully pulling buffalo chips out of a bag to make a fire. In the middle of summer on the Alkali Flats, with game scarce and water scarcer, a man had to take refreshment where he found it.

Most of the men who worked the whiskey trails between Whoop Up and Montana were failed somethings: farmers, gunslingers, soldiers, miners or cowboys. They lived for the moment they were in, damn tomorrow, or the next hour for that matter. After a trip they turned Benton inside out, blow-ing everything on poker, decent whiskey and a poke or two with one of the resident soiled doves. If they couldn't afford a dove, they visited a hurdy-gurdy house specializing in cheaper "squaws" and half-breed women. Anything left after their tubes were cleaned was spent on a bath and a "Chinaman" to launder their clothes. A few days later—washed, shaved and pockets empty but hungers slaked—they harnessed their teams and loaded up for another trip.

A few were different. They came to the Montana Territory with ideas and plans; dodging bullets along two hundred miles of one of the most dangerous stretches of land in North America was simply a means to an end. Donald W. Davis was one of them, John J. Healy was another.

Davis, the manager of Fort Whoop Up, was the most untrustworthy white Potts had ever met—and that was a mouthful. You never knew what he thought. There was a coldness somewhere deep inside Davis that Potts felt sucking at him when he stood too close. He often wondered whether D.W. would bleed if he cut him. He'd like to find out.

As much as Potts detested Davis, he couldn't help liking his boss, the stumpy, thick-chested John J. Healy. The man was a shallow stream—you could see right to the bottom, nothing hidden, nothing complicated. Vain and arrogant, he loved to boast of his exploits and he was always talking about a new, can't-miss idea. The big strike, for Healy, was just over the next rise.

Healy lived as if preparing his own legend. He loved it when the odds were tilted away from him and he could demonstrate that most men's courage had the staying power of a candle flame in a strong wind. At the height of the whiskey trade years he had plenty of opportunity to prove the truth of his belief. When he was working at the Whoop Up post, a small army of free traders descended looking to buy some ammuni-tion on credit to get even with some nearby Indians who had apparently killed two traders. Healy refused.

"You don't want to get the murderer. You want to murder and loot the village. Now you know me. I've taken my share in going against Injuns in my day. I've done my share and no man can say that Johnny Healy stood between a white man and an Injun and justice." But he wasn't about to sanction wholesale slaughter. A big Canadian among the group, George Hammond, turned ugly at Healy's words and he approached the trading counter, hands resting menacingly on the two pistols he carried.

"You think you're a pretty big man because you stood off eighteen men last winter," Hammond snarled. "But I wanna tell you it was a good thing I wasn't there!"

"You're damn right!" shot back Healy. "Because your bones'd be bleaching by the door!" Healy reached over and landed a thunderous slap across Hammond's face. Before the surprised man knew what was happening, Healy had administered a thorough beating and thrown him out the gate.

During a brief stint as Fort Benton sheriff, Healy wandered about town in shirtsleeves, apparently unarmed, bracing hard cases in the street and hauling them off to jail. Few knew his confidence was bolstered by a derringer hidden in a secret pocket—just in case his mouth or fists failed. The man had style, but he wasn't stupid.

Healy's bravado made him one of the few whites the Blackfoot didn't hold in utter contempt. But the feeling wasn't mutual. "If we had only been allowed to carry on business in our own way for another two years," he complained in his later years, "there would have been no trouble now as to feeding the Indians, for there would have been none left to feed: whiskey, pistols, strychnine, and other like processes would have effectively cleared away these wretched natives."

Most in the Montana Territory and in the whiskey posts across the border believed J.J. Healy and D.W. Davis were the kingpins of the whiskey trade. But behind them and most other traders in the North West were the Fort Benton firms of T.C. Power and, most particularly, I.G. Baker.

Isaac Gilbert Baker had gone into the fur business as an eighteen-year-old in Iowa. By the time he took over the American Fur Company's Fort Benton post in 1864, at the age of forty-five, there wasn't anything about trading he didn't know. The company abruptly disintegrated the next year when the owner, Pierre Chouteau, died, leaving Isaac and his brother George stranded in Fort Benton. But the mining boom just under way presented one opportunity and the company's trading links in the upper Missouri, suddenly available for the taking, presented another. Baker lost no time in establishing his own outfit. Initially, he kept costs down by creating temporary partnerships with free traders, thus avoiding the high cost of building and maintaining permanent posts. After a year of operation, he boasted a personal income of $7,300, the highest in Fort Benton. Within three years that kind of money was just pocket change.

As he scooped up the American Fur Company's business, Baker also built an immensely profitable infrastructure in Benton to supply the mining industry. From sluice boxes and shovels to hotel sheets, saloon whiskey and parts for river boats, he made himself as indispensable to the gold seekers as the ore itself.

It took just four years for the Bakers to become the wealthiest and most respected merchants in Benton. But Isaac and George could feel the basis of their fortune shifting beneath their feet. The newest leg of the Union Pacific Railroad was drawing trade off the Missouri and, though few realized it, the mining boom had peaked. As the Bakers pondered their future, John Healy, like thousands of others, was still searching for gold in Montana and the British Territory. Perpetually short of cash, Healy hired on with various expeditions as a guide, hoping to make his own strike on the side. On one trip south of the border, Healy didn't find gold, but he did meet Alfred Hamilton, a trader who introduced him to his uncles, Isaac and George Baker.

Healy spun them tales of abundant furs north of the border. The Blackfoot had successfully kept traders operating on the periphery of their territory. But in 1869 Healy believed the timing was perfect to take a trade expedition right into the heart of the Confederacy's land. The Blackfoot needed more guns and ammunition to hold off the Cree and Sioux raiding parties that were hitting them in increasing numbers. What's more, the Blackfoot had developed a taste for firewater. The Bakers listened intently and before Healy knew it, he and Hamilton were heading north for a trial run. Included in their trade goods was plenty of high-proof, low-quality whiskey.

In October 1869, Healy and Hamilton swaggered back into Fort Benton, their wagons tottering under piles of fur. The take—fifty thousand dollars. "[N]ot bad for a six months cruise among the Lo Family [Indians] across the border," hailed the Helena *Daily Herald*.

The Bakers could hardly believe their good fortune. As the mining boom wound down, they could simply shift their men and equipment to whiskey. Their distilleries, built to service saloons, hotels and army forts, would come in particularly handy. Healy and Hamilton crowed about the ease of their trade and how eager the Indians were for whiskey. A ragtag assortment of Métis and American and Canadian traders had been selling whiskey on the periphery of Blackfoot country for years. But no one had done it in a big way. The Baker brothers intended to change all that.

In 1870 Isaac Baker sent Healy and Hamilton north again, this time with instructions to build a permanent post. By centralizing the trade, they'd force the Indians to come to them, cutting out the roving free traders, especially the Métis, who did a good business in the Cypress Hills.

Baker had prepared well by securing a permit from the U.S. Interior Department, allowing Healy and Hamilton to carry spiritous liquors for medicinal purposes. If they were waylaid by the authorities, no one would be fooled, but the permit might oil any transaction necessary to put them on the road again. And, just in case there was trouble, Baker ensured that the licence was taken out in Hamilton and Healy's names.

Healy, who'd been trading at Sun River, intended to meet Hamilton and the wagon trains for their second run into British territory. Then he heard that the soldiers at Fort Shaw were preparing to stop him, permit be damned. Healy spread the word he was going to Fort Benton to send a telegram— giving the military enough lead time to intercept it. The telegram told his partner to meet him with their trade goods seventy-five miles east of their intended route. While the Fort Shaw soldiers were diligently searching the flats north of Sun River, Healy and Hamilton had already crossed the Marias River and were charging hard for the border.

Fort Hamilton went up that summer—eleven rough, log huts strung together inside a log fence. It didn't even last the season. A fire, accidental or deliberate, no one ever figured it out, razed the post. Still, the trade was so rich, Isaac Baker immediately commissioned a replacement. This time he hired William Gladstone, a former HBC master carpenter, to build something with a little more staying power. Baker poured $25,000 into the two-year job, four times what most trading posts cost to build.

With large, squared timbers and a thick, earth roof, Fort Whoop Up looked like a massive buffalo squatting on a rock. On two opposite corners sentry look-outs had been built and equipped with brass cannons, prominently displayed—the men were always disappointed they never actually got to shoot the cannons at any Indians, though they fired them to signal the arrival of a fresh shipment, and occasionally when things were slow they fired them for fun. Just in case all of that wasn't enough of a deterrent against attack, military-style gun place-ment slits were cut into all four walls. Over the whole thing flew the Stars and Stripes. At the peak of the whiskey boom in the early 1870s, Whoop Up pulled in the stupendous sum of five hundred thousand dollars annually for the Bakers.

John Healy pioneered the Whoop Up whiskey trade, but he was no manager. Under Healy's supervision the fort, despite the vast profits it threw off, was an organizational shambles. Men went unpaid for months, the fort was often in short sup-ply of critical commodities at key times and fewer furs than

Interior of Fort Whoop Up, early 1870s.

Isaac Baker expected came south. Then there was the vexing problem of "breakage" and "leakage"—a certain amount was expected but it was becoming an epidemic.

Some drivers carried their own custom-made spigots that they drove into the barrels to siphon off whiskey en route. Baker had tried labelling the whiskey as kerosene. It still ended up short. He wasn't sure whether the traders were drinking it or burning it. And, to Baker's thinking, far too many barrels were written off as peace offerings to the Blackfoot. Baker had tried everything to sop up the leakage, even hiring Mormon teamsters to cart the whiskey. But there simply weren't enough abstainers to go around in the Territory.

Isaac Baker had spotted Donald W. Davis working as a clerk at Fort Shaw and knew right away he'd be the perfect addition to his business. From the moment Davis set foot in Montana as a seventeen-year-old U.S. Army clerk, the reek of ambition set him apart. He'd fought in the Civil War at the age of fourteen, and after being wounded at Gettysburg, he returned to his Vermont farming family and learned bookkeeping at Poughkeepsie Commercial College. But the life of a bookkeeper, working six days a week for twenty dollars a month, held little appeal. Davis wanted wealth but he had no intention of slogging like a slave to get it. The West was the answer.

Davis chose the safe route to the frontier, joining the regular army in 1867. He got lucky in his first posting with the Thirteenth Regiment of infantry stationed at Fort Shaw, sixty-five miles south-west of Fort Benton. Endowed with a garden, shade trees, a long stretch of lawn, good fishing nearby and rife with corruption, Shaw was a comfortable step up from the dreary prison-like army posts speckled throughout the Dakota and Montana territories.

From the saddlery to the mess tent, there were endless opportunities for creaming. Four and a half million pounds of supplies were needed for Fort Shaw and nearby Camp Cooke. Fort Benton merchants were only too happy to provide inducements to anyone who helped them get a contract. The richest man in Fort Shaw was the "sutler," J.H. McNight. A sutler operated a fort's store and supplied everything from buttons to bacon. Whiskey offered the biggest margin; even with a fixed price on booze, the profit was substantial.

Thomas Power, who financed McNight with a credit line in his Fort Benton store, rewarded him well for every military order he directed his way, and McNight, as Power's conduit, favoured the officers who gave the nod to bids from his supplier. The underground economy wasn't buried very deep and the network of men kept each other alive to good opportunities. "Come over yourself and see my new place," wrote Major Upham to McNight from the Blackfoot Agency on Sun River. "Plenty of room for sinching now without being observed."

The sinching, or under-the-table deal making, was so prevalent in the Blackfoot Agency, established in Fort Benton in the late 1860s according to the Treaty of 1855, that the Indian Bureau moved it out of the town in 1870 to the growing settlement on Sun River. But the corruption was so well-established merely moving the agency didn't eradicate it.

As acting quarter-master sergeant at $26.85 a month, Davis kept the books for the military stores, giving him first-hand experience in the art of graft. But he was low down in seniority and had little chance to cash in on contracts and orders. There were, however, plenty of other opportunities to make a buck. His goal was to save a thousand dollars before his term expired in 1870. The $250 he'd already accumulated by 1868 bankrolled his operations—cashing paycheques for the men at a substantial discount, floating short-term loans at high rates and playing poker. His "wheeling and dealing" doubled his pot in two years.

Literate men with military experience and clerking skills were in very short supply. The minute Davis got his Army discharge, he easily landed a job trading for I.G. Baker at three times his previous salary, plus handsome bonuses. Isaac Baker soon dispatched Davis to operate Whoop Up, under Healy's general supervision. Davis would skim some off the top but he'd make damn sure no one else did, and he'd squeeze the last penny of profit out of the operation. What's more, Davis, who loathed Indians, would have no trouble ruling Whoop Up with the "iron hand" Baker demanded. Davis didn't think any Indian deserved to call himself a warrior. They were underhanded and cowardly, skulking around at night, slitting throats, stealing horses and ambushing sleeping traders. As far as D.W. was concerned, the Indians deserved whatever they got at the hands of whites and he, for one, was happy to do his share. However, Davis's loathing for Indians didn't stop him from quickly taking a Blackfoot wife, Revenge Walker, to ease his way into the trade.

Running a whiskey post in the heart of Blackfoot country wasn't a job for the squeamish. In the spring of 1873, two young Blackfoot warriors had slipped into D.W.'s camp on one of his periodic trips from Whoop Up to Fort Benton. They liberated his best bay mare and a scurvy little buffalo pony, said to have the surest feet on rough terrain anywhere north or south of the Missouri. The next day a livid D.W. shot the first two Indians he saw, neither knowing nor caring if they were the right ones.

The Indians responded in kind. One trader's body stopped the bullets just as well as any other. It made travelling the Whoop Up trail like being at the wrong end of target practice.

The Blackfoot gave Donald Watson Davis the name Spit-ayna, Tall Man. Well over six feet, he towered over most men in the territory. With skin pale as the mud from the banks of the White Mud River and hair as black as any young Indian buck, he could be spotted a long way off. His bushy beard stuck out like a prow and he looked all the more menacing when the dark shelf of his brow compressed into a deep scowl.

By 1873, as manager of Fort Whoop Up, Davis was drawing $150 a month, "what a man has to work like a slave for on a farm for six months," he wrote to his father. On top of his $1,800 a year, Isaac Baker offered a generous bonus, standard practice to encourage traders to turn over the maximum furs with the minimum cheating. Shirley Ashby, another Baker trader, pocketed a $7,500 bonus in 1869 after bringing in over $40,000 worth of furs.

D.W. Davis found nirvana in the whiskey trade. "I do no hard work nor have I since I came to the country and get the best of pay," he crowed after five years as a trader. "That is the reason I am not anxious to come to civilization to live as we live easy, get better pay for what we do in the states."

The Blackfoot called the area around Fort Whoop Up "Many Ghosts" or "Many Died." It had been a death zone for thirty-five years. Hundreds of Indians had died in tribal battles and three separate smallpox epidemics. Lately, they mostly killed each other in drunken brawls or fell down in a stupor and froze to death. Occasionally one of the traders amused himself from the safety of the stockade by potting a few Indians in the field below the fort. Chiefs tried to keep their bands out of rifle range during and after trading but it rarely worked once the hooch flowed. The gunfight in the spring of 1873 at Sol Abbott's Whoop Up Saloon, which cost Fred Kanouse most of one shoulder and three Blackfoot their lives, was standard fare.

Davis worked wonders maximizing profit, making one load of whiskey do the job of three. Before each sale, he floated just enough high-proof alcohol on top to ensure a good flame. The stuff tasted so powerfully of medicine, chemicals and other ingredients, the Indians couldn't tell how little whiskey was in it.

Davis also ensured there were sufficient sober traders within the fort to man the cannons and alert the rest to attack—either by whites or by Indians. Once a visitor doubted the security of Whoop Up's sod roof. Surely an enterprising Indian could simply cut a hole in it and pick off the people inside.

"Well, it's been tried," responded one of the traders.

"And what happened?" asked the visitor breathlessly.

"We lit the candles for them," the trader chuckled. "They don't do that no more."

"Lit candles for them?" asked the visitor blankly.

"Yeah, these candles," he replied patting the stock of his Winchester. "Goes right through that roof easy as anything. All you gotta do is develop an ear for footsteps overhead."

With cannons, stockaded walls, rifle slits and up to fifty armed men inside, Whoop Up traders didn't need to be quite as careful as the men operating out of hastily erected tents or the backs of wagons. Oxen and mules weren't cut out for quick getaways. The only answer was alliance. During the fur trade days of the 1840s and '50s a Cree wife was good security in Cree territory, a Blackfoot one in Blackfoot territory. But territory, as the Indians understood it, was rapidly ceasing to exist. Boundary lines were blurring as the Plains tribes became a shifting, unstable mass.

Soldiers were more powerful scalp insurance. A trader picked a respected and, preferably, formidable brave, deputizing him as a "soldier and companion." In return for bonuses like a pair of boots, a hat, extra whiskey or a double measure of flour, the soldier promised to control his band's young warriors and ensure they visited the trader in small, orderly groups. The soldier held an honoured position. Prominent chiefs like Sitting Bull, Crazy Horse, Big Bear and Red Cloud all claimed it as their right or, showing even greater power, offered the coveted position to a favoured brave.

The Whoop Up traders called their soldiers "mad dogs." They got the first taste of whiskey, an extra share of rope tobacco and the promise of more if they kept their people in line. Mad dogs patrolled the fort with war clubs, warding off the overly eager and escorting Indians away from Whoop Up after trading had finished. It was the mad dog who accepted and distributed the all-important "tail"—the gift at the end of every transaction that kept a trader in good favour. The tail, an assortment of gifts and trade goods, was intended to ameliorate the bad feelings that often arose when the Indians sobered up and found they'd traded away most of their furs and horses yet had little to show for it.

The hit-and-run tactics of the free traders, combined with the presence of the whiskey posts, wreaked havoc on the established fur trade. In just a few years a handful of men had thrown the two-century-old business into turmoil. "These whiskey men would make it very disagreeable for those who like myself, was trading with the Indians," grouched Shirley Ashby, one of many Baker employees who claimed to trade clean. "As soon as this whiskey or alcohol was within a mile or two of my trading post, the Indians would get drunk, jump on their horses, with nothing but hair lariats, and when they would arrive, they would say, 'You miserable dirty white dog. You are here with your cattle eating our grass, drinking our water, and cutting our wood. We want you to get out of here, or we will wipe you out.' They would then shoot over our heads into the goods, and I want to tell you that this was not a comfortable position to be in."

It was a fool's mission to show up in Indian country without any whiskey to trade; even worse was carrying liquor and not wanting to trade it. Viscount Milton and Dr. Cheadle made this mistake only once. Milton, a reedy, bleached young aristocrat, and his protector, Cheadle, an adventuring physician, were the Laurel and Hardy of frontier explorers.

Milton and Cheadle set off from Quebec to enjoy a season "hunting the buffalo and grizzly bear in the neighbourhood of the Rocky Mountains—a glorious life in the far West." They leap-frogged from disaster to disaster, getting lost at every turn and once nearly strangling their own guide when they mistook him for a marauding Sioux. But their biggest blunder came when they met Kekek-ooarsis, an old Cree, and his squaw mending fishing nets in an abandoned Hudson's Bay Company fishery near White Fish Lake.

> We smoked several pipes with him...and were so delight-
> ed with his urbanity that in a weak moment we promised
> to make him a present of a small quantity of rum.
>
> Alas! mistaken generosity, fruitful of anxiety and
> trouble! The old gentleman became all excitement, said
> we were the best fellows he had met for many a day,
> adding that if he might venture to offer a suggestion, it
> would be that we should fetch the firewater immediately.
>
> We accordingly went back to the lodge, sent off to
> him a very small quantity well watered, taking the pre-
> caution to fill a small keg with a weak mixture and hid-
> ing the cask in the cart. It does not answer, however, to
> dilute the spirits too much. It must be strong enough to
> be inflammable, for an Indian always tests it by pouring
> a few drops into the fire. It possesses the one property
> from which he has given it the name of firewater, he is
> satisfied, whatever its flavour or other qualities may be.
>
> We had hardly covered up the cask when Kekek-
> ooarsis appeared, accompanied by his squaw, a with-
> ered old hag, and Keenamontiayoo, "the long neck," his
> son-in-law. The men were already half drunk, singing
> away the Indian song without words, and clamorous for
> more rum. They produced a number of marten and
> other skins, and all our explanations failed to make
> them understand that we had not come as traders.
>
> After two hours' continued discussion, we doled out
> another small quantity as the only way to get rid of them.
> How they chuckled and hugged the pot exclaiming,

"Tarpwoy! tarpwoy!" (It is true! It is true!) hardly able to believe the delightful fact. At the first dawn of day they entered the lodge again, bringing more furs for sale.

Boys rode off as couriers in all directions to carry the welcome tidings to their friends in the neighbourhood. Before long, men came galloping up from different quarters, and these were presently followed by squaws and children, all eager to taste the pleasure-giving fire-water, and our lodge was soon crowded with importunate guests....

First one fellow thrust a marten skin into our hands, another two or three fish, while a third, attempting to strip off his shirt for sale, fell senseless into the arms of his squaw.

The demand was the same for all, and incessant: "Isquitayoo arpway! isquitayoo arpway!" (Firewater! firewater!) Hour after hour we sat smoking our pipes with an air of unconcern we did not feel, and refusing all requests. Afternoon came and the scene still continued. We dared not leave the lodge lest they should search the carts and discover our store.

Wearily passed the time till darkness came on and still the crowd sat round, and still the same request was dinned into our ears. But we were thoroughly determined not to give way, and at last they began to conclude we were inexorable, and dropped off one by one, immensely disgusted with our meanness.

Now and again, Jerry Potts had hired on to ride shotgun for the few bull trains that went north without a load of the "liquid problem." Once he and a young Indian named Sic O Pee took Shirley Ashby across the border, guiding him to where the Stoney Indians were congregated. It turned out to be a rich haul. The whiskey traders had not been there yet and in a few days Ashby cleared six thousand dollars in beaver and mink furs.

But usually the whiskey traders wiped the ground bare, leaving little for "dry" traders in their wake. The Hudson's Bay Company particularly felt the pinch since the traders were "officially" forbidden to include brandy, rum or whiskey in their trade goods. "Americans within two days Ride from this place with Licquor," moaned Rocky Mountain House clerk John Sinclair, "so I think there will be no trade at all at this place." Some traders boldly camped right on HBC land with rum, powder, shot, dry goods and trinkets and waylaid the Indians before they got to the gates of the post. In one trip, Thomas Bird and James Gibbons set up within sight of Rocky Mountain House, taking in 108 buffalo robes and nine horses for a single keg of rum.

Since the Indians would not come to the post, Sinclair decided to go to the Indians. Packing no whiskey, he returned from his foray with only forty buffalo robes, "too many free Traders out amongst them and all well supplied with goods & Liquor." His bleak mood blackened when he ran into a whiskey trader heading south with six thousand buffalo robes. The man hooted at Sinclair's miserable load.

SUMMER 1873

Besides his protection value, Potts knew plenty of interesting things, if only you could wheedle it out of him—a liberal pouring arm, plus a good dose of patience being the best way. He could tell you which tribes were where and which ones had a bug up their ass and were likely to settle a score with the first white they came across. He'd also know if there were any rival traders nearby—the kind who preferred to acquire their load of trade goods by taking someone else's.

The Trader handed a bottle to Potts, who poured a quarter of it down his throat with hardly a ripple of his Adam's apple, then eased himself down beside a big rock.

Shortly, the Trader had a small intense fire burning. His helper, now groggily awake, made trail bread—flour, water and salt wrapped around a stick and baked in the fire—crisp and charred on the outside, steamy hot and doughy on the inside. Gnawing the bread straight off the stick, maybe dipping it in molasses first, then washing the sticky remnants off your teeth with whiskey was as close as it got to heaven on the trail. This bread was extra sticky so a lot of washing had to be done. Potts' quart turned into a pint that was sinking fast.

Chapter 5

Warrior

Jerry Potts was one of the most dangerous men alive. He didn't look like much—short, even for the time, bandy-legged with a small, nondescript face dominated by a large drooping moustache and a penetrating set of eyes. His body was oddly clothed with many bits of two cultures—Indian brave and frontiersman with an odd dash of city slicker thrown in. Jerry Potts didn't look like much. But then, neither did a wolverine until you saw it rout a grizzly.

Though Jerry Potts made his living among whites for most of his adult life, in his heart he was forever an Indian, a Blackfoot warrior.

Whites called Potts a half-breed. He was illiterate, reading and writing not being important survival skills in the trading posts and Indian camps along the Missouri and into the North West badlands where he'd spent his entire life. One of the few printed words he recognized was his first name, occasionally pointed out to him when one of his escapades was spectacular enough to make the Helena *Herald*.

Yet Potts spoke four languages—English, Blackfoot, Crow and Cree—well enough to get along and could make himself understood in Sioux, if he cared to. He was a master tracker and horseman and a deadly shot whose coolness under fire was the sort spoken of by hard men, late at night over camp-fires. His exploits as an Indian warrior were also spoken of over camp-fires by hard men of a different sort.

Had it not been for his mother's decision to return to her tribe, Jerry Potts would have been just another half-breed drifting on the high plains of the Missouri. But his education at the hands of the Blood gave him a doctorate in survival in a place where the only diploma you earned was your own hide.

Once among the Black Elk, Potts threw himself enthusiastically into the rituals of budding braves. War had become an obsession among the Plains tribes and young men did little else but prepare for it. The more dangerous and foolhardy the game, the more its participants were admired and the winner lionized. They fought, at first barehanded, then with sticks and rocks. Knives and arrows followed with bullets not far behind. It was an exhilarating combination, youngsters bursting with their maleness, drunk with their invincibility, passionate about their honour and aching to draw blood in battle. "It was a life of savagery," wrote U.S. army officer Richard Irving Dodge.

> There is no right and no wrong to him. No softening stories of good little boys are poured into his attentive ear at a mother's knee. No dread of punishment restrains him from any act that boyish fun or fury may prompt. No lessons inculcating the beauty and sure reward of goodness, or the hideousness and certain punishment of vice, are ever wasted on him.
>
> Imagine a white boy growing up with such surroundings. The most humane of Christian gentlemen will exclaim "there is a fit subject for the penitentiary or gallows"; and yet that same Christian Gentleman believes the Indian boy to grow up and develop into the "Noble Red Man" endowed with all the virtues.

Potts earned the name Kyi-yo-kosi or Bear Child after offering his respect to the Great Spirit by submitting to the most important ritual of the sun dance. Respected elders lifted his chest muscles away from his bones, pierced a channel underneath the muscles, threading rawhide through and tying it firmly over his skin. Then they lashed him by the rawhide to a sacred pole in the centre of the ceremonies. A man could earn honour by quickly tearing himself away or by enduring the pain. Potts endured. After several days without food or water and having never once broken silence, he pulled himself free.

Once accepted as a warrior, Potts threw himself into the Blackfoot military societies, collectively known as the All-Comrades Society. The Confederacy tribes had as many as a dozen societies devoted to passing on military lore. Some of them had specific duties like policing the camps, inflicting punishment, guarding and conducting the buffalo hunt.

At twenty-three Potts killed for the first time. It was simply a drunken quarrel and at the end of it Antoine Primeau, a French Canadian, himself well-soaked in bug juice, lay dead in the dirt, with a musket ball through his eye, at Fort Galpin, Montana. There was no honour in that first death, no retribution exacted, nor even a lesson taught, but it was the beginning of the legend of Jerry Potts.

Though he killed dozens more men over the years and fought in some of the most ferocious Indian battles on the frontier, Potts always escaped without serious injury. He credited his good medicine to strict adherence to Blackfoot omens and taboos. While working at a Montana trading post, he dreamt of a cat, which was to be his special talisman against evil. The next day, he scoured the area until he found a cat identical to the one in his dream. He killed and skinned the source of his vision and wore it next to his own skin for the rest of his life.

Potts also had a war charm, purchased in the usual way from a medicine man for the usual price, one horse. Elite warriors, who had been blessed by a special vision, carried special shields, shirts and war bonnets with them into battle, passing them from warrior to warrior with ceremonial rituals and songs. But even if a warrior couldn't afford special apparel, he would have a war charm—a hawk's head, a dog's paw or a buffalo tail.

Potts' war charm and cat skin may not have had the powerful medicine of a war shirt or bonnet, which not only protected a warrior but also gave him extra powers to take scalps and bring honour to himself through his exploits in battle, but the Blackfoot concluded there must be something extraordinary about them because Potts seemed to slide out of the worst situations like a ghost slipping through a dream. In later years, after he'd beaten overwhelming odds again and again, his allies and enemies alike took to claiming that he possessed supernatural powers. He even survived a point-blank shot in battle, escaping with only severe powder burns.

Once he and a cousin were ambushed by three Crow while they were hunting along the Sun River in Montana. The cousin fell, dead when he hit the ground. Potts, whimpering and cringing like a whipped dog, tossed his rifle down in defeat. The Crow, magnanimous in victory, motioned that they were happy with a single scalp—Potts could go. Word of Potts' fluency in Crow had not spread to this particular band.

Smiling like an idiot, Potts gratefully turned his horse away but not until he heard them discussing which part of the "stupid one's" back should receive the first bullet. As the slug snicked into the chamber, Potts dove forward in his saddle,

Jerry Potts in front of his lodges with Peigan women and medicine bundle.

just in time to see his fatally wounded hat smack into the dirt.
Momentum carried him right off his horse and as he hit the
ground he rolled and surfaced with his revolver spitting. His
cousin's killer died first, followed quickly by bullets in the
backs of the two others as they turned to flee.

Potts stripped the Crow, peeled off their scalps, sorted
through their possessions, hoisted his cousin across his horse
and left the corpses for coyotes. One of his trophies from that
day was a blue steel gun. Shortly before his death, Potts
renamed his youngest son Blue Gun, to commemorate his
good fortune.

The Crow figured prominently in the creation of Potts' warrior legend. A few years later Potts was hunting buffalo alone
in the Shonkin Creek area south of Fort Benton, when he was
cut off by seven well-armed Crow. With elaborate courtesy
they invited him to visit their camp, an offer Potts could hardly refuse.

While the Crow casually arranged themselves to prevent any
escape, Potts considered his options. If he didn't somehow
vamoose, the Crow would surely serve him up a lifetime of pain
and humiliation in the next few hours. And they'd stretch out
the agony for days if he was recognized as the possessor of
many Crow scalps. They might stake him out naked in the hot
sun, fat smeared over his body and blood oozing from dozens
of superficial cuts, an invitation to an army of vermin and scav-
engers. Or they'd split his belly open and pile his guts beside
him. Either way he'd have a ringside seat at his own slow, hor-
rifying death. It wasn't the end Jerry Potts imagined for himself.

The confident Crow made two fatal mistakes. They didn't
bother to search Potts after he handed over his Henry rifle,
and they arrogantly assumed he couldn't understand their language. As they rode, the Crow laughingly discussed his future.
Should they kill him now, or take him to camp and enjoy his
screams for mercy? The consensus was for a drawn-out, entertaining death. But the leader, uncomfortable with the inconsis-
tency between Potts' idiotic demeanour and the way his
strong, wiry body radiated menace, decided it would be pru-
dent to end it right there.

As he gave the order, Potts dove off his horse, rolled, yanked
out a hidden revolver and popped up in perfect firing position.

The surprised Crow wheeled hard to take aim but Potts' bullets dropped four in quick succession. The remaining men, firing wildly behind them, hightailed it into the bush.

Potts lay panting on the ground. Four dead, three heading for camp at high speed. A satisfying conclusion, the great spirit had smiled on him once again. But an opportunity was at hand to teach the Crow a lesson. Potts caught his horse and rode towards Fort Benton, where he knew several bands of Peigan, Blackfoot and Blood were camping. With the Sioux and Crow pushing into Blackfoot territory and looking to make war at every opportunity in the upper Missouri, the tribes of the Confederacy often kept each other in sight when they moved towards a fort to trade. There would be a good supply of battle-hungry braves to play a role in the adventure Potts had planned.

It didn't take Potts long to assemble his war party. As the man to be avenged, and a warrior with a formidable reputation, he assumed the role of chief. Potts figured that the remaining Crow would never admit that they'd been routed by a single half-breed. Instead they'd return to camp and claim victory.

Stealing up to a bend in Shonkin Creek where the Crow were camped, Potts and his party lay quiet and waited. As the night descended into silence, they moved. The sleeping Crow only had time to run. They didn't get far. The night air filled with their screams of pain and terror and the sweet smell of blood was everywhere. Within minutes dozens lay dead. The attackers marched triumphantly among the bodies, dispatching the wounded and claiming their trophies. Scalping takes surprisingly little time. A sharp tug of the scalp lock to free it from the skull, then three or four quick slices and the gory treasure is free.

As Fort Benton was just settling in to sleep, Potts' war party returned, sticks festooned with still dripping scalps, their whoops of triumph audible for several miles. The townsfolk wasted little time snatching up their weapons and taking cover. The owner of the Overland Hotel eagerly handed out his whiskey gratis, praying they wouldn't burn the place down.

That night there was an orgy that boggles description—drunken carousel, scalp-dances, war-dances, discharge of firearms, hootings, yellings, howlings, cursings, personal encounters, threats against the whites, and "hell broke loose" all around. Why the whites were not all killed and every building burned down, I never knew, and I don't understand it now, for the blood-lust had taken possession both of the full-bloods and the half-breeds, and it was practically in their power to do as they pleased.

At the height of the tumult, settler Winfield Stocking and his wife, Margaret, one of only a handful of white women in the whole territory, made a run for the I.G. Baker store, the only building in town with the protection of thick brick walls. They were turned back halfway across the street by a yipping river of half-naked men, brandishing tomahawks and knives.

Stocking and his wife retreated to the cellar of their clapboard house. Stocking loaded his rifle, cocked his revolver and stood guard all night. He was never disturbed. But if he had been, he intended to save his last two bullets, the first for Margaret and the last for himself.

When the 1864 gold strike brought thousands of fortune hunters to Montana, Potts was in great demand as a guide—he brought his parties back alive. In 1868, he was guiding an expedition when two hundred Sioux attacked. Potts, George Steell and a tenderfoot were separated from the main party and chased for miles. Just as the Indians were beginning to overtake them, Potts audaciously reversed course 180 degrees, charging back through the Sioux, who were so surprised they didn't land a single bullet. With the Indians in hot pursuit, Potts and his companions hightailed it to an abandoned log cabin where they released their exhausted horses and holed up.

Their barricade withstood the first attack, with Potts killing five. When a second attack didn't materialize, Potts figured that the Sioux intended to wait until dark and burn them out. Escape was their only hope, but without horses the Sioux would catch them in minutes. At dusk, Potts slipped out with his saddle blanket and belly-crawled for a quarter mile. Once clear of the sentries, he stood up, wrapped the blanket around himself, hiding his white clothes, and strolled through the camp as if he were a Sioux brave. When he reached the herd,

Potts quickly cut out the three fastest-looking horses and, swinging wide around the camp, led them back to the terrified gold hunters. They galloped hard into the night, the two white men desperately trying not to fall off the saddle-less horses. Once they were well in the clear, Steell and his companion nearly had heart attacks when Potts let loose a triumphant Blackfoot war whoop.

Potts loved action; if none was available he'd create some. He and his drinking buddy George Star, another half-breed, could always find something to liven things up. The two men would stand twenty-five paces apart and, after a brief argument about who would have the honour of going first, proceed to trim each other's moustaches with their bullets. Fortunately, when they missed, they shot wide. Once they discussed upping the stakes a bit by shooting simultaneously. Happily, it occurred to one of them that if both died, neither would benefit from inheriting the possessions of the other. So they discarded the idea.

Aside from booze and cards, guns were just about the only source of entertainment on the frontier. Two trading partners, named Fink and Carpenter, liked to amuse themselves by taking turns shooting a cup of whiskey off each other's head. After a brief falling out over an Indian girl, they made up and decided to show their goodwill by repeating the stunt. Fink went first after winning a coin toss. Carpenter, obviously the duller-witted partner, stood stoically with the cup atop his head. "Hold your noodle steady, Carpenter, and don't spill the whiskey," instructed Fink. Moments later, Carpenter was dead with a bullet through his brain. "Aw shucks, Carpenter, you spilled the whiskey," complained Fink.

Though Potts worked for whites he wasn't above indulging in a little Indian humour at their expense. Winfield Stocking owned a splendid, big grey horse for which he'd paid $150. He was furious when he woke up one morning and discovered it stolen. After searching for days, he heard that a Peigan, living in one of Jerry Potts' lodges on the Marias River, had taken it. Stocking cautiously waited until Potts came into town before inquiring about the horse. Potts agreed that the animal was at his camp and told the man that he'd be happy to help get it back.

"Course," Potts said, "you take your chances after you leave my camp. With me you're okay, after, it's every white man for himself." Stocking took Potts very seriously. He considered Potts the best sort of half-breed—a white man's friend.

Stocking saddled up the next day and joined Potts on the fifty-mile trip to the Marias River, taking care to bring along his Winchester and a six-shooter. With them went five other Peigans, who didn't make a favourable impression on Stocking: "I would not care much for their photographs." At the camp Stocking accompanied Potts into his tent and enjoyed a fine meal of boss ribs.

> After supper Jerry sent for the Indian who had my horse. He admitted that he had the animal, and that he knew he belonged to me; but he stoutly insisted that he had bought him from another Piegan Indian; that he was willing to give him up but that he ought to be well paid for his trouble and receive a present besides, for making restitution of the property.

Potts, acting as interpreter, stifled his amusement. Stocking told the Peigan that he had nothing with him, but he would be happy to pay him at Fort Benton, but only if he took the horse with him. Potts nodded sagely. This white man had hit upon the only way he could get his horse and escape with his hide.

> Then he begun to itemize what he wanted, and I filled two pages of a blank book with memoranda before he quit—a sack of flour, so much coffee, so much tea, sugar, tobacco, crackers, and fifty other things.

Stocking and the Peigan shook hands on the bargain. The Indian would produce the horse in the morning and Stocking would provide the gifts at Benton. But fifteen minutes later the Peigan reappeared.

> "My friend, I forgot something. My squaw wants cloth enough for a dress. She wants some thread. She wants some needles," and fifty other things that I have forgotten. It was all set down in the book.

Again they shook hands on the bargain. Half an hour later, the Peigan returned.

"My friend, I forgot something. My boy wants a butcher knife. He has to have a hatchet too," and a dozen or fifteen other things, all of which I religiously set down in my book, knowing that I dare not refuse. And still he kept coming back, and adding the list of what he must have, until it was twelve o'clock, and until I had nearly filled the blank book from cover to cover.

His last demand was for an axe, which rounded out a bill of goods that would have cost between three and four hundred dollars—and as he couldn't think of anything else, he quit for the night.

In the morning, there was no sign of either the horse or the talkative Indian. Stocking asked Potts if he thought the man would be back. "Nope," he responded. Stocking then told Potts he'd pay him ten dollars if he got the horse for him. In less than five minutes, the horse was in Stocking's hand and the money in Potts' pocket.

"Go slow," he cautioned Stocking. "When you clear camp ride like hell." It was advice Stocking didn't need. "If he and his friends had overtaken me on the way to Benton, it is not likely I would be talking."

Back home, Stocking carefully secured the horse before falling into bed exhausted.

At daybreak, the Indian was at my door, in Benton, pounding on it to wake me up, and clamouring for what he called his "pay". It is needless, perhaps, to state that he never got it. I had never intended to give him anything, for I knew that he had stolen the horse, and he knew that I knew it, too.

The Peigan and Potts got the last laugh—which they had intended all along. Several days later, the horse collapsed, having been ridden to death.

Baker's Massacre

By 1865 "civilization" had begun to neuter the Confederacy in earnest as once unified tribes clashed in whiskey-fuelled brawls—Peigan against Blood, Blackfoot against Peigan. Even within the bands themselves braves, elders and chiefs disagreed over whether to kill every white they saw or trade and make peace. Even Crowfoot, the richest and most influential chief in the Confederacy, had difficulty controlling his young braves.

Jerry Potts kept his lodges away from the larger bands of South Peigan—the people of his wives—he wanted no part of their squabbles. It seemed to him that the spirits who guided the Blackfoot into supremacy over all Indians were growing tired of them and turning away. But it wasn't until the late fall of 1868 that the spirits deserted the Confederacy completely and accelerated their spiral into despair. As the rivers swelled from the late season melt, the white man stole their most sacred object—the Manitou Stone. Nearly two centuries of standing hard against the white tide meant nothing once it was torn from its rightful place.

Long before Big Dog and the shooting stick turned the Blackfoot into powerful warriors, a god placed a pebble at the top of an isolated hill. Over the years the Stone grew into a massive oblong rock no brave could move. The Stone held powerful medicine for all the Plains tribes. Many times Jerry Potts detoured miles to pass his palm over its smooth face. He left tobacco and pemmican at its base and rode away, looking back to see the light glint off its blue surface like an arm reaching to the spirits.

In 1862, Wesleyan Methodist George McDougall, his wife, Elizabeth, sons John and David and three daughters became the first permanent white family in the territory, setting up a mission they named Victoria on the Saskatchewan River, about seventy-five miles east of Fort Edmonton.

Fear made many missionaries who entered Blackfoot territory little more than children. Potts had once guided a Black Robe from Fort Benton to Fort Edmonton.

"I heard there is a war party about. Is that so?" the missionary asked Potts timidly.

"That so," confirmed Potts.

"Well, what do you suppose they want?"

"Want war."

"Is there something we can take along?" the man asked anxiously. "Something they'd like, a present? Perhaps some food?"

Potts considered. The man fidgeted, turning his hat nervously in his hands. "Food good," he finally said. He drew his eyes slowly to the man's face, coming to rest on the excellent red, Irish curls long overdue for a trim. "Hair's better."

The missionary's eyes widened when he realized what Potts was saying. He pulled his hat down hard on his head—as if an Indian knife couldn't find flesh through felt—and walked quickly off.

"Give 'em that hair, they leave you alone. For sure," he said to the rapidly departing back.

But the McDougalls, especially the two boys, were nothing like other missionaries. They didn't hide inside the fur traders' forts or their missions, and they openly admired and emulated the Indians' skill in hunting and trapping. David McDougall, who became a trader, and John, a preacher, were champion braggarts who viewed every obstacle as a contest. If a man could make 50 miles a day by dogsled, they could easily manage 70 and claim it would be a leisurely trip. Unfordable rivers had to be challenged and every feat of wood-chopping, running, hunting and log-peeling had to be bettered. "The two brothers would pooh-pooh the then world's marathon record as something they had often outdone in their youth," recalled an observer. "The missionary brother was fond of enlarging on his physical toughness—how of a freezing night he would make shift with a single blanket, wade across streams with hefty wives of less puissant fellow clerics in his arms and so on."

In 1863, John, then twenty-one, led a small provisioning party on the two-thousand-mile round trip to Fort Garry from Victoria. Characteristically, he sped ahead of the party on the last day in order to be the first one through the mission gates. "Fifty miles before dinner," he crowed, flinging open the mission door, "and both horse and rider as ready for work as ever, and I may be pardoned in saying 'that was a horse, and this was a man.'"

Whites in the West weren't so impressed. "There are three liars in the territory," the saying went. "The trader is reckoned as one and his reverend brother as the other two." But the brothers' swaggering and daring gave them easy entrée into the camps of Cree, Stoney, Kootenay and even Blackfoot, David for trading and John for trapping souls. The Blackfoot, in particular, loved showmanship. They didn't even mind being beaten at something by a white man if he put on a good enough display of bravado.

In the late 1860s, a group of Indians showed off their most sacred object to Parson John—the Manitou Stone. McDougall was certainly the first white man to be taken to see it. The Indians explained how it protected them and spoke of the horrors that would befall their people if it were ever disturbed. McDougall strode up the gentle hill with its table-like top and peered at the Stone. He didn't see an oddly coloured meteorite, polished by the years and many venerating hands. He saw a challenge. If he successfully moved it, he would demonstrate the superiority of the white man's religion and the weakness of the Indian's "dead faith." And when the prophecy didn't come true he could tell them the Great Father's medicine was so powerful he had cast aside the spell.

In late fall 1868 Parson John, with a team of white and half-breed helpers and a block and tackle, hauled the Manitou Stone to the Victoria mission's front yard.

Elders from Cree, Assiniboine and Blackfoot tribes were enraged and terrified. They took council and considered stealing it back. But they worried that such action might make things worse; if the spirits hadn't wanted it moved, surely they wouldn't have allowed it to happen. They begged the Wesleyans to return it lest the three evils foretold by the legends—disease, war and famine—be unleashed.

John McDougall scoffed at their fears, assuring them they were now under the protection of the Great Father. He urged them to listen instead to the words he read from the big black book that sat on a table by the fireplace in the mission's front room.

Shortly after the theft of the Stone, a missionary wrote a letter to the Wesleyan Society magazine. He described the Stone and the legends as an example of the "savages'" quaint beliefs. And he pointed out that none of the predictions had come to pass.

Only one white expressed unease at the removal of the Manitou Stone; William Francis Butler, who arrived at the mission in late 1870 during his investigation of the North West, commissioned by the government of Manitoba. Butler was a rare individual, able to appreciate the Indian for what he was, neither noble savage nor murdering villain.

> I have heard a good deal of persons who were said to possess great Knowledge of the Indian character. And I have seen enough of the red man to estimate at its real worth the possession of this knowledge. Knowledge of Indian character has too long been synonymous with knowledge of how to cheat the Indian—a species of cleverness which, even in the science of chicanery, does not require the exercise of the highest abilities.
>
> I fear that the Indian has already had too many dealings with persons of this class, and has now got a very shrewd idea that those who possess this knowledge of his character have also managed to possess themselves of his property.

McDougall proudly showed off the Manitou Stone to Butler, boasting about the feat of moving it. Butler gazed at the object and felt a great discomfort. As an Irishman who'd grown up with beasties and leprechauns, he wasn't about to denigrate the power of beliefs held so fervently. "[A] few months later," he wrote sadly, "brought all the three evils upon the Indians; and never, probably, since the first trader had reached the country had so many afflictions of war, famine, and plague fallen upon the Crees and the Blackfeet as during the year which succeeded the useless removal of their Manito-stone from the lone hill-top upon which the skies had cast it."*

First came war, starting just months after the Manitou Stone had been moved. In January 1869 a group of hunters in northern Montana were stalked, then stripped to their underwear by Indians. In April a wagon master was wounded. In May five

---

* The name of the stone is variously spelled Manitou and Manito in legend and literature.

men from a bull train, bound for Fort Peck, a trading post on the Missouri at the mouth of the Milk River, disappeared; all that remained were the burned-out skeletons of the wagons. Three times that spring Indians descended on Fort Benton, shooting wildly and galloping through town. In mid-July two teamsters were shot and later died. There were dozens of incidents, some reported, some not. The culprits weren't always the Blackfoot. The Sioux claimed victory in many of the raids as did the Crow. But whites were convinced the Confederacy intended an all-out assault in Montana. "Blackfoot War!" the headlines screamed as settlers demanded the army protect them.

But the U.S. army, caught between squabbling bureacracies, was practically moribund. The new president, Ulysses S. Grant, had just instituted his Peace Policy, aimed at bringing the Indian to heel with God, reason and bribes, not slaughter. The army, their skills refined by the killing of the Cheyenne, Apache, Sioux and Comanche, sat idle in their forts in Blackfoot territory. But the traders and settlers could act—and they did. Two Indians trading in Fort Benton were shot in August 1869. And a lynch mob strung up three Blackfoot supposedly responsible for the deaths of the two teamsters. One of the victims was the brother of Mountain Chief, a powerful Peigan leader.

Mountain Chief was in an awkward spot. His gut screamed vengeance but his head counselled caution. He was keenly aware of the problems other tribes were having in controlling their young braves. Whether they were bent on retaliation for years of broken promises or simply after whiskey and guns, the end result was the same—dead whites, burned settlements, pillaged horses and enough hysteria among settlers and traders to turn the flame of discontent into a fire-storm.

Mountain Chief had already extended his hand in peace three times. His mark on the U.S. treaties of 1855, 1865 and 1868 made him one of the most conciliatory of Indians. Mountain Chief saw the future. He was also concerned about the Sioux. In no time they would be swarming into Montana, pushed west by the American Cavalry. Mountain Chief wasn't sure his people could hold off their more numerous enemy.

The day after his brother was killed in Fort Benton, Mountain Chief, grieving and stone-faced, abruptly ordered a group of white traders from his camp. Two weeks later a raiding party killed former trader Malcolm Clarke in the Prickly Pear Valley.* The murder was blamed on Mountain Chief, but it made little sense. He had no history of retaliation and even if he had sought revenge, he could have had it when the white traders were in his camp.

In the midst of all this came the second evil, plague—small-pox—brought up the Missouri on a river boat. The disease struck in the fall of 1869 and stretched cruelly into the spring of 1870. Within the Confederacy the Blackfoot alone lost 1,400 and the Peigan and Blood 1,000 more, nearly 30 per-cent of the nation's population. Those who took the Manitou Stone were also punished. John McDougall's three sisters died at the height of the epidemic.

Jerry Potts had carefully skirted many encampments, wiped out to the last child. Teepee poles lurching grotesquely askew, camp-fires colder than a dead man's hands and corpses—splayed, half-eaten, bones poking through, maggot-ridden. Coyotes skulked about, fighting and chewing over bits and pieces of human anatomy.

Potts knew of braves who had killed themselves rather than suffer the indignity of disfigurement and madness. He had come across poor dead souls who had fallen and been left behind while their band was on the move, their hands flung out, their legs spread as if running from the horror.

The third evil came fast on the heels of the first two. Famine held hands with smallpox all through that terrible winter of 1869–70. Even if the decimated tribes had been able to hunt, there was little to shoot. The viciously cold winter weather combined with early summer drought and a grasshopper plague to drive the Blackfoot mainstay, the buffalo, far to the south, seeking forage. The Blackfoot had never faced such desperation. Once aloof and suspicious, many were reduced to huddling piteously around military posts, forts and missions, begging for whatever scraps they could get. Others went crazy in their des-peration for whiskey to anaesthetize their anger, pain and impo-tence. And still others tried to recapture the legend of the Confederacy. Chiefs and medicine men lost control as young warriors went renegade, attacking anything that moved.

* Now Sieben, Montana.

While the Blackfoot died and the bureaucrats argued, the people of Montana demanded protection from the blood-thirsty savages. General Alfred Sully, superintendent of Indian Affairs in Helena, had made his name in the West with a punishing series of assaults on the Sioux in the Dakota Territories in 1864 and '65. Sully believed implicitly in the salutary effects of reprisal. From the moment word of Malcolm Clarke's death reached him, he favoured a repeat of the Dakota campaign in Montana. Simply arresting the Peigan culprits would not be a sufficient lesson.

On New Year's Day 1870, General Sully and U.S. Marshall W.F. Wheeler, under the guise of a council at the Teton River Agency, issued the assembled Blackfoot chiefs a provocative ultimatum. Give us the murderers of Malcolm Clarke, he ordered, or we will "cross the line with our troops" and drag the culprits back from the land of the White Grandmother, Queen Victoria.

The chiefs were stunned. The Medicine Line provided sanctuary. On the other side the Long Knives were as impotent as castrated dogs. It was magic, this line, like a wall of friendly spirits, through which only the Indian could pass, leaving the blue coats fuming on the other side. A darkness swept across the banks of the Teton and gripped the chiefs with a chill sense of foreboding. Not only did Sully threaten to cross the border but he claimed to have the permission of the Grandmother to do so. Why had her protection of the Indian been suddenly snatched away?

Sully was so impressed with the fear he instilled in the Blackfoot that he softened his earlier recommendation. "For the present no blood should be shed, if it is possible to avoid it," he wrote two weeks later. As Sully, representing Indian Affairs, counselled caution, General P.R. De Trobriand, commander at Fort Shaw, wrote to Lieutenant-General Philip Sheridan in Chicago, urging him to deliver "a sharp and severe blow upon some guilty band as an example to the rest." That sounded fine to Sheridan. His experiences with the "butchering savages" had taught him everything he ever needed to know. "The only good Indians I ever saw, were dead," he'd stated a month earlier.

As the pressure increased from Montana citizens to ignore

the Peace Policy and do something about the Blackfoot, Sheridan, the old cavalry man, could feel his spurs tingling. "About the time of a good heavy snow," he wrote to his superior General E.D. Townshend. "I will send out a party and try and strike them. About the fifteenth of January they will be very helpless, and if where they live is not too far from Shaw or Ellis, we might be able to give them a good hard blow, which will make peace a desirable object."

Two days after Sully's caution, Sheridan sent orders to De Trobriand at Fort Shaw. "If the lives and property of the citizens of Montana can best be protected by striking Mountain Chief's band, I want them struck. Tell Baker to strike them *hard*."

Major Eugene M. Baker quickly assembled a unit, drawn from Fort Ellis and Fort Shaw, to make the assault. It had been a long time since the largely moribund forts had danced with such enthusiasm. Men who hadn't been sober in months put the bottle down. Saddles encrusted with dirt were finally cleaned and rags became valuable tender as the men frantically dug grease out of their neglected rifles.

"We're goin' Injun huntin'!" enthused the once listless corps. Veterans filled newly arrived young men with gruesome stories of what would happen to them if they got caught. "They'll scalp ya' and smoke yer hair right in front of yer dyin' eyes! Finest tobacco in the world, I'm told." A favourite tale was the plight of the Union Pacific brakeman whose train had been ambushed two years earlier. The engineer and stoker were killed and the rest escaped into the bush—except the brakeman. He was scalped on the spot with the Indian sitting on top of him wielding what the poor man recalled was a very dull knife.

Amazingly, the brakeman, still alive, staggered to the tracks and, wearing only shirt and shoes, flagged down another train. While they examined the plundered wreck, one of the trainmen found a scalp dropped in the frenzy. "My hair!" the shattered brakeman whimpered. The rescuers stuck the thing in water and sent the man off to Omaha where two surgeons tried to stick it back on. "Fella's got the ugliest looking head you ever saw," said one observer. "Poor bugger never could get a hat to fit."

At 4:00 a.m. on January 19, 1870, three hundred men left fear in their beds as morning reveille blew them instantly alert. Eugene Baker rode up and down the ranks of the Thirteenth Regiment of infantry, bolstered now by a detachment of the Second United States Cavalry. His words left little doubt as to their duty. "We're going out there to teach those goddamned Indians a lesson! I don't want any shirking. We've been told to hit 'em and by god we're going to hit 'em hard!" The air plumed with the white breath of horses and men, more eager now than ever to be off. The thermometer teased -35, but no one felt the cold.

Baker employed two savvy guides, Joe Kipp, son of fur trader James Kipp, and Joe Cobell, to lead him to the camp of Mountain Chief, reportedly on the Marias River. But he didn't know that Cobell's wife was Mountain Chief's sister. As the troops neared the river, Kipp grew increasingly uneasy. He told Baker they were headed in the wrong direction.

"What do you mean?" demanded the annoyed major. "Mountain Chief ain't there," insisted Kipp. "He'll be further north." Baker conferred with Cobell, who was determined that his wife's people not be punished for the murder. He assured Baker the Peigan lodges would soon be in view; Kipp challenged Cobell's directions again. Fed up, Major Baker placed him under arrest. "You bother me again and it's the last guiding you'll ever do. And let me warn you, if you wake them up to our coming, I'll have you shot!"

At eight o'clock in the morning on January 23, Baker and his three hundred men massed a short distance from the camp. It was eerily quiet. No dogs yipped. No children played. Little smoke rose out of the teepees.

"Now boys," said Baker. "There's the devils! In you go and clear the bastards out. I don't want no damn prisoners. Uncle Sam's got no time for prisoners. You get those squaws and young 'uns too. It's the squaws that breed 'em and they'll only grow up to be horse-thieves and hair lifters. Kill 'em all!"

Hardly had they moved when a thin, emaciated Indian emerged from one of the tents and ran towards them. He tripped but caught himself before falling. His clothes were in rags, his face haggard. Had they been closer, the men would also have seen the blackening sores covering his face. He clutched a soiled piece of paper, which he waved in front of him as he stumbled forward.

A rifle barked and Heavy Runner sprawled forward on the frozen ground, his papers of friendship still clutched in his hand. Heavy Runner had a long history of interaction with whites; he was known as a "friendly." The bullet he took was army issue but the hand holding the rifle was Joe Cobell's.

Seconds after the gunshot, the camp erupted into a mass of charging men and horses. The terrified Peigan rushed out of their tents, dragging and carrying children and frail elders. The troopers shot wildly, sometimes pumping dozens of bullets into already dead bodies. They ran their horses into the lodges, trampling them or upending them to slaughter those too sick to run. Screams and the coppery scent of blood mingled sharply in the frosty air. Baker could not have stopped the killing even if he'd wanted.

It didn't take long. By nine o'clock, 173 men, women and children lay dead, shot from every direction and into every body part possible. Only forty-six escaped, including a handful of women and children taken prisoner. A single soldier was killed. The rest suffered the odd scratch, bruise or wound—mainly from bumping into each other in their frantic haste to claim a kill.

Major Eugene Baker had conquered a death camp. Not only were the Indians in the last, fatal stages of smallpox, but he had killed the wrong ones. Mountain Chief had long ago slipped north over the Medicine Line. Even so, a blow had been struck for civilization. "The first great lesson in good manners taught the savage of this Territory," applauded westerners. "That Baker's a bell ox among sodgers, you bet!" crowed a miner. "He wiped out them Pagan redskins—made a clean shave of the hull brood!"

A month after the slaughter, a French missionary entered Mountain Chief's camp on the Belly River in British Territory. He knew nothing of the Baker Massacre or Heavy Runner's fate. The Peigan rushed him into the council tent and uncharacteristically blurted out the whole story without any pleasantries or preamble. Sick-hearted at what he heard, the missionary urged the Indians to give up their futile resistance against the white men.

"It is useless," he pleaded. "You must see that! You will all be killed if you don't now go in peace to them." The Indians, warriors and elders alike, said nothing. The priest tried again.

"Why are your faces black and your hearts so heavy? Are you not grieving for your family and your friends? They are lost to you now. Do you want others to follow? What happened is only a beginning. The Long Knives have many more canoes, more weapons than all the tribes of this land put together. Their canoes have giant guns that spit fire and kill many in one shot. They will not stop! They will keep coming until there are none of you left!"

The priest's passionate words met heavy silence. Each man studied the ground in front of him. The priest looked around. None met his eyes. His passion drained away. Mountain Chief rose and addressed the priest.

"You have spoken true, your words come straight; the Long Knives are too many and too strong for us. Their guns shoot farther than ours, their big guns shoot twice. Their numbers are as the buffalo were in the days of our fathers."

To that point his voice was quiet, contemplative. His eyes flashed and he continued sharply.

"But what of all that? Do you want us to starve on the land which is ours? Lie down as slaves to the white man, die away one by one in misery and hunger? It is true that the Long Knives must kill us, but I say still to my children and to my tribe, fight on, fight on, fight on!"

His words rang out and the Indians, to a man, were rapt.

"It is better to die thus, as a brave man should die, than to live a little time and then die like a coward. So now, my brethren, I tell you, as I have told you before, keep fighting still. When you see these men coming along the river, digging holes in the ground and looking for the little bright sand, kill them! For they mean to kill you. Fight, and if it must be, die, for you can only die once, and it is better to die than to starve."

In a quiet voice, Mountain Chief invited them to disagree "and say to this Black Robe I speak with a forked tongue." The warriors clamoured their approval and the priest watched and listened sadly as their excited words endorsed their chief.
"Kill! Kill! Kill!" they chanted.

The Battle Of Belly River

OCTOBER 1870

Jerry Potts jerked awake—woken by a tug from his horse, tethered to his wrist by a long strip of rawhide. Straining, he faintly heard the sound of hundreds of unshod hooves— Indian ponies, moving fast, coming straight at him. Pausing only to kick awake his companion, George Star, Potts grabbed his guns, slipped onto his horse and made for cover behind a clump of trees.

"Hell's going on?" asked Star as he rode up to Potts.

"Horses," said Potts.

"Figured that much," snorted Star. The two old friends quickly checked their guns and shared ammunition.

They glimpsed a mounted rider through the moonlight—a Peigan, in a hurry—they relaxed. Nearly two hundred more followed him, galloping north in the pre-dawn gloom.

"They heading to Whoop Up?" Star queried. Potts considered it highly likely. The Blackfoot had killing on their minds. Warriors clamoured for revenge after the annihilation of Heavy Runner's band. It would be suicide to strike back at the military in the States but Fort Whoop Up, with between thirty and fifty whiskey traders, most of them Americans, would be an appealing target.

Potts and Star looped around so they could approach the

throng in plain view and identify themselves before they got shot.

"Bear Child here!" shouted Potts. "Where you ride?"

"The Cree attack!" a Peigan, recognizing Potts, yelled back. "We need your gun!"

Since Baker's massacre in January, the South Peigan had crossed the Medicine Line by the hundreds for mutual protection, to take counsel and commiserate with their Blood and Blackfoot brothers. Their camps stretched for twenty miles along the Belly River from Fort Whoop Up north to Fort Kipp. The Blackfoot and Blood, with fifty or sixty lodges and around two hundred warriors, were on the river close to Kipp. The South Peigan with another 350 warriors, well-armed with American repeaters, were camped farther away near Whoop Up. In all there were 550 warriors from the Blackfoot Confederacy camped along the river.

After the theft of the Manitou Stone, the Cree had also felt the dark hand of evil but their losses from smallpox and famine were slight compared to the detested Blackfoot. Before the epidemic struck, the Blackfoot had dealt the Cree a number of humiliating losses, largely because the Cree's single-shot HBC muskets, which once had given them the advantage, were now no match for the Blackfoot's Winchesters, Colts and Henrys. The Cree and their allies, the Assiniboine, saw the devastation of the Confederacy by smallpox as a perfect opportunity to strike a fatal blow.

News of the Blood and Blackfoot congregating along the Belly River reached the Cree in the fall of 1870. Chiefs Piapot, Big Bear, Little Pine, Little Mountain and dozens of lesser chiefs gathered together eight hundred warriors. Among them was a three-hundred-strong mixed band of Cree, Saulteaux and Young Dog under the leadership of Oo-sa-us-tik-wan (Yellow Hair) and Tip-oo-es-tik-wan (Curly Hair). They were everything warriors should be—strong, fearless, unforgiving and loyal. They were also blond and blue-eyed; their faces well-stamped with the Scots ancestry of their father, HBC trader Hugh Sutherland. But the souls of the half-breed brothers were Cree.

A white man who knew Hugh Sutherland happened upon them just as they finished assembling their war party at the Red Ochre Hills. "Wouldn't you be better off between the stilts of a plough, young man, than going off to get yourself killed fighting those Blackfoot?" he asked Yellow Hair. "I have never been taught anything but fighting," said Yellow Hair with a distant smile. "I suppose I have relatives beyond the Big Water who would be sorry to see me leading this kind of life, but how can I help it?"

No one could remember when such a war party had been formed. Painted, feathered and protected by amulets, shields and medicine bundles, the scalp-hungry braves swarmed west across the Prairie. They knew they would face the superior weapons of the Blackfoot but their numbers alone and the element of surprise would be decisive in wiping out their enemies.

The thrill of war rippled through the advancing Cree and Assiniboine like an elixir. They made their way along the South Saskatchewan River and halted a few miles from the Blackfoot lodges at Whoop Up. Several braves, their courage well-known, volunteered to reconnoitre. It was a hazardous job. A good scout thrust himself right into the heart of an enemy camp, sometimes even disguising himself and walking among his intended victims. Returning to his war party, he would carry vital intelligence to the battle chief—information that could make the difference between defeat and victory.

The scouts found the 60 Blood and Blackfoot lodges strung out along the river but missed the 150 Peigan lodges spread further south. There were sentries, as expected, but they estimated barely two hundred warriors in all. Buoyed by the news, the chiefs decided to strike late the following night, after the Blackfoot were asleep.

Early the next morning while the warriors prepared themselves for battle, Chief Piapot rose and walked off by himself to ponder a troubling vision. The message had been clear, they must not fight. It was hard for Piapot to stomach. He lived to crush the Blackfoot, he dedicated his life to it. Now his vision told him to give it up. Sorrowful, but resolute, he approached the war council.

"My children," he beseeched the assembled warriors. "I had a dream last night. I saw a buffalo bull with iron horns goring, stamping and killing us. We were unable to destroy it. After long meditation, I have come to the conclusion that we must abandon this venture and return home, otherwise misfortune awaits us."

A rumble of concern and discontent filled the air. Cries of protest and a few of support greeted his words. Another chief, brandishing his shield, leapt to his feet. "My children, don't believe in a dream! Advance and capture the Blackfoot Nation, women and children. The smallpox killed off most of their fighters so we won't be opposed by any great number!" But dreams were not so easily dismissed. Piapot was a respected warrior and chief; his visions were powerful. One hundred braves followed Piapot out of the war camp, but seven hundred remained—plenty enough for two hundred Blackfoot.

That night, the war party silently surrounded the sleeping Blackfoot. A handful of braves flaunted their courage by slipping past the look-outs, then announcing their presence in the middle of the camp.

"We are here!" one shouted. "You are sleeping! I come!" another taunted. The war party, whooping and firing, galloped to join them. The pre-dawn air quickly filled with acrid smoke from their blasting muskets. Red Crow, brother of the Blood chief, and a number of squaws were killed instantly. But the Cree surprise attack didn't produce a decisive victory. Small pockets of Blackfoot, including a group of women, fought viciously, finally driving the Cree back with their superior firepower.

A few miles away the South Peigan woke up to the echoing burst of gunfire, followed shortly by messengers breathless with news of the battle. Within minutes they were on their horses and riding hard. When the reinforcements arrived, the startled Cree slowly retreated to a coulee four or five miles east and several hundred feet above the Belly River.

When Jerry Potts arrived, he found the Blackfoot arrayed on the south side of the coulee and the Cree on the north. More Confederacy braves streamed in and the Cree, though still more numerous, saw their advantage eroding. The coulee stretched from one hundred to three hundred feet wide. It was a tough place for a battle, cover was sparse and the banks steep. For the moment the two sides were locked in a stand-off. Insults were hurled back and forth. Every now and then a spectacular long shot hit home or a stone looped up into the air, descending on an unwary brave and prompting derisive laughter.

Jerry Potts studied the situation. An all-out charge was too risky. Even if they won, too many Blackfoot would die. But if they let the Cree break the stalemate, the Blackfoot would be on the defensive. In that country, with little cover, casualties would be numerous. He recruited a dozen of the best shots, all armed with the Henry repeaters favoured by the Blackfoot, and took them to a small butte overlooking the Cree position. It was a little distant for accurate shooting, but Potts compensated by concentrating his fire on selected individuals. When one fell, he targeted another.

An Indian war party was fluid, adjusting to terrain and tactic. Ebbs and flows happened in an eye-blink. The best Indian military leaders weren't necessarily great tacticians, rather those who could sense a shift in momentum and pounce upon it—or speedily retreat if the tide turned against them. The success of Potts' strategy caused unease to ripple through the Cree, as they saw dozens of braves cut down from such a distance.

Sensing the Cree vulnerability, Potts leapt onto his horse and tore around the end of the coulee, charging right into the main body of the Cree. Instinctively, his little group galloped up behind him followed by a large number of the Blackfoot. Potts could just as easily have ridden to his death alone, but he rode at the point of a wedge that cleaved and routed the Cree.

Stand off, to retreat, to rout. The main body of the Cree were forced down the coulee's rim by the Blackfoot. Scrambling for purchase, most of them stayed mounted until they hit the twenty-foot drop into the Belly River. Nearly half the horses fell, many dying from the plunge which also killed dozens of their riders. The Cree were trapped on the rocky bank or stranded hip deep in the Belly River.

The narrow river valley became a killing ground. Wave after wave of still mounted Blackfoot drove like scythes through the four hundred nearly helpless Cree; the rest were either dead or terribly wounded—only a handful managed to escape.

MOUNTAIN CHIEF, SON OF MOUNTAIN CHIEF

The greatest event of my life was in the war of the Blackfeet against the Crees at Hope Up [sic].... I was

twenty-two years old at the time. It was fall of the year
and the leaves had all fallen.... The people were just getting up in the morning when the news came that the
camp had been attacked by the Crees.

I got my best horse; it was a grey horse. My father
(Mountain Chief) led his band in company with Big
Lake who that summer had been elected a big chief. We
rode up over a ridge while on the plain below the battle
was raging.

As we rode down the hill slope, I began to sing my
war song. I carried a shield in my hand and this song
that I sung belonged to that shield. One of the medicine
men dreamed that whoever held this shield would not
be hit by the bullets. While singing, I put in the words,
"My body will be lying on the plains."

When I reached the line of battle I did not stop but
rode right in among the Crees and they were shooting at
me from behind and in front.... The Blackfeet made a
rush for the Crees and I ran over two of them before
they got to the river. As they were crossing the river, I
jumped off my horse and stabbed one of the Crees
between the shoulders. He had a spear and I took that
away from him.

I jumped off my horse again and just as I returned
there was a Cree who raised his gun to fire at me. I ran
over him and he jumped up and grabbed my horse by
the bridle. I swung my horse's head around to protect
myself and took the butt of my whip and knocked him
down. When I struck him he looked at me and I saw
that his nose had been cut off. I heard afterwards that a
bear had bitten his nose off. After I knocked him down,
I killed him. I jumped off my horse and just then I met
another Cree.

We had a fight on our horses. He shot at me and I
shot at him. When we got close together, I took his
arrows away from him, and he grabbed me by the hair
of the head. I saw him reach for his dagger and just then
we clinched. My war bonnet had worked down on my
neck, and when he struck at me with his dagger it struck
the war bonnet and I looked down and saw the handle

sticking out and grabbed it and killed the other Indian.

It was a treacherous fight. The river rocks were slick with water and blood. Smoke gathered in the hollows like fog. Guns gave way to knives, tomahawks and fists. Jerry Potts was ever in the eye of the hurricane of death, trampling, cutting, hacking and bellowing victory. "You could shoot with your eyes shut and kill a Cree," he recalled. When fifty desperate Cree escaped the river and ran for a copse of trees, Potts drove his horse over a pile of corpses in order to cut them off.

One Cree lay, feigning death. When Potts was nearly on top of him, he jumped up and fired his musket a few feet from Potts' face. Several Blood charging hard behind him yelled as their leader took the fire point-blank. In the cacophony of battle no sounds were distinguishable but no sooner was the musket's kick stilled than high whoops of delight pierced the din. Potts lived! Some spirit had reached out and deflected the musket ball, leaving Potts with only a scorched neck and ear.

The fifty Cree were overrun and wiped out to the last man before the Blackfoot turned their attention to a group of a hundred making their last stand. Howling with triumph, the Blackfoot, Peigan and Blood surrounded them. Yelling taunts and promising the cowering, weaponless Cree horrible torture, the victors advanced. Then, with the kind of mysterious, mass decision that makes a flock of birds suddenly change direction, the Blackfoot withdrew.

MOUNTAIN CHIEF, SON OF MOUNTAIN CHIEF

When we returned, I had taken nine different scalps. The Crees who had not been scalped had taken refuge in the scant woods and my father said to quit and go home. So we took pity on them and let them go so they could tell the story. I remember that we killed over three hundred and many more that I cannot remember.

When we returned we began to count how many we had killed. We crossed the creek and went to a pit; they were all in a pile. Then we were all singing around the pit and I put in the words, "The guns, they hear me."

And everyone turned and looked at me and I was a great man after the battle. Then we went home and began to talk about the battle and the Indians who were dead.

Boys too young for battle gawked with awe and envy as the victors hoisted sticks festooned with hundreds of scalps. Jerry Potts counted coup sixteen times. That night the Blackfoot celebrated with the wildest scalp dance in memory, their joy stretching into an entire week of feasting and celebration. Stores from the two whiskey forts lubricated the occasion and the traders worked day and night to supply the horde, now rich with the booty of the dead Cree.

Belly River was the last great North American Indian battle, one of the largest and most bloody ever documented. As many as seven hundred were dead or wounded, most of them Cree and Assiniboine.* There were too few of the defeated Indians left to carry away their dead so the slaughtered bodies littered coulee and copse for weeks. At night the arguments of coyotes and wolves could be heard for miles. And during the day the sky darkened with circling birds.

The white world paid scant notice. A brief report about the "novel battle" appeared in the *Manitoban* newspaper in March 1871 after Captain William F. Butler returned to Winnipeg with his report on the North West.

The Hudson's Bay Company reacted crossly to the disruption in trade caused by the battle. Isaac Cowie, posted at Touchwood Hills, deep in Cree territory, noted:

> After the defeat of the Crees by the Blackfeet at Belly River, before mentioned, I had to write off the outstanding debts, varying from fifty to one hundred dollars, of a score of the best Indians belonging to Touchwood Hills, who were slain on that occasion....

Cowie closed their accounts, "By Balance of profit and loss, £23 10s.," followed by the notation "Killed in battle with

---

* There is a considerable range in the estimated casualties from the Battle of Belly River, from a low of 53 dead Cree to a high of 350. The Blackfoot lost between fifty and one hundred.

blackfeet at Belly River."

The white world did not understand what had been averted in the slaughter of Indian by Indian. The night of the attack, every white scalp, on both sides of the border in the West, was tenuously attached. The Blackfoot were hungry for a fight, aching for vengeance after the Baker massacre. Had the Confederacy taken aim at every whiskey and fur trading post in the West, including the town of Fort Benton, no one could have stopped them.

The battle also hardened the animosity between the Cree and the Blackfoot, ensuring that fifteen years later the Confederacy would remain aloof from the rebellion that pitted Cree and Métis against white. Had the Cree not attacked, the Blackfoot might well have thrown themselves into that war and turned a slim victory for the whites into sure defeat, forever altering the history of the Canadian West.

Wolfers and Woodhawks

Wolfers and woodhawks were on the bottom of the frontier pecking order. They, in turn, scorned everyone else and each other with the kind of ferocity born of doing a job involving equal parts brawn and foolhardiness.

Woodhawks were just plain crazy. If you had no desire to live long enough to find your first grey hair, it was the perfect occupation. Superficially, hawking was a simple job—cutting cordwood to supply the river boats going up and down the Missouri. The steamboats, laden with two hundred tons or more of people and supplies, couldn't make the trip without numerous stops for wood. A single boat could put a hundred dollars in the pocket of an industrious woodhawk. Cottonwood and pine brought five to six dollars a cord from fuel-hungry riverboat pilots, but hotter-burning cedar fetched as much as twenty dollars.

Most of the easily accessible timber along the upper Missouri had been cut during the first years of the mining boom. By

1866, wood was so scarce it became legal tender, along with wolf skins and gold, at the Montana trading posts. All through this period the Sioux were moving into the Montana Territory. They began killing woodhawks, then setting ambushes for the riverboat crews at their woodyards. River boats were relatively safe, if they kept moving. Being stranded was a nightmare no pilot wanted to face. When the *Amelia Poe*, en route to Fort Benton, ran aground in 1868, 1,500 Sioux and Crow swarmed over her, fighting for the spoils.

Boat crews often cut the wood but the farther they pushed into Sioux and Blackfoot territory, the more reluctant they were to offer their services. When the crews wouldn't go, the pilots bribed passengers with cash and whiskey. If that didn't work, they prayed for signs of a woodhawk in the vicinity. After spotting Indians, a desperate pilot would pay almost anything for wood. A hard-nosed hawk might bargain for a higher price with a bit of whatnot thrown in—whatnot consisting of a barrel of hooch or a roll with one of the sporting girls on board.

As it always does, money attracts a following. Early in the boating season of 1868, Dave Haney piloted the *Peninah* from St. Louis to Fort Peck, 150 miles east of Fort Benton, at the junction of the Milk and Missouri rivers. Just south of the fort, he dropped off seven would-be woodhawks. A little later in the season, this time piloting the *Leni Leoti*, Haney saw them again—seven mutilated bodies, neatly lined up on the river bank, forty-five miles from the fort. That year pilots reported an unusual number of abandoned woodyards along the river, a sight that always drove a sick fist of fear into the guts of anyone with experience in Indian country. Official estimates put the number of dead woodhawks at fifty for the 1860s—but the real figure is probably closer to two hundred. No one knows how many hawks there were in the first place and the Sioux didn't report in with a scalp count.

When the gold dried up in Montana, so did the river traffic. Forty boats made the trip up the Missouri to Benton in 1869, the final year of the gold boom. The next year the number dribbled to a meagre eight. The several hundred woodhawks along the upper Missouri were suddenly competing for a quarter of the previous work. Add in hundreds of miners, with nothing to mine, and an assortment of odd-job men who made their living on the fringes of the gold boom and you had a Darwinian struggle for a sawbuck.

Many hawks turned to the whiskey trade, only to find it too had become crowded. A man needed a connection to one of the suppliers or his own mule or wagon train to break in. As woodhawks weren't the sort of men who saved for a rainy day, few had the resources to get their feet on the first rung of the ladder. Some of the woodhawks joined the exodus out of Benton, but many couldn't even scrape up enough cash for that. With no other alternative, they turned to wolfing.

Wolfers were loathed by Indians, white men and half-breeds alike—a rare point of agreement on the frontier. Killing wolves didn't cause the animosity; it was the method—a cowardly game of bait and wait. A wolfer brought down a buffalo, deer or some other game, then laced the corpse with strychnine. A well-baited carcass could net as many as a hundred wolves and a diligent wolfer might set out twenty or thirty traps.

Grey wolf pelts had tripled in price after 1860 when demand soared among the fashionable in Philadelphia, Boston, New York and Europe for coats and carriage robes. Fort Benton shipped thirty thousand pelts to St. Louis each year during the 1870s. At $3.00 to $4.50 for a small female pelt of average quality and up to four times as much for a prime pelt, a wolfer could make as much from two or three traps, called sets, and a bit of luck as most men did in an entire year.

But baiting was like igniting a bomb. Wolves died but so did numerous magpies, prairie dogs, skunks, coyotes—and, most importantly, Indian dogs. A single baited carcass could wipe out a band's entire dog population—a terrible blow. A strong male dog could drag one hundred pounds in a travois, far less than a horse, but when the men were hunting, fighting or dead—as many were after the smallpox and years of tribal war—the women, children and old people would often have to move camp themselves, making the dogs invaluable. For some tribes, the Assiniboine among them, dogs also held a ceremonial role. On the final day of the three-day sun dance celebration, dog flesh played an honoured role in the banquet.

In winter, when game was scarce and movement more difficult for the horses, Indian pack dogs could run down and hold elk, moose or caribou at bay. Once the hunters dragged the kill back to camp, the dogs' presence warned off marauding wolves. Even more critical in those years of tribal conflict, dogs were a band's early warning system.

Indians abhorred the wolfers' random massacre of their dogs, raging when they came across the animals' bloated carcasses. In October 1869 the Blackfoot attacked a group of thirty wolfers, stripping them of everything—skins, rifles, horses, clothing— and ran them barefoot for miles. They left the wolfers alive to spread the word—next time it would be scalps. Instead of backing off, the wolfers took to travelling in armed groups, shooting at anything even vaguely resembling an Indian. The Blackfoot, in turn, fired at anyone resembling a wolfer. Since fur and whiskey traders, prospectors, even woodhawks, all looked remarkably like wolfers, there was considerable spill-over in the Indians' retaliation. Whites and half-breeds quickly learned to say, "No wolf skins!" in several Indian languages.

Traders condemned wolfers for stirring up the Indians, who were plenty ornery as it was. Wolfers accused the traders of selling repeaters and ammunition to the Indians so they could ambush more wolfers. With that much hatred floating around, a conflagration was inevitable.

Beset on all sides, wolfers banded together to convoy pelts into Benton. Once they were in groups, the wolfers suddenly realised that twenty of them could throw their weight around far more satisfactorily than two or three. The biggest group of wolfers operating together worked the High River country, just north of the Montana border. They fancied their gang so much they gave themselves a name, the Spitzee Cavalry.* Six-foot six-inch John "Liver Eating" Johnson, the bearded and habitually unwashed sometime woodhawk and whiskey trader, was a typical member of the sixty-strong Cavalry.

Johnson earned his nickname during a battle between sixty whites and a hundred Sioux on May 9, 1869, at Musselshell, Montana. Shortly after the fighting started, a downpour neutralized the Sioux's numeric advantage. Flintlocks jammed,

---

* Spitzee being their mangled pronunciation of the Blackfoot word, *I-pit-si*, meaning high, their description of the river that emptied into both the Belly and Bow rivers during spring thaw.

sodden powder wouldn't ignite and wet bowstrings played havoc with accuracy. The whites quickly overwhelmed the Sioux, slaughtering thirty-five without a single casualty of their own. Johnson spotted a man who wasn't quite dead. Howling like a coyote, he drove his Bowie knife into the man's belly and carved out his liver. He offered it triumphantly around, impaled on the knife point. With no takers, he downed the bloody organ in a few bites.

Thomas Hardwick, a.k.a. the Green River Renegade, was a charter member of the Cavalry. He killed without passion, his face utterly devoid of emotion. At a time and place when Indian hating was a religion, Hardwick was considered an extremist.

The Spitzee Cavalry may have been little more than a bunch of thugs, but they were organized. John H. Evans, a former military captain and one-time woodhawk, led them. They even had a secretary, Kamouse Taylor, temporarily wolfing in Canada after a disagreement with the army in Montana over interpretation of the liquor trading laws. With this modicum of structure, and in a righteous fever over their right to kill wolves any way they pleased, the wolfers easily convinced themselves they were the law in the territory—the only defence against the murdering Indians and the lying traders.

In 1872 the Cavalry fought a pitched battle with the Blackfoot at Sweet Grass Hills in Montana. Scores of Indians were killed and the Blackfoot retreated to plot vengeance. Several leading chiefs didn't have to work too hard to talk their braves into an all-out war on the wolfers. The Blackfoot campaign was devastatingly effective. They scouted wolf sets and ripped the hides to ribbons or set them on fire. Sometimes, they ambushed wolfers as they returned to their baits to collect the kill. Occasionally, in a pre-emptive strike, the Indians torched the prairie, driving game and wolves out of the area.

By 1873, the Blackfoot had seriously disrupted the wolfers' business, turning the Spitzee Cavalry downright mean. They broke up into smaller groups and posted themselves along well-travelled trails. Whiskey traders got a shock to see the men blocking their way, guns levelled. The Cavalry gave them two options—sign a document promising to quit selling repeaters to the Indians or suffer the consequences. Those who saw the light and signed were sent on their way, after paying a toll fee to finance the Cavalry's clean-up operation. Traders who ignored the ultimatum were killed, the site made to look like an Indian attack.

Realizing they were on to a good thing, the wolfers blackmailed some of the smaller whiskey forts into paying fines to atone for all the trouble they'd caused by trading weapons to the Indians. In the spring of 1873, the Spitzee Cavalry swaggered into Fort Kipp and frightened the manager into giving them $1,300 worth of furs.

John Healy, figuring that Whoop Up would be next, sent a deliberately provocative message to the Cavalry.

> [I] am going to sell to the Indians anything they want to buy. I will have traders out on the prairie. You may meet some of them. Please don't interfere with any of them, as they are under my orders, and if you have anything to say, come to me, I am the one who is responsible.
>
> Yours truly
John J. Healy

Healy soon heard that his missive had had the desired effect.

> Well there was the biggest kind of roar. They held a meeting and there were hot words. The idea of one man, just one man, going against the wishes of the other white men! They could hardly believe it was true.

Healy sent away the fort's entire complement except John Tallemache, the cook, then began preparing for his expected visitors.

> I fixed everything all up. I got the little howitzer and I loaded it with six pounds of powder and on top of it I put three pounds of ball, thirty to the pound.
>
> At one end of the room I cut a piece out of the log wall and I set up the cannon so as to rake the whole store, and hung a blanket over the place so it wouldn't appear that there was anything there.
>
> I took a double-barrelled shotgun that was there, I sawed off the barrels, and I took bullets and hammered

them flat and I cut them into square slugs and loaded the gun with them. I loaded a couple of revolvers and a Winchester, and put them all on a shelf under the counter so they would be in reach of my hand, and I was ready for them.

I went about in my shirt sleeves. I was feeling just as good as I ever did in my life.

When eighteen members of the Spitzee Cavalry, headed by Kamouse Taylor and John Evans, barged into the fort, they were startled to find a clearly unarmed John Healy casually smoking a cigar and drinking a jar of whiskey.

"What are you skunks up to?" Healy asked mildly.

"There's word you're selling guns to the Injuns," accused Kamouse Taylor.

"That so?" queried Healy, in an irritatingly blasé manner. "Best we have something to eat before we get to that."

After dinner, Healy led the Cavalry back into the big store-room he'd prepared beforehand. He set himself behind the counter where his sawed off shotgun and other weapons were secreted. Healy languidly leaned back against the wall, directly beside the blanket covering the howitzer. Then he got out a fresh cigar, a big one, and lit it.

"Healy, there is a serious charge against you of selling guns and ammunition to the Injuns and we have come down to see about it," stated Kamouse Taylor.

"Well, what do you have to say about it," demanded John Evans when Healy didn't respond—just lay back sucking on his cigar.

"Guilty and you be damned!" shouted Healy, his Irish temper suddenly erupting.

The Cavalry, inflamed by Healy's burst of anger, grabbed their weapons and ostentatiously chambered their bullets.

"What right have *you* to come down here and try *me*? What are you?" he demanded, pointing scornfully at Kamouse Taylor. "A renegade from justice? You! You!" dismissively waving at the rest. "You're mad dogs...."

At that, Bedrock Jim, one of the Cavalry's real hard cases, stood up and advanced ominously on Healy followed by the other men.

Healy pulled hard on his cigar until its end was a bright red coal. Then, moving fast, he pulled out the shotgun and levelled it at Bedrock Jim and ripped the blanket off the wall, exposing the howitzer.

"If you move a hand or take another step towards me," assured Healy, "I'll blow you all to hell!" Healy emphasized his point by moving the cigar within inches of the howitzer's fuse. "Now git!" he ordered.

The wolfers vanished. "Eighteen, to one," Healy shouted derisively to their departing backsides. "Next time you'd better bring forty."

Thirteen Kit Carsons

The Thunder Breeding Hills rise like a blessing out of the long miles of prairie. Soft, undulating shadows cast a welcome to travellers from the east with promise of ample water, shelter, firewood and game within their two hundred square miles. In the evening a purple mantle creeps over them, filling the coulees with dusk. Even in the darkest night the hills stand out against the black. South of the River That Bends,* the Thunder Breeding Hills embrace river, mountain and plain. Here the spirits collide and swirl around one another, offering fearsome hints of the mysteries folded within the bosom of the hills.

Strangeness envelopes this land. A huge pile of symmetrical rock lies like a wall tumbled by a giant hand. It might have been the lodge of some powerful spirit that fell in battle. Creatures seen nowhere else inhabit the slopes and valleys— scorpions, horned toads, grizzlies and a breed of wolf so large a single one could bring a buffalo to its knees. During the driest summer the hills are green, beckoning with a tantalizing bounty of life.

Indians approached cautiously, careful not to disturb the powerful spirits and wary of trespassing too deeply into a place that might never let them go. Even the Blackfoot, who swaggered

---

* Now called the Saskatchewan.

where they pleased throughout the territory, trod lightly in the hills, such was their air of mystery, danger and supernatural power. Neither tribe nor trader ever won complete dominion over the hills, though the Blackfoot, Gros Ventre, Assiniboine, Cree and later the Sioux all claimed bits of them.

In the 1850s Métis buffalo hunters from Fort Garry carved out their own piece of the hills, which they named Montagne de Cypres for the cypre or jackpine, valued for making superior teepee poles and travois supports. In time the whites christened the area Cypress Hills, even though no cypress trees grew there.

Until 1870 each faction kept more or less to their territory. Skirmishes were frequent but battles rare. Early that year five hundred Métis, many pushed westward by the failed Riel rebellion, populated a semi-permanent tent city on the eastern periphery of the hills. To the buffalo hunt was added a considerable trade in whiskey with the bordering Indians, primarily the Cree and Assiniboine.

Whiskey traders from Fort Benton soon joined them. Within three years there were two permanent forts financed by T.C. Power—Fort Farwell owned by Abe Farwell on the west side of Battle Creek, and Fort Solomon, owned by Moses Solomon six hundred feet away on the east side. The forts weren't nearly as sturdy as the stockaded Fort Whoop Up to the east, but the whites could retreat behind the walls, shoot the log bolt across the gate and stay there until the Indians drank themselves comatose. Six free traders, loosely associated with Farwell and Solomon, worked out of the forts, and within a few minutes' walk a dozen more traders, mostly supplied by I.G. Baker, operated out of tents and wagons.

Early in the spring of 1873, a wretched band of 150 Assiniboine led by Little Soldier, staggered into a campsite south of Abe Farwell's after a two-hundred-mile death march from their barren hunting grounds to the west. Thirty had died along the way and many others were near collapse. Shortly afterward they were joined by two smaller groups of Assiniboine who were almost as destitute. In all they numbered 250 men, women and children, camped in forty or fifty lodges. They were an impoverished lot, with barely a dozen serviceable horses left and armed with ancient muskets and bows and arrows. They hoped only to rest, hunt and drink whiskey.

While the Assiniboine were recuperating in the Cypress Hills, two hundred miles to the south a group of thirteen wolfers, a portion of the Spitzee Cavalry, headed by Thomas Hardwick and John Evans, eagerly pushed towards Fort Benton. Their wagons were piled high with pelts, their tongues dry and their manhood twitching for the town's brothels. Their last night on the trail the wolfers bedded down on the bank of the Teton River, unaware that a small number of Cree, hunting far from their home grounds, had been stalking them.

On May 17, 1873, while the wolfers slept, the Cree liberated forty horses and disappeared. Furious, but impotent, Hardwick and company hitched the few remaining horses to some of the overburdened wagons and ignominiously walked into Benton, pulling the other wagons themselves. They didn't get much sympathy. Even though stealing horses was usually grounds for a lynching, no questions asked, the wolfers were so despised no one was prepared to get worked up about it. The military couldn't have been less interested; a senior officer at the garrison told the wolfers to come back later when they weren't so busy. To make matters worse, several groups of woodhawks and other wolfers had preceded them into town and had a great time taunting the Spitzee Cavalry for having their horses stolen right under their noses.

The angry wolfers whipped themselves into a frenzy of revenge. After several days in Benton's saloons, they loaded up with Henry rifles, Smith and Wesson revolvers and enough ammunition to blow away a small town. Led by "Captain" John Evans, the wolfers tracked the Cree's trail across the Teton River and north to the international boundary. At first it was simple. Even Indians couldn't easily disguise the trail of forty horses, especially when their most important consideration was to put as much distance between themselves and their victims as quickly as possible. The wolfers were in high spirits, gulping whiskey and one-upping each other with boasts of what they would do to the culprits when they caught them.

A week later the trail ran cold. They'd seen no sign of horses or Indians for several days, they'd run out of whiskey and were short of food. The wolfers decided their only chance was to head for the Cypress Hills and hope the Cree had done the same. In any event they knew they'd find whiskey and grub. On the night of May 31, the thirteen wolfers halted at the lip of a short box canyon and surveyed the two whiskey posts. Disappointingly, the only Indians around were a motley collection of Assiniboine who had hardly any horses, much less the wolfers' forty.

Hardwick and Evans loped up to Fort Farwell to find out what the traders knew. Abe Farwell told them that he hadn't seen any Cree nor any horses. And for sure this ragged bunch of Assiniboine weren't their thieves because they'd been camping there all month. Hardwick stayed at Farwell's playing cards and drinking till the wee hours. Evans left with a couple of jugs to take back to the boys. Both Farwell and Moses Solomon were anxious to be rid of the wolfers. If trouble wasn't readily available they were uniquely skilled in creating some. And the Indians hated them; the longer the wolfers stayed, the more the odds of a fight rose. Besides, the Indians were already riled.

When the Assiniboine had arrived at the whiskey posts, they traded what little they had of value for liquor and supplies. Now they were reduced to begging for whiskey and foraging for scraps. They complained that the traders had cheated them with mouldy flour, guns that didn't shoot, damp powder and heavily watered whiskey. In April, free trader Paul Rivers and his partner William Rowe were attacked and Rivers killed. Rowe, feeling his days were numbered, sold his stock of liquor to Abe Farwell and hurriedly left for Fort Benton. Shortly afterward, a drunk young Indian fired on Solomon's fort and he bolted the gate, refusing to let any of the Assiniboine from the surrounding camp into the post to trade.

June 1, 1873, dawned sharp and clear, the bite in the air spring's last kick before giving way to summer. The wolfers ate breakfast around their camp-fire before getting down to some serious drinking. From time to time they were joined by other traders. As they all got drunker, their woes increased. "It's been horrible here," moaned George Bell, Solomon's partner. "Indians're all jumped up. They've been shooting through the windows and threatenin' to scalp the lot of us."

Little Soldier, the Assiniboine chief, equally sure there would be trouble, urged his people to break camp. But one of the young braves mocked him, calling him a fearful old woman.

He brought out a keg of whiskey and declared his intention to stay. Within an hour most of the Indians, including Little Soldier, were drunk.

By mid-morning the now well-lubricated wolfers were given a fatal spark when George Hammond, a well-known braggart and bully operating out of Farwell's, stomped into camp.

"Goddamn thieving bastards!" he bellowed. "Took my horse again!" Just the day before, Hammond had ransomed the horse back from an Indian with two kegs of whiskey, a blanket and some tobacco. And now the "bastards" had gone and taken it again.

Hammond, also sauced, fulminated mightily, telling the wolfers that he intended to "clean out" the camp. It was a well-received suggestion. The wolfers gathered up their weapons and followed Hammond, ready to settle up with some Indians, any Indians. On the way to the Assiniboine camp, a half-breed pointed out Hammond's horse grazing unattended outside the post's gates. Nobody paid any attention.

Hammond strode into the midst of the Indians and, without a word, grabbed two horses. Those braves still standing objected. Hammond raged and threatened. The Indians raged and threatened back.

The wolfers were grouped in the coulee watching the action. Hammond retreated without the horses. Farwell hurried over to try to stop the impending bloodshed. But Hammond and the wolfers were determined.

From somewhere came a shot. Then another. The wolfers flung themselves down, sending volley after volley into the Indian camp. Half a dozen traders perched atop Farwell's fort joined in. A withering cross-fire from twenty repeaters pelted hundreds of bullets into the Indian camp. Any Assiniboine not immediately cut down scattered in confusion, fumbling for their few weapons. For a short time muskets battled Henrys and Winchesters. Repeater bullets slammed into one body after another as the Indians fled for the nearby bush.

The wolfers, cheering at the rout, tore into the camp, laying waste to everything in sight—kettles, teepees, drying racks. They slashed, ripped and crushed. Hardwick rode off to chase down whatever Indians escaped into the bushes. Farwell feebly tried to stop the carnage.

"We've started in," snarled Hardwick, "and we'll clean them all out if we can!"

Spitzee member Ed Legrace, riding with Hardwick, charged ahead, promptly taking a bullet through the heart for his carelessness. The wolfers' enthusiasm for bush work evaporated, but still full of blood-lust, they returned to the camp. Chief Little Soldier, so drunk he had slept through the massacre, woke up to the sight of his father's body. His wife frantically tried to lead him to safety.

"I will die here," he declared, shrugging her off, calling "White men, you will know what you have done today; you never knew a Woody Mountain Assiniboine Indian to harm a white man." A wolfer, Sam Vincent, calmly blew a hole through his chest.

An old Indian, Wankantu, sat stunned on the ground, hardly protesting as the men kicked and clubbed him to death. Bawling out a parody of the war whoop, the whites whacked his head off, drove a lodge pole through it and planted it in the centre of the camp. They looted the camp of its few remaining items of value, then burned everything else in a giant bonfire. Every man, woman and child who had not escaped to the bush was slaughtered—at least a hundred of them.* Four women were spared and set aside for later entertainment. Chief Little Soldier's wife was one of them.

> [He] grabbed me by the arm and ravished me, he remained with me all night and had connection with me many times, every time he did, he told me I would not live till morning.... The other woman can tell more than me as she had many men with her, there being only one with me.

Both forts were quickly closed and, as if to hide the evidence,

---

* The generally accepted historical death toll at Cypress Hills is twenty-two, but this is hardly likely under the circumstances. The population of the forty or fifty lodges would have been between two hundred and two hundred and fifty. The wolfers themselves boasted of killing upwards of two hundred. And judging by the fact that old men, women and children were killed, the death toll was certainly at least a hundred and most likely closer to two hundred.

torched. Every trader and wolfer pulled out within a few days. But the Cypress Hills Massacre was not to be like the Battle of Belly River, unheard and unknown in the white world. The wolfers swaggered into Benton, boasting of having "wiped out the forty lodges, very few escaping." The locals hailed them as "thirteen Kit Carsons" who had proved themselves to be "advanced guards of civilization."

Unlike the Battle of Belly River, the Cypress Hills Massacre was like a pebble tossed into a pond. The ripples carried to St. Louis, Chicago, Washington, New York, London—and Ottawa. In the capital the horrible slaughter lit a fire under the organization of the North West Mounted Police.

PART THREE

The Great March

CHAPTER 6

Departure

JULY 8, 1874

His steel sword, held proudly aloft, flamed as it caught the late afternoon prairie sun. Colonel French sat astride Silver Blaze, the animal's chestnut coat shining and his wide blaze a startling white beam. For the last three weeks the camp and parade square had buzzed with frantic activity. Now all was calm and quiet save for shuffling hooves, soft nickering and the creak of leather and wood. The North West Mounted Police were ready.

Rows and rows of troopers, horses, wagons, guns and stock carpeted the landscape, a sharp contrast of might and right against the gently rolling plain. French surveyed his creation— A Division, mounted on its bays; then B Division, all riding dark browns; C Division next, the artillery troop, with its coppery chestnuts and the two formidable nine-pounder steel field guns; D Division's mix of pale greys and creamy buckskins gave it a frontier look; E Division, snugged up behind, was aboard their blacks; and finally F Division brought up the rear on light bays.

Colonel French would lead 274 men to the West; his assistant commissioner, 26 officers and non-commissioned officers and 247 constables and sub-constables. A week earlier French had sent Sub-Inspector Albert Shurtliff, accompanied by fourteen men and seventeen horses, to establish a headquarters at Fort Ellice, a Hudson's Bay Company post 250 miles east of Lower Fort Garry. Three officers and nineteen disappointed troopers were left to police Manitoba from Lower Fort Garry and six other, even more disappointed men, had been assigned to stay in Dufferin. Along with the men and 311 horses came 142 pulling oxen, seven half-breed guides and scouts, 114 Red River carts driven by twenty Métis, plus 73 wagons, the artillery guns, two brass mortars, several mowing machines, field kitchens and portable blacksmithing forges.

The troopers, not long ago an undisciplined collection of teachers, coopers and clerks, sat tall and proud. Now a crack force with a mission, they would surge westward carrying the colours and creed of the Queen into a land of primitive savagery. The officers and men were clad in scarlet Norfolk jackets so the Indians could distinguish them from the extermination-minded American military. Black Wellington riding boots set off their pale riding breeches, and brown, leather-gloved hands confidently gripped their reins. The men's pith helmets, white and puggaree bound, gave them a dashing eastern look as if they were off to meet Gurkhas instead of red Indians.*

It was in every way a moving sight. The banners scattered throughout the corps lifted in the breeze. Even the terminally cynical Sub-Constable Joseph Carscadden found himself momentarily numbed by the glory of it all.

Colonel French allowed himself a quiet moment of satisfaction. Battling tremendous odds to reach this day, French's iron will, patience and dedication had served him well. His had been an impossible task—to create a new breed of law enforcers, neither soldier nor diplomat, but a measure of each—and do it in such a short time Wellington himself would have blanched.

---

* Puggaree is a muslin scarf wrapped around the helmet and tied in a knot with the end usually dangling down the back. It was fashioned after the British Army head gear used in India as protection from sun and bugs.

He had inherited a few good officers, his assistant commissioner, James Macleod; that very dependable Sub-Inspector James Walker; Inspector Jacob Carvell, who had fought for the Confederates during the Civil War; Sub-Inspector Ephraim Brisebois, solid and reliable; Inspector William Jarvis, a man who got things done with no fuss; Sub-Inspector Albert Shurtliff, who spent too much time lending money to the men and calculating interest owed but could account for every whip, stirrup leather and tent peg in his division. Even James Walsh was a solid man.

As he thought of Walsh, French made a mental notation to monitor him carefully. He had too much of his own mind and he always seemed to be on the verge of a disrespectful remark. Walsh needed reining in, no question about it: independent thinking and undisciplined behaviour had no place among his corps.

Inspector Theodore Richer was another officer who bore watching. He was a know-it-all, forever pushing his views in your face. He had to analyse every command as if it were some kind of parlour debate. He simply couldn't keep his mouth shut and follow orders. Still, the troopers arrayed before him were dedicated enough and during the long march, his guidance would knit them into a smoothly functioning unit.

The men looked as battle-worthy as the Queen's Hussars. More than 170 had claimed artillery, militia or constabulary service, but that was doubtful. French never admitted it to his superiors in Ottawa, nor did he discuss it with his officers, but it became obvious on the first day of training that fewer than 20 percent had any military experience whatsoever. The worst offenders in this regard were the 150 already enlisted when French was hired. They had simply not been properly screened or scrutinized.

French had done his best to weed out the weaklings and malcontents in Toronto.

On two distinct occasions, I assembled all ranks on parade, plainly told them that they would have, and must expect, plenty of hardship; they might be wet day after day, and have to lie in wet clothes; that they might be a day or two without food, and that I feared they

would be often without water, and I called on any present who were not prepared to take their chances of
these privations to fall out, and they could have their
discharge, as there were plenty of good men ready to
take their places.

French had been disappointed in Toronto with the results of
his challenge—barely a dozen men had taken their discharge.
But he knew that once he got them away from their comfortable New Fort barracks, he'd make more inroads. In Dufferin
French again hammered away at the men, putting the fear of
the frontier in them. That very morning, during parade, he
had one last go, emphasizing the deprivations they'd surely
encounter. He bluntly challenged those "chicken hearts,"
wanting in sufficient courage, to leave the NWMP. To French's
intense annoyance, just as he finished his speech, a distinct
and eerily lifelike rooster crow rose from the ranks, causing a
number of muted chuckles among the men. He chose to ignore
the impertinence but it rankled mightily.

Gratifyingly, French's tactics had prompted thirty-two men
to desert in the past three weeks. Assistant Commissioner
Macleod expressed alarm at the losses—more than 10 percent
of their entire complement. All but one of the blacksmiths
were gone, and a high percentage of those who took "leg bail"
had previous military experience.

"They have not the pluck to see this enterprise through, the
chicken hearts!" French had countered. "They have no heart,
they have no gumption. I'm glad they're gone. We are better
off without them in the coming days as we face our own hardships." Besides, French told Macleod, it was all part of his
plan. "I anticipated the backing out of a certain number, and
fortunately brought twenty spare men so that the force was
not as short-handed as some supposed."

In the midst of his triumphant survey, French let a small sigh
escape. It would be a great relief to set out at last. He was fed
up with the soothsayers around Dufferin who had criticized
everything from his choice of horses to the quality of side-arms
issued to the men. He could hardly be blamed for the handguns.
French had ordered 330 Imperial Army style Adams revolvers,
which arrived only at the last minute. When they were

unpacked, the armourer was horrified to discover bent barrels, jammed chambers and trigger guard screws missing or loose.

French abhorred negativity of any kind, and he'd taken a big dose of it in the last few weeks.

> To get badly cooked food, to be worked hard all day, and yet be pestered all night with mosquitoes is objectionable, and it is not encouraging to an ordinary individual under such circumstances, to be assured by one of these prophets of evil who are always about (but who, unfortunately, do not always flee from the misfortunes they predict), "Oh mosquitoes! you have not felt any yet; just wait till you get to the Pembina River, or the Souris."

George French shook off such sour thoughts. His men were ready. He lowered his sword. Assistant Commissioner James Macleod's powerful voice sent the command to march rippling through the ranks. The trumpets sang out. They were off.

Fred Bagley felt dizzy with excitement. His buckskin champed and fidgeted, sensing his nerves. Bagley wished his mother and father could be here. He hoped a photographer

NWMP getting ready to depart from Fort Dufferin

would immortalize the scene. Maybe his parents would read about it in the paper. He would have liked to stand in his stirrups and bellow, "Here I come, you damned whiskey traders!" Bagley was a long way behind the advance guard but he could see the dust they kicked up as they set off and hear the tremendous commotion as the cavalcade moved forward. He longed to drive his heels into his horse's flanks and gallop into the frontier.

But for the moment, it was all Fred Bagley could do just to stay in the saddle. Bedlam descended with the Colonel's sword. Within seconds a hundred men were flat on their backs—their horses galloping off helter-skelter—and they were the lucky ones. Bagley could see several unfortunates being dragged, their boots stuck in their stirrup irons. One trooper was towed directly in front of the Colonel, who had to check Silver Blaze quickly to avoid a collision.

The horses had been standing, reined in and anxious, for too long. Several of the less experienced men spurred when they should have squeezed gently and eased up too quickly on the reins instead of holding their mounts firm against the bit. Their horses vaulted forward, then jack-rabbited sideways as noses collided with tails. First one hoof was flung out in irritation, then another, and suddenly clumps of horses erupted into kicking contests. Wagons tipped; loads scattered; horses shot off in all directions and the neat rows and columns disintegrated into a snorting, crashing, cursing mass of man and beast.

Amid the calliope of noise and chaos, a long cry rang out. A rooster's crow. Once, twice, three times, then silence. In the confusion, no one could tell who made it, but a slight smirk could be detected on the face of Sub-Constable Joseph Carscadden.

JOSEPH CARSCADDEN

We moved off in beautiful order, the horses raising Cain generally, baulking, kicking, and smashing everything within reach of their heels. But this was to be expected from young, untrained horses; restive, excited and badly managed.

...I have not the slightest desire to reflect discredit on the teamsters—quite the contrary—they did much better than could naturally have been expected: for what will be the result if you place a number of Clerks, Law Students, Medical Students, Railway men, &c, on a box behind a pair of young Colts? They kick, of course,—hit the box he sits on,—probably knock the driver over. He swears like a trooper and makes the poor animals' flesh quiver under the heavy cowhide lash so kindly provided by the noble Commissioner....

But let me take another and still more common view of the case. Here we have another pair of revolutionists trying to break either their own legs or the driver's and the inexperienced youth (say, a divinity student) is doing the very best with them that he knows how—probably he would eventually succeed in quieting and subduing them, but before he has had time to do so, up comes one of those all-important personages—a Sergt.-Major, or perhaps some young scapegrace who has sufficient influence with some M.P.'s wife to obtain a commission and whom the men call an Officer (God save the mark) These individuals—the Sergt Major afore-mentioned or the influential body who thought it wise to leave home because he could not pay his washing bill, comes posting up at full gallop.

No! hold on writer, you are going too fast. Look again. Are they galloping? No! They content themselves with a snail's pace for they have not yet learnt to ride. When they reach the unfortunate teamster, they commence giving directions how to start the team, which are yet as reluctant to start as ever.

While the men on horseback desperately hauled on their reins, trying to keep their mounts from bolting, the men in the wagons had a different problem. A few were able to pull out on the first command, but only after diligent yelling and flailing by both officers and men. Most others stood fast, the horses unwilling, or unable, to pull their heavy loads one inch. Red-faced officers, "non-entities" according to Carscadden, their neat uniforms already askew, gave up trying to budge the stubborn animals. All up and down the line they unharnessed the recalcitrant beasts, hollering for replacements.

Eventually the last of the wagons moved off, with sweaty hands clenching the reins in death grips, the thought of a stampede not far from anyone's mind. The officers just had time to draw a breath of relief when the ox carts drew their reluctant attention. Pulling up the rear of the procession were the 114 Red River carts driven by twenty half-breeds—most of whom were still in the grip of an all-night drinking binge. As grog shops didn't exist on the plains, a man had to take a good memory with him.

At reveille that morning most of the half-breed drivers were still snoring—the rest hadn't even returned to camp. Carts, which French had ordered packed and ready the previous sundown, stood half-full, contents still strewn on the ground. Several sergeants set off to kick the sleeping ones awake and round up the missing. They had to be careful though; the half-breeds were independent and unpredictable. You could curse and ridicule them and they'd walk away laughing. But the next moment, they'd take offence at a passing comment and be ready to slice you open like a Sunday ham. Once a half-breed got his back up, no amount of apologizing or cajoling would rectify the situation—unless it was accompanied by a large quantity of rum and tobacco. If one walked away, the rest could just as easily decide to follow. A damnable race. But the Force needed them.

Only the half-breeds had experience with ox trains. The men considered it a lowly job, but it took skill and energy to keep an ox train moving, and in the right direction. It wasn't just a case of perching on the box, reins in hand, and shouting, every now and then, "Git along, there!" The drivers walked as often as they rode, keeping their charges in line with a nine-foot bull whip, three feet of stinging rawhide attached to a six-foot flexible handle. An experienced driver could take chunks out of an ox's hide as if he were scooping out butter or raise welts as big as sausages. It didn't take long for the oxen to develop quick reactions to the pistol shot of the whip.

The ox carts, sometimes eighteen of them strung together and driven by one man, lurched painfully slowly forward to join the train. It was then that the Mounted Police got their first taste of the ox-cart concert. The Red River cart was little more than two large wheels joined by a wooden axle with a rough box on top—simple, effective, sturdy and capable of loads that would break ordinary wagons. If anything went wrong they were easy to repair with rawhide, rope, wood or whatever else came to hand.

Occasionally, a driver tired of having his eardrums assaulted greased the axles with buffalo fat to soothe the cacophony of wood screeching against wood, but few bothered—it didn't work for long in any case, invariably getting clogged up with dirt. Frontiersmen entertained themselves dreaming up new oaths for their favoured vehicle and the concert it produced. But few were prepared for what they heard that July afternoon in 1874.

JEAN D'ARTIGUE

> I would here like to describe the noise made by the carts, but words fail me. It must be heard to be understood. A den of wild beasts cannot be compared with it in hideousness. Combine all the discordant sounds ever heard in Ontario and they cannot produce anything so horrid as a train of Red River carts. At each turn of the wheel, they run up and down all the notes of the scale in one continuous screech, without sounding distinctly any note or giving one harmonious sound.

After two hours of pandemonium, the North West Mounted Police, ragged and disorganized, but finally moving, staggered and swayed across the prairie. Not a pretty start, but the adventure had begun.

The first two miles seemed like two hundred. Officers and sergeants, hoarse with shouting, were reduced to croaking orders. While the train itself covered only two miles, the officers travelled much farther, galloping up and down the ranks attempting to instil some order. No amount of urging could encourage the half-breeds to move any faster, so they were left alone.

The seventy-three wagons driven by troopers were all over

the place. James Walsh and Sam Steele tried to bring them into line, flanking the lead animals and driving them into the main body. "Bloody hell, man! Use your goddamned reins!" Steele bellowed again and again. "Keep them on the bit! Steady! Steady!" It was useless. The men simply didn't have experience enough to hold the horses in line, and in any case, the animals were so jumped-up the men were lucky to have them moving at all. The officers gave up. As long as the wagons were heading in the right direction, there were other problems to take care of.

Fortunately, the first day was a so-called Hudson's Bay start—a practice run to check out the equipment. In truth, the Force couldn't have gone any farther if they wanted to. Darkness fell and the magnificent procession stopped. In the rush to prepare for departure, French had neglected to ensure that the scout had checked out the campsite in advance. He assumed that anyone who called himself a scout would know an appropriate spot this close to Dufferin. French balefully surveyed the site. It had neither wood nor water. "Why didn't you tell me there was no fuel or water here?" he demanded of Taylor, one of the guides. "Didn't ask me," he replied blandly.*

There wasn't any food either. After a late start, the heavy cooks' wagons and ox teams carrying the food arrived in camp long after the men had given up waiting for dinner. Most of the troopers were sound asleep when the half-breeds arrived with the last ox carts. Walking beside them was Assistant Commissioner Macleod.

On the outside, Macleod was calm, competent and self-sufficient. On the inside was a vastly different man. He pined for his sweetheart, Mary, fought a constant battle against loneliness and fretted about the men. His was the most difficult job in the Force. As assistant commissioner he was the connective tissue between French in command, the officers and the men.

---

* Each troop of fifty men camped together as a unit in large tents that slept up to a dozen. The first few nights the Force's full complement camped in close proximity, but often the terrain wouldn't accommodate everyone in the same spot—two or three troops might camp in one small valley while the rest were spread out in nearby areas. Corralling the horses varied with the circumstances but the preferred method was to string ropes between wagons and carts.

He couldn't afford to get too close to anyone but he needed the confidence of everyone.

Officially, Macleod's job was to carry out and enforce Colonel French's orders. But the Colonel had great difficulty delegating real authority and he saddled his second-in-command with enough menial jobs to keep five men busy, while retaining all the critical command decisions for himself. Because of his law degree Macleod also ended up being policeman, judge and jury for the astonishing multitude of indiscretions the men seemed able to commit. Macleod, being Macleod, didn't complain, though his senior officers were appalled that French treated him little better than a constable. The only person who knew how Macleod felt was Mary.*

JAMES MACLEOD

July 10, 1874

My Dearest Mary

I hardly know when the day ends or commences. We have at last started and have found it a most difficult business to accomplish. We have not nearly enough transport and all the wagons are so heavy that the horses can hardly draw them along.

I wish you had seen me last night. I was left behind to see everything off, and as I came along in rear of the train, a young officer came galloping up to say that there were 3 ox teams stuck and could not pull an inch further so off I had to go, sent my horse on to camp and took the oxen into my own hands. I managed to get two of the teams into camp all right and sent a pair of horses to the assistance of the third.

You ought to have heard me cursing and yelling til I was quite hoarse. It was long after dark when I arrived. The half breeds were awfully tickled when I marched in among them....

---

* Though hardly a regular mail service, dispatches and letters were occasionally given to passing traders, travellers and missionaries to take to Winnipeg. But the men received mail only once during the march.

I have been called out of my tent about 50 times since I commenced this stupid letter, and I am in very bad humour.

JM

Macleod didn't really expect things to go smoothly. Ever since he'd joined the Force as one of the original nine officers, it had been a rough, uncertain ride, full of false starts and wrong turns. But he believed that the men would whip themselves into shape once the march began. Macleod felt much the same way about the horses. But on the first day, watching them strain at the unaccustomed loads, worry settled like an undigested lump of dough inside him.

On the first night Inspector Theodore Richer, in charge of F Division, again loudly voiced his concerns about the choice of horses, their trail-readiness and the loads they were forced to pull. Richer claimed that even if they had the right horses, in perfect condition, there weren't enough of them—an expedition such as theirs should have at least one remount for every rider and several dozen more as replacements for the harness horses. Macleod thought Richer made a lot of sense, but unfortunately it was too late to do anything about it. Make the best of it, he advised Richer.

On the morning of the second day, French ordered each troop to provide its spare horses to pull the wagons. He didn't want a repeat of the first day's fiasco. But after breakfast several wagons sat horseless.

"Get those wagons ready!" ordered French.

One of the sub-constables deputized to drive that day shuffled his feet awkwardly.

"What's the matter with you? Get on with it!"

"Can't, sir. Sorry, sir."

"What do you mean you can't?"

"I don't have any horses, sir."

French took a deep breath. "And where are your horses?"

"Still with F Division, I'm guessing."

"Damn Richer!" French swore. He wheeled sharply and stormed off.

When French found Richer, he laid into him for disobeying orders, threatening everything from demotion to imprisonment if he didn't immediately comply. Hot-tempered, and still smarting over French's refusal to listen to his suggestions that they buy a string of seasoned cart horses in Dufferin, Richer shot back with equal ferocity. At least a hundred troopers were in earshot as Richer hurled invective at Colonel French.

Colonel French cut short the argument by placing Richer under arrest, which meant confining him to a wagon under the guard of a sergeant-major. The men couldn't hide their dismay. Just before departure, Inspector Charles Young, a highly experienced officer, formerly of Her Majesty's 50th Foot, had been dismissed after he got drunk and accosted French with the same vehement suggestions about the horses. (Young was replaced as inspector of B Division by Ephraim Brisebois.) Now Richer, another experienced and popular officer, was under arrest.

The six inspectors were critical to the Force's mission in the West. Once the whiskey traders were dispatched, each one would be stationed, along with a command of men, at various strategic places from Manitoba to the Rockies. Having only sporadic contact with Colonel French, police headquarters or the other far-flung divisions, they would have to operate independently. Losing two inspectors, a third of the total, within two days was a devastating blow.

The next morning, Richer, supposedly under arrest, simply walked out of camp towards Dufferin, making sure everyone could see and hear him. As he went, Richer loudly denounced Colonel French, vowing to expose his inadequacies in Ottawa, where he claimed to have high-placed friends. As Richer stalked off and his angry words faded into the distance, a frigid silence entombed the camp.

Massacre at Duck Lake

JULY 11, 1874

It was a scene right out of Dante's *Inferno*, complete with appalling heat. Squawking, flapping, death rattles, blood.

White everywhere. Dozens of men flailed away, hip deep in a muddy soup. Some threw stones and others dove head first into the carnage, grabbing whatever came to hand. All were smeared with mud and dappled with blood. Above the din rose a howling, not unlike a pack of dogs on the scent of a kill. One throwback snatched up a victim, yanked off the head and bayed with triumph.

Ducks—meaty, succulent, nourishing ducks—hundreds of them, so panicked by the onslaught of empty-bellied men they just sat and squawked, waiting for the slaughter.

Feathers covered everything. Every now and then, the blizzard of white lifted briefly to allow a glimpse of the action. In the middle stood Fred Bagley, head tufted with down, thigh deep in mud, happily holding his territory against all comers. Grinning and yowling, he clubbed everything that moved. Beside him, the Professor, Jean D'Artigue, poised and serene amidst the mêlée, might have been fly-casting on the Seine as he elegantly dispatched his targets with the flick of his horsehide whip. Off to one side, sketch pad in hand, the Artist, Henri Julien, captured the scene, disapproval etched on his face.

Massacre at Duck Lake

HENRI JULIEN

I had some qualms of conscience at killing so many inoffensive things. They lay moulting and helpless in the marshes and along the grassy margins of the rivers.

The men would go down with big sticks, knock them over the head, and catch them by the leg in their feeble attempts to fly away, and bring back a dozen of them in the course of an hour. It was butchery. There was no romance in it.

On the edge of the shallow lake, irritated officers stood shouting at the men to break off and move out of the way to give the true sportsmen a shot. They didn't dare fire lest they injure one of the troopers—though they were tempted.

James Macleod, on a rise about half a mile away, leaned against his horse and watched the mêlée through his field-glasses. He smiled at the excited "hunt" and laughed out loud when two men mistakenly clouted each other. A little duck for dinner would be a welcome change, even if it couldn't be accompanied by a decent bottle of claret. Macleod turned just as Colonel French cantered up, his scowl so deep it seemed to extend straight down to the soles of his boots.

"This must be stopped! It shows a want of discipline," charged the Colonel. "They're behaving like animals!"

"Normally, I'd agree with you, Colonel," soothed Macleod. "But this might be the time to ease off a bit. The men've had a hard four days. Letting off a little steam'll do them good."

"I don't like it. I don't like it a bit," said the Colonel crossly as he wheeled his horse around. "Handle it your way but mark my words, we'll pay the price for this erosion of discipline."

"Discipline," Macleod muttered to himself. "A full stomach'll do wonders for discipline."

Macleod slowly mounted his horse and loped towards the massacre site, carefully timing his arrival to coincide with the natural end of the high jinks. Then he could put on a little show, throw his weight around, place a few on report—just enough to satisfy the Colonel while still allowing the men their fun.

Macleod chuckled as he caught a few feathers in his hand. Good thing French hadn't noticed a number of well-lubricated officers hard at it on the duck battleground. Macleod was something of a legendary drinker himself. "As the evening wore on and the bottle circulated freely," one of his fellow officers recalled years later, "man after man disappeared, either under the table or into an armchair or some other seclusion, and when Col. Macleod assisted the one solitary survivor up the stairs to his bed, the man stopped short on the first landing and said 'By God Colonel, where d'you put it?'" Yes, James Macleod liked his whiskey, but some men have no sense. They get drinking and they can't stop and before you know it, they're up on charges in front of Macleod himself, one more bit of work to do in a day already too full.

This morning they'd passed Grant's Tavern, officially known as Pembina Mountain Depot—the last watering hole before the force reached Cypress Hills, another 550 miles west. The troopers were excited about the prospect of wrapping their lips around a bottle, but Colonel French thought he'd scotched that idea by putting the post off-limits to both the men and the half-breeds. The half-breeds simply ignored the Colonel's command, while the men immediately began scheming ways to fill up without getting caught.

Charles Grant, the tavern's proprietor, was happy to oblige. The very notion that a civilian tavern owner with three hundred parched men descending on him would voluntarily agree to keep his store locked up was ludicrous. When it came to whiskey, Macleod knew his men, troops and officers alike, were remarkably inventive. He could post a twenty-four-hour guard, and a guard to watch over the guards, and the men would still find a way to get the stuff. As for the half-breeds, they weren't subject to military discipline, or any other discipline that Macleod had yet discovered. He only hoped they wouldn't hit on the idea of storing some up for later sale to the men.

Macleod admired his commissioner. But he wondered how a man who was so capable in so many ways—a fine horseman, an excellent shot, a hard worker and a brilliant administrator—could be, to use the Colonel's favourite word, so "wanting" in common sense. Hadn't enough gone wrong in the early days of the march without adding tinder to the fire, by harassing the men over something so minor as a free-for-all in a duck slough?

After the departure fiasco (the "circus," as Sub-Inspector James Walker aptly called it), James Macleod was certain things would improve. But on the second, third and fourth days, the circus of balky horses, runaways, stranded wagons and missing ox carts repeated itself. His only consolation was that the disarray did seem to end a little sooner each day and when they eventually moved out, their formation appeared marginally more orderly.

On the second day, after a tremendous battle to calm horses and hitch wagons, Sub-Constable Joseph Carscadden had sidled up to him and said, in a reassuring tone, "Don't worry about those balky horses, Major, they won't be a problem much longer."

"What in hell are you talking about?" Macleod barked, irritated that his thoughts had been penetrated so easily, and by a sub-constable at that.

"Well, sir, it's simple. Surprised you didn't think of it yourself. Give it a week and those Toronto horses'll be so weak with hunger and broken from pulling they won't be balky any more."

It was bad enough to have a sub-constable reading your mind, but then the cheeky bastard looked him right in the eye and assumed an Irish accent.

"You could say, sir, that soon they'll be wanting in endurance, but they'll be well disciplined."

Carscadden then saluted elaborately and marched briskly away. It was all Macleod could do to stop himself from kicking the sub-constable and his smirk up and down the column. The man was too smart and too impudent for his own good. And he couldn't hold his tongue. Carscadden was Macleod's primary suspect as the perpetrator of the rooster calls. Macleod made a mental note to find some particularly unpleasant extra duty for him—a double dose of fatigue might make him rethink his sarcastic ways. Wanting in endurance! Macleod almost laughed. If the Colonel had heard that, Joseph Carscadden would be marching the rest of the way in irons.

John Palliser called this section of the North West an arid wasteland, and with good reason. Water was only a dream at the best of times, let alone during an unusually hot summer. At Fort Dufferin, Macleod had been too busy getting the horses squared away, organizing the wagons and dealing with endless disciplinary problems to pay much attention to the matter of equipment and supplies. He was appalled to discover, on the second day, that no cutlery or canteens had been issued to the men.

Worse than the lack of canteens was the absence of barrels. Even if they found water, they had nothing to carry it in. At the end of the second day, they'd been forced to backtrack two miles when their destination, the Marias River, turned out to be little more than a dry wash. Total distance that day: six miles. Fortunately, an obliging settler had hauled water to them in his wagon. He didn't trouble to hide his amusement that only eight miles out of Dufferin, the Force needed his help.

The third day wasn't much better—eight miles and only enough wood and water to make tea. To tide them over, the men had been issued a handful of the god-awful biscuits—when freshly cooked they were doughy in the centre and leaden on the outside. Since no fires meant no cooking, this batch of biscuits, now three days petrified, had been made back in Dufferin. Macleod threw his away, and to his astonishment, neither mice nor prairie dogs would touch them either. Should they ever make it back to this spot, Macleod had no doubt the wooden biscuits would still be where he'd chucked them. He decided he'd recommend them to the Boundary Commission as building materials for their cairns.

James Macleod, though at thirty-seven one of the oldest members of the Force, was blessed with an iron constitution that bore up under privation, hard work and hard riding better than any other man on the march. He had been the only one in the entire complement who didn't get seasick during the rough lake crossing the previous October, and on any given day he easily rode twice as far as any other member of the Force, checking on strays and carrying out the Colonel's orders. To Macleod, the real hardship on the trail was his separation from Mary. Loneliness gripped him and he wondered what misguided spirit of adventure had prompted him to leave a comfortable life and a wonderful woman, for the wilds of the North West. Still, he was far from alone with his sad thoughts under the starry prairie sky.

HENRI JULIEN

July 10, 1874

[Here] we first encountered the hostility of the mosquitoes. We had met them before, of course, but never in
the same way. The mosquito of the prairie must be a
distinct species in entomology. We had men among us
who had travelled in all parts of the world, and who
had been pestered by all manner of insects, but they all
agreed that nowhere had they seen anything equal to
the mosquitoes of the prairie.

I myself have hunted in the interior of Quebec, and
fished in the inland lakes of Ontario, and the visitations
of these tormentors I then thought the most intolerable
of nuisances, robbing me of fully half the enjoyment of
my sport. But the Canadian mosquito is as different
from his Manitoba congener, as is the white man from
the Indian, the civilized bug from the barbarian.

As soon as twilight deepens, they make their
appearance on the horizon, in the shape of a cloud,
which goes on increasing in density as it approaches to
the encounter.

At first, a faint hum is heard in the distance, then it
swells into a roar as it comes nearer. The attack is simply dreadful. Your eyes, your nose, your ears are invaded. If you open your mouth to curse at them, they
troop into it. They insinuate themselves under your
clothes, down your shirt collar, up your shirt sleeve
cuffs, between the buttons of your shirt bosom. And
not one or a dozen but millions at a time.

You can brush them off your coat sleeves in layers.
In the Mississippi valley, mosquitoes are warded off by
a gauze net. In our Canadian backwoods, the smoke of
a big fire drives them away. But up here, they would
tear a net to shreds, and put out a fire by the mere
superincumbent weight of their numbers.

The best proof of their virulence is they attack animals as well as men. They send a dog off howling in
pain. They tease horses to desperation. They goad even
the shaggy buffalo as vengefully as the gadfly vexed the

bull of Io.*

Often in the evening, when our tents were pitched, and we went down to the nearest brook or rivulet to water our horses, hoping that this was to be our last work before turning in for a sweet night's rest, the mosquitoes would rise in columns out of the spongy soil under our feet and begin regular battle with us. Our horses would rear, pitch and kick. We, ourselves, would be covered with scratches and blood. Our only refuge was to run out the horses to their pickets, then hasten to throw ourselves on to the ground, and cover ourselves up in blankets.

On the fourth day the men were on the move from 6:00 a.m. to 9:00 p.m. in 90-degree heat, with nary a bite to eat nor a sip to drink, except those farsighted enough to secret a store of whiskey from Grant's Tavern.

Macleod contemplated their progress grimly. Four days to travel barely thirty-three miles—an easy day's ride on a good horse—following the well-marked Boundary Commission Road, the frontier equivalent of a highway. Today, they'd actually covered eighteen miles and had enough wood purchased at Grant's Tavern to cook the ducks and enough water in the slough for the animals and to make tea. Even though the brew was muddy and filled with down and other suspicious particles, the men gulped it back thankfully before commencing their daily barrage of complaints.

Macleod should have been able to take satisfaction in finally getting in a decent day's march but their eighteen-mile day exposed a fresh, and very serious, problem—one that no one had considered. Horses with riders, horses pulling wagons, oxen pulling carts and cattle all travel at different rates. Colonel French had issued standing orders that there be no more than a mile and a half from tip to tail of the column. But by noon of day four, they had stretched themselves out

---

* Zeus fell in love with Io, the gorgeous daughter of a river god. When Hera discovered it, Zeus turned Io into a white heifer to protect her. Then Hera created a vicious gadfly and ordered it to harry Io for eternity.

over six miles of prairie. While the men were setting up camp, the cattle, ox carts and all-important cooks' wagons were hours behind. The men had pulled in to camp at nine that night, but the ox carts didn't show up until one the next morning.

Colonel French planned to average twenty-five miles a day. But if they ever reached that pace, and kept it up, before long the cattle and the oxen, hauling the bulk of their supplies, would be days behind.

The progress of the ox carts was hampered by the nature of the beast. Red River carts broke down frequently; axles snapped, wheels cracked and so on. Though they were easily repaired—a little rawhide could fix most anything in an ox cart—each breakdown brought large sections of the bull train to a complete halt. The half-breeds conferred, offered advice, shared whiskey, had a smoke, brewed some tea—and then in their own sweet time went about fixing the thing.

The half-breeds had celebrated prodigiously in Dufferin before their departure and continued to do so all through those first days. Grouchy and inattentive, several of the drivers fell asleep while driving, causing spectacular accidents. A favoured technique when they were tired or drunk was to string as many as eighteen carts together. One man, in front, would drive the whole bunch, allowing the rest to snooze. But if the driver fell asleep, the cart would inevitably go off track and turn over in a hole or get stuck, often causing a pile-up.

Colonel French quickly came to the conclusion that the ox carts were abominations and the half-breeds were an evil curse sent to try him. They paid little attention to his orders and even had the cheek to imitate his accent. After the difficulties of the first day, the exasperated Colonel ordered Macleod to oversee the half-breeds—let him sort out the wretches.

Macleod never admitted it to French, but he quite liked the half-breeds. He was secretly pleased when the men praised his strength, clapped him on the back and told him he was the best frontiersman they'd ever seen who didn't have a drop of French or Indian blood. It was a small conceit, but Macleod felt flattered. He wasn't really bothered by the carping of the men, either. None of them had been prepared for so many missed meals, thirst and fatigue this early in the march. And the myriad other problems that seemed to sprout up like weeds could be handled, as long as the men's morale remained good. A man, days without food, can walk hundreds of miles to safety if his spirit remains strong. But men of weak spirit can be defeated by trifles—unerringly Colonel French had found just such a trifle.

After two days without so much as a nibble for the animals, and with predictions from the half-breeds that no good grazing would be had for many days yet, French was forced to act. On the second day, he sent back two wagon loads of "superfluous" items to Dufferin to be replaced by two wagon loads of oats for the horses. It was the correct decision, the smart decision, the military decision—but it was a disaster.

The "superfluous" items included much that made life worthwhile; maple syrup, tobacco, toiletries, blankets, surplus clothing and books. In effect, the men were left with what they were wearing and two thin blankets each. Macleod had tried diplomatically to explain to the Colonel that he was dealing with a breed of men quite unlike those he was used to in the Imperial Army, the Irish Constabulary or even the Canadian Militia.

These men came from diverse backgrounds. Many were better educated than any of the officers and others had more real military experience. They came from six provinces and seven different countries. It was hard to make any generalizations about them, other than that they weren't stupid. They all knew it was going to get very cold on the trail. And if they didn't, the Colonel had told them so in his scare-away-the-chicken-hearts speeches. French liked to dwell on the fact that the boundary survey had been snowed in by a three-day blizzard in early September the year before. These men could add one and one. Here it was July 11; at the rate they were travelling, they would still be marching in October. What would they do then to keep warm?

A Plague of...

At the end of the fifth day, Fred Bagley lay quietly in his bedroll. Chingachgook and Indian princesses, usually frequent visitors to his dreams, had been absent for days. For one thing he was wide awake, couldn't have been more wide awake, had never been more wide awake. Yet he had never been more exhausted, not having really slept for two whole days. Last night, after several fitful hours, he'd briefly dozed off, only to be jolted awake by an all-hands call to calm the horses. Out into the thundery, rain-swept night he'd dragged himself to quiet the terrified animals. They were still so spooked from the stampede back at Dufferin, any little lightning flash threatened to set them off.

Half-asleep, patting and muttering reassuringly every few minutes, Bagley stood in the pouring rain with the rest of the troopers, hanging on to halter ropes. Bagley wondered how the horses had the energy to be spooked, the way they were dragging themselves along. God knows, *he* didn't have the energy. All night, sullen men groused and promised horrible revenge on whoever had convinced them to join the North West Mounted Police. They damned Colonel French in many creative ways, stopping only to comply with occasional bellowed orders from the sergeant-majors. Some began to think that Willie Parker and Sub-Constable Brown, who came down with typhoid and had to be taken back to Dufferin, were the lucky ones.*

Major Macleod had been everywhere that night, clapping some men on the back, joking with others, trading jibes, and now and then settling matters with a harsh word. Once he put his hand on a trooper's shoulder in what looked like a friendly gesture, but Bagley knew better, having caught the man's pained grimace. A good half of the men felt like dropping the halter ropes and walking back to Fort Dufferin. Had James Macleod not been there, they probably would have done just that.

---

* Brown died, as did Sub-Constable McIntosh, who was left behind in Fort Dufferin with typhoid.

Taking shank's mare back to civilization would not have been too great a hardship. They'd covered just forty-two miles since leaving Dufferin. It would be a hard walk, but a determined man could do it in a day. Every night the air swelled with angry desertion talk, and fifteen men had slipped out of camp since their departure only four days ago. But even at their current molasses pace, Bagley estimated they'd soon pass the point where desertion was a realistic alternative.

That morning, the beginning of the fifth day, reveille had sounded at 3:30 a.m., convenient since the men were all still up anyway, holding on to the horses. Three hours later, after saddling and harnessing, wringing out tents, manhandling the sodden canvas into the carts, striking the camp and checking equipment, they ate breakfast. Three stale biscuits each, edible only because the wet weather had softened them sufficiently for teeth to penetrate.

Colonel French's plan had been to cook fresh meat every night, rather than travel burdened by heavy bags of pemmican, dried meat and other provisions. It was a plan Fred Bagley approved of highly. He adored the smell of food roasting over a fire. In Dufferin, he'd enjoyed standing around the fire after supper with a cup of tea, as the men smoked and told wonderful lies, stories of great sexual conquests, battles fought and hardships endured. This was the life he'd left home to find.

James Macleod

Colonel French's plan was great as far as it went, which was nowhere. The herd of cattle meant to provide the fresh meat was so far behind the column that Bagley hadn't even seen them for two days. And even if the cattle had been miraculously able to keep up, so far there had been enough wood for only a single evening fire. On top of it all, at three of their five campsites there'd been no food or water for the horses. The only things the Force seemed to have in abundance were mosquitoes and those damnable biscuits. Bagley didn't know whether to curse or bless the cooks' foresight in making a huge supply before they departed.

On Sunday, July 12, day five, they'd marched only nine miles; even so it had taken them until nine that night to do it. As usual, the cooks' wagons were nowhere in sight. Bagley heard Inspector Walsh and Sub-Inspector James Walker discussing supper, and his ears pricked up eagerly. But his hopes of a nice slice of brisket were dashed when Walsh said he doubted the wagons would appear for hours yet. Three more biscuits.

The grumbling men settled in for the night about 11:00 p.m., having beaten off the last onslaught of mosquitoes, which seemed to have multiplied tenfold after the previous night's rain and were positively attracted rather than repelled by the latest bug repellents—oil of juniper and liquid ammonia—dreamed up by the Force's doctor, John Kittson. Then the heavens opened once again. The same amount of rain that fell during the entire previous night poured down in a scant forty-five minutes, accompanied by the requisite thunder, lightning and wind.

Water poured through the tent walls and, defying the laws of nature, seemed to flow upward in streams through the flaps. Long after the deluge stopped outside, it continued inside—leaking, dripping and oozing through every seam and dozens of pinprick holes.

There was one innovation in this prairie storm. The rain had been preceded by five minutes of hailstones the size of walnuts. Men who'd gone outside to see what was going on retreated quickly from the pounding. With the hail came a sudden drop in temperature so that Bagley's soaking clothes had turned into a chilly cocoon.

In truth, wet, cold and hunger weren't the only sources of Bagley's discomfort. He'd expected—even looked forward to—privation and hardship as the lot of the true frontiersman. But he hadn't expected to be laid low by anything as mundane and unheroic as his bowels. He'd been alternately feeling hollow, queasy and, after the duck feast, unpleasantly stuffed.

Today his innards staged a full-scale rebellion, catching him short while riding. As a result, his grubby breeches now sported a nasty stain in an embarrassingly obvious spot.

Lying in his damp blankets, shivering and miserable, and smelling his own rank self and the dank oily canvas, Bagley slowly became aware of a soft but distinct pattering noise on the tent surface. He peered around him. The rest of the men were sound asleep, some of them lying in puddles of water. In one corner a man groaned softly, elsewhere someone whimpered. At 3:00 a.m., with sleep impossible, his bowels bubbling ominously and reveille only half an hour away, Bagley decided to get up and investigate.

He grabbed his carbine and slowly crawled out of the tent. It was first light, enough to see by, but everything was just a little out of focus. As his eyes adjusted, Bagley couldn't believe what lay in front of him. Nothing he'd read, not Fenimore Cooper nor the five-penny Westerns, had prepared him for what he saw. Everything, wagons, tents, the ground, was carpeted with little death heads on tiny bodies, dark as night.

Bagley realized with a start that he was looking at grasshoppers—millions, perhaps billions, of them. The men had caught sight of them yesterday, massed on the horizon like storm clouds. The insects were still a long way in the distance, but as the sun set, they completely blocked its last rays. The grasshoppers shifted and twitched. Bagley stopped to listen—not a hum exactly, more a high-pitched screeching, like a million tiny violins. He had a sudden urge to go charging through them, like a child scattering seed pods in a dandelion field.

The grasshoppers had muffled all the normal pre-dawn camp sounds. No cattle lowing, horses whickering or birds chirping—just those violins. Over on the far side of the field, Bagley could make out the shape of a man holding a carbine, a sentry fast asleep and covered with grasshoppers. The carbine, sticking up in the air, was thickened considerably by its insect jacket.

Bagley caught a wisp of smoke over by an ox cart, a hundred feet away. Squinting hard, he saw that it was Major Macleod, with a ground sheet over his shoulders, smoking. Macleod beckoned him over with a smile and a wave of his hand. Each step Bagley took towards Macleod was accompanied by a sickening crunch and crackle as he squished grasshoppers. He tried tiptoeing, then shuffling, but finally he steeled his heart and marched over the bodies.

"Well, Fred, it looks like God has paid us a visit today," Macleod said languidly.

"God?" questioned Bagley.

"Who else put these beautiful creatures here for us to enjoy?"

"I never thought of it that way, sir."

"Well, Fred, there's beauty all around us if we look for it. Granted, it's been hard to find lately."

Macleod sighed to himself. It had been a brutal few days. He'd just pulled in an hour ago with the last of the tail-enders. On the trail, the rain had filled the baked hollows, turning hardpan into bog that grabbed and sucked at every wagon and cart wheel. Just about at the end of his own endurance, Macleod made a last check for stragglers and found a young sub-constable weakly trying to extricate his wagon from a bog. Macleod harnessed his own horse to it and managed to pull it out. He saw that the tired, hungry recruit wouldn't make it into camp if he had to drive the wagon so Macleod helped him onto his own horse and sent him ahead.

Macleod hauled himself into the wagon, yelling and whipping the animals into action. As he drove, he grew uncomfortably aware that he was all by himself at the tail end of the column, easy pickings for any of the rumoured Sioux in the neighbourhood. On the second day of the march, the Force had met a number of Métis fleeing the Sioux. They'd happily filled the men's ears with tales of atrocities. And yesterday, they'd met one who said a band of fifty warriors was raising hell around Pembina Mountain Depot. There was also an unconfirmed report that the Sioux had snatched a woman from Grant's Tavern shortly after the force passed. Colonel French took the reports seriously enough to order, for the first time, an armed advance guard and the distribution of ammunition among the men.

Macleod prayed that he didn't come across any ambitious Sioux. Not only was he alone, but he had only his side-arm, having left his carbine on his horse.

The rainstorm smashed into Macleod about a mile out of camp and he hunkered down, his head bowed to his knees to protect his face from the barrage. When he got into camp he was startled that no sentry challenged him. All the guards were slumbering heavily, despite hail, rain, thunder—not to mention the Sioux warning. Since it was almost dawn he decided not to wake them up; he'd deal with their laxity later. He rummaged about the camp hoping to find the remnants of last night's supper. Nothing. A good smoke might take away his hunger pangs. Shortly after he'd settled down, the grasshoppers descended.

Macleod came back to himself and noticed Fred Bagley still standing there, apparently waiting for him to respond to a question—one that he hadn't heard. He shrugged off his lethargy to attend to the boy. Tears welled up in Bagley's eyes. For a moment Macleod had forgotten just how young the lad was.

"Here now, boy, what's the problem?" he asked softly.

"As I was telling you, sir, it's my stomach. I didn't make it off my horse and, uh, I made a bit of a mess of myself," Bagley said morosely.

"Son, half the men have their sphincters clenched as tight as steel drums right now," said Macleod, not completely stifling a laugh. "I don't know if it's the water, the food or the goddamn biscuits."

Macleod took a handful of mud off his boots, slapped it on the back of Bagley's pants and rubbed it in. "Now nobody'll be any wiser," he said.

Macleod lounged against the ox cart, watching the prairie sun rising. As the light hit them, the grasshoppers began to glisten—iridescent, dazzling colours, shimmering like a mirage. For a moment Macleod believed his own comforting words.

Reveille sounded and he heard the waking men exclaiming at the sight of the grasshoppers taking flight.

SAM STEELE

July 13

The air for a height of hundreds of yards was full of them, their wings shining in the sun, and the trees, grass, flowers, and in fact, everything in sight was covered by them.

Even the paint and wood work of the wagons and

our carbines were not free of their attacks, and our tents had to be hurriedly packed away to save them from destruction.

Beautiful they are, thought Macleod, and perhaps truly a gift from God, but as he watched the grasshoppers consuming everything in sight, it occurred to him that when they had been spotted on the horizon yesterday, the horde was heading east. In other words, the Force was marching straight into ravaged territory.

Chapter 7

The Death of Romance

JAMES FINLAYSON

July 14

Reveille at 3:30 a.m. on the march at 7 a.m. After marching about six miles we suddenly came upon a range of rugged hills, called the Pembina Mountains. We had to double our teams to ascend the opposite side owing to a deep valley running between, through which runs the Pembina river. We halted for dinner in the valley. Very windy with lots of dust, distance from here to Dufferin 65 miles, camped on the open plain near a swamp.

No water. No wood. No supper. The bull train did not get in till after midnight therefore no provisions.

Among Colonel French's many weighty concerns, the ox carts—that "imposition of the country...a style of vehicle more in accordance with the 1st than the 19th century"—with their countless axle and wheel breakdowns, proved to be his greatest aggravation. But the carts were nothing compared to the spawn of Satan that drove them.

No amount of threatening could induce the ox drivers to move out on schedule, usually 5:30 or 6:00 a.m. If they even showed up at the rest stop for lunch, it was just as the main body was pulling out again. Then, contrary to his most explicit orders, they'd insist on staying for their own rest, which meant, of course, they didn't get into camp until long after most were asleep. After arriving past midnight on the fourteenth, they flatly refused to start with the rest of the troops the next morning.

Colonel French found the half-breeds' independence irritating—their insolence unbearable. They made jokes in a strange mix of French, English and Cree, then laughed as soon as you turned your back. During one contretemps, the Colonel had furiously reminded them *he* paid their wages and he could dismiss them and see to it there were no pay packets waiting for them when they returned to Winnipeg. "*Oui, mon Colonel,*" answered one of the cretins. "Dat's good idea. We go back now."

French wished he'd ignored the "experts" who assured him that he needed half-breed drivers. The Colonel peppered his reports with complaints of their carelessness with the animals and their unreliability. "The half-breeds and oxen could not be got to start on time, and did not arrive until 3 or 4 in the afternoon, marching in the hottest part of the day. There appears to be no system amongst them, they are consequently not in camp yet, 11 p.m., and probably will not start in time to-morrow."

After dealing with the half-breeds for a week, the Colonel concluded that any idiot could do their job so he assigned sub-constables as additional ox-cart drivers, to provide a "leavening" for the breeds. The men might not be experienced, but they would more than make up for that, he reasoned, by doing what they were told, when they were told—a refreshing change. Extra drivers allowed the long trains to be split up, no more than three or four carts per man, thus eliminating, at

Ox cart and driver

least in theory, the multi-cart pile-ups. The Colonel was confident that the additional drivers would vastly increase the ox trains' speed.

JEAN D'ARTIGUE

July 15

It is useless to mention how we greeted such an order, and I believe had we not been a long distance from any settlement, the Colonel would have had to make the expedition alone.

What military commander, who respects his men and wants to be respected by them, would have thought (I do not say dare) to have placed them on the same footing as those who worked for mercenary motives.

The members of the Mounted Police had sworn to keep the British flag unstained; while the half-breeds had only engaged to work for so many dollars a month. No comparison could, therefore be made between us; and it was more than discouraging, on the morning of the 15th to see some of our men, in their uniforms, driving oxen with sticks.

Joseph Carscadden had a more practical reason for being irked at ox-cart duty. "Many of the drivers are half-breeds whose pay varies from $2 to $5 a day. The red-coats pay is 75 cents," he grumped, "but they are Mounted Policemen and as such are bound for three years, so their dissatisfaction is of no moment, though of course the half-breeds must be satisfied."

FRED BAGLEY

My first experience of cart driving was rather disastrous. Having conquered my initial fear of the oxen, and finding them moving too slowly, I ventured to hit the lead ox a resounding thwack on the back with a stout stick, whereupon all three set off on a mad gallop (and couldn't the little beggars go) across the prairie, scattering on their way the various sacks of sugar etc., which constituted their loads.

As I could not stop them, nor keep up with them in their wild stampede, and it almost seemed to me at the time that only the barrier of the Rocky Mountains would prevent them from reaching the Pacific coast, it came in the nature of a Godsend, when Colonel Macleod happened by on horseback, who, after a hearty laugh at my predicament halted my runaways and sent some men to help me gather and reload my scattered cargoes.

This incident inspired me with a little more respect than I formerly had for my speedy little beasts, and I decided then and there that moral suasion was to be preferred to a big stick when dealing with Red River cart oxen.

Jean D'Artigue

July 16

And yet, notwithstanding my disgust, I could not help being somewhat interested and amused when, the next morning, it fell to my lot to drive a train of these carts. Being a new hand at the work, the foreman of the half-breeds very kindly harnessed my oxen, and arranged them in order for starting, the strongest ox in front, the next strongest tied to the back of the first one's cart, and the weakest one behind and that tied to the second cart.

On starting we received three biscuits each, on which to make our noonday meal; it being expected that we could not keep up with the main column, and be able to take our dinner with them.

By mid-morning the troops were far out of D'Artigue's sight; at midday the wagons had disappeared too. Travelling until nightfall, his party hoped to catch up, but the tired oxen had slowed to a crawl, forcing the men to stop. It was then they realized that all their provisions were in the wagons, miles ahead and the three paltry biscuits issued for lunch were long gone. Cursing the saints and the maker of this vast, waterless, woodless prairie, the men set about trying to make themselves comfortable for a night on the ground, without even a single blanket among them.

"I've never heard such complaining," one hale voice boomed out of the darkness.

"Oh good," snapped D'Artigue, "a Diogenes among us."

"Come now, what are you complaining about?"

"Look around you," spat another trooper. "I can't see a damn thing *not* to complain about!"

"My friends," Diogenes pressed on, "you do nothing but grumble, now against the government, and then the Commissioner, but you should remember we were prepared for this before leaving Toronto."

"Nothing," a sour trooper interjected, "could have prepared me for this."

"If my memory serves me rightly," lectured Diogenes, "the Colonel told us then that we might at times be without food for two or three days at a time, and have to camp on the open prairie with nothing but the canopy of heaven for covering." One of the men began to protest but Diogenes overrode him. "If you are not men enough to endure what you signed up for, then perhaps you should go home!"

"Splendid idea!" chorused the men.

"Surely you knew what to expect," shot back Diogenes. "Of what do you complain then?"

"We complain," responded one man with exaggerated patience, "of having to drive ox carts."

"And you forget," interjected D'Artigue, "that if the Sioux were in the neighbourhood, they could easily get the better of us, and take possession of the oxen and carts that are scattered along the road for several miles."

Diogenes dismissed their carping with a stern reminder that things could—and certainly would—become much worse. His prediction didn't seem to bother the rest of the men, who quickly fell asleep, but the more sensitive D'Artigue tossed and turned until dawn when he got up, determined to catch up to the rest of the Force. One man in a group of three hundred is surely harder to kill than one in a party of six.

"Anyone with me?" he inquired loudly, trying to roust up some companions. "Bugger off, Frenchy," was the only reply.

"I'm off then," he announced, still hoping for some company, but not seeing a flicker of movement. D'Artigue harnessed his oxen and hurried them off, with visions of catching the Force in the middle of an ample breakfast. Within a few hours he found them, or at least found where they had been. One look at the dry creek bed and the complete absence of grass told him they'd broken camp early to look for water and forage.

> Increasing the pace of my oxen, I continued to advance, and then began in reality the hardships of privation. I was all day consumed by a thirst that all the ravines which I crossed could not quench. When night came two of my oxen were tired out. What was I to do? Beat them unmercifully as the half-breeds did till they would fall? I had not sunk to such a degree of cruelty.
>
> I chose the wisest course, set them at liberty, and with the third proceeded as fast as possible on my journey. About eleven o'clock the sight of deserted wagons proved that I was not far from the camp, though I could not as yet see their fires. Very soon, however, I was arrested by the usual challenge:
>
> "Who comes there?"
>
> "A famished man," I replied, and the sentry allowed me to pass without further explanation.
>
> They had located their camp in a valley, on the banks of a small brook. The men were lying around the camp fires, being too fatigued to set up tents. It mattered very little to me where I slept, the main point being to get something to eat from the kettles which remained near the half-extinguished fires.
>
> My search was at first fruitless, and I visited no less than five divisions before finding provisions at the sixth. Stealing my way over the sleeping men, I found a large kettle of cooked meat, a box of bread, and a kettle of tea.* Seated on the ground, with the meat between my

---

* What he likely came across was the remains of the officers' rations. A quantity of bacon and salt meat (probably pork) was brought along but there is no indication of the troopers ever eating any of it—except by theft.

knees, the bread on one side, and the tea on the other, I made a meal that only a hearty man, having been two days without food, could dispose of. In fact, it was nearly daylight when I had fully satisfied my appetite, and, making my way to my own division, I climbed into a waggon and was soon fast asleep.

Ox-cart duty wasn't all privation, but one needed a larcenous nature to capitalize on the opportunities.

FRED BAGLEY

This was the most severe jolt Romance had been given since we left Toronto, but it was not without its compensations.

For inasmuch as the brigade of carts as a whole contained a variety of foodstuffs in bulk it was sometimes possible for us cart drivers by careful selection to get enough food from several carts for a substantial meal, and thus avoid, for the time being the eternal wet and dry or 23 of the main column. This was all very well when there were enough carts together to supply a varied, if not very luxurious menu....

Sub Const. Jean Claustre and myself, each with three Red River carts and oxen, found ourselves separated from the rest of the Brigade, by some miles, and very hungry. His loads consisted of flour only and mine solely of sugar. Happened to come on to a small pool of stagnant water, and nothing wherewith to make a fire, we made a splendid meal of flour paste and sugar.

Rest

Colonel French was right. The "leavening" of men among the half-breeds moved the ox train along much quicker, which allowed him to up the pace of the entire Force. After averaging only 8.8 miles per day in the first five days of the march, French pushed the troopers to average 26 miles from the fifteenth to the eighteenth of July. But the solution to one problem exacerbated two others. The more distance the Force covered, the more spread-out the column became, with many wagons and carts lagging up to half a day behind the rest. And as they ate up the miles, the horses began to fail.

JAMES FINLAYSON

July 15

On the march at 7 a.m. After marching twelve miles we halted at Beaver Creek for dinner.

Much dissatisfaction was manifested by the ox drivers at not getting in in time for dinner before the main body moved off. Country through which we passed hilly and some places stoney. Slept out all night with the sky for a cover.

For supper, *nothing!*

July 16

Reveille at 3:30 a.m. Many of the boys who came in late last night, were put under arrest for not turning out at roll call, one *Slap Jack* per man for breakfast, lucky to get that. On the march at 5:30 a.m. Arrived at Turtle Mountain after dark and camped near a small stream. Distance from here to Dufferin 120 miles.

Had supper, the same as I had for dinner namely *Nothing*!

COLONEL FRENCH

July 17

Overshot the proper watering place and consequently had a long march in the heat of the day; several horses played out. The oxen did not start with us, and saw nothing of them all day. Left a few men behind with

McLeod [sic] to repair carts. Boundary Commission road apparently changed, make[s] the road longer. Did not arrive at Turtle Head Creek until after 9 at night, and then found no grass. Used some of last years B. Com. hay, but the horses did not care for it; did not pitch tents, men lying under waggons, &C.

With the longer marches, the horses were rapidly consuming the precious oats brought from Fort Dufferin. Twice, when reasonable forage was available, French ordered a group of men to cut feed with the haying machines but the eastern horses, unused to prairie grass, refused to eat it. "Government horses," disparaged the Artist, who'd been enjoying regular meals from the officers' special rations, "like Government men, being used to feed well, are apt to become too dainty."

Oats are a fine feed supplement but they burn fast and hot in a horse's belly. For endurance work, only steady hours of grazing each day can keep muscle from eroding. But with the frequent summer storms and the threat of another stampede, the division commanders didn't dare let the horses loose to graze. As the wagons were usually so far behind, they were rarely available to pen the animals in at night and there was no wood to build a corral. The only alternative was tying or hobbling tightly, neither conducive to grazing—even if there had been good forage available. (Macleod's prediction of a country ravaged by grasshoppers was unfortunately proving all too true.) The western mustangs ate whatever was available, but any advantage they had was wiped out when their loads were increased to save the eastern horses.

On Saturday, July 18, reveille sounded at 3:00 a.m. Within a few minutes, groggy troopers crawled out from under wagons and pulled themselves upright, trying to work the kinks out from a night spent sleeping on stony ground. No matter which way they lay, rocks of unbelievable sharpness poked into every part of their anatomy. They peered into the darkness, sniffing hopefully, praying by some miracle that the cooks had found wood. But the wagons had arrived only a few hours earlier, after the punishing twenty-eight-mile march of the previous day, and the cooks were sound asleep. That meant no breakfast but the men did make tea, water, for once, being abundant.

French ordered pull-out for 4:00 a.m. Fifteen minutes before departure, the men of E Division stood clustered together, their horses still unharnessed. The division commander, Jacob Carvell, hurried over to his second-in-command, John McIllree.

"What's going on here? We won't be out for another hour at this rate!"

"They won't budge," replied McIllree. "They say they're not moving until they get more rations."

"More rations? There aren't any more rations! Am I supposed to go out and shoot a buffalo for their breakfast?"

"Can't say as I blame them, sir," McIllree reasoned. "You couldn't keep a mouse alive on what we're feeding them. I really think they mean it."

Carvell took one look at the grumbling men and knew McIllree was right. He had to get them moving; if this kind of dissension spread, they might as well give it up and go back to Dufferin. By scrounging and raiding supplies intended for successive days, Carvell managed to cobble together enough food to give the men a hint of what a full breakfast was like. He should report the incident to Colonel French and see that the men were disciplined for breach of orders; that would be the proper thing to do. It took him only a few seconds to decide the progress of the march would not be improved by an investigation and the ensuing punishment.

Later that same day, two horses stopped and lay down. No amount of blandishment or beating could get them up again. Colonel French ordered the animals left on the road, with the faint hope that "the Boundary Commission people may find them." The next day two more were abandoned to the same fate. Those few officers and men familiar with the ways of horses weren't surprised. They'd seen the horses steadily deteriorate since departure. But the bulk of the men were stunned. One day the horses were tired and poorly fed, the next day they were left for dead. Even the dimmest members of the troop began to wonder about their future.

HENRI JULIEN

To wind up all our sensations of this day, we saw the

prairie on fire in our rear.

The spectacle was sublime. The crackling flame, the lurid light, the heavy masses of smoke rolling low at first over the surface of the grass, then mounting higher and higher, till, caught in a stratum of breeze, they veered and floated rapidly to the east, formed a scene of impressive grandeur.

Julien enjoyed the spectacle from a distance but those more directly threatened were less enraptured.

SÉVÈRE GAGNON

While we were getting dinner ready, a spark coming from God knows where sets the prairie on fire to our left. Fortunately the wind was blowing from the West and protected us; in a moment, everything was on fire to our left. The fire followed the wind. We greatly feared for part of our escort which had been left behind.

JAMES FINLAYSON

Hunger and thirst is two of the worst complaints among the boys. Some of them were caught in a Prairie fire and had a very narrow escape. In some instances horses were quickly unharnessed and mounted by the teamsters and galloped off in haste for some place of safety. Fortunately no one was hurt and nothing lost. When we came up, the country was burnt black. Camped on the edge of the burnt Prairie by a swamp.

At 9:00 p.m. on the eighteenth the main body of the Force arrived at the Souris or Mouse River. The ox carts didn't even begin arriving until after ten the following morning. Macleod pulled in in the afternoon and the final ox cart showed up late in the evening of the nineteenth.

Eleven days, 181 miles, thousands of biscuits, one duck supper, one pancake breakfast, no buffalo, no Indians, no Indian maidens, no adventure. Taken altogether, the accomplishments seemed meagre, the privations many, the rewards few. But on Sunday, July 19, day twelve, hope returned and the future reacquired its rosy glow. All it took was a rest—the first since leaving Dufferin. After nearly two weeks of being led to campsite after campsite, with no wood, water or forage, for the first time the guides' promises of Shangri-La held true. The campsite was a beautiful green bowl nestled intimately among a group of hills. "Enchanting," declared no nonsense Sub-Inspector Sévère Gagnon.

The first bend of the Souris delivered in abundance everything that nature had withheld until now. Two cattle were slaughtered. Enormous fires were kindled. Songs could be heard drifting out of the tents and troopers wandered among the divisions, visiting friends they had seen only in passing since leaving Dufferin. All were exuberant at the prospect of a feast. "The usual run of men are pretty much like animals," observed Henri Julien. "Feed them well, keep their stomach full, and they will work cheerfully."

Fred Bagley washed his pants. Many of the men swam and lounged for hours in the river, their skins finally restored to white. The cold, clear water soothed their sunburned, dust-blasted, insect-ravaged skin. A gentle breeze from the river made the summer heat more bearable and the softer ground

Repairing an ox cart in camp

allowed them to sleep comfortably for the first time since
Dufferin.

John McIllree, at last, enjoyed the recreation he'd been
anticipating when he joined up.

JOHN McILLREE

The Souris is a clear rapid river, and it is a great treat to
get a bathe in it, as this prairie dust makes us as black
as a nigger. Had Divine Service this morning.

Fishing tackle was issued, and I tried my luck, but
did not see a fish. I do not think there was one caught.

Some ducks and prairie hens were shot. Plenty of
food again. Horses much played out. Took them all
down to the river and gave them a thorough washing all
over. A day's rest is not to be appreciated until you have
worked hard for some time.

While the men were luxuriating, Colonel French sat for
hours in his tent, planning, calculating, worrying.

Temperament and training made George French an aloof
man. The welfare of the entire Force was his responsibility. He
couldn't afford to become concerned about the problems of
individual men. His distance from his troopers would have
had few repercussions in a military organization. At Kingston,
for instance, he had remained happily ensconced in his office,
managing the overall affairs of his command. Under him were
a number of officers with rigidly defined duties and under
them men with clearly defined jobs. Untouched by responsibility for day-to-day affairs and rarely seen by the men, French
thrived as a commander, earning deserved praise for the
smooth functioning of his unit.

But the North West Mounted Police was far from a military
organization. The recruits were volunteers—not conscripts,
policemen—not soldiers. What's more the Force was brand
new and heading into the unknown; they had no tradition,
culture or precedent to rely on and no manuals to consult.
Procedure had to be invented on the spot. A standing order
written up one day could easily be made ridiculous the next by

changing circumstances.

In French's British military experience, transgressions were punished swiftly and severely. A man could be flogged or clapped in irons for a smart remark. Sergeant-majors dispensed their own brutal form of justice to keep soldiers in line. Desertion could be punished by death. But the Mounted Police Act forbade corporal punishment. The men could only be confined to quarters—useless on the march since there were no quarters—or fined, regardless of the seriousness of the offence. Since the men wouldn't actually see any pay until they got back to civilization, the last proved a weak weapon at best.

The march forced the Colonel into constant contact with the men, which made him uncomfortable. He rode among them day after day, but he never developed a feeling for them or an understanding of their problems. It never occurred to French that a good word here and there could go almost as far as three square meals. After the prairie fire, rather than congratulate the heroic men who risked their lives to protect wagons and teams, he fumed because he was unable to catch the culprit whose "carelessness" caused it in the first place.

The troopers might have accepted French's aloofness and his criticisms, but they couldn't stomach his ceaseless investigations into trivial offences and his relentless insistence that his officers place men on report for minor transgressions.

Men amusing themselves after hours

JOSEPH CARSCADDEN

I left the team in a stationary condition with several important nonentities (all speaking at once) giving vast information to the young driver—including a choice vocabulary of oaths, curses and denunciations, until the youth becomes angry and swears in return.

You look surprised; well it is a fact, for the youth is not acclimatised yet. He is not accustomed to be treated like a good or bad dog as the case may be. He is not yet toned down to our most worthy Commissioner's level.

All in good time my young teamster wait until you are marched up to the orderly room [tent] a time or two. You'll cool down.

"O, but," I hear him say, "If I don't do wrong they cannot march me up there."

Foolish young fellow make your mind up, for guilty or not you will be no more exempt than the worst character in the Force. Then when you are brought up, you will be fined; whether guilty or not, for the very fact of your appearance before our noble Commissioner as a prisoner constitutes a crime and you must suffer accordingly....

Was it intended by the M. Of Justice (I say him because he is our head and to him alone, can we look for Justice) that men should be harassed with fines continually from $5 to a months pay even for the most trivial circumstances and often were men fined without the shadow of a charge being substantiated against them.

On the morning of July 20, Sub-Constable Pierre Lucas, who'd been out all night after being left to tend sick horses, showed up in a froth of excitement.

"There's Sioux about!" he babbled to the sentry. "I just escaped! It was awful! They got one of my horses and nearly got me."

Lucas explained that he'd been attacked the previous night, managing to drive off five naked marauders but losing a horse to an Indian bullet. "I do not believe his statement," French stated flatly, but he couldn't shake his story, despite a lengthy cross-examination. Most of the men believed that Lucas had

shot the animal himself and invented the story to escape punishment, but many privately wondered what they'd have done
in his place.

JEAN D'ARTIGUE

What could he do? Certainly his orders were to remain
there until someone was sent to his rescue. But then, he
was alone, unprotected and without provisions. So he
concluded the best thing to do was to shoot the poor
dying brute, and proceed on his journey.

Being well aware that if he told what he had done the
Commissioner would not only fine him, but make him
pay about two hundred dollars for the horse, he declared
with great earnestness that he had been attacked by five
Sioux, and that, making a vigorous resistance, he won
the day, losing nothing but one horse which was killed in
the fight. Everyone was convinced that the story was a
fabrication but nobody could prove it.

Diarrhea, Dust and Disobedience

Reveille blew at 3:30 a.m. on Tuesday, July 21. A parade, of
sorts, had been held most mornings since their departure from
Fort Dufferin—largely scraggly, disorganized affairs, often with
the previous evening's late arrivals missing. This day, Colonel
French rode up and down the corps, enjoying the effect his
decision to halt for two days had had on the deportment of the
men. Rest and cleaning had spruced them up dramatically.
Tack and guns had been cleaned of two weeks of dust and
grasshopper carcasses. Even the horses, enjoying their first
proper grazing since Dufferin, seemed to have a strut in their
step. This morning everyone would start together, and on time,
as vital repairs had been made to wagons and carts.

But throughout the inspection, something niggled at French.
Then it came clear: there weren't enough horses—taking a

quick count, he estimated fifty missing.

"Where are the rest of them?" he demanded of Macleod.

"Some are down, five or six, I think. The rest can't be ridden or harnessed."

"How many?" barked the Colonel.

Macleod reported that thirty-five were still so stricken with saddle and harness sores, split hooves, tender backs, pulled muscles and lameness, they couldn't be ridden. Nine more were too weak to get up at all, let alone pull a wagon. It was sobering news. With every horse healthy, they had barely enough for the troops and wagons, leaving only a handful for replacements.

The Colonel held a hasty council among the senior officers, who stressed that something would have to be left behind to lighten the horses' loads, perhaps one of the nine-pounders, a haying machine or even one of the blacksmiths' forges.

Colonel French wouldn't hear of it. Such talk smacked of negativism and defeatism. Besides, abandoning government equipment would be difficult to explain to Hewitt Bernard back in Ottawa. Embarrassing questions might be asked about why the equipment was brought along in the first place. Instead, French ordered a constable and five sub-constables to provision themselves with seven days' rations and "bring on those horses that could not keep up."

His officers' concerns didn't go entirely unheeded. "I insisted on the men dismounting and walking on foot every alternate hour and I propose continuing this to relieve the horses."

FRED BAGLEY

July 22

Many of the men were not very well pleased at the prospect of walking in riding boots over the parched prairie, in scorching hot weather.

Sergeant Smythe, who was most outspoken with his objections, deciding to disobey the order climbed into the cook wagon, and on the Commissioner happening to catch him there and threatening to put him in arrest, declared:

"I don't care what you do. I joined a mounted force, not a foot one, and as I don't feel well to-day, I must ride on something either a horse or a waggon. It is immaterial to me which."

The Commissioner, with a grim smile on his face which seemed to express: "Now what can one do with a guy like that?" rode off, without further comment, while the Sergeant retained his seat amongst the pots and pans.

Discipline suffered a set back there and then.

The boy Bagley, temporarily exempt from ox cart driving, not possessing the "nerve" of the Sergeant, conscientiously plugged along doing the stipulated hours of riding and walking and on taking off his boots when a short distance from camp after a long, hot march found his feet both blistered and bleeding. Whereupon Captain Walker, a handsome giant of a man, carried him pick-a-back the rest of the way to camp.

The men walked, rode and drove through the shimmering heat, which shot up to 99 degrees by early afternoon. Their necks and faces, inadequately covered by their fashionable helmets, burned to a deep, raw red and their throats, parched of water, were scoured by the dust. The charms of the Souris seemed a distant memory. Added to their woes were bowel problems, now epidemic among officers and men.

SURGEON JOHN KITTSON

I observed that Diarrhoea was always on the increase immediately after the consumption of Fresh Meat. The better class of Half-Breeds will not eat the Meat of worked or travelled animals; they say the flesh is poisoned. Our experience would lead to the same conclusion, but there is no doubt that the sudden change from salt meat to fresh meat has some weight in explaining the cause of the "Prairie Cholera."

Half-Breeds are not subject to the malady, their food being the same when hunting as when at home, consisting of jerked meat, Pemmican and Marrow fat.

Opium, always the principal ingredient of anti-diarrhoea mixtures elsewhere, was of secondary importance with us, enormous and repeated doses being taken in the same case without the least benefit.

Kittson racked his brain and pored over his medical journals for a solution. He remembered that Ipecac, a medication made from ipecacuanha, a South American plant, had been successful in controlling dysentery during the Crimean War. He busied himself among the ranks, dispensing twenty to thirty grains per man. But the diarrhea kept coming. Finally, he hit upon Trinitrate of Bismuth—a gastric sedative—tripling the normal dose and adding in opium for good measure. It worked reasonably well, though many of the men were startled to find that their stools turned black.

HENRI JULIEN

We also suffered a great deal from blistered and cracked lips due to the dry state of the atmosphere and the high head winds constantly sweeping over us. Glycerine we

Sick Parade

found no preventative. The best treatment was the immediate application of caustic.*

In the early afternoon of July 22, the advance guard spotted a bright gleam in the distance—the second bend of the Souris River. But this time, instead of gentle banks covered in grass and wood, the river flung up an obstacle course of precipitous drops and rock outcroppings. Somehow the Force had to get across it, but by the time they reached the river, the sun was already heading for the horizon. Hobbling on blistered, aching feet, the men gripped reins and harness leads and prepared to descend.

SÉVÈRE GAGNON

It was about midnight when the last waggon could cross over. A good part of the convoy has been left on the other side of the river.

Two belonging to my troop nearly got fatally wounded; one was kicked on the head by a horse, while leading it by the bridle, the other one fell between the legs of his horses running away down a steep hill.

HENRI JULIEN

We had a very hard time here. There was a bridge at the first ford, but not at this: the banks were quite steep, and the wagons of C Troop having got entangled with the bull carts, the one retarded the other. The consequence was that several wagon-boxes were smashed. Our two pieces of artillery were the most difficult of all to manage, weighing 4,400 pounds. Not being a soldier, I never saw the use of these two nine-pounders. They were always in the way. Retarded our march, took up the time of several men and the service of several good horses. They were not fired off even once at an enemy,

---

* Caustic is a substance, like carbolic or silver nitrate, which burns organic tissue and was frequently used for surgical purposes.

and, in fact, had hostilities been encountered, would have been of less use than the rifles which the gunners should have carried.

But I suppose they looked military, and had therefore to be dragged along with us, as much for show as for anything else.

The near calamity of the crossing completely escaped Colonel French's attention. "[H]indermost wagons delayed several hours," was the only hint in his diary that a large group of exhausted men huddled on the wrong side of the river that night. But he did attend closely to the "continued" inattention of the men and his problems with the infernal half-breeds, most notably their leader, Drever, Mr. D.

COLONEL FRENCH

July 23, 1874

A, B, and C Troops had 12 horses missing, kept them all back until they were found. A lot of oxen and cattle not to be found, just like Mr. D's carelessness.

McLeod as usual, was in the rear, and would not let any carts start until the cattle were found, much to the disgust of the half-breeds whose motto appears to be "the Devil take the hindermost" as long as their own four carts and oxen are all right.... A horse died from rupture, over-driven by a half-breed.

Fred Bagley, back on ox-cart detail, plodded along, his mind drifting in and out of daydreams about home. He wondered if his mother would be shocked at how thin he'd become. She certainly would be aghast at how filthy the men were. The glorious bath in the Souris was now all but forgotten, dirt having settled back on him like a familiar coat. Despite it all, Fred Bagley felt pretty good about himself. The doctor's nostrums had calmed his bowels and hearing the other men complain bitterly about their stomach ailments made him realize he had stood up to the indignity as well as anyone. And, if truth be told, he didn't even mind the ox-cart detail too much, except for the noise. The half-breeds were wonderfully entertaining, though he couldn't understand half of what they said. He would, however, have liked a little more excitement. A buffalo hunt would be nice; whacking ducks with sticks didn't exactly compare. An Indian or two would be even better. His hopes were raised when a couple of Boundary Commission men from the United States brought them a warning.

Henri Julien

July 22

While employed in making hay, on the opposite side of the line, some Sioux came to them and levied blackmail in the way of crackers, pork and other eatables. We put on double pickets to guard our horses against these cowardly marauders.

All the next day Fred Bagley's head swivelled like a top, his eyes straining hard to spot a fabled redskin. But he saw nothing and was infuriated that evening to learn someone else had been luckier.

John McIllree

July 23

Started at 5:00 a.m. sharp. E Troop to the front. Reported that Indians were in the woods around the camp. One was certainly seen by one of our officers. After we left the Souris, the country was just the same barren waste, and the day was extremely warm. We only went about 12 miles today, and stopped at the Rivière des Lacs, which was nearly dry.

Close to the River is the Hill of the Murdered Scout. Some Indian murdered another up there with a stone. The stone that he committed the deed with is still lying there and the murderer cut out a full figure of his victim in the turf about 12 feet long. Slept nearly all the remainder of the day.

Several giant footprints had also been carved in the turf near the figure of the slain man. The stone particularly fascinated Fred Bagley. He gawked at the rusty-coloured stain spread over it. Blood, the half-breeds insisted, still there from the heinous deed many years ago. Lichen, scoffed the sceptical. One of the men started to cart the ten-pound stone away as a souvenir, but the half-breeds stopped him, warning that the stone's powerful medicine would bring horrible suffering upon anyone who interfered with its resting place. They reminded the man that Indians, likely relatives of the murdered one, had been seen in the vicinity. The trooper laughed, but later Bagley saw him surreptitiously drop the stone. He half thought of retrieving it himself but decided if there were evil spirits about, he'd just as soon not aggravate them.

Colonel French was pleased at how well morale was holding up in the face of adversity. "Great Rivalry between the Troops as to who should be off first. A troop got off at 3:30," he noted with satisfaction on July 24. The men would have damaged themselves laughing if they'd seen his diary entry. Dust, not zeal, spurred them from their beds before dawn. Every day they faced a mix of soot and debris from the prairie fires that insinuated itself into every orifice and, if there was a wind, scoured exposed faces mercilessly.

INDIAN FIGURE ON MURDERED SCOUT HILL.

Hill of the Murdered Scout

Even when no wind stirred up the gritty dust, the horses' hooves sent clouds of it cascading onto the men riding behind. The first troop to depart could spread out and ride in comfort, leaving those behind to choke in their wake. When the last troops pulled into camp, throats and eyes raw from irritation, faces inflamed from sunburn and insect bites and coated with sooty particles, they looked as if they'd spent the day brawling.

On the twenty-fourth the rush to be first was given added impetus. There'd been no water the night before and none that morning. The guides painted tantalizing pictures of St. Peter's Springs, an abundant oasis, only a short march away. But if the Apostle had ever been that way, he hadn't stopped to drink recently.

JOHN McILLREE

July 24

Started at 5 a.m. Travelled all morning over the same dreary waste and heat oppressive. No wood or water.

About noon we arrived at St. Peter's Spring, which was a fraud as there were very little signs of water. We stopped there to rest and immediately began to clean out the Spring and dig other wells. After a good deal of manual labour we got a good supply of water from the spring and we managed to water most of the horses.

The water was splendid, as cold as ice. It was a sight to see the flocks of birds coming to drink; looked like they had not seen water all the summer. Horses played out badly all the morning and we had to leave several behind us, one of which is since reported defunct.

Sweet Sorrow

JEAN D'ARTIGUE

...finally on Friday, the 24th of July, we arrived at

Roche Percée. But what a change since our departure
from Dufferin!

We had set out full of hope, mounted on excellent
horses, accompanied by waggons carrying our supplies,
and followed by carts laden with the same, but our
hopes were doomed to bitter disappointment.

No romantic incidents occurred; no encounter with
the Indians and the whiskey-traders and on our arrival at
Roche Percée the column resembled a routed army corps.

For a distance of several miles the road was strewed
with broken carts, and horses and oxen overcome with
hunger and fatigue.

This was the natural result of the Commissioner's
blunder before leaving Dufferin, in ordering us to carry
our supplies. During the whole of Saturday, horses and
oxen which had been unable to keep up to the column,
continued to arrive in a deplorable condition.

Was it in this manner that the Canadian Government
had intended the Mounted Police to be managed and
directed?

Certainly not!

Could Colonel French have done better than he did?

Certainly yes!

Colonel French was beside himself. Incredibly, after only four
days of marching, the horses and men were in worse condition
than when they had pulled into their rest stop at the Souris
River.

Everywhere the Colonel turned, someone had let him down.
He cursed his guides—supposedly expert frontiersmen who
could rarely find wood, water or grazing and had only a vague
idea of the Boundary Commission trail they were following.
Nor had their legendary marksmanship bagged them anything
more than the occasional hawk, duck or grouse. As for scouting, they were never willing to actually ride far enough ahead
of the corps to do any.

French cursed Edmund Dalrymple Clark, the young nephew
of Sir John A. Macdonald who had been given both the paymaster and quartermaster positions. French stripped Clark of

the quartermaster title, but the "disorganized state" he'd left behind meant the Force departed poorly equipped, missing obvious items like cutlery and canteens. They had too much flour and not enough oatmeal, endless salt but too little tea. With only the payroll to worry about, Clark still couldn't seem to get the men paid on time while they were in Lower Fort Garry and Fort Dufferin.

French's efforts to rest the horses had been thwarted at every turn. Even his utmost vigilance couldn't stop the men from sneaking unauthorized rides, and when he did a wagon check, he regularly found men napping amidst the supplies. His officers, reliable enough in other matters, too often turned a blind eye to these transgressions. French could not get it through their heads that serious disciplinary problems inevitably grow out of laxity with seemingly minor offences. They are like hairline cracks in a dam—ignore them and sooner or later a break will occur.

Sub-Inspector Albert Shurtliff had also let him down. Shurtliff and fourteen men had left a week before the Force and travelled straight to Fort Ellice, a Hudson's Bay Company post, seventy miles to the north of Roche Percée. Their task was to establish the Force's headquarters there. After the argument among the officers in Dufferin about the horses, Colonel French conceded nothing but hurriedly sent a messenger to Fort Ellice, just before the Force departed, ordering Shurtliff to rendezvous with them at Roche Percée with as many horses as he could spare.

The Mounties at Roche Percée

COLONEL FRENCH

July 25

Shurtliff came in about 11 a.m. and reported his arrival. He is camped 10 miles west, at Wood End Depôt, on the Boundary Commission road, has been there for four days; has only 6 horses for me, having sent some to Fort Garry to draw out provisions for his own party.

Chapman [a constable] and Dr. Nevitt [the Force's Assistant Surgeon] arrived, bringing letters; they left the iron hopples behind, left one horse on the road played out, not to be wondered at considering the thoughtless way they drove, starting late and driving fast.

French peevishly upbraided Shurtliff, harshly dismissing his explanation that he had no choice but to send his extra horses to Fort Garry to bring food back for his starving men. Fort Ellice, like everywhere else, had been devastated by grasshoppers, and the Hudson's Bay men at the post weren't about to turn over horses to the Force when they faced a long lean winter without supplies from Fort Garry. In any case, Shurtliff argued to the obdurate Colonel, the six horses he did bring left only eleven to spread among his fifteen-man command.

Even his "right hand," James Macleod, was failing to move along the half-breeds and their infernal ox carts. He couldn't fault Macleod's work habits, but he was far too soft on the men and had become positively cosy with the drivers, who now behaved as if Macleod, not French, were commander of the Force. As for the half-breed drivers and their chief, William Drever—what sin had French committed in a previous life to have them foisted upon him?

It all amounted to a disgrace. The line of march—more a zigzag—was habitually spread over ten miles. They looked more like a group of chimney sweeps heading to work than a military force. Supplies were low, the horses were deteriorating and even the men were starting to break down.

For several days John Kittson, the surgeon, had been warning him that a number of the men were sickly. After they pulled into Roche Percée he reported that at least five could go no farther. French told Kittson sharply that he wouldn't put up with slackers and malingerers, but the doctor assured him the illnesses were genuine. As the surgeon was a good man and unsympathetic to laggards, French doubted that anyone one could fool him for long. On the sick list Kittson included one case of phthisis (tuberculosis), one of prostatic abscess, a severely sprained ankle and two men seriously debilitated by diarrhea. As well, he advised French that a dozen or more men needed to be watched carefully.

It was clear to the Colonel that if the present state of affairs continued, the Force would—sooner rather than later—end up stranded somewhere on the prairie with nothing to eat except their dead and dying horses. The time had come for decisive action. The original plan had been to take the whole Force to Fort Whoop Up, dispatch the whiskey traders, then send half the troop, with the cattle and machinery, north to Fort Edmonton for the winter to help with the Indian problems there. But if any of them were to make it to Whoop Up by the fall, they could not afford to be burdened by sick men and ailing horses. No matter the cost, the Force had to move faster. French decided to break up the train, "taking with the main body merely what is absolutely necessary."

SÉVÈRE GAGNON

Important News:

My troop is changing its direction; we will take charge of the largest part of the heavy convoy, and all the cattle to be distributed to the farmers, and will follow the Northern route to Edmonton; we have still about 850 miles to cover.

The season is so far advanced that it is doubtful to believe we will be able to pass by the Bow River with the whole convoy and reach Edmonton before winter; this explains our new direction. We are 258 miles from Dufferin according to our odometer. It is stormy.

French couched his orders in such a way as to make it seem as if he had planned it all along, and the universe was merely unfolding as it should. But many knew better. Sub-Inspector

Cecil Denny noted gloomily, "Hundreds of miles remained to be covered, and the prospects for a successful termination to the journey began to look none too rosy."

JEAN D'ARTIGUE

Under these circumstances, the Commissioner adopted the most unreasonable and incredible plan that ever originated in one man's brain—placing in the hands of Inspector Jarvis a dozen good men of his own division, with instructions to proceed to Edmonton, via Fort Ellice, with twenty-four waggons, fifty-four carts, fifty-five of the weakest horses, a large number of oxen, and a herd of cows and calves.

A dozen half-breeds were also given him to assist in driving the carts; and besides the above, he was instructed to take as far as Fort Ellice, five or six sick men and two or three wagons. As for myself, although a member of B Division, for some reason never known to me, I was transferred to Inspector Jarvis' command.

Having only sick horses, or horses reduced to mere skeletons, and considering we were going *via* Fort Ellice and thus would have to travel at least nine hundred miles before reaching our destination, was it reasonable on the part of Colonel French, to expect us to reach Edmonton before the coming winter?

For my part, I do not think he expected for a moment that we would be able to go any further than Fort Ellice, a distance of 130 miles from Roche Percée. But if he did, he thereby tacitly acknowledged that Inspector Jarvis was better able than he to direct the expedition. For travelling 900 miles with sick horses and heavy waggons was a very different thing from travelling 270 miles with horses that were at least in good condition at the outset.

The sudden change shadowed the troops' seven-day rest at Roche Percée with foreboding. The four officers and twenty-seven men set to march north had grave doubts about ever

making it to Fort Edmonton.* The 244 men continuing on to
Fort Whoop Up, with fewer supplies, fewer horses and a
smaller corps, also felt vaguely uneasy about splitting the
ranks so early in their mission. Still, even with the pall cast
over them by French's orders, the magic of their verdant
campsite soothed and healed. "The valley is just about the size
for our camp," wrote Sévère Gagnon, "and there is a nice pasture for our cattle; it is all surrounded by hills and rivers; really the very place for a picnic."

FRED BAGLEY

July 26
Church parade a.m.
   The service consisted as usual of the reading by an
Officer of excerpts from the Scriptures, and the singing
of a few well known hymns during the rendition of
which the men seemed to be impressed with the solem-
nity of the occasion, but later on some of them shocked
the Commissioner with their ribald songs and speech.
   Oh well; "Single men in barracks (and camp) don't
grow into plaster saints."
   Our evenings in this comfortable camp were
enlivened by the music of a Band composed of a fife in
the capable hand of "Bill" Latimer, and a drum impro-
vised from a tin dish, and played upon with tent pegs by
that accomplished British Army drummer Trumpeter
Frank Parks.

The assistant surgeon, Dr. Richard Nevitt, who had returned
to Fort Dufferin in the first week accompanying William
Parker and the other man stricken with typhus, brought the
most welcome of all things from civilization, a fat pouch of
letters. He also brought shocking news. American papers were
reporting that the Mounted Police had been wiped out by the
Sioux. Colonel French was horrified. He rushed to his tent

---

* Of the total, Shurtliff, one officer and seven sick men were assigned to
stay at Fort Ellice.

and penned a long dispatch to Ottawa, assuring the government they were all still alive.

When Nevitt handed out the letters, Fred Bagley hopped eagerly from one foot to another, waiting for his. He was bitterly disappointed when the bag emptied with nothing for him. He tried to hide it but, for the first time, homesickness welled up in him. He didn't want to go back but he would have given a great deal to feel his father's heavy hand on his shoulder and hear his mother's comforting voice.

Bagley couldn't keep the covetous look off his face, watching the other troopers rip open their envelopes and devour the contents. Several of them felt sorry for Bagley and read bits of their own letters to him. Soon letters were being passed back and forth as if they were community property.

Bagley decided to lift his spirits with a little hunting but as a sub-constable, and the youngest one at that, he found himself at the end of a long line for the shotgun.

FRED BAGLEY

One shotgun had been issued to each Troop, and theoretically it should have been of benefit to the men, but, as some one remarked, "What is one shot gun among fifty men." Furthermore; officers' servants were many, and nearly all mighty hunters. And so...

NWMP camp at Roche Percée

JOHN MCILLREE

July 25

Did nothing in particular all day, but loafing round the camp. A good many ducks were shot by the men today....

July 26

Nearly had a stampede in afternoon owing to some one, by careless shooting, putting a bullet into one of our horses. Slept most of the afternoon. Went up to the top of the highest hill in the evening and the view was very pretty. Turned in early.

July 27

Still in camp.... Went out with gun in the afternoon but got nothing but hawks and muskrats.

In addition to shooting up the countryside, the men explored the unusual rock formations that gave Roche Percée its name. The half-breeds explained that a giant cavern beneath the monolith was an age-old Indian hiding place and sanctuary. On one rock they found a name etched that Fred Bagley excitedly declared was none other than that of the famous American Indian fighter, General George Custer.

HENRI JULIEN

This singular rock is a white sandstone of wind formation, running up like a crest from the bottom of the Souris Valley. At its base, it measures about 35 feet in height, and the base is about 140 feet. Some parts are softer than others, and from the combined influence of wind and rain, fissures and holes have been worn through it. On different parts of the rock are cut the names of people who have passed by and many hieroglyphics which, of course, remain a mystery to us.

Henri Julien had not suffered the men's dreary routine of

biscuits and tea. He was treated as an officer and throughout the march enjoyed a batman and officer's rations. But when Albert Shurtliff brought along a wagon load of pemmican, he felt it his journalistic duty to sample the concoction.

HENRI JULIEN

We had pemmican for the first time and found it very good. It is made by roughly pounding dried meat placed in a bag of raw buffalo skin with the hair outside. Boiling tallow is next pounded in. It then hardens and will keep for years. It is much improved by mixing cherries in it, and using marrow instead of tallow.

Dried meat, the jerked meat of South America, is prepared by cutting thin slices of the flesh along the grain and drying them in the sun, on willow or dogwood scaffolding. This will keep very well.

Both pemmican and dried meat are very wholesome. Indians and half-breeds will live on either for days and weeks and prefer it to any other prepared meats.

The marrow is prepared by breaking the bones and boiling them. The marrow floats and is poured into bladders. On cooling it hardens to the consistency of butter, and protected from the action of the air in bladders, it keeps very well. It is used instead of butter in the kitchens and on the tables of the half breeds throughout the North West.

Pounded meat is dried meat pounded till the fibre is all separated. It looks for all the world like short tow.* Eaten with marrow I found it delicious.

After the first sampling, the men and officers fell on the pemmican, declaring it "first rate stuff." In no time they cleaned out the entire wagon load.

Major Macleod, who tucked in with the rest, wondered how different their experience would have been over the last two

---

* Short tow are the ends left over after braiding or twisting flax and hemp into rope.

weeks if they'd replaced the heavy artillery guns with pemmican—conservatively, that would have provided two to three
weeks' extra rations; but most importantly, it could have been
eaten on all those days when there was no fire or the cooks'
wagons lagged hours behind. Their walking larder, the cattle,
had given them exactly one meal so far.

Sending the bulk of the animals north with Jarvis was the
right decision, but it gave Macleod the shivers nonetheless.
The cattle gave him a sense of security—once they were gone
there would be nothing to fall back on. When the "larder" left
on July 29, along with 25,000 pounds of flour and wagon
loads of other supplies, Macleod felt the line between survival
and death would narrow to almost nothing.

In Dufferin the troopers had spent three weeks assembling,
packing and loading for their long march. Here in Roche
Percée they had only a few days to dismantle it all. "At work
dividing stores for Edmonton, Fort Ellice and Bow river. Have
to superintend the whole work myself," Colonel French complained. Never a friendly man, he became increasingly aloof
and prickly. He spent hours drafting pages of orders for
Inspector Jarvis, instructions covering every possible contingency, including what to feed the men, how much and how
often. "Writing official reports and letters, sending off pay
lists &C., did not get to bed until after 12 and up again at
4:00 a.m," he wrote plaintively.

Chapter 8

On the Road Again

$\overline{A}$t 6:00 p.m. on Wednesday, July 29, 244 officers and men pulled slowly, noisily away from Roche Percée. Colonel French had decreed a 10:00 a.m. departure but the horses weren't in any hurry to be saddled and harnessed again. Though only a month old, the cavalry saddles ordered from England were starting to disintegrate. Packing in the panels had shifted, making the saddles lumpy and uncomfortable on the horses' backs. The harness buckles were rusting and corroding, and the troopers had to struggle mightily to thread straps through and fasten them. After an eight-hour "circus" the men finally wrestled the animals into their tack and traces, packed the last of their supplies and moved out to the bawling commands of their sergeants.

The troopers were fed, rested, clean and hopeful the worst of the march was over. Their horses had perked up wonderfully and the wagons were lighter since they'd left most of the heavy machinery and "superfluous" supplies behind. They still had over 600 miles to go, but they'd come 270 miles since Fort Dufferin and now they were seasoned, with calloused backsides and a far better idea of what to expect in the days to come.

As they departed, one man stood staring balefully at the retreating column. Sub-Inspector Sévère Gagnon's face displayed a mixture of dismay and anger. "My horses," he muttered woefully to himself as he watched them go. Gagnon always put the horses of his troop first. He hectored his men to clean hooves regularly, search for saddle sores, treat insect bites and bandage strained legs. And no matter what time they arrived at a campsite, he insisted his weary men rub the horses down and take care of any damage from the day's march.

Gagnon fussed and fretted over the animals, making constant trips to veterinary John Poett for poultices, liniment and other medication. The harassed Poett had his hands so full with dozens of ailing animals, that he turned over a portion of his medical equipment to Gagnon, telling him to handle all but the most serious problems himself. As a result of his care, Gagnon's A Division had the healthiest horses in the company.

After French decided to separate the troops, he personally selected the wagons, carts, livestock and horses that would accompany Jarvis. Gagnon was horrified when he discovered A Division's mounts were to be replaced by a selection of animals from other divisions. "[A]lmost every one is sick and many are the refuse of other troops," he moaned. "They have taken our horses from us and they were the best of the force. People would be amused to see these poor skin and bones horses and the heavy loads they have to pull."

Gagnon knew the temper of his division matched his own glum mood. It wasn't so much that they'd been left behind—cut adrift, the more uncharitable claimed—it was the formidable task they faced in the weeks ahead. How did they stand any chance of making it to Fort Edmonton, nearly nine hundred miles away, with such a small number of men, when marching only 270 miles from Dufferin to Roche Percée had almost destroyed the entire complement?

Inspector Jarvis had been left with Gagnon, Sam Steele, and eighteen constables and sub-constables, including Jean D'Artigue. Shurtliff and half a dozen sick men would ride along with them as far as Fort Ellice. As well as lightening the main Force's load, French saw his new plan as a way to rid himself of the most detested of the half-breeds. He assigned twelve of them, including the loathsome Mr. Drever, to accompany Jarvis. Somehow, with this handful of men, they were to ferry twenty-six wagons, fifty-seven ox carts with their sixty-three oxen, eleven breeding bulls, fifty-two cows and forty-five calves to Fort Ellice, then take half of those wagons, horses and supplies, and a third of the cattle on to Fort Edmonton. The prospect depressed even the most incurable optimists.

JEAN D'ARTIGUE

I learned from some of the men that the Apostle of Temperance was one of our party; and wishing to know what he now thought of the great wisdom of the Mounted Police, I was very anxious to see him. But I had some difficulty finding him; nobody could tell me where he was.

Giving up my search, I was returning to my quarters, when seated on a hill that faces Roche Percée, I beheld a member of the Mounted Police who appeared very much absorbed in thought. I went up to him, and, sure enough, he was the man I sought.

"Well my friend," said I, "I am very glad to hear that you are going with us to Edmonton." But, seeing that he took no notice of my remark, I shook him, shouting at this time: "Ha! father of the braves are you asleep." He lifted up his eyes, giving me a reproachful look, as much as to say: "how dare you disturb my reveries," and sorry to have gone so far, I was about to apologize for the liberty I had taken, when he now seemed to realize that no offence was intended, for his face assumed a mild appearance, and, as an answer to my enquiry, said,

"Would to God, I had never seen this day."

"Why, what is the matter with you?" said I.

"Why do you ask me that question?" said he, "don't you know as well as I? Have you not also been detached from the main column where glory awaited us, to go, not to Edmonton, for we can never reach there, but to

Fort Ellice, which place we may reach, but never pass, at least this year."

"But then," said I, "if we did not go, other men would have to go in our stead."

"All I have to say is this," said he, "if the corps had been well directed, it would not have been necessary to send this detachment to Ellice. All this is the result of having taken with us our supplies. Now the evil is without remedy, and if the whiskey traders are as well organized as they are said to be, the expedition will surely prove a failure."

This said, the templar resumed his thoughtful appearance, heedless of my presence. I therefore returned to the camp, reflecting on what a change had come over this man in so short a time. On our first meeting in the [train] cars, he was full of hope, and possessed a fine appearance; but now he was completely discouraged; his castles in the air had vanished, and his person displayed the utmost neglect.

"What is the cause of all this," thought I, and I found the answer in the mismanagement of our commander-in-chief.

While D'Artigue and his fellow troopers contemplated their fate, the rest of the Force marched off into the sunset. Despite the late start, they managed to cover nine miles in three hours, a respectable distance for the first march after a long rest. They camped that night at Wood End, a Boundary Commission depot on Long River.

All during their week at Roche Percée, the men had remained oblivious to the significance of the depot's name, despite the fact that Inspector Shurtliff had camped there for four days while waiting for the Force. That night Colonel French, while discussing the route ahead with the guides, discovered, to his dismay, the name Wood End meant just that— no wood beyond it. He hurriedly altered his plans. They would remain at the depot for a day to cut wood and bake enough rations for three days. "Biscuits," the men thought gloomily, when they heard the news. "More damn biscuits."

FRED BAGLEY

July 31, 1874

Road making parties very busy.... Long River consists mostly of small pools of water and a lot of mud. Loud guffaws from some of our cultured "Old Country" men when a senior Officer, erstwhile Major in the Canadian Militia shouts swampward:

"Are there any water down there in the Crik?"

The long layover at Roche Percée, the unexpected decision to send a party to Fort Edmonton and the unscheduled stop at Wood End ate away at the men's confidence, in Colonel French's judgment. Here they'd been on the road again, ready to eat up the miles, only to stop for an entire day to gather fuel.

Men openly wondered why wood-cutting parties had not been sent from Roche Percée, as many of them had been idle during their week's rest. And why hadn't the Colonel ordered a road-building crew to prepare a crossing of the Long River for them in advance? Those with a little more imagination began to question the reliability of the scouts and guides, who should have warned French that the depot marked the beginning of a vast stretch of treeless plain. Some of the troops, ignoring Colonel French's direct order, made only desultory efforts to gather wood. "Those troops who did not carry enough wood on their waggons are now beginning to feel the effects of their thoughtlessness," French commented smugly, five woodless days later.

None of these concerns made too deep an impression on Sub-Inspector John McIllree, who had more important things on his mind.

JOHN MCILLREE

Went down early in the morning and had a bathe in the Long Creek which runs through the valley, which I enjoyed muchly. Saw some fish and went down after breakfast to make war on them but after a couple of hours work and a good wetting, I gave it up as a bad job. We have not caught a fish so far.

A few days later, to his delight, a large flock of ducks, obviously not wise to the earlier massacre, appeared. McIllree's troop happily slaughtered a hundred with sticks and stones. Colonel French, in a rare moment of leisure, picked off twenty-five with his shotgun.

After a twenty-six-mile march on August 3, the men settled into camp at Everlasting Song Creek, only to be startled awake by the first storm in some time. It seemed as if the clouds had been saving themselves for a furious lashing. The men thought themselves old hands at the thunder and lightning business, but each one threw something new at them.

JOHN MCILLREE

August 3

Went to bed. It was lightening at the time. I had got to sleep, when I was woke up in a short time by the wind which was blowing a hurricane. The first thing I knew was the curtain of the hut blew up and I nearly got smothered with a load of dust and gravel. The next

John McIllree (fourth from left) on patrol, early 1880s.

thing was the tent went bodily up into the air, followed by my helmet and sundry tin plates, blankets &c. I grabbed my clothes and got some of them on and went about camp.

I could not help laughing. Nearly every tent was down, and the men were rushing round in their shirt tails or other equally classical costume trying to find their raiment. It *blew* and rained and hailed for some time and then it quieted down, and the clouds broke, and the moon came out and revealed our misery in full.

The only one who looked anyway comfortable was our Captain, Capt. Carvell who never stirred out of his bed. He has an immense oil sheet so he just rolled himself in it and lay quiet.

I was disconsolate at the loss of my helmet as I do not own anything else to put on. I was very tired so I crept under a waggon and was soon asleep.

HENRI JULIEN

My tent was blown completely away, and so were many others in camp, only one square tent remained in a semi-erect position.

These military tents are a fraud on the prairie, as we had more than one occasion to experience.

As usual, the half breeds managed such things better. There is nothing better than their low-roofed tent, with a base forming an oval and the door at one end. It is supported by two poles and a cross bar and measures 15 ft. in length by 11 in breadth. It is the warmest, easiest to set up, and all together the most comfortable.

Next day the troopers baled themselves out of the storm's aftermath and stuffed sodden tents and supplies into wagons. It made for a miserable day. The heavy, wet canvas increased the pulling horses' load and the troops, riding in front, churned up the muddy track, which bogged down the wagons even more.

Shortly after stopping for lunch on August 4, John McIllree, manfully shrugging off the loss of his helmet, made a joyous discovery. Not far off, he spotted a small herd of beautiful antelope on the rise of a hill. His blood surging, he checked his ammunition and waved at fellow sub-inspectors Jack French and Cecil Denny, to join him in the hunt. Henri Julien hurried along behind.

HENRI JULIEN

August 4, 1874

The deer had begun to show themselves in considerable numbers, and we were naturally looking out for some sport to relieve the distressing monotony of the march.

Five antlered beauties approached the outskirts of the camp in a body. Jack French, scenting the battle from afar, made for them. He crept along slyly, carefully in true Indian fashion, till within 400 yards, when Denny went rushing down like mad, scaring the animals away.

Jack French was so furious that he felt tempted to give the intruder a taste of his load, while the sporting qualifications of "Texas Jack," as Denny was nick-named, became the byword of the force. That night, we had pemmican instead of venison.

DR. RICHARD NEVITT

He [Denny] is to begin with an Englishman, son of an English Clergyman. Dean Denny (I believe) of Exeter. He has been in the States for some years and according to his own story has spent a good deal of money there trying to farm.

He is young, only 23, and fine looking with quite a handsome face. He is quiet and gentlemanly in his deportment. He might be called a little strange at times, but I suppose, he like others gets a fit of the blues at times. He is very generous to me and as far as I can learn to all others.

The officers, at least some of them, tease him a good deal about his American experiences and he is given to drawing the long bow at times. But he is very consistent and sticks to a story no matter how improbably it might appear.

That night a disconsolate, and much abused, Cecil Denny went to bed, dismayed that his reputation as an avid adventurer and skilled outdoors man, which he had worked so hard to cultivate, was in tatters. The next day "Texas Jack," assigned to rear guard, mooched morosely along, his mind drifting and his eyes half focused on the horizon. Then something moving in the distance drove him upright in his saddle. Antelope! He looked around quickly to see if anyone else had spotted the animals. But the rest of the men had fallen into that state of semi-somnambulism that overtook most of them each day after several hours on the trail.

Denny had to make a fast decision. Should he go after them himself or recruit a few good shots to bring the antelope down? He opted for greater glory. He would bag a fat specimen and triumphantly present it to French and McIllree, both of whom had been ignoring him since the unfortunate incident. No one noticed as Cecil Denny reined his horse and cantered off.

With his eyes fixed on the antelope and using the hillocky land to shield him, Denny carefully swung wide to approach them from behind, keeping downwind. Anticipation tingled his spine. Then his horse's head dropped forward and Denny, who'd been fixated on the antelope, quickly gathered his reins and urged the animal on. The next moment he pitched forward and his horse squealed in panic. How odd, he thought in a brief instant of clarity; there is no hole or rut, this is solid ground—why am I falling? Then everything dissolved into frantic thrashing.

Quicksand sucked the horse down to its knees, belly, then withers in seconds. Denny somehow vaulted out of the saddle, scrambled furiously like a giant spider to find solid footing and lay panting with fright on the ground. He gasped as he watched his horse disappearing. The animal finally settled, entombed in a death grip, grunting in terror and discomfort. Only its head was visible, poking bizarrely out of the ground.

Denny tried to grab the bridle but he couldn't get close enough. What a fiasco. First he'd messed up the hunt and now this—he'd never live it down. At least his nickname, Texas Jack, though facetious, had a hard-nosed ring to it—he shuddered to think what the men would call him after this.

As Denny glumly considered his reputation, it suddenly occurred to him that he couldn't see any sign of the other troops. He wondered, in addition to his other problems, if he were lost. "Hello! I say, anyone! Help!" he hollered again and again. The breeze took his words and scattered them. Denny turned slowly around, willing himself to calmness. He remembered riding hard to the west to get behind the antelope—but where was west and how far had he ridden? He traced the route with his finger in the dirt, figuring the angles and looking at the sun. That way. Pointing himself in what he hoped was the right direction, he resolutely trudged off.

Denny walked for hours without finding a trace of the Force. His feet swelled and his throat ached with thirst. He could hardly believe it when he saw a figure far ahead, a man riding and leading a horse. But the man was moving away at an angle. Never had Cecil Denny run so fast. As he got near enough to make sure the figure wasn't an Indian, Denny painfully cleared his parched throat and, after a few false starts, produced a serviceable yell.

Major Macleod wheeled around and grabbed his carbine when he heard the shouts.

Then he relaxed as the exhausted Denny collapsed at his feet, as if in worship. "Sir, oh thank God!"

"Would I be right in assuming you need help?" Macleod queried, once Denny had righted himself.

"Help's not the half of it!" Denny exclaimed. He described the desperate straits of his horse and told Macleod he doubted if the poor animal was still alive, or even if they could find him. "Though I marked the spot as well as I could," Denny added.

"Let's see if we can find him again, shall we?" Macleod said calmly, handing over the reins of his spare horse.

Some hours later they were both a little surprised to discover the horse, head still sticking out of the sinkhole as if it had recently been decapitated. Macleod had spent so much time helping stranded wagons and bogged-down oxen he'd taken to setting out each morning with a spare horse fitted with a lasso harness. After several missed attempts, he tossed a loop around the animal's neck and tied the rope to his harness. Both men and the horse pulled and heaved. The stranded animal did nothing at first, lethargic and resigned to its fate. But as its rescuers raised it a few inches, the horse tasted freedom and fought furiously to dig itself out. Finally it struggled to firm ground, alive, but unable to carry a rider for weeks.

While Cecil Denny had had enough excitement to keep him jittery for days, the rest of the men yearned for some diversion. As the memory of Roche Percée's lushness and bounty rapidly retreated, the days collapsed into each other and the monotony of the prairie drained their energy. The men began to feel as if they were marching on a treadmill.

HENRI JULIEN

The effect of this loneliness upon the imagination is very singular. The eye dwells on vacancy, tired at glancing at the blue sky above or the brown earth beneath. A feeling of weariness creeps over you, interrupted at intervals by vague longings for something beyond the far low line of the horizon, which is ever barred across your vision.

The silence is oppressing. It is in vain that you attempt to relieve the tedium of conversation with your companions. Besides that, the stock in trade of chatting is soon exhausted in these wilds, whither nothing from the other world reach you; the very labour of talking becomes tiresome and you fall to meditation. You throw the reins on your horse's neck and let him jog at will, while your eyes roam over the waste and your thoughts wander as the winds.

This has truly been called the "Great Lone Land." Its silence and its solitude weighs on you like a mechanical power. The breeze circles around your brow and bears no odour of flowers on its wings. There are no green trees even on the water's brink, and hence no wild birds carolling among the boughs. It is a real desert; a land of desolation; and it will remain such until the white man settles upon it and turns the waste into a garden.

The men of the North West Mounted Police would not have been cheered to learn that one of their number wasn't suffering at all from boredom.

> Dufferin
> August 4th/74
>
> My Dearest Father
> Did dear Mother receive my letter that I wrote to her from here about five or six weeks ago. I think I wrote it in pencil, if so were you able to make out the writing. I have much to be thankful for since then, as I have had a very severe illness of Typhoid fever, but I am getting quite well & strong again now.
> ...one of the two fellows that was sick, named Fortescue, sergt Major of B or A Troops is nephew to the Archbishop of Canterbury, so you see we have some gentlemen in the force as well as some cads.
> This is a great place for wild flowers the place now is very gay with beautiful marigolds & other flowers. In fact I have a beautiful nosegay right in front of me now which I gathered this morning & they are quite a treat in the house.
> We heard of the force some time ago that they were going along capitaly & were over three hundred miles from here & about sixty miles south of Fort Ellice, the men were in good spirits & the horses holding out good. This is a good country for sport, plenty of prairie chickens, & pidgeons. There is also a beautiful little lake about a mile from here which is always covered with wild ducks, so when I get well I shall likely have some good sport as I have my faithful gun with me. Now Dear Father I think I must conclude with fondest & best love to you all
>
> > Believe me
> > Ever your most affectionate son
> > Willie Parker
>
> Remember me to all my old friends

Henri's Adventure

Since the second day of the march, Colonel French had been plagued by the nagging feeling that his guides didn't really know where they were or where they were going. Shortly after leaving Roche Percée, the nagging intensified into near panic. "On Monday my sketch of the Boundary Commission Road will give out," he admitted in the privacy of his diary, "and I shall be completely in the hands of the guides who will, doubtless, make marches in accordance with their lazy ideas of a day's work."

The next day French confronted his guides in an attempt to determine exactly what they knew. It was a task he'd attempted many times in the past, but the half-breeds were so skilled at evasion and so unwilling to give a straight answer that they usually slid out from under his interrogation. But this time French came armed with a new tactic. "Had a long pow wow with guides. Found that one of them was a regular imposter, by asking him the distances apart of certain places, knowing the true distance myself. This one says he speaks Blackfoot, I hope his Blackfoot will not be such an imposition."*

The Colonel's worst fears were realized two days later, on August 4. The Boundary Commission Road, which they'd been following since Dufferin, ended and promptly the whole Force was lost. Welch, one of the older guides, confidently insisted that they'd soon find their way again, but the Colonel became more and more exasperated as they rode aimlessly for miles looking for any sign of a trail.** By the time they found the hint

---

* Colonel French didn't expect to arrive at the Cypress Hills, on the edge of Blackfoot Territory, for another three weeks, but he was distressed to think that once he got there he might not be able to communicate with them.

** Little is known of the half-breed or Métis guides. When they are mentioned it is usually only by their last names, which vary considerably in their spelling. Henri Julien took the most interest in them. "Welse [Welch] was a Scotch Métis, who understood neither English or his father's Gaelic, but jabbered all the Indian languages, Sioux, Cree, Assiniboine, and weighed 235 pounds, and, though over 70 years of age, had not a grey hair on his head."

of an old route, everyone was exhausted and bad-tempered.

The problem of direction grew even more acute because the Palliser map French carried, and notes from the Boundary Commission, indicated they were approaching a hellish range of rocky hills that rose to several thousand feet above sea level. It was imperative they find the easiest route through, in order to save the horses. Every day the terrain, though treeless, grew more rugged with rock strewn everywhere and ravines, carved by ancient rivers, taxing the men and horses to the limit. In Roche Percée they had found coal for the forges and were able to repair the wagons and re-shoe the horses. But they couldn't carry much of the coal with them, and the horses could not continue on such rough ground without good shoes.

COLONEL FRENCH

> After leaving the B.S[urvey] road, I surveyed our route as well as (under the circumstances) I could. It entailed on me a very large amount of extra work. I had to be on the alert to take the altitude of the sun and find our latitude. I plotted out the work and marked it on Palliser's map. At night I had frequently to wait up until 1 or 2 a.m. to obtain the magnetic variation of the pole-star.

Colonel French kept meticulous track of their progress via his prismatic compass and an odometer attached to his personal wagon, but knowing where they were had little to do with knowing how to get where they were going. By now the guides' failure to guide and the scouts' failure to scout had become abundantly clear to the men, who were keenly aware that zigzagging their way west would not improve their chances of reaching Fort Whoop Up before winter.

Being lost on the seemingly endless prairie was a secret fear of many of the men—a considerable number of whom had become separated from the main body at one time or another. Those assigned to heavy wagons, broken equipment, ox carts, the artillery pieces or sick horses inevitably found themselves plodding anxiously along, far in the Force's wake, eyes squinting ahead, hoping to catch a glimpse of other troopers.

Many privately wondered if the entire Force, spread out as it was over miles, and riding tired horses, could do much more than hold off a surprise attack of Indian warriors. But no one believed they'd survive an encounter with the Indians alone or in one of many small groups that were regularly separated from the main column.

JOSEPH CARSCADDEN

I shall also remark that although the Commissioner was so careful of himself and his men whilst travelling thru the dangerous parts of the Blackfeet country—arming the men and supplying them with ammunition—he did not scruple to leave single men out on the prairie, alone for days and nights together.

Now if there could be any danger for 300 men in a foe's country what would there be for 1 or 2 men? And often would single men be ordered to remain behind with some old sick horse or ox.

When one or more troopers didn't show up in camp at night, the drill was to fire rocket flares to help orient them. But French habitually waited as long as possible lest the flares upset the horses or set fire to the prairie. The first night out of Wood End, when a trooper went missing, an over-eager sub-constable had lit a rocket and sent dozens of horses stampeding out into the night. It took the men hours to round them all up.

On the evening of August 4, the Force arrived at their campsite, only to find themselves short two men who'd been riding with the main body. Normally French wouldn't have worried much about it, confident they would straggle in eventually. But this time was different. One of the missing was Henri Julien. It was one thing to misplace a trooper or two, or a half-breed, but losing the Force's official artist would be difficult to explain to his superiors in Ottawa. French had the camp combed. No Julien. The last anyone had seen of him was in the early afternoon during Cecil Denny's unfortunate antelope-hunting episode.

HENRI JULIEN

I was bound to have my own private adventure, and I had. I started one afternoon, with Page, one of our half breed guides, for a duck hunt on the prairie. About five o'clock in the afternoon, we came to a lake which, to our delight, we found covered with coveted birds.

Page had a shotgun; I had only my rifle. His chances were, in consequence, far superior to mine. He took up a position on one side of the lake and plied his weapon to his heart's content. I went over to the other side of the water in quest of adventure. Sitting on my horse, [Old Rooster] hardly expecting such success, I spied a fair chance at a shot, and, aiming my rifle, I brought down a duck, stricken to the heart with a ball. Too well pleased with my success, and forgetful of the risks which I ran, I immediately leaped from my saddle, dragging my horse by the bridle, I turned to the water's edge.

...[A]s I stooped to pick up the duck from the margin of the lake, the horse seized his opportunity and broke away, as a civilized horse would have done, he scooted away in a directly opposite line. Nothing would do but I must take after him. He did not go fast, being intent on teasing me, rather than anything else, so I ran along side of him, but whenever I reached out to seize the bridle, he would shy his head, kick his heels, and look around me, as if to say "O no, not if I knows it."

I ran about 8 miles, dropping my duck in disgust on the way. I was amused at first, then I got vexed, then I swore, but all was useless. At last, resolved upon being philosophic and employing strategy I got ahead of Old Rooster and got up a conversation with him.

I promised him all sort of things, and talked to him like a father. He was actually fooled. He turned his head to make sure that I was in earnest, when I made a desperate plunge and seized the bridle. He had sense enough to see that he was fairly caught and he fairly capitulated.

I got on and struck for the line of march. But here another disappointment presented itself. Instead of continuing the direct route mapped for the day, the caravan had deflected at an acute angle, and after several hours ride I failed to come up with it.

As twilight turned to black, French stirred the camp into an uproar over the missing artist. The half-breed had since returned to camp and, when questioned closely, revealed exactly what French expected—nothing. Page pointed out the general direction of their hunt, and mentioned the lake, but refused to take responsibility for a man silly enough to go charging off into the wilderness without waiting for his companion. The half-breed claimed to have had a good look around for Julien but failing to find him did the only sensible thing in his opinion—returned to camp and ate his supper.

Inspector Brisebois led a squad up and down the column but found no sign of the artist among the stragglers. French ordered rockets sent up and then astounded everyone by commanding that one of the guns be readied to fire. After dragging the cursed things for an entire month, they were finally to earn their keep. With every man holding horses, the ninepounder split the night air with its bark. Still no Julien.

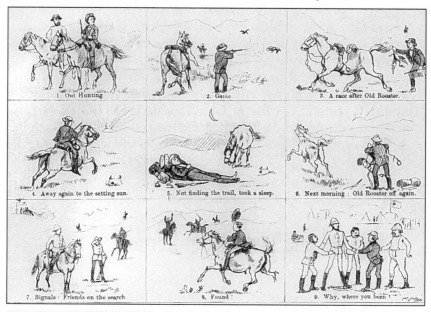

Henri Julien's adventure with Old Rooster

It was now far past sunset, night was gathering in its shadows, I was tired and I made up my mind to give up the pursuit for the evening. So I halted in a sheltered hollow, dismounted, made a pillow of my saddle, tied down my horse with the bridle to his pastern, and stretched out to sleep, supperless, wearied and disgusted.

The mosquitoes were buzzing in the millions. I wrapped my hands in two handkerchiefs, thrust them in my pockets, covered my face, and still they pestered me beyond endurance. The next day my hands and face were all blistered. I slept thus as best I could till about three o'clock; next morning I awoke to find that my rascally horse had broken from his fastenings and had scampered off over the prairie. Another chase and another series of vexations. At last I caught him about six or seven miles from where I had left my saddle.

As dawn broke, a search party pulled out of camp. Within an hour a yell went up as a small, forlorn figure appeared in the distance. Julien was a slender man and careful about his appearance, even in the wilds. But after his night alone he seemed to have shrunk by half. His hair stood on end, his clothes were filthy and his face was smeared with dirt from his futile efforts to ward off mosquitoes.

Julien attempted to affect his usual *savoir-faire*, but no one was fooled. Trembling visibly and babbling slightly, the artist couldn't contain his joy at being rescued. He smiled as they rode into camp and the men cheered his arrival. But beneath his bravado and sun-blistered skin lay the discernible pallor of fear.

Old Wives and Played-out Horses

FRED BAGLEY

August 6
Marched at 6 a.m. About 11 miles and halt at coulee at

11 a.m. In afternoon some, but not all, reached summit of Dirt Hills. Steep climb took severe toll of animals, especially gun horses. Column scattered all over the Hills. At least 10 miles distance between advanced parties and rear Guard. Column split up into a dozen small camps.

The Dirt, Dirty or Dung Hills, as the men variously called them, were almost the undoing of the supply end of the Force. The five-mile, thousand-foot climb proved impossible for many of the wagons and the artillery guns. The horses that did make it to the top just stood for a time, legs splayed, heads down and coats mottled with sweat and lather from the 90-degree heat. No amount of whipping and cursing could get the guns up, and the artillery detail was forced to spend the night on the hillside until reinforcements came from the main body in the morning.

Colonel French had no alternative but to order a day of rest. For once they were fortunate enough to find a campsite with wood, decent water and food. A lovely and unexpected spring at the top of one of the Dirt Hills proved an excellent spot for drinking and provided a rare delicacy—frogs. They were as thick on the ground as ducks had been at the massacre site a few weeks earlier. The first troops there eagerly snatched them up, stuffing them into sacks and carting them back to their camp-fires. Joseph Carscadden and two others from his troop collected and devoured 150 of them, "and it was the most delicious meal we had on the march."

The men lamented the loss of the Professor, Jean D'Artigue, to Jarvis's company, since he undoubtedly would have given an impromptu lecture on the preparation of a complementary sauce and the selection of a correct wine to fully enjoy such a feast. He might even have been prevailed upon to describe a similar repast, *avec la mademoiselle*, on the banks of the Seine. "I soon lost my prejudice against the French for eating frogs," admitted Irishman Edward Maunsell.

The first day past the Dirt Hills, Colonel French, as was his habit, ranged up and down the column, reprimanding shirkers and ensuring that every trooper rode for no longer than an hour before walking. His horse stumbled over a clod of dirt, unearthing a bony protuberance. Something about it made the

Colonel dismount and pick it up. French slapped his riding gloves against it several times to reveal a skull, long since bleached and picked clean. He shoved it into his saddle-bag for later examination.

At their camp on the bank of Old Wives Lake, the Colonel took it to one of the Métis.

"Well, Paul, what do you make of this?" asked the commissioner. "I can't tell if it's an Indian or white man."

The Métis took the skull from the Colonel and examined it carefully from every angle, then declared that it was certainly an Indian—perhaps one of the Cree women who gave this place its name.

By now, a number of other half-breeds had joined them and freely offered their own thoughts on the skull's origin. Amid verbal flourishes and gesticulation, the story of Old Wives Lake emerged. Years before, a party of Cree passing nearby had in their group a number of old women. They made camp that night but were barely asleep when sentries alerted them to the presence of Blackfoot.

At this point, a brief but spirited argument sprang up among the Métis. Half maintained that it was a party of Assiniboine not Cree that had abandoned one of the old women who was hindering their progress. The other half, just as vigorously,

Crossing the Dirt Hills

argued for the story the way it was being told. Finally, it was agreed that the second story would be told in full after the first; that way everyone could decide for himself which version he preferred.

The Cree men, women and children hurriedly slipped away, leaving the old women behind to pretend that the camp was still occupied and provide whatever token resistance they could. The ruse worked, allowing the band to escape. The Métis, whose story-telling ability was well-known, drew a crowd of men and officers eager for a diversion.

"Please, what happened to the women?" asked Fred Bagley.

"Dey dead," responded the Métis. "Maybe here's one."

"This is barbarous, infamous, cruel!" exclaimed Henri Julien, who'd joined the throng. "Imagine abandoning the aged and infirm to their fate. Heartless. Absolutely heartless."

"Damned right, Artist," exclaimed Carscadden loudly. "Absolutely barbaric! Filthy practice! Never catch us leaving anybody behind. No, sir. We're civilized people. Would never leave anyone behind." The last was spoken to the Colonel's rapidly departing back and the stunned silence of the onlookers.

Colonel French was forced to call another halt on August 9 at Johnson's Lake. It was only one day after the last rest stop but French had pushed the pace to thirty miles the previous day. As a result, a large number of the wagons didn't arrive until midnight, with a sizeable contingent not getting in until the next morning. The men were grateful, as many had been stricken once again with diarrhea and some could barely get on their horses, let alone walk one hour out of every two. But no amount of digestive upset could hold John McIllree down.

JOHN MCILLREE

Got up at 6 a.m. and was agreeably surprised to find a nice sandy beach to the Lake. I took a walk for about 2 miles along the beach. Saw geese, ducks and plover and stoned a skunk to death.

Had a bathe on my return but the water was very shallow. You had to walk out about a quarter of a mile or more before you could swim. The water is very alkaline and it rather upset our constitutions both men and beasts.

After dinner I took the gun and went for a walk, but I got nothing but a lot of big plover. Saw a very good mirage in the evening. It looked as if a big island was floating down on us and it lasted some time.

The game from Roche Percée and biscuits from Wood End hadn't lasted long. By the time they reached the Dirt Hills, most of the men were reduced to small bowls of porridge for every meal and the officers were warned to cut down their bacon rations. Even the dreaded biscuits were endangered as the baking powder barrel was nearly empty. Fortunately, they were fairly close to the Boundary Commission depot at Wood Mountain and with a little luck the depot would have rations to spare.

The only man French felt he could rely on to get there and back in the minimum time, with the maximum supplies, was Major Macleod. He gave him ten men, a train of wagons and bowed to the inevitable—pemmican. The frontier staple he had spurned in Fort Dufferin, in favour of cattle to be slaughtered en route, was now essential—especially since the cattle were gone. After six days of hard riding, Macleod returned with 4,700 pounds of pemmican and baled dried meat. They would have to parcel it out carefully though. Even 4,700 pounds would not go far among 244 hungry, overworked men.

Increasingly, the deteriorating horses preyed upon Colonel French's mind. After jettisoning the excess equipment at Roche Percée, he had been convinced he had enough animals to get him to Fort Whoop Up. But only fourteen days later, when the North West Mounted staggered into a campsite on Old Wives Creek, four horses died almost immediately and another lingered for a day before finally giving up. The men didn't look much better than the horses. Their uniforms were invisible under a coating of trail dust, caked thickly in their underarms and clotted in their neck creases. The crotches of their breeches acted like catchment basins for sand and soot and their faces were smeared with dirt and blood from mosquito bites. Any square inch of cloth that showed through sported a variety of food stains—since the men had no cutlery, it was difficult to be fastidious about table manners. Buttons were missing, seams split and bony knees poked through holes in their breeches. Their boots were the worst of it.

A few men had kept their own boots, against orders, and with their government issued pairs, they were in good condition from the knees down. But the rest struggled with broken heels and soles beginning to crack from miles of walking over hard ground in riding boots meant only for stirrups.

In contrast, the Colonel was always impeccably turned out. He prided himself on his ability to maintain his and his horse's appearance. He thought it so crucial for the morale of the men that the commanding officer look commanding that he kept his batman currying his horse and attending to his kit for long hours.

Sooty Sons of the Plains

Fred Bagley was blue. He'd left home nearly three months ago, on fire with dreams of adventure. But thirty-six days into the frontier, he had yet to find any. Granted, they'd had stampedes and storms and all the promised privation and more, but the heart-stopping thrills of the Wild West eluded him. Where were the whiskey traders, the gun fights, the buffalo and most especially the Indians? Where was the romance?

Bagley tried to cheer himself up with a review of his conduct and deportment, which he modestly concluded had been exemplary. He drove and trudged alongside his oxen from breakfast to midnight on many days and had become so skilled he could harness them as quickly as the half-breeds. Bagley rode better than almost anyone and had marched until his feet were bloody. As he demonstrated his strength, skill and stamina, he found the older men increasingly treated him as an equal.

Though Fred Bagley's previous life had been calm and sheltered, he discovered, to his great pride, that he possessed a cool head in an emergency. A few days earlier, while driving his ox carts across a corduroy bridge, his second ox lost its footing. Grunting and scrabbling to maintain its balance, the ox tipped the cart, which sent the animal somersaulting over the edge. With legs locked, the other oxen braced themselves against the drag. Bagley leapt from his seat and peered down, horrified to see the squealing animal dangling upside down with the goods from the cart scattered into the muddy creek.

Bagley took stock. He'd faced a similar situation when he first started driving the ox carts, but this time he was alone, and something had to be done immediately. There was no hope of being unexpectedly rescued by Major Macleod—not twenty minutes earlier he'd seen him galloping off in the other direction, doubtless on another errand of mercy. He knew he had no hope of pulling the ox back onto the bridge, and if he didn't act fast, the stricken bull would pull the whole lot down after him. He ran back to his cart and dug out a knife. Grimacing and muttering apologies to the poor beast, he sawed through the traces and watched as the ox fell bellowing into the creek, where it landed with a great crash, remarkably unhurt.

Bagley earned praise from the troopers, officers and even a back slap or two from the half-breeds for his bravery and quick thinking. It made him feel better about the dried meat he'd stolen earlier and secreted in his pockets to chew on during the long day. The ox incident certainly ranked as adventure, but not the sort Bagley had dreamed of during training in Toronto and Fort Dufferin. More than anything he fantasized about rescuing an Indian maiden. But to date, he hadn't caught sight of an Indian of any sort, maiden or otherwise.

Jean D'Artigue, heading north with Inspector Jarvis' party was somewhat less thrilled at the prospect of confronting the red man.

JEAN D'ARTIGUE

After leaving Roche Percée, I did not sleep in the tents with the other men, preferring to sleep outside, under a waggon or a tree. And that night, after spreading my blankets under a waggon, I laid down, placing my loaded carabine on my right side, and my revolver on my left....

I dreamed that we were encamped where we were in reality; that I was under a waggon, and I saw Indians crawling like snakes thorough the grass and coming towards the camp. Taking hold of my carabine, I tried to rise, but in vain, I could not move. I then attempted to shout, but could give no utterance. I was in great agony, which was increasing as the Indians were getting nearer and nearer.

Already I could see their painted faces, their naked breasts, and their heads adorned with hair and quills. When within fifty yards of the camp they suddenly made a bound which was followed by fearful yells that no pen can describe. Death stared me in the face. I collected all my strength to rise, and this time succeeded so well, that I fell back senseless to the ground, having knocked my head against the axle of the wagon.

When my senses returned I was still lying on my back, the carabine grasped in my right hand, and the revolver in my left. Everything was still with the exception of the horses which were tied to the waggons and eating grass we had mowed for them the night before. This was only a dream, but of such a horrible nature, I did not care for a recurrence of it.

On August 12 at Old Wives Creek, Fred Bagley's wish finally came true. An Indian. Only one, but word rippled through camp that this Sioux brave was an emissary sent to greet them and announce that his chief wished to hold council the next day. The troopers had heard many stories of Sioux ferocity, but the Indians were so small in number—only seven teepees,

Sioux camp at Old Wives Creek

containing about thirty men, women and children—and so obviously friendly that everyone immediately relaxed.

Colonel French extended an invitation to meet the next morning and feverishly set about preparing for the visit, personally checking and double-checking all preparations. He was determined to impress upon the Sioux his authority and his peaceable intentions. He knew that Indians loved ceremony, so he would put on a good show. That afternoon, a detail of men busied themselves, erecting two tents and joining them to form a large pavilion and making rough benches for French and the senior officers. Another group unpacked gifts—trinkets, tobacco, cloth, etc.—that Lieutenant-Governor Morris had sent along for negotiations with Indians. Colonel French carefully instructed his orderly on the proper preparation of minutes, with a precise inch of margin on each side of the page.

Fred Bagley's depression was gone as if it had never existed. Tomorrow he would be one of the buglers to trumpet their arrival. At dawn Bagley was awake, madly sprucing himself up, shining his bugle and preparing for the great event. At ten French sent a messenger to inform the Indians that the chief of the Red Coats was ready to take council with the Red Children of the Great White Mother. They walked sedately towards the pavilion in a single line, the chief in front, carrying a special shield attesting to his position, and the wives behind. As they walked, the Indians chanted a long, low rhythm, loud enough to be heard above the trumpets.

Fred Bagley had difficulty concentrating on his job of heralding the Indians. For one thing his lips were so blistered, cracked and swollen from the days of wind and sun, he could barely purse them, let alone press them against the mouthpiece of his bugle. For another he was so fascinated by the Indians he couldn't keep his mind on the notes. The Sioux arrived at the makeshift pavilion and solemnly shook hands with everyone.

HENRI JULIEN

We at first met them with closed lips as we did not know what to say. The usual How-do-you-do would have sounded ridiculous and the Happy-to-see-you would have been a lie on our lips, as they were a most wretched lot of the grand and proud Sioux.

However, we soon got into the How of our red brothers and "How, How" in higher tones was heard all round. After they were squatted, the men on one side of the pavilion and the wives on the other, the pipe of peace, of red stone, inlaid with silver, and having a long flat stem, was filled with kinnie by the chief's henchman and passed around filling the air with white smoke and peculiarly agreeable odour.*

Col French had his staff and other officers about him, all in full uniform, some sitting on rude benches and others—myself among them—squatted in front of the Colonel's table in the most approved fashion.

The force were elbowing each other outside of the entrance, trying to get a glimpse of what was going on inside.

For half an hour they smoked, neither side saying a word. Finally a warrior, acting as the chief's spokesman, rose to speak, in Sioux. Pierre Léveillé laboriously translated the Sioux into English and then in turn translated the Colonel's words into Sioux. The process was slow as his facility with Sioux was shaky.

"The great spirit gave the land to all his children," the man declared grandly. "We want to know why you come here and where you are going. All who have hair on their chins are rich; we have clean chins and are poor. I am telling no lies. We had horses and land on the other side, but the Yankees lied to us. They gave us drink and killed us and took our lands away. The Sioux wished to keep quiet, but the Yankees wronged them and drove them away with their big guns.

"England never did that to their red children. What now is wanted? We have nothing to kill the buffalo with; we want guns and ammunition, we can get nothing without arms; nothing to use against the Yankees when we go against them. They will kill us.

---

* From kinnikinnik, a low-growing aromatic shrub.

"We heard you were coming, a big man. I will get my children to help you where you go."

When the Sioux finished his speech, the Indians again shook hands vigorously with everyone in the pavilion. French took this as a sign to reply. "My brothers wish to know why we come this way," French began. "I will tell you. The White Mother who lives beyond the great waters sent me. She heard the Yankees came to kill you and give you bad whiskey."

Fred Bagley sat in the back of the tent making himself as unobtrusive as possible. He had been assigned other duties but couldn't resist the lure of their first Indian powwow—attending was worth the risk of being put on report. But events weren't proceeding as he'd fantasized. Though the Colonel was orating with a solemn and funereal air, the group of Sioux next to him were chattering back and forth and periodically breaking into laughter.

Bagley had expected the Indians to be awed or, at the very least, respectful. As he stared at them, trying to determine the cause of the levity, one of the braves turned and winked broadly, just like a white man. Shocked, Bagley glanced around to see if anyone else had caught the exchange. But all continued as before—had he imagined the wink?

"The White Mother has white children, and red children, and black children," French continued sonorously. "She loves them all alike."

The great powwow

As the Colonel paused to allow the interpreter to catch up, the brave who had winked uttered a rapid string of Sioux, which was followed by the wildest eruption of laughter yet. But this time the Indian turned to Bagley and said sotto voce, in very distinct English, "Well, it seems to me the Great White Mother must be a bitch in heat that lays with any cur."

Fred Bagley wouldn't have been more shocked if Chingachgook had materialized and kissed him full on the lips. He didn't know whether to be insulted and demand satisfaction over this great slur on the Queen's rectitude, or laugh. He compromised by maintaining a disapproving silence and a cold glare.

"She sent these braves to punish those that kill them," Colonel French continued, motioning towards the troopers standing guard. "We have been travelling in this direction for three moons, and will go on for the space of another moon. We want to capture those who killed the White Mother's red children. We do not want the land of the Dakota nor anyone else's. We have guns only for our warriors but will give you ammunition, calico and tea."

French presented the Indians with over ten pounds of black plug tobacco, flour, cloth, tea and flint with promises of ammunition to come. The Sioux received the gifts graciously, carefully counted everything, wrapped it all in a blanket, then left the pavilion.

Colonel French was delighted. His first powwow had gone without a hitch. The Sioux had seemed particularly appreciative of his personal assurances that they would be protected. "The interpreter tells me that this party of Sioux have given me the name of Wachasta Sota, which signifies, I believe Man with Power," he wrote happily in his diary.

JOHN McILLREE

The Indians came over and had a pow wow this morning. It was not at all an interesting affair. There were no big Chiefs and the speakers were poor and our interpreter was poor. We sat and looked at each other for about half an hour and smoked, when one of the braves got up and shook hands all round, saying how-how or something like it. He then proceeded to make a speech commencing by wanting to know why we were coming through their country, which was a beastly piece of cheek as they are Sioux that have been driven out of the States but they ended by begging for flour and ammunition.

Two or three made speeches and professed great love and esteem for us. We gave them some flour and calico and powder balls and flints, and after sitting and looking at each other for another half hour, they left.

They are a very plain, dirty looking lot. The women are very ugly and the boys about 16 or 17 are decidedly the best looking.

Fred Bagley didn't give a fig what others thought of the Sioux; they were Indians, the real thing, his first contact with the frontier denizens. Perhaps a little grubbier than he'd imagined and less exotic in their appearance than he'd hoped—no bare-breasted Indian princesses—but they were Indians and that was enough for a fifteen-year-old in the Great Lone Land.

Bagley spent as much time as he could lurking around the Sioux when they came into the Force's camp, which was often. The second day of the Sioux visit Joseph Carscadden, of the razor tongue, strolled up to Bagley, who was talking with several other troopers. Carscadden told them he thought the Indians were around so much, poking into everything and generally making themselves at home, they might as well be offered a commission in the Force.

"Oh! Look out!" Carscadden warned, silencing their laughter. "Nonentity approaching."

An officer joined the men and stood companionably with them as they watched the small group of Sioux squatting around one of the division's camp-fires.

"I say," he remarked. "I have been studying the language of these savages. I do declare they sound exactly like Irishmen."

The men looked at each other, not knowing whether to laugh or take him seriously.

"Yes, indeed," piped up one of them. "I do believe you are exactly correct. In fact, just yesterday I listened to them myself and I know they are pure Irish for I heard one of them call the other Dick Murphy."

"Indade and begorra!" said the officer in a mangled accent. "They are Irish, I am now sure of it."

Carscadden shook his head in wonderment as the officer walked away.

"Can you believe it?" he said, casting his eyes to the heavens. "This is a being we have to obey. Of course, no one ever said officers are required to be intelligent. Perhaps it is better for us that they are not."

JOHN MCILLREE

After breakfast took the gun and went for a walk. I went for about 6 miles down Old Womans [Wives] Creek and when I got that far I had nothing. The Creek was nearly dry and there were very few ducks and those very wild. I came across a small lake then where I shot 8 ducks in a few minutes, and I could have shot lots more but it was very hot and I did not care to carry more. I had a wash and a rest and struggled home to camp. The Prairies are on fire on the West side of the Creek and are burning furiously.

Lots of the Indians loafing about camp. They are a horrid nuisance. They come in and sit down in the tent, and they will not budge for hours. They are a nasty begging lot and will sell anything they have got. I always thought the Indians valued their scalps and would not part with them, but one of our men got one for two plugs of tobacco.

Dr. Kittson could hardly wait to get his hands on the Indians. What a clinical cornucopia they presented! What specimens! He saw right away that they were riddled with delicious medical conditions. It would be a challenge to treat them and record their responses to white man's medicine. It meant a paper at least and perhaps an appearance before a prestigious medical congress. But first he needed permission.

The chief consulted their Pa-ge-we-chas-ta (Medicine Man or more correctly Herb Man) and came to the conclusion that they would allow the pale-faced Medicine Man to treat their sick, and a good proportion of the whole number was immediately paraded in the Chief's capacious Lodge—three men and five women.

The men were affected as follows:—One case of Pannus (Blooded Eye), nearly blind. One case of Sciatica of seven years standing (effects of a fall) and one case of Shaking Palsy (Paralysis Agitans). These were not encouraging and the women less so. Two cases of confirmed Dyspepsia and three cases of Phthisis....

I had ample occasion to exhaust the Medical Service on these poor unfortunates, but to no purpose. With one exception they all gave up my Prescriptions after a few trials.

This exception was the case of the Sciatica; he was blistered, cauterized, injected hypodermically; he seemed to delight in the agony, but to no purpose, and I fear the reputation of the pale-faced Medicine Man to be a low ebb among the Sooty Sons of the Plains.

That such diseases as Consumption and Dyspepsia should be common among the Indian Women did not surprise me, two diseases which, par excellence, follow in the wake of want, hardship and exposure. The cruelty they have to bear at the hands of their Lords and Masters is incredible. Pope must have had them before his mind's eye when he wrote the lines:

"Fixed like a Plant on his peculiar spot to draw nutrition, propagate and rot."

I was repaid by getting lively specimens of their "blood purifiers," [lice] a great nuisance to the Prairie wanderer and against catching them it is useless to guard one's self. They lie dormant on Camp grounds, long deserted, and brought to lively and tormenting activity by coming in contact with a warm body. We got rid of the few we caught in this place by the free application of Mercurial Ointment.

Fred Bagley was desperately envious of the constable who managed to trade for a scalp. He would give almost anything for such a trophy, though he'd never be able to show it to his mother. Unfortunately he, like most of the men, had little to offer, having sent virtually all their personal effects back to Dufferin on the second day of the march. If he thought he could get away with it he would have traded his bugle and claimed it had been stolen, but the risk of getting caught was too high and, in any case, he had already been put on report once for misplacing it. Men pulled buttons off their uniforms, scrounged tobacco and cast around for any object that might tempt the Indians, but not be missed by the Force. Bagley managed to scrape together enough bits and pieces to trade for two pairs of moccasins soled with thick buffalo hide. He got them in the nick of time; the only thing holding his riding boots together was strips of rawhide wrapped around the boot uppers.

The Indians gestured to him and waved their bows and arrows. Bagley wondered if they wanted him to shoot, or perhaps wanted to shoot him. The Sioux set up a target and took turns plugging it with arrows. Bagley was so enthusiastic he clapped and cheered every time they hit the mark. He would have liked to try but was unsure of how they might react. The Sioux behaved as if the camp, and everything in it, was available for their use. But he wasn't sure if they felt the same about their own belongings.

After the shooting demonstration the Indians, men and women, formed themselves into a circle and began chanting and singing. Then the dances began. First one for rain and then one to celebrate all the scalps they had taken—and would take.

"What're they saying?" Bagley asked one of the half-breeds who arrived to watch.

"Dey talkin' 'bout war and all peoples dey killed. Dey say dey squash Blackfoot under moccasins. Heroes, dey all big heroes. Now dey gonna tro' all white men out of country, kill 'em too, I guess."

Bagley's eyes widened.

"Not you," the half-breed hastened, "Redcoats okay."

The troopers applauded heartily as the Indians hopped and weaved back and forth. After the dances ended, a group of men jumped to their feet to show off their own skill with a little impromptu jump and bump. Apparently offended, the

Sioux sat down and watched stoically, neither smiling nor clapping. As the men grew more raucous, determined to out-hop and bob the red man, the Indians, disgust plain on their faces, stood up and left.

HENRI JULIEN

For the fellow who had fed his mind with Cooper, Schollcraft, Longfellow and other poets or novelists, the sight of the Indian himself is a disappointment. In vain do you look for the type of a Pontiac or an Uncas. Still less are you blessed to behold a Pocahontas or a Minnehaha. The men are dirty and ugly, low browed, dull eyed and brutish in appearance. The women, even the budding girls, have not a single feminine grace. The men must be hard up indeed who takes such for a wife.

And still, like their sisters the world over, these women put on airs. They have a certain grotesque coquetry about them. They cast sheep's eyes at you, and squint to see whether you are admiring them. If they catch you laughing at them, as is generally the case, their black eyes flash fire of indignation, and they strut away with an approach to offended dignity.

PART FOUR

Den of Iniquity

CHAPTER 9

Interlude

JOHN McILLREE

   August 17

Pemmican is first rate stuff. It is buffalo meat chopped up small and run into skin bags with melted fat, when it becomes a *very hard* compact mass. Another small band of Sioux came in today, and they all moved to the N of us about 2 miles.

It is great to see their procession. They have a few carts and for the rest, they cross some of the tent poles across the ponies' backs with the ends trailing along the ground and their goods tied across on the poles. The dogs are harnessed up the same way on a smaller scale. The horses are led by the women and naked boys.

Major Macleod was delighted at how the pemmican and dried meat heartened the men who dug into it with such gusto and capacity that Colonel French cut them off, sequestering the remainder for emergency use. Macleod felt confident that the pemmican would stretch their stores enough to get them to the Cypress Hills, where the half-breeds assured him they'd find more game than an entire country could eat. But would the horses make it? If they failed, no amount of pemmican would save the Force.

While at Wood Mountain, the Boundary Commission quartermaster, Captain Herchmer, had told Macleod he had excess oats to sell. When Macleod returned on August 10, Colonel French agreed he should go back and collect a load. On the fourteenth Macleod set off again with sixteen carts. Though he knew the Colonel might baulk at the expense, even during these desperate times, he decided to buy every cup of oats the Boundary Commission could spare, regardless of the price.

Once the decision was made, he reasoned, it would be difficult to overturn.

COLONEL FRENCH

> I find he has purchased 60,000 lbs. of oats from the Boundary Commission, and, although the price is high, I approved his purchase.
>
> Oats, at any price, is a Godsend to the poor horses. I purchased a fine horse from Herchmer. Macleod got a poney, and I got five from a half-breed.
>
> Every little helps.

Major Macleod made record time, travelling almost non-stop, getting to Wood Mountain and back in three days, with the wagons pulling into camp a day behind him. Four days later he set out again, this time with Sub-Inspector James Walker, twenty-seven men and twenty-seven ox carts, for the Boundary Commission depot at White Mud River a little farther west, where the rest of the oats were stored. Nine days of hard riding later Macleod's party, wagons overflowing with oats, caught up to the Force.

The Major's three arduous trips in the August heat added three hundred miles to his own personal log. Each time he returned, the men greeted him with loud cheers. Macleod enjoyed the fanfare but privately rued the abysmal command decisions that had made the trips necessary in the first place. If the senior officers, including himself, had made even a few correct decisions in the beginning, the Force wouldn't have been continually short of food, water, fuel and fodder. When he was feeling particularly gloomy, Macleod concluded that if they'd made even one correct decision before starting out— finding a single person who'd actually been where they were going—they wouldn't be in such a mess now.

The arrival of the oats was particularly fortuitous. Since leaving the Boundary Commission trail, the Force had to build its own roads through terrain that became progressively hillier as they marched west. Fatigue parties cut gentler approaches to rivers and coulees, constructed bridges and created rope systems to lower the heavier wagons down sharp inclines. Though they had little progress to show for it, the men and horses were pushed to the end of their endurance every day— no man or beast could keep that up for long. Colonel French thought he had unloaded all the excess at Roche Percée but he was forced to lighten the load once again.

COLONEL FRENCH

August 19

Marched about 9 to a pond about 2 miles north west of our old camp; formed a depot there, leaving Constable Sutherland and 7 men (5 of whom were sick), also a half-breed, 26 sick and weak horses, and a dozen wagons. Marched 12 miles more in the afternoon, and camped on creek.

The gun teams doing well. The boundary commission horse and the stallion drawing well.

With their typical rough humour, the men named the outpost Cripple Camp. But the implications of leaving a small group of ailing men and animals to fend for themselves on the edge of Blackfoot territory wasn't lost on the troopers. While five sick men were being marooned at Cripple Camp, one of the invalids who'd been sent back to Dufferin in July, was making do.

WILLIAM PARKER

Dufferin
August 19th/74

My Dearest Mother

I hope you were not frightened when you heard of my recent illness. For your dear old boy Will is again on his pins, I am happy to say, and is very nearly as strong as ever he was. I have a splendid appetite and as we live very well here, there is no doubt about me being my own self again.

We are very jolly here nothing much to do, there are

five of us altogether, one Sergt & four men, all the work we have to do is to attend to three horses & cook for ourselves which is very easy as we have a nice kitchen to do it in.

In a few days I expect we shall be having some grand dinners as I am going to get out & shoot prairie chickens, which are very plentiful around here. Mr. Almon invited me to dinner one day last week they are quite fashionable up here dinner at six, it was the first time that I tasted prairie chicken they are delicious, something like a pheasant in size & taste, I spent the evening there & enjoyed myself very much.

> Ever your affectionate son
> Willie Parker

As they pressed on, a new irritation plagued the men. Swarms of flying ants descended on them, winnowing under their clothes, flying up their nostrils and stinging them in the tenderest places. When they sat down to eat, the ants flew into their mouths and covered their food. But, since their meals had once again declined to a biscuit, a square of dried meat and muddy tea, the problem was minimized.

JOSEPH CARSCADDEN

August 22nd

Marched 25 miles and halted at Slap Jack Hill; so called from the peculiar nature of the cakes baked by our cook here. It may seem a slight thing to name a place by, but reader, remember that slap jacks are no slight treat for a starving man.

One of our men found the large shoulder blade of a Buffalo and labelled it "Diamond's Spoon." This man Diamond was a big fellow, and his mouth being in proportion, his comrades thought this bone would save him much time in eating.

As always, the more enterprising tended to miss fewer meals.

FRED BAGLEY

August 22nd

Raining all last night. Buffalo chips wet. So no meals.
But carts containing the bales of dried meat are
unguarded, so we fill our pockets with the brittle dried
meat, and carry on...no fires no supper.

Colonel French had fussed and fretted every day for six
weeks about their daily mileage, or more correctly, lack of it.
Suddenly, inexplicably, on August 25 he lost his compulsion to
push as far ahead as fast as humanly possible. During the next
three weeks the Force covered only 114 miles and didn't
march at all on twelve days.

Despite the slow pace and frequent stops, the Colonel was
remarkably sanguine, almost as if he were relaxing on holiday.
He worried less, became more interested in his surroundings
and found the leisure to hunt more frequently, to the dismay
of certain officers. "Stopped about 10:30 where there were
any amount of duck. The commissioner got there ahead, shot
a lot and frightened the rest away," the sportsman, John
McIllree, wrote peevishly in his diary.

Everyone agreed that the Colonel was a marvellous shot
with any weapon he took into his hands. Once he'd potted
twenty-five ducks on the wing, a feat no one else in the troop
could hope to duplicate. On another occasion he'd brought
down a giant white pelican that stank of fish and measured
eight feet from wing-tip to wing-tip. The creature caused quite
a stir until Joseph Carscadden sourly related Coleridge's story
of the Ancient Mariner who shot an albatross and was cursed
to spend eternity

> Alone, alone, all, all alone,
> Alone on a wide wide sea!
> And never a saint took pity on
> My soul in agony.

Towards the end of August, after ten days of non-stop trail
building, the Force came upon the steep banks of Strong
[Swift] Current Creek, rising out of the Cypress Hills. Having

learned the lesson of the plains rivers, they immediately sized this up as a particularly hazardous crossing, with erosion having created a precarious overhang at the lip of the bank and a fast-flowing stream below. French ordered a fatigue party to level their approach to the water. No sooner were the men at work when they stopped to gawk at a singular sight: the Colonel himself, pick in hand, digging away furiously in their midst. Shortly, most of the men were leaning on their picks and shovels, watching their commissioner work harder than any two of them put together.

The Colonel's brother, Jack "Irish" French, rode up.

"An' is it standin' there ye are an' lookin' at the Commissioner workin'?" he boomed.

The younger French's sally raised a great roar of laughter among the men, who dug into their work with unaccustomed vigour. Jack French, though he had a temper like a flash flood, could raise a smile in anyone, including his brother. He was gifted with all the personality and easy charm the Colonel lacked. During the worst days of the march, the men responded to his wit. No matter how late they arrived in camp or how awful the conditions, a rich Irish baritone could be heard calling out to his batman.

"Did you fayed my horse yet, Hardy?"

Every night Hardy would reply, "Yes, sir, I fed him."

"Well, fayed him agin, that way you'll be sure of it."

As they neared the Cypress Hills the troopers began encountering more traders, heading back to Fort Garry. The first group of them had appeared while they were still parlaying with the Sioux, and the men vied for the chance to conduct a search for whiskey. Ouillette, the half-breed owner of the wagon train, submitted with a gracious but amused smile as a battery of men turned his eleven carts inside out, finding not a drop of liquor. A week later they came upon a train of twenty-six carts and three traders camped at a nearly dry creek bed. Several officers and a party of men did their duty but, again disappointingly, no sign of the evil liquid. "Honest traders!" remarked Henri Julien approvingly.

It didn't occur to the officers or men that the traders were going the wrong way to be loaded with whiskey. Any wagons heading south or east of the Cypress Hills would naturally already have sold their contraband.

The day they conducted their second whiskey search, the Force met up with two more traders camping in the middle of a field of three-foot-high cactus. With them was Père Lestaing, a Roman Catholic priest travelling to Fort Edmonton. Clad in full—though dusty—regalia, he caused quite a stir among the men, who were getting a little sick of the sight of each other. He met with the commissioner and agreed to hear confession for the Catholics among the men. Even Joseph Carscadden, who had little truck with authority figures of any kind, pronounced the no-nonsense Father "agreeable" after a brief conversation.

The next day the priest solemnly wished them all well and encouraged them to think of God in the days to come. Kindly, he neglected to add that he believed they would need a great deal of help from the Almighty if they were to survive. Three weeks later, Lestaing met up with Inspector Jarvis's party, which, contrary to all expectations, had not only made it to Fort Ellice but was slogging mightily towards Fort Edmonton. The men listened eagerly as Lestaing gave them news of their comrades, but his final words hit them like a fist in the gut. The priest had been appalled at the troopers' condition. His nineteen years on the frontier told him that it was highly unlikely the NWMP would ever reach their destination.

Searching traders' carts

A Métis accompanying Père Lestaing was the brother of Pierre Léveillé, one of the Force's guides. French immediately offered him a job, eager to engage anyone with the faintest idea of the country beyond the Cypress Hills. His confidence in his guides had ebbed so low that he hauled Sub-Inspector McIllree off his wagon and Texas Jack Denny out of the rear guard and sent them out searching for anything faintly resembling a road or trail. They might not know anything about the route ahead, but French could at least count on them to tell the truth about what they found. A week earlier he had hired on another scout, but quickly doubted the wisdom of his decision. The man showed up with a guide Macleod had hired at Wood Mountain to help them get through the Hills.

Unlike the other half-breeds, who gave a faint nod to civilization in their dress and manner, this one looked and behaved as if he had lived every second of a hard life in the wilderness. Dressed in skins, with a bushy beard and wild hair, he earnestly told French he had trapped in the vicinity of Fort Whoop Up and knew the country well. The Colonel didn't like the look of him, but he was desperate. No amount of dead reckoning would get them to the Bow River, which would lead them to Whoop Up. He needed someone who could distinguish one barren hilly lump from another and then find the easiest way through them.

FRED BAGLEY

A man named Morrow or Moreau of "Dan'l Boone" like appearance and garb, came into camp with one of Colonel Macleod's guides, and although he is suspected of being a spy of the "Whoop Up" lot Col. French engaged him as a scout.

The new guide raised a shiver of excitement in the men. For the first time, here was someone who had actually been into the whiskey traders' dens of iniquity. The fact that "Dan'l Boone" Moreau was taciturn and kept to himself only enhanced his allure. When they could get him to utter a word or two, what Moreau (a.k.a. Morse) said sent Bagley's heart

racing.* Parcelling out sentences as if they were precious
gems, the guide told them he had seen the whiskey traders
barricaded behind fortified block houses that were connected
to underground magazines and hiding holes.

French didn't trust the new guide a bit. He was suspicious of
the man's convenient appearance just as they approached the
Cypress Hills, where many traders sold their whiskey. The day
after he hired on, the guide asked permission to leave camp
and retrieve some ammunition he'd cached. When he didn't
return precisely on time, the Colonel sent Inspector Jacob
Carvell and Acting Constable Bill Latimer to arrest him.
Moreau reappeared just as the pair set out and French rescind-
ed the order, but his suspicion remained.

The men were torn between their own interest in the scout
and the Colonel's obvious distrust, until Dan'l Boone won
them over a few weeks later with some skills he'd learned to
while away winter nights in snowbound cabins and tents.

JOHN McILLREE

Doing nothing in particular. Nothing to read and nothing to do, the latter something wonderful to relate.
Went to sleep in afternoon. Our guide went out and
shot an antelope.

In the evening we were amused by our scout Morrow
performing some slight of hand tricks which he did very
well. He also gave us a most perfect imitation of a musi-
cal box. He did it some how with his throat and his fingers in his ears for notes. It was very well done.

Moreau also brought some sensational news from Wood
Mountain. He reported that the depot had been recently
robbed by Sioux and, in a separate incident, some Indians and
one white man had been killed on the Boundary Commission
Road. The white had been tied to a tree and tortured to death

---

* Like many of the Métis or half-breeds, this man is referred to only by
his last name, which is spelled many different ways in the various
accounts.

by knife slashes. The work was attributed to Blackfoot Indians who "did not fancy our coming into their country."

With Blackfoot territory looming, the news galvanized the men, who suddenly developed a keen interest in the care and maintenance of their carbines. The Colonel issued lengthy and detailed orders to tighten security—for once all hands obeyed with alacrity.

FRED BAGLEY

As these Cypress Hills are the stamping and fighting ground of Gros Ventres, Sioux, Crees, Assiniboines, Bloods, Piegans, Blackfeet and Sarcees it is considered "enemy" Territory, extra precautions are taken to ensure the safety of the Force, by increasing the Guard by adding 30 more men to it, and by placing sentries in the lines of each Troop, and a cordon of sentries surrounding the camp.

Horses are to be kept within the lines each night and not to be turned out to graze until daylight. Extra ball ammunition is issued, and orders given that every man must sleep in his ordinary clothes, and keep carbine and revolver ready for immediate use if necessary.

Fred Bagley's enthusiasm deflated considerably when he was assigned to advance guard. The Force was moving so slowly because of all the road work that the advance guard could precede the line on foot, so Bagley, as trumpeter, stumped along, instrument in hand. The duty was particularly onerous because they'd entered a part of the country where the mud adhered to the feet like glue, building up until the men felt as if they had anvils attached to their boots. Not only did the walking exhaust him, but it gave him no opportunity to filch snacks from the wagons.

As they marched deeper into enemy territory, the Colonel formed a mobile Lancer Troop to protect the advance guard and ensure that no one slipped through their cordon. As an additional precaution, the men were ordered to march at all times in their scarlet tunics and belts so they wouldn't be mistaken for American cavalry.

"Looks like business," noted Sub-Constable James Finlayson hopefully.

Romance Returns

SEPTEMBER 2

It was only mid-morning, but Fred Bagley was exhausted. He had blown reveille at 3:00 a.m. and he'd been walking one hour, riding the next, since seven. His feet were in good shape and the mud didn't stick to his Sioux moccasins as readily as it did to boots, but he'd rather be doing almost anything than walking. The last two days had been cold and rainy—at night he'd wakened often, gripped by a chill that made him ache with the effort of shivering. Fortunately, their last campsite had good wood and passable water, which meant fires to get warm by and hot tea, with fewer of the muddy additives they found at so many watering holes. It was pure pleasure not to have to strain the inky water through his shirt.

Fred Bagley pondered his fatigue. After all, they'd marched only thirty miles in the past seven days and though there was endless road work, he was getting plenty to eat, thanks to the pemmican. Bagley concluded it wasn't the work that tired him, it was boredom. Ever since the Indian excitement at Old Wives Lake, the monotony had ground away at him. The days had become indistinguishable, just like the rolling, treeless terrain.

They had seen very few Indians and, with the exception of the traders and that very nice priest, virtually nothing of any note had happened. Previously, when he had time on his hands, he'd found hanging around the half-breeds the perfect cure. But lately those usually happy-go-lucky souls had become testy and ill at ease. When he tried to steer conversation around to the Blackfoot, they clammed up entirely. As he was ruminating about this sad state of affairs, he heard a horse come up from behind. He swivelled his head—Colonel French.

"Good morning, sir," he said brightly. Bagley always tried to be bright with the Colonel.

"What do you make of that out there?" French asked, pointing to the horizon where Bagley could just barely see a dark mass, moving slowly.

"I can't make it out, sir. Maybe they're Indians," Bagley said eagerly. That made sense, since their last campsite had recently been vacated by Indians. Judging by the quantity of debris, there must have been hundreds of them.

The Colonel rode out to the left flankers of the Lancer Troop and Bagley could see them conferring. Suddenly, French spurred his horse into a flat-out gallop. Bagley heard the men shouting but couldn't make out the words. Behind him a great commotion erupted as Major Walsh shot out of the ranks, driving a wagon and lashing his team for more speed. Two of the scouts appeared out of nowhere and quickly caught up to French. Then Bagley heard the cries. Buffalo!

COLONEL FRENCH

I took a carbine from one of the men, and made after them, headed them and turned them towards the train,

Buffalo hunt

fired at one which dropped back, and was despatched by someone else; three went across the creek, I went after them, and was joined by the Scout Morreau and Levallèe [Léveillé], we shot each one.

I fired into the Scout's buffalo as he stood at bay, and dropped him. This was a very fine beast about 10 years old. He made when dressed, 953 pounds ration meat.

FRED BAGLEY

Buffalo steaks for dinner and supper. Gorgeous. Some of the men could not wait for the meat to be cooked, but ate it raw. Half-breeds cutting slices to carry on. There being no grass or water we made about 20 miles without halting....

John McIllree was riding listlessly near the front of the column when he heard the shouting. His heart leapt as the cries of buffalo reached him. No more puny prairie chicken, ducks and plover. This was the real thing—buffalo! McIllree spurred his mare towards the source of the action at a dead run. He pulled her up just as a rifle went off and he saw a huge animal pitch forward onto its knees. McIllree was bitterly disappointed his gun had not brought it down.

JOHN MCILLREE

There were some more going over the hills but they were too far and I did not want to blow my mare. It turned out that there were six bulls and the Colonel headed them off and brought them back pretty close to the line of waggons.

There was some great shooting and between them they managed to shoot five of them. We cut them up and got the meat on ox carts.

We made about 15 miles and camped for [the] day in a hollow surrounded by hills where there was a creek and a good spring.

Any amount of buffalo meat for dinner, tea and everything else, but it was beastly tough. These were all old bulls. Night quiet and not so cold.

At first, Henri Julien had surveyed the action from the safety of the ranks. His ordeal out on the prairie had lessened his craving for the hunt. But buffalo were different. He must bag one; what a story to take back to his friends in Montreal. The next day he rode over to two of the troopers—a pair who seemed to have a reasonable grasp of horse and gun—and suggested they try for a kill. They wouldn't go haring off like maniacs, they would do it scientifically. The three men pulled away from the column and headed for a series of gullies and bluffs, hoping to surprise some animals hiding there. They moved quietly and stealthily but saw only rocks.

HENRI JULIEN

My comrades fell back, but determining not to be balked, I took courage and "went it alone." The road was very discouraging. The declivities and ravines were covered with boulders and cut up with holes. Scrambling through as well as I could, I rode on in that direction and was rewarded by the sight of a grand skedaddle.

Three fine bulls leapt up from their lair and darted across the plain. Of course here was my chance and I followed.

Two of the stronger bulls got away from me, but the third remained within range and I let fly at him. My first shot took effect, but it did not retard the progress of the goaded animal. So away in his wake! A second successful shot, but still the brute pushed forward. He fell on one knee as he felt my second ball, but immediately rose and fled for his life.

I pushed a considerable distance and had a third shot which proved fatal. The noble animal stopped, fell, quivered and died. My companions standing on a hill watched my chase in the prairie below and when they beheld my success sent up a cheer. When I got off my horse to survey my victim, I found that I was nearly half dead myself.

Riding at such a pace over rocks and drifts, holding a heavy rifle poised in my hands, loading and firing, anxiety and a keen desire—all these had completely exhausted me, my back was nearly broken, my knees and ankles were peeled.

And my poor Old Rooster, to whose honour it must be said, that he did his whole duty on that eventful day, his flanks and belly steamed with sweat and blood. In my excitement I had spurred him unmercifully, and my rowels were all bent.

For the next two nights camp was livelier than it had been in weeks. The men debated about the taste of the buffalo and traded opinions about the massive animals. They were all awed by the size of the beasts. The great brown bodies lying still on the ground were larger and more powerful than anything they could have imagined. The sheer quantity of meat was staggering. Though few had been impressed by their first look at Indians, the thought of bringing down one of these giants with mere bows and arrows instilled in them respect for the red man.

Seventeen hundred and twenty pounds of meat from two buffalo disappeared quickly into the bellies of the men. Without rationing, the ravenous troopers easily wolfed down up to five pounds at each meal. But Colonel French's pleasure in the hunt was spoiled by the usual men for the usual reasons. He was furious to discover that nothing remained of the other three buffalo brought down by the half-breeds. Instead of dressing the meat, as ordered, the half-breeds had merely sliced off enough for their own use and left the carcasses where they lay. When he reproached them for their lack of frugality, they shrugged, telling him that if they needed more meat they'd shoot another buffalo. The Colonel stalked off, fuming.

It was a sore point among the men that only the officers, the half-breeds and the artist got in on the first buffalo action. But the scouts assured the eager men they'd get their chance. These buffalo weren't even a herd, just a few renegades away from the main group. For the next five days every eye in the

Force watched the horizon keenly and every carbine sat lightly in its place. On September 7 the men were rewarded.

The call went up and reverberated through the ranks. The officers could not have contained the onslaught if they'd wanted to. This time there were at least fifty bulls, cows and calves, and not a man in the Force intended to let them get away without contributing a bullet to their deaths. Every trooper on a horse thundered off in chase of the buffalo; drivers leapt out of their carts and wagons and ran on foot. Within moments, the cavalcade looked as if a tornado had whipped through it and snatched up all signs of life as every piece of equipment was abandoned in the communal hunt lust.

Somehow none of the men got winged during the fusillade—enough bullets flew in the next thirty minutes to wipe out a small town. John McIllree was ecstatic as he helped bring down three buffalo. But he wanted his own and galloped his horse for three miles after some surprisingly speedy cows before they gave him the slip. One trooper howled with rage when his ammunition gave out; he clubbed his prey with his rifle butt until another rode up and finished off the charging beast. The din was terrible—cows bellowing, calves bawling, bulls roaring, rifle reports and men screaming and shouting in exultation.

The old bulls among the herd put up a valiant fight. If they weren't killed on the first shot, they wheeled into their tormentors, scattering men and horses everywhere. And once they got their dander up it could take a dozen or more shots from the carbines to finish them off. More than a few troopers were pitchforked over an enraged buffalo's head.

Even the terminally sceptical and professionally unimpressed Joseph Carscadden found himself caught up in the frenzy.

JOSEPH CARSCADDEN

We were crossed today by two large herds of Buffalo after whom all our mounted men gave chase, you may guess we had a lively time just then; we killed 20 cows & 1 old Bull that nearly took the lives of several of our men before he gave up, those old bulls fight desperately for life and woe be unto him who wounds them slightly and is not prepared for the result.

The bull comes bearing down on his enemy and if you have not a good horse to leave him behind with, or a good rifle to finish his day with you may calculate upon going up pretty high in the air on his horns, unless the hunter is a very good marksman, the rifle will not save him as a flesh wound merely adds fuel to the flames and enrages the animal more and more.

I should here remark that from the peculiar construction of the Buffalo, a novice would think that he was taking a fair aim at the beasts heart, when such an aim would no more carry that bullet to the animals vital parts than it would to heaven, the Buffalo has got a false backbone, I cannot call it by any better name, this false or top bone is about 1 foot above the real back bone in large animals....

The simple novice will fire about 8 inches too high, which spot is protected by numerous oval bones which fence off the bullet and flatten it as a stone wall would.

Into the Valley of Death

The buffalo blessed the troopers with bountiful meat and their chips provided fuel in a woodless territory. The food came at a critical moment. Their pemmican was now almost gone, and other supplies were so low that Colonel French ordered the baking powder ration reduced for the second time in so many weeks and flour cut to two and a half cups a week per man.

But for everything the buffalo gave, they took away more. Though men had full bellies, the quantity and richness of the meat, after weeks of privation, caused a volcanic upsurge in diarrhea. And what the buffalo provided in meat for the men, they took away in forage for the horses and water for both. They had gnawed to the roots what little grass the fires and drought had left behind, and they churned every water hole into a muddy wallow flavoured by urine and feces. One otherwise pristine water hole was spoiled by a huge rotting buffalo carcass lying in the middle of it.

The very availability of the meat created problems. Killing the beasts took time and energy. The Force was slowed by the hunt, and the chase tired the horses even further. Then the carcasses had to be skinned, dressed and loaded into wagons to be carted back to camp. The men had to hunt regularly because there wasn't enough salt to cure it all, nor enough barrels to store it.

But the most serious problem caused by the buffalo was psychological. From the first kill on September 2 to the mass hunt on the seventh, the officers and men of the NWMP were gripped in a collective euphoria, enthralled with the hunt, the kill and the feast. The buffalo made all their other troubles seem to vanish. But they didn't.

The men were still wearing down as they marched an hour and walked an hour. Their stamina was still eroding day by day under the burden of heavy road building. The horses were still teetering on the verge of collapse. Grass was still rare and the oats that had kept the animals alive to this point were gone. The men seldom had either wood or water, much less both. And underlying it all was a new threat—cold. A crust of ice had appeared on the water the morning of September 6.

Even with their stomachs full of buffalo meat, two months on the march had begun to exact their toll in earnest. Every night that first week in September a few more men didn't have the strength to put up their tents. Others were too exhausted to eat supper or strain the foul mud for tea. Even the most dutiful had trouble staying awake on guard duty. Many were put on report and fined for dereliction of duty as they lost their carbines, misplaced bullets, forgot to hobble their horses, dozed in the saddle or fell asleep driving the wagons. Some began having difficulty accomplishing previously simple tasks like saddling their horses. Piece by piece the North West Mounted Police were falling apart. But their infatuation with buffalo masked the breakdown and obscured the now everpresent danger from Indians as they moved into territory claimed by the Blackfoot but constantly invaded by the Sioux, Assiniboine and Cree.

After the Force's first contact with the Sioux on August 12, no one took them seriously as a military threat. Even Jean

D'Artigue, who had had nightmares about them in anticipation, dismissed them after laying eyes on the dreaded warriors of the American West.

JEAN D'ARTIGUE

> But the Indians were so effeminate, one would never have thought that they were of the same nation that had a few years before committed such depredations in the State of Minnesota.... [T]hey did nothing but encumber our camp, with their squaws and papooses, and devour the remains of our meals....
>
> "For Sioux," said a sub-constable one day, "they seem very cowardly."
>
> "The word cowardly is not expressive enough," said the Apostle of Temperance, "if all the Indians resemble them, I tell you frankly that I would not be afraid to meet a score of such braves."

The half-breeds disagreed strongly with the troopers' contemptuous dismissal of the Sioux, cautioning that you couldn't judge them until you saw their ferocity in battle. Despite the reports they had received in Fort Dufferin of Sioux raids and atrocities and the warnings from the half-breeds, the NWMP, to a man, were convinced these Indians would cause no more trouble than a group of children at a Sunday picnic. No extra guards were mounted, no additional ammunition was handed out, and the Force allowed the Sioux to roam about their camp fully armed.

A suspicious frontiersman might have interpreted the Sioux's keen interest in the NWMP camp, the men and, most particularly, the nine-pound guns, as a military reconnaissance.

After Old Wives Creek Sioux sightings became so commonplace, not even Colonel French bothered to comment on them. The Force came across campsites recently abandoned by several hundred Indians, and they frequently spotted them crossing the trail, far in the distance. Little did the men know it, but the Sioux's presence had a purpose. Even when they weren't visible there were indications they were around. Numerous inexplicable stampedes plagued the troopers. The situation became so serious that French ordered the men "to keep all horses tied up after dark, no matter how little chance they may have for feeding." Still, they managed to bolt.

But one savvy Indian fighter among the Force eventually came to the right conclusion.

FRED BAGLEY

> Our half-breeds suggested a snake in the grass was the cause, but it is more likely that it was the proximity and smell of Indians, who although out of sight of us have been watching us all the way through the Cypress Hills.

On September 4 the Force had been so preoccupied with watching out for buffalo and road building through the hilly terrain that when the Sioux launched an attack, no one noticed. After a fifteen-mile morning march, the main body stopped for dinner at 1:00 p.m. They moved on again at three o'clock just as the stragglers were pulling in for their break. The main body pushed on for five more miles before a deep, long coulee stopped them cold; they wouldn't be able to cross it without considerable grading. Colonel French elected to make camp at the bottom, while the fatigue parties levelled

Sioux on the march

the incline on the other side. The remaining troopers roped the wagons down the slope with their wheels tied off. It was a precarious business and they nearly lost the guns, in spite of dozens of men on every rope as they were lowered.

The Force was oblivious to the fact that fifty Sioux warriors had been shadowing the column since dawn. Vantage points were excellent in the hilly terrain studded with coulees and ravines. As they watched patiently, the Indians amused themselves discussing the Red Coats' horsemanship and wondering why the hapless ones always seemed to choose the most difficult route. In the morning the Red Coats passed a number of ideal ambush sites, but the Sioux war chief elected to bide his time. Though the Force spread itself out more with every hour, both horses and men were still relatively fresh; late afternoon or evening would give them a greater advantage.

The afternoon played itself out perfectly. The bulk of the men were far out of earshot, occupied in getting the wagons down into the coulee; five miles away a group of vulnerable stragglers plodded along.

It would be a classic Sioux ambush. The Indians slipped down the back of a hill and up the far end of a ravine that the Red Coats would soon pass. They'd wait in the ravine until the perfect moment, then gallop up as one to overwhelm them. Before the whites knew they were being attacked, they would be dead. With luck no one would live long enough to sound an alarm. In any case, the main body was too far away for a rescue.

Just as the first riders were emerging from the ravine, an Indian pony stumbled and a sharp-eyed sub-constable caught the movement. Fearing they were Blackfoot, the sub-constable shouted out the alarm and twenty troopers clumsily converged into a skirmish line, carbines drawn and pointed towards the sighting. They hadn't practised this manoeuvre since Fort Dufferin and they weren't battle-hardened Texas Rangers but, with the element of surprise gone, the troopers—gripping their carbines anxiously—were enough to give the Sioux pause.

The Sioux were as the prairie weather, transforming themselves from a full-out attack to retreat in a heartbeat and from a war party into a trading party just as quickly. They had long experience at prevarication and obfuscation and, though they weren't Irishmen, there was a touch of the blarney about them.

The war chief barked a command and forty-three of the warriors melted down the ravine as if they never were. Six others rode out with the chief, ostentatiously lowering their Winchester and Henry rifles and approaching the Red Coats with happy gestures and broad smiles. The Red Coats relaxed when they saw it was only the Sioux and calmed even more when the chief began conversing with the Métis drivers in French. One of the sub-constables asked why they had loaded and cocked their rifles, if they had peaceful intent. The chief quickly responded that they'd mistaken the Force for Blackfoot and only a fool would not have readied himself for battle. No one asked how a noisy contingent of Mounted Police and half-breeds with wagons and carts could ever be mistaken, even at a distance, for the stealthy Blackfoot.

The Sioux returned to the main body with the stragglers, and Colonel French graciously invited the would-be raiders to spend the night in camp. He knew they would do so anyway, better to make the gesture as one ally to another. "We gave them some tea, buffalo meat, biscuits and ammunition, which apparently much pleased them. A few small presents go a long way in showing the Indians that we come as friends."

That night the Indians entertained the troops with singing and dancing.

The next day, Colonel French had no more time for Indians, friendly or otherwise.

COLONEL FRENCH

September 5

Our guide knows the road no further, and we are in the hands of Morreau, the Scout, whose reputation is doubtful; however, having kept a careful record of the angles and distances since leaving the B.C. road, on the 3rd August last, and this checked by observations for latitude and magnetic variation will enable me to keep a close check on him.

If Palliser's map is correct (which it is certainly not in some places), we are now 83 miles [west] from the Forks of the Bow and Belly rivers, and 18 miles north...

September 6

Started at 2:30 p.m. to get pasture, which the Scout reported five miles ahead. He brought us a very northerly course. I objected to halt in the coulé which he pointed out as there was no grass there, sent him on to another one about 1 1/2 miles, when he returned, and had the assurance to state it was the Belly River, and that we were at our journey's end, and that the Bow River was just a mile down.

I told him we were at least 70 miles from Bow River and asked him to show me Bow River, and on going to the place indicated, found it was merely a turn of the river. We have in fact struck the South Saskatchewan half a day sooner than I expected, but an error of 8 or 10 miles in Palliser's map is a trifle. The Scout insists that the Forks are 12 miles to the north.

I took it as a special dispensation of Providence, my having kept a careful record of the angles and distances since we left the B.C. road.

There is not a soul in camp that knows this place, and the Scout has brought us nearly a day's march out of our road during the last two days, and he would make it still worse to-morrow.

I am not quite certain whether his actions are due to ignorance or design. He is the greatest liar I have ever met. He is suspected as being a spy of the whoop up villains, but there is nothing definite or tangible to show this.

Although I have never been here I will do the guiding myself tomorrow. If I could have relied on Palliser's map I would have taken this duty sooner.

Theirs Not to Reason Why

September 8, the sixty-third day of the march, started like any other. Reveille at 3:00 a.m. and pull-out at five. They weren't delayed by breakfast because a steady prairie drizzle had turned the buffalo chips into a sodden, unignitable pudding and the remaining slabs of buffalo meat stayed piled in the wagons. With no fire or forage for the horses, a lunch stop wasn't necessary either. The column briefly paused at midday but got underway again shortly, movement being preferable to standing around shivering in the rain.

They kept moving until well after dark, searching for a campsite. They gave it up at 10:00 p.m. and stopped in the worst possible location, perched on the lip of a high and steep ravine that led down to the South Saskatchewan River. They were exposed to the elements without a scrap of cover or the slightest break from the wind. Water had to be laboriously hauled across the river flats and up the bank for two miles. The grass, as usual, was poor. Their buffalo chips were liquid. No fire, no food.

Shortly after they bedded down, the drizzle turned into a downpour and the north-west wind whipped itself into a squall that gathered momentum over miles of untreed prairie and relentlessly beat down on the troopers and animals. The officers and men huddled under their two summer-weight blankets, dressed in every scrap of clothing they possessed. Mumbled prayers were heard sporadically and the occasional

The storm in camp

sob and moan came in on the wind. Few slept.

When reveille sounded weakly at 3:00 a.m. even the bugle notes seemed to have a resentful tone to them. Colonel French ordered a 5:00 a.m. start, but the weather was so bad he relented and sent a party of men with the horses down into the ravine for shelter, water and, if they could find it, grass. The delay gave him the perfect opportunity to investigate a serious infraction committed during the night.

The combination of almost nightly stampedes and deteriorating weather forced the Colonel to order all available wagons and carts circled every evening for safety and shelter. A ring of sentries guarded the perimeter of the camp, with others stationed at each division and at the commissioner's tent. Another one walked an endless tour around the circled wagons and carts, keeping a watch on the animals penned inside and the supplies.

Shortly after reveille French learned that biscuits were missing from a barrel in one of the cooks' wagons. Livid, he ordered up the sergeant-majors and commanded them to bring in all the night sentries, dressed exactly as they'd been on guard duty. These were difficult times but Colonel French wouldn't abide thievery in his command.

Shortly, the stiff and grumbling sentries were assembled in the orderly tent. Major Macleod entered the tent, expecting it to be empty, and was surprised by the gathering. He caught the eye of one sergeant, who merely shrugged his own confusion.

Their attention shifted to Colonel French when he strode briskly into the tent.

"Attention," barked the adjutant, and the men pulled themselves into some semblance of the position.

French, lips compressed into a hard line, appraised the lot.

"We have a damnable thief among us," he charged, staring at each, one by one.

This was hardly news. Thievery had been a way of life among the troops since the beginning. Every troop lifted pots and pans, clothing, even saddles from the other troops—but it was considered more healthy competition than outright stealing. And Fred Bagley was far from the only one to help himself to unguarded supplies when hungry. What pilferage was serious enough to make the Colonel so enraged?

French launched into a vigorous harangue, touching on the subjects of discipline and orderliness, placing particular emphasis on the importance of honesty. Gradually it dawned on the dumbstruck men that they were being accused of stealing something—but what?

French signalled his adjutant, who stood fidgeting off to one side. The man stepped forward and began searching each sentry's pockets. Colonel French hovered over his shoulder inspecting the lint, dirt, gravel, tobacco shreds and horsehair accumulated over the past ten weeks. Three times he gave the arrest order. Without any explanation, he dismissed the rest of the sub-constables.

All were baffled at the turn of events, none more so than the three arrested men who wondered what the debris in their pockets had to do with anything.

"Biscuits were stolen from the wagons last night," announced French. "I concluded it could only have been the sentries who took them. I have just found crumbs in your pockets. Have you anything to say before your punishment is assessed?"

The men babbled their denials incoherently, talking over each other. For two and a half months the cursed biscuits had been the staple of their diet. Morning after morning they stuffed the beastly things in their pockets to nibble on during the long day. How could crumbs *not* be found? Major Macleod numbly wondered if he had crumbs in his overcoat pocket. It was only by a supreme act of will that he didn't check.

"Silence!" thundered the Colonel. "A man owns up to a mistake! It does you no credit to lie in the face of solid evidence. Put them in irons!" The last was addressed to the adjutant.

For a long moment everyone stood silently, paralysed in disbelief. Then Major Macleod stepped forward, placing himself between French and the men. He snapped to attention and vigorously saluted.

"Begging your pardon, sir," he said, as neutrally as possible. "Could we have a private word?"

"Request denied," snapped French. He gestured impatiently at the adjutant. "You have your orders!"

"I'm sorry, sir, you can't do that," countered Macleod, in the wary yet reassuring tone one uses on a dangerous dog.

"What are you talking about?" the Colonel asked threateningly.

"I'm sorry, sir. As a lawyer it is my duty to advise you that your actions constitute a breach of the law. Our regulations give you no authority for such a course of action. It is very clear."

"Regulations be damned!" shouted French, rapidly losing control. "These scoundrels are guilty! They must be punished!"

"I'm sorry, sir, I can't allow this to happen," Macleod said firmly. "You haven't a shred of real evidence. Even if you did, we've got a lot more serious problems than a few missing biscuits. I can't allow this. I won't allow this."

Macleod, still at attention, hadn't raised his voice once during the confrontation, but the steel in his tone finally gave the Colonel pause. He had endured the endless insubordination of the half-breeds and the subtle insolence of some of the men; he'd even been forced to dismiss Inspectors Richer and Young in Dufferin for arguing with him. But this was different.

Major Macleod, his "right hand," was threatening mutiny if he didn't back down. The Colonel turned to the sergeant-majors to order the arrest of his second-in-command. Not a one would look their commissioner in the eye. French knew he was lost. Suddenly a great tiredness overcame him.

The confrontation between Macleod and French stretched out agonizingly for the onlookers. In reality less than a minute had passed. Macleod snapped to attention and saluted again.

"Right then, I'll see to the loading up, sir." Macleod turned to three sub-constables and the sergeant-majors. "Off with you, now. There's plenty of work to be done."

Colonel French stood stiffly alone in the tent for some minutes, then slumped down in his chair. Nothing was seen of him for several hours until, just before pull-out, he emerged while Major Macleod was busy on the far side of camp. French sent the adjutant out to re-arrest the three sub-constables. In a flat staccato, he read the new charges. Since they hadn't guarded the biscuits well enough to prevent the theft, he found them guilty of dereliction of duty, and fined them fifteen dollars—twelve days' pay.

Macleod had new problems. After an hour of desperate effort, the men still couldn't get the horses up the bank from the river where they'd taken them for water. The animals' hooves scrabbled ineffectively at the scree as if held back by unseen hands. With the sergeant-majors bellowing from above, the men beat and screamed at the horses, trying to drive them up the slope. Eventually most acquiesced but five toppled over, falling with a sickening thud. The men hauled at their halters, begging them to move. Some were in tears at the sight of the gaunt animals lying on the slope, their dull eyes registering nothing but resignation. Ten horses died that morning before they left camp and seven others, near death, were left behind to be brought along slowly by Tommie Lake and a party of sub-constables.

The terrible sights and sounds of the dying horses haunted some of the men for the rest of their lives. They christened the place Dead Horse Camp.

Though the bone-chilling cold remained, the rain mercifully stopped at 10:00 a.m. when the Force staggered off. The sky even cleared a little and the men had a brief glimpse of Trois Buttes to the south in the Montana Territory; but it wasn't a reassuring sight, for the hills were topped with a bright, white cap of fresh snow. Then, as quickly as the sky opened, it closed again, bringing an all-day rain.

They managed only thirteen miles that day, as fewer than a third of the horses were capable of supporting a rider. Every couple of miles the Force halted to catch its breath. At each

Dying horses

stop the men and horses huddled together for warmth. Hardly a word was exchanged—they were too exhausted, hungry and forlorn even to curse their plight.

Two more horses died as the men pulled into camp at 9:00 p.m., bringing the death toll since they left Dufferin to forty-eight.* The animals were left as they lay. Their campsite was awful again, on the lip of a steep ravine, with the river—which French assumed was the South Saskatchewan—three miles away, down the slope and across a valley. But they had little to choose from.

JOHN MCILLREE

> The country is a barren waste. You would think along a large River like this that there would be some good grass in the valleys, but there is not a blade. The horses are getting weaker every day from want of enough food, and a good many of them are worthless for work.
>
> The Buffalo chips are getting soaked and as there is no wood it is hard to keep up a fire. All together our prospects are not very bright. Winter is fast approaching and we have nothing but our Summer clothing with us. I suppose it will all turn out all right, but there are some hard times before us.

The men lethargically went about the business of setting up camp, knowing there would be no supper because they couldn't find wood or dry chips. "Three of B Troop's boys went after water tonight and got lost so they lay out all night," James Finlayson wrote glumly in his diary. "We are used to that sort of work in the cold now." Joseph Carscadden's pessimism dove to new depths: "[I]t looks very much like starvation so much so that we must keep moving ahead or sure death awaits us...."

As the wind freshened and the temperature plummeted, John Poett, the veterinary surgeon, began to panic about the horses.

---

* The number of horses that died varies somewhat in the different accounts since the men, by now, were split into two groups, but this estimate is reasonable when all the reports are taken into consideration.

He noticed some of them wouldn't drink even when they were standing in water. He could pull their skin away from the bone and it tented up, a sure sign of severe dehydration. With their protective layer of fat gone, their coats had lost their resilience and ability to withstand the cold and constant rubbing of saddle and harness. The festering sores on their thin, tender skin defied all Poett's potions.

The necks of many wagon horses were ringed in blood from the irritation of the pulling collars. John McIllree could not get one of his horses to lean into the collar, so he tied the animal's tail directly to the wagon to relieve the strain. The animal pulled the wagon willingly for the rest of the day.

The horses' feet were also in bad shape. The rocky terrain had worn their shoes down to almost nothing and with no wood to fire up the forges, no new ones could be made. After days of marching, the delicate, fleshy frog underneath the horses' hooves was a pulpy mass.

John Poett worried that with all the other problems, the rain and cold would chill the weakened horses so much that they would soon die en masse. He wanted the men to try to keep the horses on their feet, but realized it was a useless suggestion; the men were in no condition to stay awake all night to prevent their horses from lying down. Once the animals were down, the odds were that they'd never rise again. At Poett's urging, Colonel French issued controversial orders on September 9. "I had a blanket taken from every officer and man last night so that each horse was covered and protected from the cold rain and wind."

JOSEPH CARSCADDEN

I shall never forget the sufferings of this night. In order to let the reader understand the situation allow me to explain.

On our march from Dufferin to this place we were allowed 2 blankets. This was ample covering in summer but now it is not and we can scarcely bear the cold and look at our poor horses standing there in the corral shivering, what shall we do for them, nothing except give up one of our blankets to them and shiver & shake ourselves. Yet hard as it is, we must do it and here we are now this fearful cold night with just one blanket and that a single one; but wait till we get a good warm supper and then we can better stand the cold, let us look around and find some wood and make a warm fire.

The search is instituted but poor fellows in vain, there is no wood within miles of you, then what can we do, take some of the old wooden ox carts and burn them, yes, that will be a happy way of getting out of the difficulty but would it be allowed.

No Sir!

Our noble hearted Commissioner will not permit this waste of Government property, and what on earth are we to do for supper simply nothing, you cannot have any supper tonight. Oh misery we must go to bed.

What do I call it? Bed?

No, no we cannot call a stretch on the grass with a saddle for our pillow and one blanket around us by such a sweet name, well we must lie down on the grass as I have described, hungry eyes starting and trembling in every limb with the intense cold.

As the wind howled, the men huddled together as best they could, trying to draw a little warmth from bodies pressed against one another. Added to the noise of the wind and rain was the snarling of wolves as they fought over the dead horses. All the candles had run out the night before. Without camp-fires or other light, the prairie dark settled over them with a heavy, ink-black hand. Many troopers muttered prayers, others lay quietly shivering, gripped with melancholy.

Then out of the dark a stentorian voice lifted, singing "God Save the Queen." It was the singing Irishman, Staff Constable Frank Norman. No matter what the hour or how wretched their condition, Norman's rich voice could usually be heard at night solo or pulling along a chorus of others. He often added his own words, as he did this night.

Confound their politics,
Frustrate their knavish tricks,

And get us out of this damn fix.
God save all here.

The troopers had heard it before and several joined in, but the ditty petered out into silence and, for once, no chuckles accompanied the verse. The men lay still again, each alone with the darkness, depression and wolves.

During the night Poett prowled among the horses. He could see that the blankets were doing the animals little good. He searched out the Colonel, who was still awake—as most of the men were—and made an urgent proposal.

JOSEPH CARSCADDEN

This night when our sufferings were almost unbearable, our Old Surgeon made a very humane suggestion to the Comr which I really wonder he did not carry out as it would only have been consistent with his other acts viz: that we the men should turn out of our tents and put the horses in them instead.

This would certainly have been an improvement to our poor horses but what of ourselves, this veritable nuisance of a Vet Surgeon must have considered that the men of this force were extremely docile to be ordered out of their only shelter like a dog and not rebel but the Comr seemed to know how far he dare go. He well knew that if the screw were tightened any more just then it would be snapped asunder like a thread and he wisely considered, perhaps I had better say no and cunningly desisted from following up the would be vets suggestion.

JAMES FINLAYSON

September 10
Reveille at 4:30 a.m. B Troop refused to leave camp until they had breakfast which put us about three miles in the rear. The reason we would not leave without breakfast was very good, namely we had no dinner or

supper yesterday and a fellow can't go far with an empty stomach.

The weather getting very cold. I have put on drawers. Have worn undershirts all summer.

The NWMP pushed on because they had nowhere else to go. Most of them were still damp from the day before, and the strong wind and rain soaked them instantly again. They resembled zombies. Most were leading, almost dragging, their mounts. Some of the horses and men seemed to be leaning on each other, their mutual distress evident.

The men's footwear could hardly be called boots any more. Some had only shreds where the soles once were. As they walked now more than they rode, their feet were cut and bruised from flint-like rocks. Large blisters swelled where their skin rubbed against bits of leather or was irritated by the debris they could no longer keep out of their boots. Most of the uppers had split down the seams and the men wrapped twine or makeshift rope from their horses' tails to keep the boots from disintegrating entirely. Others simply gave up and abandoned them, going barefoot or binding their feet in cloth or crudely made saganappi—rawhide fashioned from buffalo skin. One man slopped along in carpet slippers. Few could walk normally any more and their hobbling gate made them look more like a parade of terminally ill patients than a march of policemen.

In a regular command Colonel French would have flourished. He was capable and determined. Anything physically possible he was willing to attempt personally. But here, out in the middle of the wilds, he didn't know what to do. He had no resources to fall back on, and every decision he made seemed to drive them further into trouble. For the first time in his life, George French was helpless.

COLONEL FRENCH

September 10

I begin to feel very much alarmed for the safety of the Force. If a few hours' cold rain kills off a number of horses, what would be the effect of a 24 hours' snow storm. On the 20th September last year there was a three days' snow storm in the district between the Cypres Hills, Wood Mountains and the Old Wife's Creek. I cannot possibly get back there until the first week in October.

If I could get 5 or 6 tons of hay cut to bring along in our waggons to meet such a difficulty, I would feel more at ease, but the buffalo have scarcely left a blade of grass over 3 inches in length.

Made 7 miles, but had to halt as the rear guard was delayed several hours owing to Mr. B. not having obeyed my positive order with reference to a horse left behind close to last night's camping ground.

A river runs into the Saskatchewan. I am doubtful whether it may not be the Bow River...

French sent parties out in every direction to fix their location, discover a trail or at least locate a decent camping spot. He ordered Sub-Inspector Vernon Welch to go west and look for grass and the elusive Whoop Up trail. Cecil Denny went north with Pierre Léveillé to search out Fort Standoff—the rumoured whiskey post, the Old Bow Fort of the Hudson's Bay Company, the Bow River—anything. French even ordered them to bring back some Indians to help them, any Indians, even if they had to lasso them to do it.

FRED BAGLEY

September 10

The commissioner and his guides seem to be very hazy as to where we are. No one seems to know. Scouts sent in every direction. Looking for Old Bow Fort.

Everyone glum and low spirited. Future prospects gloomy. Cold wind and rain. Threat of snow. Six buffalo killed.

Even the most hardened sceptics were bred to have an innate trust in the capabilities of the officer class. The Colonel's obvious dismay and confusion shook the ranks to their core.

JOSEPH CARSCADDEN

I believe that there is an old proverb which says "That there is no black cloud but has its silver lining," well it may be true but it seems very much like a lie just now. Amongst the men, you can hear the doleful question put in many dolorous voices, How are we to get home? This is beyond human power to answer as you can hear some poor fellow answer, "God knows I don't."

The cold still continues intense even the Comr, who usually has so impassive a countenance and who can fine any individual on any or no charge without the slightest change of countenance or features, begins to look more down mouthed...he feels his responsibility in bringing a lot of Troops and animals into a position when he cannot see his way out of it.

Turning Tail

On the morning of September 10, Cecil "Texas Jack" Denny faced his scouting mission north with elation salted by little jolts of trepidation. His party selected four of the toughest and healthiest mustangs and set out along what they thought might be the Bow River. French ordered them to search for any signs of the whiskey trading post the reports said had been erected somewhere along the river. They were also to keep an eye out for Indians of any tribe and try to approach them for information about their whereabouts.

Denny had successfully refurbished his reputation after the unpleasant incidents with the antelope and the quicksand, having killed numerous antelopes and two buffalo and having acquitted himself well after being assigned to help scout earlier. Now Colonel French was entrusting him with his own independent command. True, his men consisted only of three half-breeds, but among them was the legendary Pierre Léveillé, "a prairie hero" who topped six feet in his moccasins and weighed

in at over three hundred pounds. Any unease he felt lifted at
the thought of this enormous man at his side. Originally sent
by Lieutenant-Governor Morris as chief scout and interpreter,
Léveillé had become the Colonel's trusted confidant.

Denny had also heard that Léveillé's French father had
served under Napoleon at Waterloo before coming to Canada
and settling at Fort Garry, where he married a half-breed
daughter of Alexander Mackenzie, the first white man to cross
to the Pacific. Pierre Léveillé was reputed to be an extremely
dangerous man to cross, especially once he'd made his mind
up—reportedly he had been one of the few Métis who went
against Louis Riel in the 1869–70 Red River uprising. Cecil
Denny liked a man with a story—he had one himself. How
could he get into any trouble with such a one at his side?

Denny's expedition got off to a capital start. They spotted
buffalo within a few hours, easily killing one. Shortly after
carving out the best bits, they came across a creek flowing
from the river, which actually had some wood on its banks.
They built a fire and roasted buffalo steaks for breakfast.

Pushing on into the afternoon, Denny felt better than he had
for weeks. This was more like it, Texas Jack loping along, a
trio of savvy guides at his side, sure-footed Indian ponies
beneath them and the West stretching out before them. No
wonder so many of the men were depressed. Even with plenty
of food and water, plodding along day after day was stultifying, enough to kill anyone's spirit.

Denny marvelled at how little it took to alter one's perspec-
tive. The prairie, viewed by a half-starved, thirsty and
exhausted man walking on tatters instead of boot leather,
appeared both dreary and ominous. From the vantage point of
his noble steed, his belly full of buffalo, the bald terrain took
on a harsh beauty.

They paused at a high point along the river and surveyed the
gash of a deep gully that swooped in to meet the river. Denny
started as one of the guides called out, "Look!" Two Indians,
on foot, scampered towards the gully. Denny's party spurred
their horses, trying to cut them off, but the braves disappeared
into the ravine. Denny signalled his men to move closer. He
didn't want to provoke the Indians but he'd been ordered to
get information.

Suddenly one of the half-breeds reined his horse to a skidding stop. One hundred yards away, at the edge of the gully, stood the two Indians, along with forty-eight others, all with rifles pointed in their direction.

The Indians were on foot but looked very menacing. Still, Denny concluded that they were safe for the moment—men on foot could hardly overtake their ponies. If the rifles remained silent and they got close enough to persuade the Indians they were peaceable, Denny was sure they could give him some valuable information to take back to Colonel French.

Denny nodded to Léveillé, who stood in his stirrups and boomed a greeting in Cree. The Indians hollered back in a different language. Their tone was threatening.

"What's he say?" queried Denny.

"Dunno," Léveillé replied.

The Indians slipped back over the edge of the bank, leaving only their heads and guns visible. It looked as if they expected battle. As Denny was pondering his next move, one of the Indians stood up again and began making an elaborate series of signs.

"What's he saying? What's it mean?" Denny asked Léveillé excitedly.

"Dunno."

Denny leaned forward and tried to make out what the Indian was waving. By squinting hard, he brought into focus a brown, shrivelled object tied to the end of a stick—it looked like a scalp. Denny turned to consult the half-breeds only to find them reining their horses around and spurring for the horizon. He was horrified. In a second, the only thing left of his companions was the dust of their rapid departure. Texas Jack was alone—facing the Indians. Denny liked to think of himself as a courageous man but staying there, unprotected, within bullet range of fifty Indian guns, was a folly not worth pursuing. He wheeled his horse and galloped frantically after them.

When Denny finally caught up, Léveillé and the two others were heading straight back to camp. Denny begged them to continue but the half-breeds swore the Indians were a war party of Sioux who undoubtedly had reinforcements, with horses, in the neighbourhood.

Denny argued, cajoled and threatened. Finally, by promising to give the gully a wide berth and retreat at the first sign of trouble, he got their agreement to continue—but only at night. Denny preferred the daytime since his red coat could be seen clearly, but the half-breeds were adamant. They continued forty more miles up river with no change in the barren, hilly country.

Early in the evening on the second day, Denny looked ahead at the river and saw it blocked with a solid dam of brown. Buffalo, thousands upon thousands of them. Bobbing and fighting against the fast-flowing river, they surged across it and stormed up the bank. Denny was awestruck by the magnificent beasts.

Colonel French felt besieged on all sides. The confrontation with Macleod, conflicting information from the guides and scouts, the shattered state of his troops and the continued deterioration of the horses left him floundering. He patched one problem only to have another spring up. And no one, from the fifteen-year-old assistant trumpeter Fred Bagley to Colonel French himself, had the foggiest idea of precisely where they were—or how to get from here to Fort Whoop Up—except, perhaps, Moreau.

Dr. Kittson in his tent

COLONEL FRENCH

> Our guide Morreau says that "Whoop Up" is only 40 miles off, but he is such an out and out liar, and hitherto has proved so utterly useless as a guide that no one believes him.

Getting lost reflected very poorly upon the commander of an expedition. Water, food, forage and the elements were all beyond his control. He could hardly be blamed if the prairie grass had been burned by fires, eaten by locusts and ravaged by buffalo. Nor could anyone fault him for not anticipating the seriousness of the drought, even though explorers John Palliser and Henry Youle Hind had called much of the southern plains an "arid belt" that supported little life. But losing his way was a different matter. He had guides, scouts, a map and compass. He took regular readings with his sextant. How was it possible to be stranded here on the Bow River, assuming it was the Bow, like so many children wandering helplessly in the woods?

JAMES FINLAYSON

> September 11
>
> We are lost on the prairie and no one knows where we are.... Horses and oxen dying fast. Provisions getting scarce things look very dark. No buffalo seen today. Weather very cold.

FRED BAGLEY

> The depression seems to have affected Sub Constable Thornton very seriously and he presents himself before the Comr and demands his immediate discharge saying, "I joined this force to fight for Queen and country but so far have fought only hunger thirst and cooties."
> He was sent to the Dr. for mental examination.

Colonel French concluded that the Force had three choices; they could go south towards Fort Benton and hole up for the winter, north to Fort Edmonton and do the same or turn around and go home. He made up his mind—he would do all three. But, with his command collapsing around him, it was essential that he present a united front to the Ottawa politicians who would demand an explanation for the radical change in plans he intended. Colonel French summoned his officers and under the guise of consultation gave them their orders.

COLONEL FRENCH

September 12

There is but one opinion regarding the portion of the Force going back, viz., that it should return forthwith.

All feel satisfied that it would be impossible to take the stores through to Edmonton, owing to the condition of the horses. A post on this part of the Bow River or Belly River is out of the question, as there is neither grass or wood here, and not much wood apparently on Bow River near the junction.

The Sweet Grass Hills of West Butte, near Boundary Line, promises well for a post: good grass, good wood, and water, and only about 80 miles from Benton, an important point as we will have to obtain our provisions there in any case. I understand that the whiskey traders are not here now, but are about Benton, and [propose] remaining there till the Force returns. A post at or near the Boundary Line will spoil their little game....

Although most of the ruffians were murderers from Benton, "Whoop Up," as far as I can understand, is the only Fort which has a local habitation as well as a name. It is principally a trading post of the firm of Baker, & Co. of Benton, highly respectable merchants who do not sell whiskey or spirits.

Major Macleod and the five inspectors were bewildered at the new information presented by Colonel French. Where had it come from? They had all read the reports in Dufferin that portrayed the whiskey traders as a murderous, immoral lot, working out of numerous forts, including the infamous Whoop Up.

Less than a year earlier, Colonel French had begged a further 150 troops from the Government of Canada, in order to deal with the "five forts between the Milk River and Edmonton, one of them containing 100 outlaws and desperadoes, and mounting several guns." He had left Dufferin preparing—indeed, hoping—to fight. And on August 12, exactly one month earlier, the Colonel had written to Colonel Hugh Richardson, of the Department of Justice, via the Wood Mountain Depot, repeating his belief that there were five hundred outlaws waiting to ambush them at Bow River.

Now, out of the blue, the Colonel announced there was no threat, insisting that Fort Whoop Up was somehow a legitimate trading post, owned and operated by upright merchants. French explained his plan; a contingent would go back East, another group would take the sick horses and men to Fort Edmonton and a third contingent would remain in the west for the winter but would not bother about the supposed whiskey fort. Their job would be to build a post near the border to discourage any renewed interest in the whiskey trade. Macleod and the inspectors exchanged questioning looks, before coming to the unanimous agreement that it would be best if Colonel French returned, as fast as possible, to Manitoba with a contingent of troops.

JOSEPH CARSCADDEN

The extermination of this den of Smugglers was one chief object in going so far west, but I hear you say why didn't you go there and complete your work. That is a question for you intelligent reader, for you to solve—none of the M.P. [mounted police] can.

Our Comr hired a guide who was well acquainted with the locality of the Smugglers and would, without doubt, have conducted us to them. But there happens to be a half-breed in our train of whom we have since been informed that he had a personal interest in the prosperity

& continuance of this band of Smugglers.* He makes himself particularly agreable to our Comr by bowing & scraping before him, and whispering soft words in his ear. He always called the Comr by some sweet names as my dear Col and my dearest Comr this affection called forth our Comrs warmest feelings and gained his best esteem.

This half-breed knew well how to get on the soft side of the Comr and when this point was achieved, he would chuckle to himself and say all was right now, the Smugglers were safe as he could persuade the Comdr from following the Guide, when the time came. And persuade him he did, for when we were within a few days march of this Fort, the half-breed begins to frighten the Comr by saying the Guide is not to be trusted and a lot more such stuff, till finally the wily breed gets the place of [the] guide himself and our friend guide is watched and his instructions and directions are unheeded.

The breed is in favour & has got the confidence of the Comr and guides us safely and surely, not towards but away from the Smugglers Fort.

The reader is now informed why we travelled so far west and are now returning home without finding our goal or accomplishing our errand.

On the evening of September 12, French ordered preparations to begin immediately for their trek south to the Sweet Grass Hills. There he would split the troops, leaving some to stay in the West for the winter with the heavy equipment and

---

* This half-breed is never identified but it is almost certain Carscadden is talking about Pierre Léveillé as the one favoured by French and Moreau as the one discredited by him. Léveillé is the only one who Colonel French ever has anything positive to say about. Moreau was the only one familiar with the territory beyond the Cypress Hills and he was hired to guide them to Whoop Up. When Moreau told Colonel French they were only forty miles away from Whoop Up, they were actually fifty miles away—almost dead on in terms of frontier navigation. Léveillé's interest in the "prosperity" of the whiskey trade was likely surmised because his brother had worked for the traders in Cypress Hills.

sick horses and the rest he would personally lead east, to winter in the Force's new headquarters at Fort Ellice.

But before they set out the next day Colonel French, still behaving erratically, abruptly decided to send the Fort Edmonton contingent off immediately without waiting for Cecil Denny's report. Denny's party was overdue and rapidly moving into the category of presumed lost. Without his information, Major Walsh, commanding the Fort Edmonton bound troops, would have no idea what to expect. Even so, French ordered Walsh to form a party of seventy men with fifty-eight horses to march north and meet Inspector Jarvis.

In the morning of that same day, Sub-Inspector Welch, sent out by French to look for forage and the Whoop Up trail, returned having found no road, no grass but thousands of buffalo swarming south. The buffalo's southern movement meant they had just been through the country Walsh would be travelling into, fouling whatever meagre water was available. But French affirmed his orders and Walsh prepared to swim his party across the river where they'd camp, before heading to Fort Edmonton.

COLONEL FRENCH

September 14

Two men came in, also Sergeant Lake. Two out of the three horses paralysed by cold and hunger died, making 9 horses killed in 36 hours from this cause. A good many in camp look as if they have not much longer to live. Denny's party not in. I must leave this p.m., and strike south. Ice on water last night. Observed for latitude and magnetic variation....

Very anxious about Denny's party, and fear they may have come to mischief....

Oxen starving now. The horses can pick up a little of the grass left by the buffalo but the poor oxen cannot do this. On following up the Force, overtook an ox-waggon, 3 miles out, completely played out. Carvell and I put our horses in, and took it on to Camp. 5 oxen unable to reach Camp.

As the Force prepared to move out on the fourteenth, the men discovered that Major Macleod, along with his horse and saddle, were missing. There was no clue as to his whereabouts. Colonel French ordered a pull-out, but left a party on site with instructions to wait until the assistant commissioner returned. The men were distressed at leaving without Macleod but reasoned that if anyone could handle himself in the wilds, it was the Major. Ever since the biscuit crumb incident, men of all ranks had relied increasingly on him. He spent his great endurance and physical strength freely comforting individual men, interceding in the escalating disagreements among troopers and blunting the more autocratic of the Colonel's orders.

Macleod had been deeply concerned about Texas Jack's fate but even more worried about what his disappearance might portend. If his party had been attacked by Indians, then Walsh and his men would be riding into sure disaster. It would be very easy to cut off and wipe out seventy inexperienced and weak men with played-out horses.

Knowing that Colonel French was in no mood to grant him permission for anything at the moment, and unwilling to ask anyone else to go in his stead, Macleod had saddled his horse and slipped out of camp shortly after supper on the thirteenth. He forded the river and rode hard along the bank, quickly picking up Denny's trail. But thousands of buffalo soon obscured the tracks. Darkness fell but Macleod doggedly headed in the direction where Denny's trail had led.

By two in the morning Macleod still hadn't found them. He knew that he ought to turn back, but he stubbornly kept pressing farther and farther. Buffalo had been passing all around him in the dark. Once he'd been almost jostled off his horse by the animals. At first light he saw several dim shapes in the distance and assumed they were more buffalo. But as he got closer, he was delighted to see Denny and the half-breeds—unhurt and apparently none the worse for wear.

"Fancy bumping into you boys," drawled a smiling Macleod when he rode up.

Macleod, Denny and the half-breeds pushed their horses all morning and into the afternoon, but still couldn't make camp until the early evening. Macleod had no doubt they could easily catch the Force as long as they stuck to the plan of going to

Sweet Grass Hills. But with French changing his mind by the hour, goodness knew what their destination might be. As they rode into the abandoned camp, Macleod was happy to find the hunter himself, Sub-Inspector McIllree, patiently waiting for them, the rest of the Force having left at 4:00 p.m.

Denny's curiosity about the horseless Indians gnawed away at him. When they caught up to the main body on the evening of the fourteenth, he sought out the discredited scout Moreau and told him of the encounter, described the Indians' gestures, clothing and what little he could see of their guns. The frontiersman grunted periodically and snorted derisively when Denny said the half-breeds had identified the Indians as Sioux.

When Denny's story wound down, Moreau squatted and began tracing two faces in the dirt with a stick, each displaying a distinctively different series of slashes on the cheeks, representing paint marks. Moreau stood back, admiring his work. Denny pointed to the one on the right. "Assiniboine," the scout stated emphatically.

Denny later learned that Moreau was right. "They had been one hundred miles up the Bow River from the point where we had met them, and had attacked a party of white men who were camped in the valley with two or three wagon-loads of goods for trade with the Blackfeet. They attacked at night, stole all the horses, killed one man, captured and burned the wagons, and destroyed the goods they were unable to take with them. They were later attacked in turn by a large party of Blackfeet, but got away after losing all their horses."

Denny was disgusted. How could Léveillé, whom French praised as the only half-breed worth a damn, have mistaken Assiniboine for Sioux? He could see them clearly and, what's more, could hear their language. Denny was also dismayed at how little attention Colonel French paid to his report and how eagerly he listened to Léveillé.

COLONEL FRENCH

They had been up the Bow River for about eighty miles, and gave a dreadful account of the country; neither wood nor grass, country very rough and bad hills ahead.

Mr. Levaille (who was in charge of the party of half-breeds selected by his Honour to accompany or precede the force with Indian presents) was with Mr. Denny and placing great reliance on his judgment I asked him if the party could get through to Edmonton.

He stated it would be almost impossible to take the horses through, and that we would certainly lose most of them if we tried. With much reluctance I had to counter-order the Edmonton party, and instructed Inspector Walsh to follow the main party south to the Three Buttes.

The abrupt turn southward had lifted the men's spirits. The sky cleared and the tall snowy hills of Trois Buttes poked through the clouds. When they reached the Buttes, also called the Sweet Grass Hills, French would split the Force into those divisions staying in the West and those returning to Manitoba.

JOSEPH CARSCADDEN

At last. At last.

Oh! The Long looked for order it has come.

Homeward March and with smiling faces we retrace our weary steps and face the East again. Happy thought we are going home.

EDWARD MAUNSELL

This march had all the appearance of a retreat.

FRED BAGLEY

Sub constable Thornton, who demanded his discharge a few days ago, appears to have recovered his normal mental health after Dr. Kittson had pointed out to him that allowing him to leave us here, where we are surrounded by hundreds of miles of bald headed prairie in every direction, with not a vestige of wood or water would mean his certain death either from starvation, or at the hands of hostile savages.

The Force marched nine miles towards the Sweet Grass Hills, which was about all the failing oxen could manage. Their campsite looked "moist" and Fred Bagley's troop quickly dug a hole and waited anxiously for hours, hoping it would fill with water. Finally, unable to wait any longer, the men prostrated themselves at the edge of the hole and sucked at the mud.

Colonel French continued to perform his duties, drawing up his orders, dispatching his scouts, conducting the morning parade, but he was an automaton going through the motions of a shattered command and unfulfilled mission. He seemed to care little that the troop was once again spread over miles of country, that all the men were now walking full time, and any pretence of care for equipment or arms had long been abandoned.

On the third day of the retreat a group of the half-breeds exacted their revenge on the Colonel for his two and a half months of complaints and disdain.

On September 15, after a 5:00 a.m. reveille and a 7:00 a.m. start, the Force stumbled six miles before stopping for lunch at a shallow prairie lake, three miles long and a quarter mile wide. Colonel French proposed calling it "Commissioner's Lake." The half-breeds enthusiastically endorsed the idea.

Working with a sense of purpose for the first time since the march began, they erected a sizeable cairn of stones on the lakeshore. They then assembled themselves in a rough formation, stood at attention, and fired off fourteen ragged volleys, each followed by a sarcastic cheer. "Hurrah for Le Colonel!"

Chapter 10

Benton

Jerry Potts led a string of six horses into Fort Benton. Since he had quit working for the whiskey traders in 1872, Potts had spent his time building up his horse herd—through various means. Now he had nearly one hundred, not all first-quality perhaps, but few among the Blackfoot could match his numbers—nothing like Crowfoot's herd of four hundred horses, but one of the biggest in the Confederacy none the less. Horses were wealth to the Blackfoot, and by this measure Jerry Potts was rich. He was also pleasantly surprised to find a ready market among whites, who couldn't seem to hang on to their animals for long. Potts was careful to keep his branded horses away from his white customers. They took a dim view of being offered horses bearing the U.S. Cavalry brand.

At first Potts concentrated on pack horses and remounts for hunting. Buffalo ponies weren't much to look at, small, wiry and often scarred from gores and falls, but they were valuable even in those dying days of the buffalo hunt. Lately he had started breeding and trading race horses, one of the Blackfoot's great passions and a growing one in the white world—a recent race in Fort Benton had paid three thousand dollars to the winner with thousands more wagered by eager spectators.

When Potts pulled into Benton on the morning of September 24, he went straight to I.G. Baker's store, selling his six horses for $75 each. Isaac Baker, who made the deal himself, bubbled with glee about the arrival of the British Red Coats, expected within the next couple of days. He told Potts that they would be a boon to business and soon he'd be needing many more horses. Potts nodded noncommittally, took his money and strolled over to the saloon in John Lilly's Dance Hall.

The missionaries north of the Medicine Line had told Potts a year ago about the Red Coats coming west. And he'd been hearing about their progress since the end of August, when they'd first moved into Blackfoot territory.

Potts found it hard to believe that anyone could be as inept as the Blackfoot stories, told with much amusement, made these Red Coats out to be—and still be alive. They had been surrounded variously by Blackfoot and Sioux and didn't seem to notice let alone take adequate precautions. Potts concluded they were either incredibly foolish or incredibly brave.

During the day the Red Coats resembled ants running helter-skelter around a trod-on ant hill, but at night they were so inattentive even a one-legged white man could sneak up, slit throats, lift scalps and take horses without anyone waking up. Not that anyone would want the horses—they were nothing but bone and hide.

A few weeks back, a Blackfoot party had watched the Sioux's aborted ambush against the Red Coats. When the troopers drew their rifles, most of the Sioux melted away. Just as the Blackfoot were starting to think that perhaps these white men weren't as helpless and stupid as they appeared, the Red Coats inexplicably escorted seven of their would-be attackers into camp and greeted them as friends, feeding and sheltering them for the night. The next morning the Red Coats sent the Sioux on their way with gifts of tobacco and ammunition.

For the past couple of weeks the Red Coats had been stumbling around like drunks, about a hundred miles north of the Medicine Line. His last information put them near the Sweet

Grass Hills, desperately needing supplies. Several times, Potts had thought of loping north to see what was going on, but never got around to it.

If they were in half as bad shape as the stories made out, Potts reasoned the Red Coats would need horses. The only place to get them was Fort Benton, which was why he was here with $450 in his pocket. Potts arrived early in the day, as he'd planned, to take care of business while everyone—including himself—was still sober. Horse trading was horse trading. Drinking was drinking.

Potts knew that the only reason the Blackfoot were leaving the Red Coats alone was because they'd promised Parson John, the Wesleyan missionary John McDougall, to wait for a message sent personally to them by the Great White Mother—after that, all bets were off. The Parson claimed that the Red Coats would stop the whiskey trade and protect them from the American military, who they feared would cross the Medicine Line in retaliation for the Indian raids along the Missouri. Crowfoot and the other chiefs had taken Parson John's gifts to seal the bargain.

Potts chuckled to himself at the thought of Parson John's latest adventure. The man had sand—no question. After meeting with the Blackfoot, he paid a "diplomatic" visit to some of the whiskey forts. It was God's work, the Parson was reputed to have said, allowing the sinners a last opportunity to repent. But Potts thought it was more likely that the Parson, hardly the most humble man in the territory, couldn't pass up an opportunity to gloat about his part in the coming of the law.

John McDougall considered himself fearless. He'd yet to meet anything he couldn't conquer, except for the smallpox that had taken away half his family. Among the wild savages he had never encountered a situation he couldn't handle and even the most ferocious warriors came to be impressed by his ostentatious displays of valour. But the whiskey forts were a different matter. The men inside were of the worst sort: lawless, godless, arrogant and violent—and that was when they were sober. They recognized no higher authority than Colt, Winchester and Henry.

But John McDougall had a message to deliver and if he did it right he would have the satisfaction of chasing these men from their dens long before Her Majesty's troops showed up to rout them. In mid-September, Parson John and his small party paused for a moment on a rise and looked down at Whoop Up, the American flag flying overhead. Squat and solid with its poplar and cottonwood logs rising to stockades on each corner, the fort would repel anything but large-calibre cannon. He could see no movement, nor hear any sounds of habitation. Close by lay another whiskey post; this would be the one belonging to J.D. Weatherwax. McDougall elected to visit it first.

Next to the Baker and Power companies of Benton, J.D. "Waxy" Weatherwax was the biggest whiskey trader in the territory. His fort, also sporting the stars and stripes, sat in a beautiful valley. The timbered shoulders of the rivers sloped up into the prairie and down into rich bottom land.

McDougall's party rode slowly down into the valley with their carts following behind. An unaccustomed tremor vibrated inside Parson John. He pulled himself a little higher in the saddle and set his face in a look he hoped was both uncompromising and peaceful, the first to give them pause and if that didn't work, the second to calm any anxiety about his presence. He checked his cart. Its small Union Jack was still there, lifting slightly in the breeze.

Weatherwax's post was smaller and looked less the impregnable fortress than Whoop Up, but it was still substantial with a solid door and rifle loops cut in the walls. McDougall rapped on the timbers and had barely settled back to wait when he heard the rasp and rattle of a log bolt being pulled back.

"Greetings!" an unexpectedly cultured voice welcomed them cheerily. McDougall introduced himself to the proprietor, who shook hands with a firm, confident grip. McDougall was surprised at the sight of Weatherwax. The man was tall, slender and well-groomed, in an oily way. He spoke with exaggerated grace and his gestures were almost courtly. There was a slickness about him and McDougall mentally dubbed him the "Spaniard." He didn't trust, for one instant, the crafty look in his eyes, and even his polished English smacked of deception.

The Spaniard busied himself for a moment, handing out presents to emphasize his pleasure in seeing these visitors. Cautious though he was, McDougall was secretly delighted when Weatherwax produced several cans of fruit and pressed them on the Reverend. He had been in the West for fourteen years, since he was seventeen years old, and in all that time had never enjoyed such a delicacy. While he was examining the cans, a filthy man sidled up to him.

"Old Waxy must be mighty happy to see you if he's givin' up his peaches," the man cackled. "An' I'll give you this for free too. If you're headin' across the line you're a lucky man."

"Why would that be?" McDougall asked politely.

"'Cause I'm Fred Watcher. Dutch Fred they call me. If you mention my name anywheres in the territory of Montana you'll live like a king. Go see Heddy in Benton at the hurdy-gurdy. Tell her I sent you and she'll fix you up with someth'n pretty to take care of Ol' Willy." Watcher grabbed his crotch and bared a handful of tobacco-stained teeth at the Reverend. "Don't matter what you want. Dutch Fred's name'll git it for you."

McDougall assured the man he would keep his kind offer in mind the next time he visited Montana.

After the Spaniard had finished doling out his gifts, he stood beaming. McDougall noticed that for all the man's geniality and hospitality, he didn't invite them inside. The Spaniard's composure slightly unnerved the Parson. He found himself blurting out his news about the coming of the North West Mounted Police. "Yes, gentlemen, we are glad to see you travelling through our country," Weatherwax said, gripping the Parson's hand and ignoring his words. "We wish you heartily a bon voyage!"

McDougall and his guide rode away from the fort and forded the St. Mary's River to get to Fort Whoop Up on the other side. There wasn't a soul around and the place was so quiet it could have been deserted. The Reverend pounded on the solid front gate. Minutes went by and no one came. He pounded again and waited some more. Eventually the gate swung open and J.J. Healy bade them come in.

"I'm afraid there is only myself and Jimmy here to welcome you," Healy said, wobbling slightly and emanating a rich and sour odour of whiskey and sweat. "Jimmy's a bit under the weather, if you know what I mean." The man in question sat slumped on a wooden crate; he would not be moving for some time.

"Unbuckle and lay off your armoury for the moment, Parson John. I'll make you some lunch and you can give me the news."

Healy informed McDougall that his "boys" would be back shortly. They had gone south to interview the Boundary Commission men—"interview" being code for selling hooch. Plotting the 49th parallel was slow, tedious, thirsty work and the traders found the BC men to be steady customers for the slightly better class of booze they reserved for whites. As they ate, McDougall explained that the police were coming to bring some law to the West and make life safer for both red and white.

"Oh, but Parson, we don't need any gov'nment in this country! We are the gov'nment. Yes assuredly, we traders do our best to keep out the rough element."

Doubt wrote itself over John McDougall's face.

"Why just recently, Happy John Wallace came right in here and said he aimed to run this territory. Yes indeed, he was going take care of everything for us. Well, we took care of him. We planted him in the garden at Standoff.

"And then there was that river-boat fellow. He had aspirations too. We stretched him right out beside Happy.

"Let's see. There's more. Oh yes. Crazy Harry come up with a few ideas. He didn't like what we had to say and went foolish like a mad dog. We laid him out at Freeze-Out. I guess there's a few more at Slide-Out and you'll notice a bump or too outside these very walls."

McDougall found the long list of carnage absorbing, in spite of himself.

"I'll tell you this, rev'rend. These were bad men. We couldn't allow them to live in this fine country. No sir, Parson John, we don't let any really bad men stay in this Whoop Up region."

McDougall told Healy that was all very well and good, but like it or not, the law was coming in the form of three hundred trained guns and that was that. Healy chewed thoughtfully on the damp end of his cigar, as if calculating the odds. Finally, he drew a long breath and let it out in a resigned sigh. At that moment both men heard a commotion outside the fort. Bullets ricocheted off the log walls, followed by a tide of yelling. Healy rose and stretched. "That'd be the boys."

Healy pulled open the gate and two dozen men piled

through as if the devil were on their tails. The Boundary Commission men had insisted on sharing their whiskey. Soon they all had a snoot full, and one thing leading to another, the whole camp, including the "boys," swung into a wild and very satisfying donnybrook. The "boys" resembled nothing that the Parson had seen during all his years on the frontier. Many had fresh scrapes on their faces and several were still dripping blood. They were swaggeringly drunk and each had enough guns visible on his person to arm a small posse. All in all they were the most hard-bitten bunch of men ever to cross the Parson's path.

"Who's this sorry son of a bitch? Stand the bastard up and I'll plug 'im!" demanded one particularly awful looking customer on seeing the Parson.

"Hey, what's he doin' with that foreign thing?" The man leaned over, nearly falling off his horse in the process, and poked at McDougall's Union Jack.

"This is the Reverend Dr. John McDougall," Healy soothed. "He's told me the Queen's got some sort of police coming our way."

"Police! Police! We heard about 'em. They're stuck somewhere round Wood Mountain, so the Boundary boys say."

John McDougall had done his duty and passed on the message from the lieutenant-governor. He hoped the warning would do the trick and no blood would be shed. Before the arrival of the "boys," the Parson might have been inclined to linger. Instead he said a hasty adieu. After loading up the cart, McDougall's party recrossed the Belly River then pointed north for the trip back to the mission at Morley, which he, his wife and his brother had established the year before. When they got to the top of the bank, they sat down to enjoy the Spaniard's canned fruit. They had just levered the tins open with their knives when they heard a furor across the river.

It was the "boys" galloping right at them through the trees, hollering, swearing and shooting their pistols skywards. If possible, they were drunker than before and they were after him, plain as could be. John McDougall didn't run. Even if that had been his inclination, he couldn't outdistance them with his carts. He steeled himself for the confrontation—perhaps he could bluff them out.

The party thundered up, eyes crazy with whiskey, guns protruding from every pocket and belt. But instead of launching an attack as he expected, they begged him to come back to the fort. Apparently, shortly after McDougall had left, a group of men had come in from the north-east, where they'd had a skirmish with some Indians. They got away but one of them was shot up and needed attention. When Healy had introduced the Reverend to the "boys" he bestowed upon him the as yet unearned title of "Dr."

McDougall had a hard time persuading the men that a doctor of medicine and a doctor of divinity were entirely different professions. He offered to come and say a prayer for the man's soul. But they declined his offer and rode off in disgust, leaving Parson John to his peaches.

McDougall was satisfied with his visit to the infamous den of iniquity, and as he rode north he congratulated himself on becoming the "John the Baptist" of a new regime that the Mounted Police would undoubtedly bring to the West.

Best Wishes

FRED BAGLEY

September 18

Reveille at 6 a.m. Frosty morning. Snow! Marched at 8. Six miles, and halt on Milk River Ridge. Rocky Mountains visible far to the West. From our elevated view point on the Ridge the prairie, as far as the eye can reach, in every direction, appears to be literally black with countless numbers of buffalo. Thrilling sight!

...camped in a valley of the "Trois Buttes". Splendid water, and good grass. Rock caves, and curious rock formations. Indian paintings and etchings on rocks in caves. Seem to be very old.... I, and several others carved our names in the sandstone walls of cave.

September 19

Splendid camp. But we are a tough looking mob of

Soldiers of the Queen. The sentry on the Commissioners tent in rags, and with gunny sacks wrapped around his feet. Muster parade, and inspection of horses and saddles.

The system our Veterinary Officer has of prescribing carbolic acid for all the ills of our animals causes some of our halfbreeds to raise a laugh now and then by shouting in unison "Fetch along de carbolique, der's going to be a stampede."

Just before noon on the twentieth, a weary Major Walsh led B Division into the Sweet Grass camp. Six of their horses had died since leaving the South Saskatchewan River even though they had travelled at a snail's pace, stopping frequently in order to keep the nearly dead oxen from lying down in their traces. The oasis of green that greeted the troop raised smiles and deep sighs of relief, but Walsh's face was compressed in a deep frown. Four days ago he had given Sub-Constable Thornton, now recovered from his depression, permission to hunt for antelope and he hadn't been seen again. He delayed the troop's departure and sent out search parties, but no one found a sign of Thornton. Walsh decided he must press on to the Sweet Grass Hills, or he'd lose so many horses and oxen the men would have to pull the wagons themselves. But leaving a man behind sat like a stone in his gut.

Walsh found a completely different band of men at the Hills. They were as ragged as they'd ever been, but a light shone in their eyes that he hadn't seen since they'd left Dufferin. As his troopers dragged themselves into camp, a great commotion erupted. Cheering and cursing were accompanied by a symphony of crashing pots and pans. Sergeant Frank Spicer exploded into view riding a buffalo calf and sawing away at its throat with his knife. Geysers of blood spurted out as the bawling animal careered through camp-fires, scattering food and equipment in every direction.

The cooks flung mud and invective angrily in his wake. The men, dodging the missiles, charged after Spicer, eager to be in on the kill. Finally, having left most of its blood in a gory trail through camp, the calf sank to the ground. The red-splattered

Spicer leapt off, bellowed his triumph, knife raised to the heavens.

FRED BAGLEY

September 20

This evening an overgrown lout named McHamish threatened to kill me after I had smacked him on the mouth with my small fist for stealing my drinking "cup." But that red headed Irishman "The Leaping Goat" McKibben seized him by the throat, and promised to knock his head off if he didn't "lave the boy alone." The drinking "cup," the cause of all these warlike enthusiasms was an empty baking powder tin picked up at Dufferin camp, and since carefully treasured by me.

The next morning Walsh barely restrained himself from shouting with joy when a gaunt, bewhiskered man wobbled into sight. Thornton had become lost while hunting and his horse collapsed, forcing him to set out on foot. Fortunately he could see the Three Buttes clearly to the south and he plodded along for five days and over eighty miles, half-mad with hunger and thirst. Colonel French promptly fined him $150 for losing his horse.

At Sweet Grass Hills, Colonel French split up the company. D Division, and E Division were destined for the East and the Force's winter headquarters. B and F were to head west and search out a site to build their first permanent post. C Division would join them, coming along more slowly with the artillery and the remaining heavy equipment. After a trip to Fort Benton for supplies, Colonel French would meet up with D and E at Wild Horse Lake and go east with them. Macleod would go with him to Benton, then rendezvous with the men staying in the West.

FRED BAGLEY

September 22

This is my sixteenth birthday. Sounded Reveille at 6
a.m. Breakfast at 8 of buffalo meat, bread and tea. Fine
morning.

September 22, 1874, was the last time many of the officers
and men would ever see Colonel George French. At dawn the
Colonel and nine men set out for Fort Benton. With him rode
Major Macleod, Sub-Inspector Ephraim Brisebois, Assistant
Surgeon Richard Nevitt and Pierre Léveillé, along with two
half-breeds and three sub-constables, one of whom was to be
mustered out because of illness. Fred Bagley was distraught
that the Colonel had taken his buckskin for the trip. A few
men stood on the edge of camp as they departed.

JAMES FINLAYSON

He left here with the best wishes of the men. That he
may never come back.

With the troopers' silence at his back, French quickly put
distance between himself and the Force. Their lightly loaded
carts and wagons flew across the prairie; forty-two miles the
first day, fifty-two the second and thirty on the third, despite
making eleven crossings of the snaking Teton and Marias
rivers. Averaging that pace, even allowing for rest stops, the
Force would have covered the distance from Dufferin to
Whoop Up in four weeks.

When the ten men arrived at Benton around noon on the
twenty-fourth, the saloons, hurdy-gurdy joints and whiskey
shanties emptied as their denizens clamoured for a look at the
British lawmen who had come to seize control of the territory
north of the Medicine Line. Though it was only midday, a
good number of the crowd were already well-braced. Even the
troopers of the 7th Infantry, who came out of their rickety
garrison, had made a start on the day's tippling. The rowdies
shouted greetings, catcalls and a few suggestions about where

the men could get a poke for a good price.

Isaac Baker pushed his way through the throng to welcome the North West Mounted Police to the town of Benton. He made a short but fulsome speech, offering them the co-operation of the peace-loving residents. The irony of the situation wasn't lost on those sober enough to notice it. Here was the chief whiskey trader himself, Isaac Baker, grandly laying out the red carpet for the lawmen who intended to put him out of business.

But Baker's primary skill as a businessman was his ability to adjust to the changing tide of circumstance. As the leaves were turning in 1874, Baker scented another change in the wind. The Baker firm had enjoyed a highly profitable five-year run, but the days of the whiskey trade were clearly numbered. The Indians were still thirsty but they were dying so fast there soon wouldn't be any left to trade with. Moreover, any fool could see that the buffalo were disappearing. When they were gone what would the Indians have worth trading for? As Isaac Baker stood in the ruts of Fort Benton's main street, he sniffed gold in the pockets of the North West Mounted Police.

Ever since 1869, when J.J. Healy demonstrated the profits to be made north of the Medicine Line, Baker knew the young country spelled prosperity for anyone clever enough to seize the moment. For years he'd cultivated an extensive correspondence with key people in Ottawa, currying favour, making contacts and educating himself about Canadian politics and business. He knew the police were coming long before anyone else in Benton. He also knew that a railroad would likely soon follow. A railroad meant labourers, settlers, mail contracts, supply contracts and all manner of business having to do with opening up the Canadian frontier. And whoever provisioned the NWMP had the inside track on outfitting the railroad.

Colonel French was surprised and delighted to find such a warm and civilized welcome in a frontier outpost. The two other partners in I.G. Baker and Company, the Conrad brothers, Charles and William, were the descendants of a fine old Virginian family and both had served as officers in the Civil War. And whatever Isaac and George Baker lacked in pedigree they made up for in hospitality, immediately taking the Colonel in hand, insisting that he and his officers join them for supper and be quartered that night in Isaac's own home. The men, the half-breeds and the horses would be seen to in the livery stable down the road.

At last the Colonel was among his own kind, men who understood the affairs of the world and whose lives were not narrowly governed by the petty basics of daily life—food, drink, shelter. At dinner he was more relaxed than he'd been for days, even, to Major Macleod's amazement, offering an amusing story of his days as a young officer.

Though the transportation centre for northern Montana for years, Fort Benton was a scruffy, grubby town, even more so in the last few years, after the Montana gold rush had died. It looked as if someone had made great plans, then abandoned them. Even the garrison was neglected and run down, its adobe walls propped up in places with poles and boards. Plenty of money still flowed through the town but most of it was poured down throats, spent in the hurdy-gurdies or loaded in the river boats for St. Louis. Amidst it all, Isaac and his wife had carved an oasis, a home filled with fine furniture imported from the East, table linens and high-quality cotton curtains on the windows.

Business wasn't discussed during the meal or dessert— ambrosial bowls of fresh fruit—but as soon as the port and cigars were brought out, Baker cordially asked Colonel French how he and his partners could assist the North West Mounted Police in their admirable mission to stamp out the whiskey trade. Major Macleod produced a long list of supplies required to re-outfit the Force, everything from bullets to blankets. Baker assured him that filling these needs would be simplicity itself. Why, just that morning he'd bought an excellent string of Indian horses, from a reliable breed, that would serve them very well.

Colonel French steered the conversation into conditions across the border in whiskey country. Baker told French that neither his firm nor any of the other reputable Benton merchants would sully themselves with such a vile trade. But he allowed there were hard cases who drifted in and out of Benton and were generally believed to be up to no good. As for Fort Whoop Up, Baker admitted that his firm had occasionally outfitted traders who might then have used the fort as a base of operations. But who could control where a man went once his wagon was full?

"Sometimes we've hired a bad apple," one of the Conrad brothers put in, "but when we find out, we put it right fast."

After some thought, Baker offered the services of Charles Conrad to help Major Macleod and his men find Whoop Up and facilitate any urgent commercial needs that might crop up in the coming days. Baker neglected to mention that Conrad knew the way to Whoop Up like the back of his hand, having ferried numerous loads of whiskey there. Nor did he point out that one of Conrad's first acts as a partner in Baker's company was to build Fort Conrad in the British Territory—one of the forty or so forts operating in the North West between 1869 and 1874.

When the Colonel launched into a bitter complaint about the quality of the guides and scouts he'd been forced to use, Baker offered a solution.

"Got just the man for you! Savviest little bugger you'd ever want. Speaks all the Indian languages and he can track a four-day-old passing-of-wind. None too clean, of course, but he's your man."

Colonel French then raised the topic of the Cypress Hills massacre. Here, regretfully, neither the Bakers nor the Conrads could help. Doubtless an unpleasant incident. One heard rumours. Difficult to sort out the truth. Probably blown out of proportion. They all agreed that if some unfortunate killing had taken place, the likely culprits were the same hard cases involved in the whiskey trade, or wolfers, or both.

After toasts all 'round to the future of the North West, the officers settled into the first real beds they'd enjoyed since leaving Toronto. Suddenly their future seemed more secure. Before he turned in, Baker sent a hand to make sure Jerry Potts was sober come the morning.

Colonel French was up early the next day and, as Major Macleod saw to the supplies and horses, conducted his enquiries into the Cypress Hills matter. He recruited a "confidential agent" who provided a list of suspects and their whereabouts, as well as a general description of the events. By dint of careful and exhaustive questioning, French was satisfied he'd "obtained the full particulars as to the murders at the Cypress

Hills" and was confident of "nailing all the ruffians at once."

Of course, the Colonel could have saved considerable time and effort by strolling across the street to the Elite saloon and listening in, as John Evans and his ilk were fond of regaling the crowd with dramatic tales of their exploits at Cypress Hills.

His enquiries concluded, French found that Major Macleod had the supplies well in hand. He approved the fifteen horses already selected, fourteen of which were to go back East with French and one to stay with Macleod. The colonel carefully inspected the goods purchased by his second-in-command—a wagon, a double harness, corn, oats, boots, moccasins, stockings and gloves—before pronouncing them suitable. He was extremely pleased with the quality, remarking to Macleod that the prices were "generally very low."

COLONEL FRENCH

September 26

Started at noon, rather a poor start, half-breeds suffering from the extra stock of liquor laid in. Some horses baulky. One of them broke the pole of the waggon, had to camp and send back for another.

September 27

A good deal of trouble getting up hill with horses. I have only three half-breeds, a guide, a drover, 2 men and myself to manage everything. I drove the waggon, purchased two more new horses on the road. We now have 4 carts, one waggon and 31 horses to look after, our hands are full. Kept going until 10:30 p.m., made about 33 miles.

James Macleod never saw Colonel French again. After meeting up with his troops, who had covered nearly seventy miles after he left, George French turned his back on the West and never returned. Though he remained Commissioner of the North West Mounted Police until 1876, de facto command of the Force was transferred that day to a middle-aged lawyer who missed his sweetheart.

Major Macleod and Ephraim Brisebois stayed in Benton for several days to complete the ordering of supplies for the winter. Macleod met with "the breed" Jerry Potts. He described the camp where he'd left the rest of the men under the command of Inspector William Winder. Potts considered for a moment before informing him that his men were camped about thirty miles east of the Whoop Up trail. Though French had ordered him not to inspect the alleged whiskey fort, there were too many inconsistencies for Macleod to swallow. He sent a dispatch to Winder ordering him to move camp to the trail in preparation for a final push to Whoop Up. As soon as Macleod, Brisebois, Conrad and Potts departed, Isaac Baker hustled off to Helena where he ordered twenty tons of supplies, notable enough to warrant a report in the *Herald* on October 9.

Marching to Many Ghosts

Jerry Potts took his small band of six North West Mounted Policemen in hand the minute they left Fort Benton, and they were happy to let him. After a couple of hours on the trail, he pointed them in the right direction, then rode off without a word. When he returned, there was a fat deer laid across his saddle. "Grub," was all he had to say before he vanished again.

Potts seemed to know what every strange noise, scratch mark in the dirt and puff of smoke in the distance augured. He had the gift of appearing when needed, then disappearing again at will. When Major Macleod's batman was clumsily kindling a fire, Potts sidled over and, seeming only to pass his hands over the wood, had it roaring instantly.

The next day, while listening to Conrad and Macleod converse, Potts whipped around, drew his revolver and blew the heads off two huge jack-rabbits racing by, fifty feet away. His gun was in and out of his holster, and his attention back to the conversation, before the men could react. Conrad and Macleod gaped at this casual display of marksmanship.

"Grub," Potts explained again matter-of-factly, but Macleod thought he saw the tiniest smile lurking in the corner of his mouth, or perhaps it was just the stretch of his lips clenched on his cigar butt. That night Potts foraged in a creek bed and found a quantity of onion-like growths, which he threw, along with fresh potatoes from Benton and the rabbit meat, into a pot. One man swore that not even his mother could make such a delicious stew.

The next day a trooper let out a strangled yell. He pointed just off the trail where an Assiniboine Indian lay, as punctured by bullets and arrows as any seamstress's pincushion. After recovering from the shock, the sub-constable asked Potts what he thought had happened.

"Whiskey," replied Potts, as if that single word explained every horror and debasement in the Territory.

Potts took an immediate liking to Major Macleod, who often rode ahead talking with him. This surprised Charles Conrad, who had never heard Potts speak more than two or three words at one time—he didn't really converse, he listened, he grunted and that was the end of it. Conrad worried—whatever were they talking about?

From right: Dr. John Kittson, James Macleod, Dalrymple Clark, a Constable,
a few years after the march west

Conrad had caught Macleod looking penetratingly at him several times; it was a discomforting hangman's gaze. In truth, it was hard for Conrad to disguise his true self. Outfitted in his riding gear he looked rather more like the whiskey trader he was than the general manager of a Fort Benton store.

Potts was happy he didn't have to guide the one they called the Colonel; he hadn't liked the look of him—all jumpy inside. But the white chief's tall horse was another thing. Potts imagined the chestnut stallion as stud of his herd. Good thing that temptation had ridden away. Potts was also glad that the Colonel's giant half-breed wasn't coming with them. The big man stank of Cree; if they travelled together, doubtless there'd be a reckoning.

The rest of the whites were appallingly inexperienced even after three months on the trail. And by the great spirits, where had they gotten those horses and what had they done to them? He'd never seen animals so wretched and Macleod told him these were the best of the lot. Potts could only shake his head. The men weren't much better off than the horses; they and their clothes looked like they'd been flayed with a bull whip. With the exception of the Colonel, who was quite pretty, their ravaged faces told of men who'd been pushed to their limit.

Potts was well used to working for whites, but he was equally accustomed to an undercurrent of resentment for their dependency on him. Most of the whites he knew spent a lot of time making sure everyone understood how important they were. Potts didn't mind bragging—the Blackfoot made an art of boasting—but a man should have some action to back up his words, a deed behind his stories.

These men were different. They didn't try to hide their delight in his skills and were eager to learn. And it seemed to matter less to these whites that he was a half-breed. After instructing the young cook in the art of prairie fire making, using stones to hold the heat when wood was scarce and making a dirt berm around the fire to concentrate its intensity, Potts looked down into his eager face. The boy brought to mind a buffalo calf separated from its herd—helpless. He handled his gun as if it were a stick, he made too much noise when he walked and he rode like a sack of buffalo chips.

Still, there was something in his eyes. Potts thoughtfully

fondled the cat skin hanging from his neck—maybe these were the ones to stop the bleeding of his people. Then and there Jerry Potts decided he'd help these men all he could.

While Macleod and his party were still in Benton, Inspector Winder with B, C and F Divisions marched west to rendezvous with them. The troops returning East had taken the pick of the horses, leaving the lame, sick and starved discards for the men staying in the West. There weren't enough horses and oxen left to pull the wagons, so they leap-frogged ahead with some of the troops and supplies, then returned with the fittest animals to help haul the remainder.

JAMES FINLAYSON

Sept 27

Most of us washing our clothes. Washed my clothes and had to go in my drawers and no shirt on until my clothes dried.

If the people of Canada could see us now with bare feet, not one half clothed, half starved picking up fragments left by the American Troops and hunting Buffalo for meat and have to pay for the ammunition used in killing them. I wonder what they would say of Col. French?

Sept 29

Reveille at 4 a.m. Teamsters were told off to go back after the guns and the balance of our waggons. Not having enough horses to move all at once. If Canadians knew what this expedition will cost I think Col French would very soon get his discharge.... The guns came into camp at 5 p.m. Had rabbit and prairie chicken for supper. Weather beautiful.

Sept 30

Reveille at 6 a.m. On the march 9 a.m. Leaving the guns behind again. Two men of C Troop deserted last night. Hard driving using up the horses. Marched ten miles and halted for one hour to let the horses feed.

Having no water we had no grub. Marched five miles and camped. There is a nice well here dug by the "Boundary Survey" Party. Had nothing to drink from nine in the morning till seven in the evening. Hard times. W fine. Country level.

Oct 1

Reveille at 6 a.m. On the march at 8:30 a.m. On the same job today. Our mess cart broke down 1 1/2 miles from camp. I stayed with it until a wheel was sent back. The prairie caught fire and burnt over a very extensive piece of ground.

Great joy today when we struck the Fort Hamilton or Fort Whoop up trail. A mule train passed through camp from Hoopup. We searched them for liquor but did not find any so they [went] on to Benton. Rocky spring camp. Mounted guard at 6 p.m. W fine.

Oct 2

Reveille at 6 am. Relieved off guard at the same time. Marched six miles and camp on Milk river. The river banks are lined with Buffaloes there must be at least ten or fifteen thousand. The largest herd we have seen. Weather fine. Country sandy. Very hard pulling.

Oct 3

Being in a stationary camp there is not much to do. On Buffalo chip fatigue for our mess cook and in the afternoon out skinning and cutting up two Buffaloes. Robinson of F Troop blew off one of his fingers by a shot gun bursting. Weather a little cold.

On October 4, 1874, Jerry Potts guided his party to the main body of the Force at its camp on the Milk River just off the Whoop Up trail. He was startled at the wild cheering that accompanied their arrival and heard Macleod's name mentioned over and over, as if he were a victorious warrior returning from battle. Jerry Potts thought he'd seen and experienced just about everything the frontier had to offer. He'd been in the thick of battle in all its dreadful, exhilarating glory, he'd seen entire tribes decimated by smallpox, many times he had lain on the ground and felt the tremble of a hundred thousand buffalo hooves reverberating through his body. He'd come across his own people strung up by their necks with the white man's rope and he'd beseeched the spirits for strength when the willow stick pierced his breast muscles during the sun dance.

But Jerry Potts had never seen anything like what stretched out before his eyes. Potts gaped at the astonishing array of clothing. Some of the men wore nothing but ripped long-johns and tattered bits of fabric wrapped around their feet. One trooper had strapped gloves to his feet and tied them with saganappi, another sported what had once been a pair of boots but now had neither heels nor soles. There were men standing around with shirts and no drawers, in coats with no sleeves, hats with no crown and trousers ripped off at the thigh or knee. Their hair was filthy and matted, and tangled beards adorned most chins. Their faces were indistinguishable under a layer of soot from prairie fires and they reeked like week-old carcass.

In a makeshift corral of wagons stood listless, four-legged skeletons. Macleod had been right. Compared to these wretched things, his animals were the picture of health. A good half would never work again. They ought to be put out of their misery then and there. Potts wondered how the men got these pathetic beasts to walk, let alone haul or carry anything.

JAMES FINLAYSON

Oct 4

A party of men with forty horses and three oxen returned to Spring Creek camp to fetch up the guns and waggons left there. Col Macleod arrived from Fort Benton. Had a splendid roast of buffalo for dinner.

Oct 5

Reveille at 6 a.m. Had *three* potatoes for dinner, quite a treat. Have had none since we left Lower Fort. Mounted guard at 6 p.m. Fine weather.

Oct 6

Reveille at 5:30 a.m. It is just one year today since I listed. Then I was in Toronto, now I am on guard on the prairie a long way from home.

The guns with the remainder of the Train arrived today. A B Troop horse died today. Relieved off guard at 6 p.m. Weather fine.

Oct 7

Reveille at 5:30. The force moved off at 7 a.m. Leaving 11 men and one officer to guard seven loaded waggons that they were unable to take along with them.

I was left behind as one of the guard. A party of traders passed our camp who were duly searched no liquor found. We clubed together and bought 100 lbs of flour from them for twelve dollars and a five gallon keg of syrup for twelve dollars. Going to have a blow out tonight.

Jerry Potts watched the 140 remaining NWMP mount up for the final two-day push to Whoop Up.

"They don't look like much but they're good boys," said Macleod, as if reading Potts' mind.

Potts grunted noncommittally.

"They're good boys," insisted Macleod. "Soft outside but hard inside. They won't run. They'll fight."

"Maybe," allowed Potts.

Macleod chuckled. The relationship between the two men had deepened in the last week. As much as the times would allow, the half-breed warrior and the assistant commissioner of the Mounted Police were friends. Potts liked the way the white man looked him in the eye when he spoke. Macleod also asked his opinion about things other than how far such and such was and how long it would take to get there. He waited patiently while Potts thought questions over and listened carefully as he phrased his replies. It was the first time that a white man had ever treated him as an equal—Jerry Potts liked it.

James Macleod quickly understood that Jerry Potts was far more than a simple frontiersman—his experience, skills and blood made him a perfect tutor and provided an entrée into the Blackfoot Confederacy. From what he knew of those suspicious and fractured, yet still powerful people, he would need an intermediary like Potts to gain their trust. But what Macleod liked best about Potts was that he delivered—often far more than he was asked.

That first day of the final march to Whoop Up, Potts vanished shortly after the troops pulled out of camp. One moment he was riding alongside Macleod, the next he was gone. Just when Macleod was readying to halt the troops for lunch, he spotted Potts resting in the shade of a cottonwood tree. Lying across a nearby rock was a well-fatted buffalo calf, shot, gutted and ready to roast. At supper time, Potts led the troops off the established trail for thirty minutes until they reached a sylvan spring with the best water they'd had since Dufferin. After that, he had the Mounted Police in his pocket.

The troopers adored Jerry Potts. He exuded a confidence that none of the half-breeds on the march possessed. Though he spoke sparingly, they often suspected he was pulling their leg. When one of the troopers asked him what lay on the other side of a prominent hill, Potts simply responded, "Nudder hill."

Early in the afternoon of October 9, the North West Mounted Police finally confronted the evil they'd set out to vanquish—Fort Whoop Up. Macleod had heard many conflicting stories about the fort. When he received his commission in 1873, he'd carefully read the myriad reports and correspondence on the whiskey trade. They were written by sound men, some he'd met, all he knew by reputation. The men were either living in the West like Reverend McDougall, or inspecting the West as agents of the government, like Captain William Butler or Colonel Robertson-Ross. They all agreed there was a serious problem; as many as five hundred American desperadoes were selling firewater to the Indians and slaughtering whoever got in their way. Up to one hundred bandits were reportedly headquartered right here at Fort Whoop Up.

On the other hand, Colonel French, acting on mysterious information, had inexplicably declared that the fort was the property of I.G. Baker and that it was used only for legitimate purposes, not for liquor trafficking. But when Isaac Baker and the Conrad brothers vehemently denied ownership of the fort,

Colonel French had remained silent. They confirmed that they never trafficked in whiskey. It was at this point that James Macleod had decided that he would go to Whoop Up to find out for himself what was really going on.

On the matter of Whoop Up, Potts, for the first time, wasn't much help.

"Bad medicine. Many ghosts," was all he would say, stroking the stock of his Henry rifle.

There, in the valley below, was reality at last—a formidable reality at that. Built of enormous logs carefully dovetailed altogether and one hundred yards square, Macleod estimated it could easily accommodate a hundred men—all of whom, if the reports were correct, were waiting to fight it out with the NWMP. Commanding the approach were two old, but very serviceable-looking guns. Poking defiantly up from one of the bastions was the American flag. Over it all hung a death-like silence, eerie in its completeness, as if nature had swallowed all sound. So this was Many Ghosts, thought Macleod. He could almost feel them.

Macleod didn't believe for an instant that this fortress was built for simple trading. Even with only a handful of experienced gun hands defending the fort, considerable blood would be shed if it came to a fight. He looked at his ragged army,

Fort Whoop Up before the arrival of the NWMP.

now half its original size. They'd come so far. He didn't want a single man to die from a whiskey trader's bullet. For the first time, the Major was grateful to Colonel French for his stubborn insistence on bringing along the horse killers—the nine-pound field guns. It might take all afternoon, but he could pound the fort into kindling if he had to.

Macleod sent several parties out to scout for ambushes and had the men of C Division set up the two mortars and two artillery guns. He spread the remainder of the men out in an attack formation they hadn't practised since Dufferin. Still the silence. Macleod ordered the fort hailed. But even a sergeant-major's hurricane-force voice couldn't provoke a response.

After the stalemate had lasted for some minutes, Potts motioned Macleod onto his horse.

"Where are we going?" asked Macleod.

"Fort," responded Potts, riding off.

The fascinated troopers watched their commanding officer and the half-breed lope down into the valley and across the flats to the dreaded Whoop Up. Potts pounded on the massive gate with his rifle butt. After a considerable delay the gate swung open. A gaunt, grizzled specimen stood there, smiling broadly. Dave Akers had been kicking around the territory for years, mining, wolfing, woodhawking, whiskey trading, whatever brought in a buck. Macleod demanded to know if he was the owner of this fort.

"That I am," he responded genially. "Been expecting you. Supper's on."

Macleod informed him that there were accusations of whiskey trading with the Indians and that he was commencing a search of the fort. Akers waved them in.

The NWMP poked into every nook and cranny and, though they found plenty of empty barrels and a strong overriding odour of whiskey in various places, there was only enough alcohol around for personal use. There weren't a hundred men inside, nor even a dozen, just Akers and some Indian women— wives of traders in the area, Akers explained, *fur* traders.

"Got the squaws cooking up some buffalo," said the beaming Akers, repeating his supper invitation. Macleod accepted, but with the demeanour of a man smelling a rat.

Supper was a fine spread. Roast buffalo, canned peaches,

potatoes and fresh baked bread. Macleod, using all his lawyer's skills, threw probing questions at Akers but couldn't smoke him out.

Macleod contemplated the situation. It stank to high heaven, no question about it. There was no way this mangy customer owned or operated Whoop Up and there was plenty of evidence that the fort was the base of a sizeable whiskey trade. Akers was too cagey to fall into any of his traps, but Macleod thought he saw a way to poke a hole in his story.

Macleod leaned forward and explained that the Force intended to stay in the territory for the winter, but with cold weather long overdue, he doubted they would have sufficient time to build adequate shelter. Akers nodded in understanding. Winter, he agreed, could be brutal in this part of the world. Then Macleod played his final card, offering to buy the fort from Akers for ten thousand dollars.

The surprised Akers sputtered. This was a contingency that I.G. Baker hadn't considered when he created this straw man. Akers glanced furtively at Charles Conrad. Equally furtively Conrad shook his head once. Neither the Bakers nor the Conrads wanted to risk the fort's history fouling up their fledgling relationship with the North West Mounted Police. Better to cast Whoop Up adrift. It had paid for itself hundreds of times over anyway. And besides, the whiskey trade was almost dead.

The furtive exchange between Akers and Conrad didn't escape Macleod's notice. His suspicions were confirmed. Talking to Akers but watching Conrad with a hawk's eye, Macleod spoke.

"So your story is that you own this fort and that it was never used for whiskey trading," he said, his voice heavy with doubt.

"Yes indeed, that's right, sir." A vigorous nod of assent from Akers.

"Well," thundered Macleod, getting to his feet. "Let this be fair warning. From this day on, I'm the law out here and I'll arrest anyone I even *think* is trading whiskey." He then paused and glanced pointedly at Conrad.

"I've got the authority to try any man and with a wink from Ottawa, I'll hang him."

Epilogue

After the showdown at Fort Whoop Up, James Macleod asked Jerry Potts to find a suitable site for the first North West Mounted Police fort—above all else, he told him, it must be easily defensible. Potts took him to a spot on the banks of the Old Man's River, about twenty-eight miles from Whoop Up. Macleod hired the I.G. Baker firm to begin construction of the fort, which the men insisted on naming Fort Macleod. D.W. Davis, most recently manager of Whoop Up itself, supervised the work.

Macleod wasted no time in routing the whiskey traders. The primary merchants behind the whiskey business, T.C. Power and I.G. Baker, abandoned it the minute the NWMP arrived, but there were plenty of freelance sellers and the third largest whiskey trader in the territory, John "Waxy" Weatherwax—Parson John McDougall's "Spaniard"—persevered.

Towards the end of October 1874 Jerry Potts led the Mounties to a whiskey post where five men, including

Kamoose Taylor, were arrested, and sixteen horses, buffalo robes, guns and ammunition were confiscated. The five men were all employed by Weatherwax, who promptly bailed out four of them. (He neglected to spring the fifth, William Bond, a black man. Bond later escaped.) Weatherwax continued to sell whiskey to all comers, boldly frequenting Fort Macleod to socialize and play cards with the Mounties. But, on February 17, 1875, Waxy's luck ran out—Macleod, acting on Jerry Potts' information, arrested him for trading whiskey to the Indians and handed him a six-month prison term and a three-hundred-dollar fine. The organized whiskey trade was finished.

As he moved to stamp out the liquor traffic, Major Macleod also began to establish a rapport with the Blackfoot Confederacy. Having confirmed his initial impression that the Mounties could become valuable allies for his people, Jerry Potts toiled ceaselessly to create an understanding among them. He spent hours with Macleod, instructing him on the ways of the various tribes, appropriate modes of greeting, how to smoke a peace pipe, and the significance of gifts and whom to give them to. Macleod then invited all the major chiefs to parlay; Crowfoot of the Blackfoot, Bull Head of the Peigan and Red Cloud of the Blood. Potts travelled from tribe to tribe delivering the invitations personally. After their meeting, Bull Head was so impressed with Macleod that he gave him the chief's own name, Stamixotokan.

Jerry Potts' tutoring, coupled with Macleod's respectful attitude and diplomatic skills, led to a close relationship between the Confederacy and the Mounties, which cleared the way for the Blackfoot Treaty, signed in September 1877. As he penned his assent on the document, Red Cloud recalled his first meeting with Macleod. "Three years ago when the Mounted Police came to my country, I met and shook hands with Stamixotokan at the Belly River. Since that time he has made me many promises and has kept them all—not one of them has been broken. Everything the Mounted Police have done has been for our good." Crowfoot expressed similar sentiments.

The work of Macleod and Potts was an important factor in keeping the Blackfoot out of the second Riel uprising. If the Confederacy had thrown its support in with the Métis and the Cree, it's possible Canada wouldn't exist as the country we know. Riel would certainly have triumphed in the 1885 Rebellion and much of the prairies might now be an independent, Métis-led country. Not only that but if Blackfoot had retreated into the Rockies and mounted guerrilla warfare against the whites, it would have taken decades longer for the Canadian Pacific Railway to be built. And British Columbia, already impatient with Ottawa's foot-dragging on the railroad, would probably have left Confederation.

Canada's treatment of the Plains Indians is far from the even-handed benevolence that history has usually recorded. There were many dark and desperate times ahead for the Plains Indians after the NWMP arrived. But the presence of the Mounties at least prevented their extermination and shielded them from some of the worst horrors suffered by tribes south of the border.

ON THE TRAIL TO EDMONTON WITH INSPECTOR JARVIS

On November 1, 1874, Inspector Jarvis and his twenty-two-man contingent stumbled into Fort Edmonton after a gruelling eighty-eight-day, nine-hundred-mile journey from Roche Percée. Though they had followed an established HBC trail, it was in terrible condition for most of the way, forcing the men into a brutal daily regime of road and bridge building. The final seventy miles to the fort were the most difficult.

SAM STEELE

Our progress was slow and the going very difficult. Our loose horses often fell, one fine animal being lifted bodily by Carr and myself at least a dozen times by means of a pole. The other horses had to be helped along in the same manner....

The trail was worse than any we had encountered. It was knee-deep in black mud, sloughs crossed it every few hundred yards, and the wagons had to be unloaded and dragged through them by hand.

Many small ponds covered with a thin coating of ice

lined the side of the trail, and gave us much trouble while we were engaged in unloading the wagons. The poor animals, crazed with thirst and feverish because of their privations, would rush to the ponds to drink, often falling and having to be dragged out with ropes.... It mattered not how often they were watered, the same performance had to be gone through time after time.

A dozen oxen and ten horses died en route and most of the remaining horses succumbed soon after arriving at Edmonton. Despite the troopers' travail, their slog north had none of the turmoil that plagued the march from Dufferin to Sweet Grass Hills. Officers worked alongside the men, tending cattle and standing guard, hauling horses out of bogs and generally pitching in.

JEAN D'ARTIGUE

To travel in such a country under these disadvantages and labouring under the unfavourable circumstances in which we were then, required a leader of sound judgement, and great ability. And such a man we had in Inspector Jarvis.

He was as fond of short marches as Colonel French was of long ones; and he was right; for the proverb, "slow but sure" is always the safest to follow in long marches. Taking advantage of the best camping places to be found, Inspector Jarvis would order a halt, four or five times a day in order to give the horses and oxen time to feed.

And the result of such a course was soon felt; the animals began to recover rapidly, and even most of the sick men were soon able to resume their duties. I must add that since we were detached from the main column, we were living together like a family. No more of this quasi-discipline; no more days without food.

We performed our duties not only for our country's sake, but to please our commander. Every heart was beating for Inspector Jarvis, and if he had asked us to follow him, even to the North Pole, not one of us would have refused.

Jarvis, Sévère Gagnon and the rest of the men took considerable satisfaction from accomplishing what others thought impossible. Even Macleod expected them to give up and winter in Fort Ellice. But being freed from the command of Colonel French imbued the men with renewed strength and fortitude. And even during the worst days of their trek, hints of normalcy popped up every now and then.

JEAN D'ARTIGUE

[A] romantic scene took place in our camp. A sub-constable had fallen in love with an Indian maiden. This did not at all please the Apostle of Temperance who accosted me with intense emotion, saying: "I can't tolerate such a scandal. How I repent having enlisted in the Mounted Police."

"What scandal," said I, "I don't understand you."

"Do you know," said he, "that Sub-constable V. has become enamoured of an Uskinik squaw? He wants at any cost, to take her to Edmonton and marry her. Did you ever hear such a disgrace?"

"I don't understand, what there is about that to displease you," said I. "For my part, I don't see any inconvenience in her coming with us, if she will agree to be our cook."

"Foolish man," said the Apostle of Temperance, walking away, "you are making a jest of what, to me, is a serious matter. If he takes her along, I shall go no farther."—and, in truth, we were all opposed to the project of the unhappy sub-constable.

Approaching the camp I heard bursts of laughter, and entering, I witnessed a touching and somewhat romantic scene. The poor broken-hearted lover was embracing his fiancée, bidding her a last farewell. But alas! for the constancy of human hearts Sub-constable V. soon proved the adage: "Hot love is soon cold," and his cheerful demeanour showed that with him, at least, "out of sight" meant "out of mind."

HEADING HOME WITH COLONEL FRENCH

The men of D and E Divisions were in high spirits when they set out for the east, and home. They had all the best horses, selected by Colonel French, and carried only food—no artillery, mowing machines or other heavy equipment. Though their horses still looked like walking cadavers, the men were so eager to get to Fort Garry they would have carried the animals on their shoulders if they had to.

FRED BAGLEY

September 28
Reveille at 6:30 a.m. Sub Const. Bill Latimer and myself out hunting for antelope all day. As our clothes were still spread out to dry, after the "boiling" process our costume consisted of sacking around our feet and waists, and anything but clean helmets on our heads. Very warm day.

JOSEPH CARSCADDEN

We are pestered at night with Wolves. They are here by the hundred and are no doubt hungry for they like to keep very near us. Too near to be safe. No doubt these wild animals think our frames of horses would be worth a picking and maybe they have some intentions towards ourselves, for it takes us all our time to keep them off at night.

FRED BAGLEY

September 29
Colonel French arrived in camp about 7 p.m. from Fort Benton...was accompanied by some tough looking, Montana broad cloth garbed Yankees, and a few fine looking Blackfeet Indians. So nice looking, indeed were

they that some of our men mistook them for squaws until one of the bucks, by an indescribable gesture proved that he was of the male persuasion.

Colonel French brought a supply, purchased in Benton, of socks, moccasins, brogans, dried canned potatoes in tins similar to 5 gallon coal oil cans, also two teams of horses, and a few cayuses. The foot wear brought from Benton was a God send for us as many of the men were marching either barefoot, or with gunny sacking wrapped around their feet.

My buckskin mustang in very poor condition after the trip to Benton.

JOSEPH CARSCADDEN

The Comr brings with him in addition to the stores from Benton, the unpleasant information that we are not going to Fort Garry, but to Fort Pelly a place about 500 miles from the nearest point of civilization where we are to remain all winter.... [W]e trudge along discontentedly and moodily toward Pelly.

FRED BAGLEY

October 14

As we expect to reach the H.B.Co's Fort Qu Appelle tomorrow we receive orders to make ourselves and clothes as clean and presentable as possible. As the clothes of most of us are little better than rags this will be no easy matter.

CLEAN AND PRESENTABLE. Rather a large order for a dirty, lousy, ragged and hungry mob such as we now are, and utterly impossible to carry out, or at least it will be no easy matter.

JOSEPH CARSCADDEN

This march to Qu'Appelle seemed more tedious than any other part of the journey, chiefly I suppose because we were more anxious as we came nearer the end of our journey to see the place we had to inhabit all winter, but also because the roads were miserable and the country thro' which we passed looked anything but encouraging as it was simply a bed of cinders....

[W]e did not look much like English Subjects nor any other beings of the white race. The black dust and cinders did their work on us with a vengeance.

FRED BAGLEY

October 16

One man from each tent fitted out with "clean and presentable" clothes, and sent in to the Fort to get tobacco, pipes, and other small necessaries.

Recent newspapers received by Mr. McLean, the Chief Factor here contain astonishing accounts of our progress and condition. One account has it that we have been wiped out to the last man by the Blackfeet. Prayers being said in all the churches of Eastern Canada for our welfare.

JOSEPH CARSCADDEN

This tedious march lasted ten days when we arrived at Qu'Appelle, tired dejected, foot-sore, heart-sore and hungry, yes hungry for we had again run short of rations. But surely the Comr will purchase extra provisions for us here and show that our former privations and starvations were merely caused by want of judgment on his part and that he would have prevented it all if he could.

Now is the time for regaining at least in some measure the men's esteem and confidence. But does he attend to this point and secure the men's comfort, no, not by any means. What does he care for the poor grovelling creatures' esteem, not he, he is their Commander and has no ideas or feelings in common with Sub Constables and what is the consequence of this treatment.

Do the men more alertly obey his orders & do they place confidence in him as able to direct their movements? Do they show their zeal by endeavouring to save their horses, their waggons and government property in general? Do they serve their Queen and country willingly? To all these queries I am sorry to say I must answer an emphatic and undeniable negative.

But to proceed, when we arrived at Qu'Appelle the men purchased flour and other necessaries at their own expense and glad they are to get a sufficient meal even under these conditions. $15 a bag for flour is of no consequence we must have it at any cost.

The Force stayed for only one evening and the following day at Fort Qu'Appelle. After a five-day march, Colonel French made camp about ten miles outside Fort Pelly, then took all the officers, except one, and rode ten miles north to Swan River to inspect the barracks. They returned that night with the grim news that not only were the barracks unfit for habitation, but there was very little hay after the Hudson's Bay Company lost three hundred tons of it in a recent fire. French decided to take D Division, with six officers and fifty men, to Fort Garry, leaving E, consisting of thirty-two men and six officers, to winter in Swan River.

JOSEPH CARSCADDEN

October 23

[T]he Comr starts for Fort Garry with D Troop and leaves E Troop under command of Inspector Carvell to fight their way thro' a "North West Winter" house-less, shoeless and I might say without any clothing to protect them.

So we scowl farewell to the Comr and hope that we

may never see his smooth sleek face again.... Our parting with D Troop is warm and sad, for few of us expect to meet again, as every one is determined to leave the Force by any means in his power, honourably if possible, but if impossible, dishonourable.

Willie Parker, assigned to Swan River, left Dufferin on October 4, joining up with Inspector Dalrymple Clark and nine constables. It had taken him three months to recuperate from the typhoid, which had left him a 120-pound weakling. Easy living had pumped him up to 170 pounds and he was eager to leave the Red River for the wilderness. Two hundred miles into their trek to Swan River, they met the returning Colonel French.

WILLIE PARKER

The column was a wonderful sight to see, straggled out for two or three miles. Nearly every man was walking; horses were like laths, swaying and wobbling from side to side; an odd team of horses every once in a while fell down, to be replaced by saddle horses.

The men appeared rosy and in the best of health, but oh, what a sight! All were virtually in rags, no hats, most of them with no boots and several wearing their own makes of moccasins made from the rawhide of buffalo. Nearly all were growing beards....

That evening in camp was a joyous one. They had not heard anything from the outside nor received any mail for months and we had brought a heavy mail for them. It was amusing to see them get supper by making slap-jacks, which were as black as a hat, but good eating at that. They said they had not seen butter for months, and had to use axle grease to fry them with. We built big campfires and for two hours sang most of our favourite songs. One composed by a Mountie was:

Pass the tea and let us drink.
To the guardians of our land,
You bet your life it's not our fault
If whiskey is contraband.

FRED BAGLEY

November 14

The uniform of Trumpeter Fred A. Bagley, of the North West Mounted Police Force consists, at the present time of rough red shirt, moleskin trousers (barndoor), brogan shoes, and long stockings, topped off by a disreputable helmet, all miles too big for him. Ichabod. The glory has departed.

JOSEPH CARSCADDEN

[W]e had to stand in water over our ankles with pieces of boots on our feet, then our suffering really begun, the water was freezing cold, but not cold enough to make ice in one night able to bear us. So here we are breaking thro' ice and splashing thro' water making hay for our horses. But thro' all these difficulties we manage to cut some 90 tons of hay and stack it ready for use.

After remaining in tents until it was so cold that we could not remain in them any longer, we are moved into a hovel that defies description, however I shall endeavour to represent it to my best ability.

This shanty was built of logs crossing one another at the ends like a snake fence and between these logs you can see the beautiful snow coming down in flakes and thro' these chinks and crannies you can hear the wind howling and whistling.

We have six stoves and a large log fire going all the time and yet many a blue face can be seen. Such is the place the Comr leaves us in. The men are employed in fatigues all the time from day-light till dark but we do not grumble, we are aware that Inspt Carvell is doing his best to make us comfortable. I might add here that we burn about 4 cords of wood per day. The thermometer varying from 35° to 45° and 50° below zero.

FRED BAGLEY

November 23

Stock taking all day. After supper Captain Carvell issued an order to continue the work through the night. All hands refused to obey the order, whereupon he, after conferring with Troop Sergeant Major Mitchell, told us that he did not intend to *order* us to work all night, but if we would carry on voluntarily he would compensate us by issuing extra rations, and giving us a holiday to-morrow.

As this seemed to be satisfactory to the men, work was continued, and finished a little after 12 midnight, and the men had supper of rice, bread and tea.

JOSEPH CARSCADDEN

I must say however that Inspt Carvell done his best to make us as comfortable by buying boots and clothing for us at the Hudson Bay store, but the Comr so soon as he hears of Inspt Carvells just treatment to his men, writes to him thus; the men are not entitled to those things, charge them to their account.

Aside from the cold, insufficient rations and wretched conditions, boredom eroded whatever was left of the men's morale. Colonel French, comfortably ensconced in Winnipeg, provided no cards, games, books or even newspapers to help the men while away the long dark hours after their daily work was finished. At one point the supply of candles was cut off. Instead, moulds were sent and the men told to make their own. Sub-constables Bill Ouzman and Joe Woods laboriously made a deck of cards out of envelopes, painstakingly painting on the numbers and including a full set of royalty for the face cards. They sang, danced with each other, endlessly told stories and jokes, but under the surface they were a tinderbox waiting to ignite.

It all started innocently enough at Christmas dinner. The men had worked hard to decorate their "hovel" for a band of local Indians and half-breeds who had been invited to share the meal.

JOSEPH CARSCADDEN

December 25

The Indians remain with us for three days and keep dancing all the time. I may here remark that these Indians are the dirtiest ever we came across. They are of the Ojibwa Tribe and not numerous. They are poor hunters, in fact we consider them the lowest order we have seen.

After Xmas they become very familiar with us and some of them were living with us nearly all the time. Of this we did not complain altho' they were eating our limited supply of rations. But by and by our officers think it is compulsory on us to feed them.

Three weeks after Christmas, with the Indians still in and around the barracks, an ailing woman escorted by three braves arrived. Inspector Carvell was away for a two-day jaunt around the neighbourhood, leaving the visiting Captain Shurtliff as the ranking officer. Shurtliff sent the Indians over to the kitchen for food, but McCarthy, the troop cook, after feeding them once, flatly refused to give them more. Shurtliff immediately fined him ten dollars for disobeying orders, whereupon McCarthy demanded justice from a higher authority. Shurtliff responded by imprisoning him in the guard tent.*

The entire troop—except Sergeant-Major Mitchell—rose up that night and, after a "pretended furious attack," snatched McCarthy from the tent and let him escape.

FRED BAGLEY

January 17, 1875

After the Sergeant Major, and the Guard had made a futile search for him the Captain ordered a parade of

---

* Though Fred Bagley's diary says that Carvell was the Captain in question, it is clear from subsequent documents that Shurtliff was the officer present and that many felt if Carvell had been there during the initial stages, the incident never would have escalated as it did.

the whole Troop, and while he was soundly berating them for their mutinous conduct, and threatening continuing punishment, the cook, suddenly appearing to spring from nowhere, was discovered sitting beside the stove.

The Captain then ordered Sam Orr, and Bill Ouzman, whom he considered the ringleaders of the mutiny, and McCarthy into close confinement in the Guard tent, which, strange to relate, was done without any objection from the erstwhile mutineers. He also placed the remainder of the Non Coms and men concerned in arrest. There was no further trouble.

January 18

Acting Sergeant Crawford, and Sub Const. Smith were this morning "warned" for Guard, but refused to take charge of the Guard tent and prisoners, claiming that they themselves were prisoners.

The Captain held an "investigation," and found the mutineers guilty of insubordination. He handed out sentences as follows: All Non Coms concerned reduced to the ranks, and fined 30 days pay each, and each mutineer Sub Const. fined 30 days pay.

To add insult to injury he also ordered the release, without punishment, of the cook—the cause of all the trouble.

Nearly identical mutinies or "bucks," as the men called them, occurred at Fort Macleod and Fort Edmonton. Both resulted from a mixture of arbitrary regulations imposed by headquarters, boredom, harsh conditions and the exorbitant prices charged at the HBC posts for basic supplies—supplies many of the men thought should have been purchased for them by the NWMP. The men were also angry at not having been paid since they left Dufferin the previous July. Eighteen men deserted Fort Macleod that first winter and many more were simply waiting for their money before hoofing it across the border.

JOSEPH CARSCADDEN

Another matter I must refer to which may seem a small thing to strangers, but certainly not to us. When the Comr went to Garry he left us with a few pounds of Government tobacco in store. Now what are we to do without any of the weed which is such a relief to habitual smokers. Nothing so far as the Comr is concerned but another means is offered to us which of course we must accept.

Our Pay Master residing in Garry sends up by the government carts a large quantity of tobacco and other things. He sends them up of course at the expense of the government and of course we expect that he will let us have what we want at reasonable prices, but is this so, judge for yourself reader.

We apply for some tobacco at his Store and enquire the price of it, and we are told that the smoking tobacco...sold in civilization at 80 cents per lb. or 20 cents per plug, four plugs making one lb., cost here 50 cents per plug or $2 per lb. Now is this fair? I leave it to any unprejudiced person, is this a fair or decent profit to ask? But we must buy it for we cannot do without tobacco.

I will not say that this money making and mean trick was a preconcerted plan between the Comr and our Pay Master but our Comr has enough to answer for without imputing this to him.

FRED BAGLEY

March 3

I have managed so far this winter to get a little joy out of life by going out every day possible on snowshoes, with Linklater, the Interpreter, trapping rabbits and foxes, which are numerous. Snow very deep. He showed me many a "wrinkle" of the trapping business, and found me an apt pupil.

The fox skins, after being tanned, were made into caps for the men, the head and tail of the skin being brought together and the tail hanging down the wearer's back, the top being left open. They are comfortable and picturesque.

Sub Const. Sam Orr chopped his finger off to day while chopping wood.

March 5

McCarthy, the cook, received his discharge for the Force. He applied for it some time ago, and now seems to be very pleased at receiving it.

General Orders received state that Sergeant C.W. "Charlie" Thompson is reduced to the ranks for applying directly to Ottawa for his discharge instead of sending his application through the Captain and the Commissioner. This does not bother him a great deal, as he was already reduced to the ranks on the 18th. of January last for taking a prominent part in the mutiny.

March 30

Patches of earth are beginning to appear under the influence of a hot sun. What few horses we have are picking up in health and strength.

I "smoked" my deer skin, but made a very poor job of it. Having made a smoke tent of the skin I was called away temporarily, and when I returned found that the "smoke" had blazed up, and blackened the skin in places.

JOSEPH CARSCADDEN

We came here with 60 horses and some 80 head of cattle including bullocks, cows and calves. Of this large stock there now remains living at the date on which I write (March 30) 23 horses and 9 head of cattle all the rest are gone to sleep. The sleep that knows no waking. Thro' what cause? Oh, the old one, starvation. There are lots of oats here but the Comr orders before going to give the horses only 4 lbs. per day and the cattle as little as possible, consequently death must ensue as there is no nourishment in the hay.

Veterinary surgeon J.L. Poett, in his November 12, 1875, report to the Ministry of Justice, written after visiting Swan River, emphasized that riding horses should receive "not less than 10 lbs. of Oats, per diem and those employed for draught purposes, no less than 12 lbs." The report in many instances appears to be an oblique criticism of Colonel French. For instance, on his orders, the horses didn't receive more than five pounds of oats per day at any time during the Great March. "The horses belonging to the Department of Public Works are fed upon 17 lbs. of Oats per diem, the consequence is they very seldom lose a horse, and their horses are always in fine working condition," he noted.

FRED BAGLEY

April 2

By this mail came news that on last Christmas day Corporal Baxter and Sub const Wilson were frozen to death while on patrol between Fort Kipp and Fort Macleod. That was 3 months ago, yet this was the first word we had of it. This gave us some real idea of our complete isolation from even our own comrades in the NWMP and the rest of the world.

Made myself a pair of trousers out of my deer skin. They are similar to those of the rest of the Troop. Sewn with a three cornered needle and deer sinew, and with plenty of fringes up and down the outside seams.

Mine, though, are a little different to the others, in that when cutting them out I failed to match the blackened parts properly. The consequence was that after I had finished, and donned them, expecting to create a sensation, (in which I was not disappointed), a view from the front showed the right leg black, and the left one white. The view from the back showed the colours reversed. Well Bond Street London is a long way from here, so, who cares?

April 13

We now have bread and pork 3 times daily. And such

pork. All fat, several inches thick, and of almost rainbow colours, yellow, and various shades of green predominating. The men have named it "Rattlesnake" or "3 foot" pork. Those who cannot stomach it, and there are many such, must be content with bread and tea. But Linklater and I manage to get the occasional rabbit.

May 13

Some amusement caused daily by Sub Inspector Frechette attending all morning stable parades clad in pyjamas, riding boots and spurs, cloak, and helmet.

May 24

Queen's birthday was celebrated in truly loyal style by a programme of sports, including carbine shooting matches, mule racing, horse racing, and in the evening a snake killing match by sides of 7 men each. The number of snakes killed by the 2 sides chosen was exactly 1,110 — all within half an hour.

May 27

Our kit bags, which we left at Dufferin last were returned to us from Fort Ellice to day. They were nearly all empty.

June 6

This day, being the anniversary of our departure from Toronto last year, recalls thoughts of "Home Sweet Home"—sweeter now than ever to many of us. Many of our men really very ill from home sickness.

June 15

A Board of Officers inspected the "Rattlesnake" pork, and condemned it as unfit for food. No comment was made on the fact that it has been issued daily to us since last Fall.

Colonel French sent a dispatch to Inspector Carvell on June 26 informing him that he was on his way to inspect the Swan River troops. As the day approached, Carvell sent Bagley out with his field-glasses to give them early warning of the Colonel's approach.

JOSEPH CARSCADDEN

...[W]e look forward to his arrival with anything but pleasure. The only act he could do on his arrival which would cause the men of this Troop to feel rejoiced to see him, would be to grant one and all that which they ardently desire and pray for, viz. their discharge from the North West Mounted Police Force.

On the morning of July 7, a year less a day after their departure from Dufferin on the Great March, the E Division "ragamuffins" assembled themselves for inspection by their commissioner. Colonel French rode to the parade ground and stopped dead.

"What is this, Captain Carvell?" he demanded.

"My troop, sir, on parade as per orders for inspection by you."

French stared at the men lined up before him. The troopers' uniforms consisted of deerskin jackets and trousers festooned with fringes, huge fox-fur caps with thick tails hanging down their backs and tall Métis-style moccasins on their feet. Most of the men sported heavy, tangled beards, bushy moustaches and long, unkempt hair. They looked more like mountain men than Mounties. Here and there French could see the remnant of a scarlet tunic—nothing else identified them as members of the North West Mounted Police.

"Good God," French cursed in disgust as he spurred his thoroughbred hard and galloped off.

THE REST IS HISTORY

COLONEL ARTHUR FRENCH

After he returned to Manitoba, Colonel French's behaviour grew more erratic and testy by the day. His entire command was in disarray, no fewer than three mutinies were taking place within the Force, officers and men were resigning or deserting in droves and subordinates were complaining about him to Ottawa. But French was preoccupied with his accommodation and other matters. He refused to move into the quarters assigned to him in Fort Dufferin and was conducting a running squabble with Ottawa about salary and expenses owed to him. It all proved too much for Hewitt Bernard, still deputy minister of justice. He telegrammed to French in mid-January 1875, demanding an explanation "for your complete disregard for orders."

"I have slaved night, noon and morning in the public interest and I feel I have deserved a little more consideration," French responded peevishly. It was only because Bernard ordered French to return to Swan River that he grudgingly did so in July 1875. Previously, French had paid little attention to the complaints of the men or officers about the deprivations at the miserable outpost. As soon as he arrived, he began ordering a long list of comforts, including a piano, books and good-quality furnishings.

On July 22, 1876, George Arthur French was fired. In his less than three years as commissioner of the NWMP, more than two-thirds of the original 319 men and officers resigned, deserted or were discharged. More than 150 horses and hundreds of cattle died, either on the march or in its aftermath. But the stain of Colonel French's unhappy command of the NWMP didn't impede his subsequent career. He served in Australia and India, and when he retired in 1902 as a major-general, he was knighted by the Queen.

JAMES MACLEOD

James Macleod became Commissioner of the North West Mounted Police in 1876, the same year he married his sweetheart, Mary. He served in that position for four years—one of the most turbulent times in the history of the Force. He was never really happy with being an intermediary between the Ottawa politicians and bureaucrats—few of whom ever travelled west—and the realities of life on the frontier. He resigned in 1880 to take up the position of stipendiary magistrate for the North West. Imperial and exacting as a judge, he didn't suffer fools or frivolous cases, once warning a repeat offender that if he appeared on charges again Macleod would personally burn down his house, sell his belongings and run him out of the territory.

Jerry Potts continued to be a close friend and Macleod tried to tutor him in the ways of "civilized life"—with varying success. Once Macleod visited Potts and was astonished to see one of his wives using a child's chamber pot as a drinking cup. He hastily explained its correct use. "You white people are crazy," an incredulous Potts responded. "You got plenty of open prairie all around and yet you use a good cup like this for kids to piss in."

JERRY POTTS

Jerry Potts interpreted for, guided and educated the Mounted Police for twenty-two more years. His colourful life and frontier skills have overshadowed his other contributions to the west. Bear Child also had the gift of diplomacy, frequently dealing with incendiary situations and diffusing them calmly. Sam Steele called him "a master of finesse" whose "influence with the Blackfoot tribes was such that his presence on many occasions prevented bloodshed." In addition to his early work creating an understanding between the Blackfoot and the Mounties, Potts played a critical, if unsung role, keeping his people out of the 1885 Riel Rebellion.

But Jerry Potts remained Jerry Potts until the day he died. Once, after helping the Mounties arrest some whiskey smugglers, Potts guarded the prisoners in the back of the wagon while a constable drove to Fort Macleod. When they arrived, Potts and the two prisoners were discovered sleeping peacefully after having drunk all the whiskey. With no evidence remaining, the two men were set free. Despite his long association with whites, Potts remained Indian in spirit, belief and manner until the day he died of throat cancer in 1896. Three of Jerry Potts descendents; Henry, Janet and Tyrone Potts, went on to serve as Mounties.

FRED BAGLEY

Fred Bagley's "six-month" trial with the NWMP grew into a twenty-five-year career. Fourteen years passed before he saw any of his family again, this time as a staff-sergeant. Fred Bagley had another reunion, in the early 1920s, when he attended a meeting of retired NWMP members.

> Among the members present I noticed a bearded man, evidently hailing from some outside point, casting curious glances in my direction whenever my name was mentioned during the course of the meeting.
>
> After the business of the meeting was concluded this man approached me and introduced himself as ex Constable Fred P——
>
> "Well, you are the son of a gun who stole my horse in Dufferin!" he accused.
>
> It was my B Troop friend of the mustang incident! I immediately countered with "I hope you enjoyed your drink," and "Where is that fifty cents I loaned you?" After a few hearty laughs together we adjourned to fight our battles o'er again.
>
> I rode this mustang—when I was not walking, or driving ox carts—during the whole of the '74 march. He lived to the good old age of 32 years, and was known throughout the Force as "Old Buck," or the "Bagley Pony."
>
> In the year 1898, owing to his great age and infirmities his life was humanely ended by Captain Deane, the O.C. of K Division, who thoughtfully sent me the last photo taken of him, together with one of his shoes, and his near fore hoof with his last troop number (K1) thereon, all of which are now highly prized mementos of my "Old Faithful."

Fred Bagley married Lucy May Kerr-Francis in 1890 and they produced six daughters. When Bagley retired as a NWMP major in 1899, he was still only forty-one. In subsequent years, he served in the Boer War and the First World War, worked in the Calgary Land Titles Office and later in the

Banff Museum of Natural History.

Bagley's trumpet was never very far away. From 1903 to 1920, he conducted the Calgary Citizens' Band. He died in 1945 at the age of eighty-seven.

HENRI JULIEN

Julien left the Mounted Police at Fort Qu'Appelle in mid-October 1874, returning to his "little cabinet" at the *Canadian Illustrated News*. "Our mission was over," he wrote in his diary. "My trip has been worth a great deal to me in health, experience and knowledge. I would not exchange it for many a more pretentious voyage." Julien died in 1908, having established himself as one of the premier cartoonists and illustrators of his generation.

JACOB CARVELL

After the awful winter of 1874–75 at Swan River, the put-upon inspector of E Division went on leave in the summer of 1875. He promptly deserted when he was safely over the American border.

JOHN MCILLREE

The great hunter had a painful setback at the onset of the march back east. "Have been laid up for some little time with piles and am badly chaffed so that I can hardly walk," he wrote ruefully in his diary, while noting the abundant game around him. "I lie on my back all day and as I have nothing to read it is pretty slow."

McIllree's devotion to hunting and a propensity to unload his problems on others earned him the nickname "Easy Going Old John Henry." McIllree became assistant commissioner of the Mounties in 1893 and remained in the position for eighteen years.

JEAN D'ARTIGUE

Despite his initial misgivings, D'Artigue went on to serve with the NWMP for six years. In 1882, his charming book *Six Years in the Canadian North-West* was published. Shortly thereafter he left the New World and returned to France, presumably to take up school teaching once again.

CECIL DENNY

Cecil Denny resigned from the NWMP as an inspector in 1882. Over the ensuing years he worked at various jobs, including Indian agent, rancher, fire ranger, police magistrate and archivist for the Alberta provincial library. In 1922, he inherited the title of baronet, becoming Sir Cecil Denny.

WILLIAM PARKER

Willie Parker served for thirty-eight years, retiring in 1912, with the rank of inspector. He developed a reputation as a raconteur and a practical joker.

JOSEPH CARSCADDEN

True to his word, Carscadden resigned shortly after Colonel French's inspection of E Division at Swan River. Little is known of him after that. He may have farmed in the vicinity of Clover Bar, Alberta, before moving into a cabin on his brother's property near Fort Saskatchewan. His diary didn't surface until 1983.

JOHN J. HEALY

After the whiskey trade died, J.J. Healy drifted from one thing to another, including editing the first Fort Benton paper and serving as its sheriff for a brief time. He bought a schooner and followed the gold rush up to Alaska and the Yukon, getting shipwrecked three times in the process. He didn't find the mother lode in the north so he returned to the west, eventually settling in Seattle while continuing to prospect in Washington, Oregon and California. When he died in 1909, he was putting together an expedition to return to Alaska and search for cinnabar or quicksilver.

D.W. DAVIS

Davis became Canadian manager for I.G. Baker & Company and supervised a profitable business with the Mounted Police, the C.P.R. and the Indians who had treaty money to spend after 1877. Like many traders, Davis cast off his country wife, Revenge Walker, and married a young Fort Macleod schoolteacher in 1887. Just days after their marriage, he took her to the nomination meeting and put his name forward to run as the first member of parliament from the North West Territories.

Old habits died hard with D.W. While canvassing for votes, he took a sleigh full of hog carcasses with him. Each carcass was stuffed with bladders of whiskey. Of his four half-breed children, the two boys returned to the ways of their Indian people and one, Charlie, became a minor Blood chief. His white children, especially Rider Davis, a prominent lawyer and Fort Macleod mayor, were never comfortable with their half-breed siblings. After two terms as member of parliament, D.W. followed Healy to the Yukon to search for gold. He died there in 1906.

JACK FRENCH

Beloved as he was by the men for his wit and humour, Jack French had a bad temper, which plagued him throughout his years with the Mounted Police. He was killed at Batoche during the Riel Rebellion.

John McDougall

The self-described "John the Baptist" of the new era brought to the West by the Mounties became a leading citizen of the wild frontier. His missionary work continued for forty-three more years but, true to form, he didn't limit himself to converting the savages. Little of significance happened in the West that didn't have Parson John involved, from the Riel Rebellion to the coming of the railroad and visits by royalty. Braggart though he was, Parson John's fearless and muscular christianity was probably the only kind that would have survived in that contentious time. And though he often treated the Indians as a king might his subjects, he fought hard for them and their rights until the day he died.

"We companioned them in sorrow and in joy, in fasting and in feasting, in peace and in war; were in all things like them, without in any sense compromising either principle or manliness."

Sam Steele

Sam Steele thrived once the Force became established in the West. He adored the freedom of their far-flung outposts and revelled in the power a single officer had over hundreds of miles of prairie and its scattered inhabitants. When the CPR came to the West, Sam Steele was in charge of protecting the road crews. He liked to boast that not a single rail was lost to thieves or vandals while he was guarding the line. In 1898 he was posted to the Yukon and served there until he ended up on the wrong side of a disagreement with corrupt but well-connected politicians and civil servants in Dawson and was removed from the Yukon.

Steele went on to fight in the Boer War, playing a role in the Breaker Morant case. He worked briefly for the British Army prior to the First World War and helped organize and train Canada's wartime militia. All the while he was still a member of the North West Mounted Police, though several senior officers spent a great deal of time trying to get rid of him. Steele's remarkable career was dotted by escapades caused by his two-fisted drinking. He died in 1919.

JAMES WALSH

Like Steele, Walsh was a man who thrived in the West, as long as he was unfettered by bureaucrats, politicians and interfering senior officers. He became renowned as "Sitting Bull's Boss," and the intensely romantic side of his nature loved his international reputation as the man who controlled the great Sioux warrior chief. Flamboyant and vain though he was, Walsh was also sympathetic and more than a little outraged at the treatment of the Sioux by the Americans. He became as close to Sitting Bull as any white man could and began to wonder if there wasn't a way to keep the refugee Sioux safe in Canada. His sympathy won him no supporters in Ottawa, where government officials wanted Sitting Bull's Sioux out of Canadian territory and didn't care what the Americans did with them. Walsh was removed from his post and eventually was forced to resign in 1883. After following the Klondike gold rush he became Administrator of the Yukon and eventually was reappointed to the Force. He died in Ontario in 1905.

By the end of 1885 Sir John A. Macdonald's invention, the North West Mounted Police, the force that most expected would be needed for only a few years to straighten out the frontier, had become a full-fledged presence in the young Dominion. Over a thousand Mounties were spread out in more than two dozen detachments in the North West, which had become a very different place. The Blackfoot Treaty had been signed, Sitting Bull had been routed from his Canadian sanctuary and returned to face arrest in the United States, Indians from the Great Lakes to the Rockies had been shepherded on to reservations, the buffalo were just a memory, Louis Riel was dead and the last spike of the Canadian Pacific Railway had been driven home.

Law enforcement was far from the Mounties' only task. Aside from busting bootleggers and keeping the peace, they fought fires, distributed seed and food to Indians and settlers, delivered babies, performed minor surgery, escorted prominent citizens who came for a tour of the Wild West, quarantined the contagious and became remarkably self-sufficient at everything from farming to sewing. They also established themselves as the best drinkers in the West. "Whiskey hunting is not popular with the corps; and a man who persistently prosecutes for this offence is looked upon with contempt," admitted John Donkin, a trooper of the time. The chorus of the Mounties' unofficial theme song illustrates the point.

> Then pass the tea, and let us drink,
> We guardians of the land,
> You bet your life it's not our fault,
> That whiskey's contraband.

Soon settlers would come pouring into the Prairie and shortly the Klondike gold rush would funnel a stampede of eager miners into the North. Towns such as Regina, Edmonton and Calgary would blossom to become respectable and prosperous. Throughout it all, the Mounties were there. As a new century dawned, it would be easy to forget the privation, terror and disaster that accompanied nearly three hundred young men when they marched off on the Great Adventure. Their trek came as close to fiasco as anything else in Canadian history, but it was a glorious one. Without it the character of the West and the people in it, Indians and white alike, would likely be vastly different.

Somewhere, Joseph Carscadden is smiling sourly. Nearby the Apostle of Temperance is distressed that his moral vision never came to pass. Not far away John McIllree is off hunting and Fred Bagley ponders the acquisition of another buckskin. Jean D'Artigue is regaling a café audience with his exploits in the North West. And Jerry Potts is patiently waiting to save them once again.

Chronology

—1806: Explorer Meriwether Lewis shoots a Blackfoot, causing thirty years of war and much destruction.

—1827: Kenneth McKenzie goes to work for the American Fur Company.

—1831: Blackfoot burn McKenzie out of his first post.

—1831: McKenzie establishes Fort Union.

—1836: McKenzie hires Andrew Potts.

—1840: (approximately): Jerry Potts born.

—1841: Andrew Potts murdered.

—1841: George French born.

—1845: Texas becomes a state.

—1847: U.S. war with Mexico ends.

—1855: Treaty of 1855, first Blackfoot Treaty in United States.

—1857: John Palliser surveys Rupert's Land.

—1859: Father Lacombe brings nuns from Montreal to start a school north-west of Edmonton.

—1862: George McDougall and family become first white family in the Territory, seventy-five miles east of Edmonton.

—1862: Minnesota Massacre.

—1863: January 1, Lincoln declares all slaves free.

—1864: I.G. Baker takes over American Fur Company holdings.

—1864: Gold Rush in Montana.

—1868: Late spring, theft of Manitou Stone.

—1869: Fall, smallpox strikes Blackfoot; famine hits in winter and continues on into 1870.

—1869: Healy and Hamilton's expedition north into the heart of Blackfoot Territory.

—1869: Sir John A. Macdonald conceives of a mounted police force.

—1869: Ignatius Donnelly advocates Texas-style absorption of Manitoba by United States.

—1869: Late in year, first Red River Rebellion flares.

—1870: January 1, General Sully's ultimatum to Blackfoot.

—1870: January 23, Baker Massacre.

—1870: Summer, expeditionary forces travel west to Manitoba over Dawson Route under command of Wolseley.

—1870: October, Battle of Belly River.

—1870: Adams Archibald sends William Butler west to investigate.

—1870: Healy and Hamilton return to Blackfoot Territory to build Fort Hamilton, which promptly burns to the ground. Construction of its replacement, Fort Whoop Up, begins immediately.

—1871: Treaty of Washington, United States recognizes Canada's existence as a nation.

—1872: Lieutenant-Governor Morris repeatedly warns Macdonald about growing problems in the West.

—1872: Spring, Jerry Potts avenges the death of his mother, then quits the whiskey trade.

—1872: Fall, Robertson-Ross travels west, also to investigate conditions.

—1872: Fall, Hewitt Bernard begins drawing up plans for NWMP.

—1873: May 3, Bill introduced by Sir John A. Macdonald re formation of NWMP.

—1873: May 23, NWMP Bill receives royal assent; provision also made for a lieutenant-governor for territories.

—1873: June 1, Cypress Hills Massacre.

—1873: July, Morris sends Macdonald a long confidential report re-emphasizing lawlessness in West.

—1873: September 20, Morris raises stakes, wiring to Macdonald, "What have you done re police force. Their absence may lead to grave disaster." This apparently galvanizes Macdonald, who tells Dufferin that the "massacre...has so greatly excited the red men that we have decided to send the Force out before the close of navigation."

—1873: September 25, first nine officers appointed. W.O. Smith, W.D. Jarvis, C.F. Young, James Farquharson Macleod, W. Winder, J. Carvell, J.M. Walsh, E.

Brisebois and E.D. Clark. Simply called Mounted Police.

—1873: October 18, Colonel French hired.

—1873: November 1, first contingent begins arriving at Lower Fort Garry.

—1873: November 5, Sir John A. Macdonald resigns.

—1874: March, French instructed to recruit the rest of the complement, three divisions totalling 150 men.

—1874: June 6, second contingent leaves Toronto.

—1874: June 19, first and second contingents meet in Dufferin.

—1874: July 8, start of Great March.

—1874: July 11, Duck Lake Massacre.

—1874: July 14, Colonel French orders sub-constables to drive ox carts.

—1874: July 19, arrival at Souris River.

—1874: July 21, Colonel French orders sub-constables to walk an hour, then ride an hour.

—1874: July 24, arrival at Roche Percée.

—1874: July 29, Inspector Jarvis instructed to take cattle and wagons to Fort Edmonton.

—1874: August 13, powwow with Sioux.

—1874: September 2, first buffalo sighted.

—1874: September 9, Colonel French orders that the horses be given one of the men's two blankets.

—1874: September 12, Colonel French declares that Fort Whoop Up is run by honest merchants and announces that he will lead half of the troop back to Manitoba.

—1874: September 20, arrival at Sweet Grass Hills.

—1874: September 22, Fred Bagley's sixteenth birthday.

—1874: September 24, Jerry Potts arrives at Fort Benton. Later that day Colonel French and Major Macleod arrive.

—1874: September 29, Colonel French rejoins D and E Divisions heading back to Manitoba.

—1874: October 9, Jerry Potts, Major Macleod and remainder of Force arrive at Whoop Up.

—1874: October 15, D and E Divisions arrive at HBC Fort Qu'Appelle.

—1874: October 23, Colonel French divides men again, leaving E Division to winter at Swan River while continuing on to Winnipeg with D Division.

—1874: November 1, Inspector Jarvis and his command arrive at Fort Edmonton.

—1874: December 4, Colonel French arrives at Winnipeg; remainder of D Division arrives three days later. Great March officially over.

—1875: January 17, mutiny at Swan River.

—1875: July 7, Colonel French's last inspection of D Division.

—1876: June 25, Battle of Little Big Horn.

—1881: October, Shoot Out at the O.K. Corral.

A NOTE ON DISTANCES TRAVELLED

Colonel French's odometer indicated that the Force as a whole had travelled 849 miles from Dufferin to their oasis at Sweet Grass Hills. Those who went on to Whoop Up covered more than 900 miles while many individuals, such as Sub-Inspector Denny and Major Macleod added hundreds of miles to their total with various side-trips—including getting lost.

The three divisions which marched from Fargo to Dufferin covered an additional 160 miles while those who returned from Sweet Grass Hills to Swan Lake covered an additional 432 miles and those who went all the way to Winnipeg added 328 more.

Those troopers who accompanied Colonel French from Sweet Grass Hills to Winnipeg covered a total of 1609 miles. French, who kept meticulous notes of his own mileage calculated that he covered 1959 miles from the beginning of the March to his return.

Acknowledgments

Acknowledgments are the curse of the book writer—not because they aren't necessary and valuable ways to give small thanks to those who've helped but because they are the last thing done in a book, when writers—at least these writers—are at their least capable. As a result, every acknowledgment we've done has missed people who've richly deserved our thanks. We apologize in advance.

As their contribution to The Book, our girls, Quinn and Claudia, once again shouldered the burden of increased household chores and distracted and/or testy parents. Fiona Griffiths gave us her staunch support, particularly in taking over charitable duties at the eleventh hour and willy-nilly dispensing Rescue Remedy for our ailments. Peter and Pat Griffiths were wonderful during our painful move from Victoria to Toronto. To all our friends and family we've ignored for the past year—sorry, we're still alive.

We had thought this book was dead, derailed in 1990 by our family difficulties, but the publisher of Penguin Books, Cynthia Good, never lost faith, reviving it in 1993, then patiently standing by as we found *The Great Adventure* and then took forever to finish it.

Legendary editor David Kilgour was his usual pillar of strength, delving into his formidable bag of tricks to bring the book to fruition. Wendy Thomas, copy editor, did yeoman's work, keeping everything straight on a complicated manuscript—the chronology is in large part her work. Jem Bates elevated our prose wonderfully in the final stages, Molly Brass contributed two marvellous maps, Wes Lowe did the beautiful cover and Lori Ledingham provided air traffic control.

Researcher extraordinaire Raelen Willard did wonderful work for us in Montana. At the Glenbow Archives, we were once again warmly welcomed and ably assisted by the archivists. In Ottawa, though sadly depleted by budget cuts, the staff at the National Archives of Canada soldiers on. Particular thanks to Louise Bertrand for sorting out an upsetting shipping problem. Also a special thanks to the Public Archives of Manitoba for their patience as we slowly worked our way through the Morris papers.

Canadiana has become a popular collectors' item, making books for research and reference very expensive. Margaret Browning, of Victoria, her father an ex-RCMP officer, loaned us books very early in the project and patiently waited for their return. Mrs. N.R. Crump, of Calgary, loaned us books as well as papers from her late husband Norris's considerable collection. If he hadn't devoted his life to the CPR, rising to its presidency, doubtless "Buck" Crump would have become an important historian. Mr. Crump urged us to write a book about the NWMP; sadly we were unable to consult with him during its writing. A special thanks to Aquila Books of Calgary for diligently hunting down damaged—hence less expensive—books for us. Robert Stewart, of Ottawa, generously lent us a copy of his fine book on Sam Steele.

Historian Hugh Dempsey deserves a special word of acknowledgment. He has tirelessly worked as a writer, and for many years the archivist at Glenbow, to preserve the history of the West, both White and Indian, most particularly the Blackfoot. Dempsey is surely the most under-appreciated writer in this country. His output is prodigious, his research meticulous and his style excellent.

Finally, a grateful thank you to the Canada Council for considering this book worthy of support.

Selected Bibliography

BOOKS

Adams, G. Mercer. *The Canadian North-West: Its History and Its Troubles*. Toronto: Rose Publishing Co., 1885.

Anderson, Samuel. *The North American Boundary from the Lake of the Woods to the Rocky Mountains*. London: Royal Geographic Society, 1876.

Atkin, Ronald. *Maintain the Right: The Early History of the North West Mounted Police 1873–1900*. New York: The John Day Company, 1973.

Atwood, Mae, ed. *In Ruperts Land: Memoirs of Walter Trail*. Toronto, McClelland and Stewart, 1970.

Ballantyne, Robert Michael. *Hudson Bay, or Every-day Life in the Wilds of North America, being six years' residence in the territories of the Honourable Hudson's Bay Company*. Edmonton: Hurtig Publishers, 1972.

Barron, Laurie F., and Waldram, James B., eds. *1885 and After: Native Society in Transition*. Regina: University of Regina, 1986.

Begg, Alexander. *History of the North-West*, 3 vols. Toronto: Hunter, Rose & Company, 1895.

Berry, Gerald L. *The Whoop-up Trail: Alberta–Montana Relationships*. Edmonton: Applied Art Products Ltd., 1953.

Brown, Dee. *Bury My Heart at Wounded Knee: An Indian History of the American West*. New York: Bantam Books, 1970.

Butler, William Francis. *The Great Lone Land*. London: Sampson Low, 1872.

————. *Far Out: Rovings Re-Told*. London: Sampson Low, 1881.

————. *The Wild North Land 1873*. Edmonton: M.G. Hurtig Ltd., 1968.

Cameron, William Bleasdell. *Blood Red the Sun*. Edmonton: Hurtig, 1977.

Cashman, Tony. *An Illustrated History of Western Canada.* Edmonton: M.G. Hurtig, 1971.

Cavell, Edward. *Journeys to the Far West.* Toronto: James Lorimer and Co., 1979.

Chambers, Captain Ernest J. Coles. *The Royal North-West Mounted Police: A Corps History.* Toronto: Coles Publishing Company, 1973.

Cheadle, Walter B. *Cheadle's Journal of a Trip Across Canada, 1862, 1863.* Rutland, Vermont: Charles E. Tuttle and Company, 1941.

Chittenden, H.A. *The American Fur Trade of the Far West.* Stanford, California: Academic Reprints, 1954.

Connell, Evan S. *Son of the Morning Star: Custer and the Little Big Horn.* San Francisco: North Point Press, 1984.

Cowie, Isaac. *The Company of Adventurers, A Narrative of Seven Years in the Service of the Hudson's Bay Company during 1867–1874, on the Great Buffalo Plains.* Toronto: Briggs, 1913.

D'Artigue, Jean. *Six Years in the Canadian North-West.* Toronto: Rose and Co., 1882.

Dempsey, Hugh. *Crowfoot: Chief of the Blackfoot.* Edmonton: Hurtig Publishers, 1972.

————. *Charcoal's World.* Saskatoon: Western Producer Prairie Books, 1978.

————. *Indian Tribes of Alberta.* Calgary: Glenbow Museum, 1979.

————, ed. *Men in Scarlet.* Calgary: Historical Society of Alberta/McClelland & Stewart West, 1973.

————, ed. *William Parker: Mounted Policeman.* Edmonton: Hurtig Publishers, 1973.

Denny, Sir Cecil E., Bart. *The Law Marches West.* Toronto: J.M. Dent and Sons, Canada, 1972.

Dodge, Richard Irving. *The Plains of North America and Their Inhabitants.* Edited by Wayne R. Kime. Cranbury, NJ: Associated University Presses, 1989.

Donkin, John G. *Trooper and Redskin, Recollections of Life in the North-West Mounted Police.* Toronto: Coles Publishing Company, 1973.

Dufferin & Ava, Marchioness of. *My Canadian Journal 1872–8.* Toronto: Coles Publishing Company, 1971.

1873–1974, Mountie: A Golden Treasury of Those Early Years. Don Mills: Collier-Macmillan Canada Ltd., 1973.

Finerty, John F. *War-Path and Bivouac or The Conquest of the Sioux*. Norman, Oklahoma: University of Oklahoma Press, 1961.

Fumoleau, Rene. *As Long as This Land Shall Last*. Toronto: McClelland & Stewart Ltd., 1973.

Goetzmann, William H., and Williams, Glyndwr. *Atlas of North American Exploration: From the Norse Voyages to the Race to the Pole*. New York: Prentice Hall, 1992.

Grant, George M. *Ocean to Ocean*. Toronto: James Campbell and Son, 1873.

Greeley, Horace. *An Overland Journey: From New York to San Francisco in the Summer of 1859*. New York: Alfred A. Knopf, 1963.

Haley, James A. *The Buffalo War: The History of the Red River Indian Uprising of 1874*. New York: Doubleday & Company, Inc., New York, 1976.

Hamilton, J.C. *The Prairie Province*. Toronto: Belford Brothers, 1876.

Harmon, Daniel Williams. *A Journal of Voyages and Travels in the Interior of North America*. Toronto: The Courier Press, Ltd., 1911.

Healy, W.J. *Women of Red River*. Winnipeg: The Women's Canadian Club, 1923.

Hearne, Samuel. *A Journey from Prince of Wales's Fort in Hudson's Bay to the Northern Ocean Undertaken by the Order of the Hudson's Bay Company for the Discovery of Copper Mines, a North West Passage, etc., in the Years 1769, 1770, 1771 and 1772*. Toronto: Macmillan Co. of Canada, 1958.

Hill, Douglas. *The Opening of the Canadian West*. London, England: Heinemann, 1967.

Hind, Henry Youle. *Narrative of the Canadian Red River Exploration Expedition of 1857 and of the Assiniboine and Saskatchewan Exploring Expedition of 1858*, 2 vols. London: Longman, Green, Longman and Roberts, 1859.

Horetzky, Charles. *Canada on the Pacific*. Montreal: Dawson Bros., 1874.

Horrall, S.W. *The Pictorial History of the Royal Canadian*

Mounted Police. Toronto: McGraw-Hill Ryerson, 1973.

Howard, Joseph Kinsey. *Strange Empire: A Narrative of the Northwest*. New York: William Morrow and Company, 1952.

Innis, Mary Quayle. *Travellers West*. Toronto: Clarke, Irwin & Company Ltd., 1956.

Jenness, Diamond. *Indians of Canada*, 5th ed. Ottawa: The Queen's Press, 1960.

Kane, Paul. *Wanderings of an Artist Among the Indians of North America*. Rutland, Vermont: Charles E. Tuttle Co., 1968.

Keenleyside, Hugh L., and Brown, Gerald S. *Canada and the United States: Some Aspects of Their Historical Relations*. New York: Alfred A. Knopf, 1952.

Kelly, Nora. *The Men of the Mounted*. Toronto: J.M. Dent & Sons, 1949.

Lamb, W. Kaye, ed. *The Journals and Letters of Sir Alexander Mackenzie*. Cambridge: Cambridge University Press, 1970.

Lord, John Keast. *The Wanderer, At Home in the Wilderness*. London: Robert Hardwicke, 1867.

MacEwan, Grant. *Colonel James Walker: Man of the Western Frontier*. Saskatoon: Western Producer Prairie Books, 1989.

MacGregor, James G. *Vision of an Ordered Land*. Saskatoon: Western Producer Prairie Books, 1981.

Macleod, R.C. *The NWMP and Law Enforcement, 1873–1905*. Toronto: University of Toronto Press, 1976.

McCourt, Edward. *Remember Butler: The Story of Sir William Butler*. Toronto: McClelland & Stewart, 1967.

McDougall, John. *Saddle, Sled and Snowshoe*. Toronto: William Briggs, 1896.

————. *In the Days of the Red River Rebellion*. Toronto: William Briggs, 1903.

————. *On Western Trails in the Early Seventies*. Toronto: William Briggs, 1911.

————. *Parsons of the Plains*. Edited by Thomas Bredin. Canada: Longman, 1971.

McLean, John. *Canadian Savage Folk*. Toronto: William Briggs, 1896.

————. *The Indians: Their Manners and Customs*. Toronto: William Briggs, 1889.

————. *McDougall of Alberta*. Toronto: The Ryerson Press, Toronto, 1927.

Messiter, Charles Alston. *Sport and Adventures Among the North American Indians*. London: R.H. Porter, 1890.

Milton, Viscount, and Cheadle, W.B. *The North-West Passage By Land*. Toronto: Coles Publishing Company, 1970.

Monaghan, Jay, ed. *The Book of the American West*. New York: Bonanza Books, 1963.

Morris, The Honorable Alexander. *The Treaties of Canada with the Indians of Manitoba and North-West Territories*. Toronto: Belfords, Clarke & Co., 1880.

Nevitt, R.B. *Winter at Fort Macleod*. Edited by Hugh A. Dempsey. Calgary: Glenbow-Alberta Institute, McClelland & Stewart West, 1974.

Newman, Peter C. *Company of Adventurers*, Volume 1. Toronto: Penguin Books Canada Ltd., 1985.

————. *Caesars of the Wilderness*, Volume 2. Toronto: Penguin Books Canada Ltd., 1987.

Nix, James Ernest. *Mission Among the Buffalo*. Toronto: The Ryerson Press, 1960.

O'Meara, Walter. *Daughters of the Country: The Women of the Fur Trades and Mountain Men*. New York: Harcourt, Brace & World, 1968.

Overholser, Joel. *Fort Benton: World's Innermost Port*. Helena, Montana: Falcon Press Publishing Co., 1987.

Parsons, John E. *West on the 49th Parallel: Red River to the Rockies 1872 to 1876*. New York: William Morrow and Company, 1963.

Sharp, Paul F. *Whoop-Up Country*. Helena, Montana: Historical Society of Montana, 1960.

Smith, Cynthia M., and McLeod, Jack, eds. *Sir John A.: An Anecdotal Life of John A. Macdonald*. Toronto: Oxford University Press, 1989.

Southesk, The Earl of. *Saskatchewan and the Rocky Mountains*. Edinburgh: Edmonston and Douglas, 1875.

Spry, Irene M. *The Palliser Expedition: An Account of John Palliser's British North American Expedition, 1857–1860*. Toronto: Macmillan Canada, 1963.

Stanley, George F.G. *Birth of Western Canada: A History of the Riel Rebellions*. Toronto: University of Toronto Press, 1973.

————. *Mapping the Frontier, Charles Wilson's Diary of the Survey of the 49th Parallel, 1858–1862*. Toronto: Macmillan of Canada, 1970.

Steele, Samuel B. *Forty Years in Canada*. Toronto: McGraw-Hill Ryerson Ltd., 1972.

Stewart, Robert. *Sam Steele: Lion of the Frontier*. Toronto: Doubleday Canada Ltd., 1979.

Thomas, Lewis H., ed. *Essays on Western History*. Edmonton: The University of Alberta Press, 1976.

Turner, C. Frank. *Across the Medicine Line: The Epic Confrontation Between Sitting Bull and the North-West Mounted Police*. Toronto: McClelland & Stewart, 1973.

Turner, John Peter. *The North West Mounted Police: 1873–1893*, 2 vols. Ottawa: King's Printer and Controller of Stationery, 1950.

Tyrrel, Joseph B., ed. *David Thompson's Narrative of His Explorations in Western America, 1784–1812*. Toronto: Champlain Society, 1916.

Utley, Robert M. *The Lance and the Shield: The Life and Times of Sitting Bull*. New York: Ballantine Books, 1993.

Van Kirk, Sylvia. *Many Tender Ties: Women in Fur-Trade Society in Western Canada 1670–1870*. Winnipeg: Watson & Dwyer Publishing Ltd., 1981.

ARTICLES, PAMPHLETS, GOVERNMENT REPORTS, THESES AND UNPUBLISHED MANUSCRIPTS

Bagley, Frederick Augustus. *The '74 Mounties: The Great March across the Plains*. (GA)

Dempsey, Hugh. *A Blackfoot Winter Count*. Glenbow Museum, 1965.

————. *Blackfoot Ghost Dance*. Glenbow Museum, 1968.

————. *A History of Rocky Mountain House*. Canadian Historical Sites Occasional Papers in Archeology and History # 6, 1973.

————. *Jerry Potts, Plainsman*. Glenbow-Alberta Institute, 1966.

Goldring, Philip. *The First Contingent: The North-West Mounted Police, 1873–1874*. Canadian Historical Sites Occasional Papers in Archeology and History #6, 1979.

————. *Whiskey, Horses and Death: The Cypress Hills*

Massacre and Its Sequel. Canadian Historical Sites Occasional Papers in Archeology and History # 21, 1979.

Historical Society of Alberta. *A Chronicle of the Canadian West, North-West Mounted Police Report for 1875.*

Johnston, Alexander, comp. *The Battle at Belly River.* Lethbridge Branch, Historical Society of Alberta, 1966.

Long, H.G., ed. *Fort Macleod: The Story of the Mounted Police.* The Fort Macleod Historical Association, 1958.

Macleod, R.C. *The North-West Mounted Police 1873–1905: Law Enforcement and the Social Order in the Canadian North-West.* Ph.D. Thesis, Duke University, 1971.

Royal Commission on the Liquor Traffic 1896. Toronto: Coles Publishing, 1973.

Royal North-West Mounted Police. *Reports 1888–1889.* Toronto: Coles Publishing, 1973.

Shaeffer, Claude E. *Blackfoot Shaking Tent.* Glenbow Museum, 1969.

Stacey, Beverley A. "D.W. Davis: Whiskey Trader to Politician." *Alberta History*, Summer, 1990.

The Boundary Commission NWMP Trail Association. *An Astonishing Cavalcade: The 1874 Route of the North West Mounted Police Across Manitoba.* 1994.

Tobias, John L. "Canada's Subjugation of the Plains Cree, 1879–1885," in *Readings in Canadian History: Post Confederation.* Edited by R. Douglas Francis and Donald B. Smith. Toronto: Holt Rinehart and Winston of Canada, 1986.

ARCHIVES AND LIBRARIES

Detroit Public Library
Fort Benton Archives
Fort Macleod Archives
Glenbow Library and Archives, Calgary (GA)
Hudson's Bay Company Archives, Winnipeg
Medicine Hat Museum and Art Gallery
Montana Historical Society Archives, Helena (MHSA)
National Archives of Canada, Ottawa (NAC)
North Dakota Archives
Provincial Archives of Manitoba, Winnipeg (PAM)

RCMP Archives, Regina
Sir Alexander Galt Museum and Archives, Lethbridge
Smithsonian Institute Archives
University of Toronto Archives
University of Calgary Archives

DIARIES

Bagley, Fred (GA)
Carscadden, Joseph (GA)
Denny, Cecil (RCMP Centennial Archives)
Finlayson, James (NAC)
French, George (NAC)
Gagnon, Sévère (NAC)
Julien, Henri (NAC)
McIllree, John (GA)
Parker, William (GA)

ARCHIVAL COLLECTIONS

We consulted too many collections to list every one of them
but the following we found particularly useful in researching
the history of the North West Mounted Police, the Canadian
North West and the American West:

National Archives

Record Group 10	Department of Indian Affairs
Record Group 13	Department of Justice
Record Group 18	RCMP (including Official Correspondence, Indexes and Registers, Division and Detachment Records, Dominion Police Records and Service Records)
Butler, W.F.	MG 29 B13
French George A.	Letterbook and miscellaneous correspondence, RG 18, Vol. 3545, Series B3

Irvine Family   MG 29 E111
Julien, Henri   MG 29 D 103
McDougall, John   MG 29 C23
McDougall, William   MC 29 E 15
Morris, William   MG 29 C8
Smith, W. Osborne   Letterbook, RG 18 reel T-6268
Steele, S.B.   MG 29 E55
Walsh, Cora   MG 29 C45

Glenbow Archives
Bagley, Frederick   M43, 44, 2111 files 1–8
Carscadden, Joseph   M6608
Clark, Simon J.   M228, 229
Davis, D.W.   M304
Denny, Cecil   M318
Jarvis Family   M584, 4015
Macleod, James   M339 (file 1), 776, 780–783,
                                  785, 1257, 2820, 3625 m
                                  3939, 4135, 4851
Macleod, Norrie   M775
McDougall, George and John   M727–730, 732, 733, 2718,
                                  3022, 3215
McIllree, John Henry   AB McIllree
Parker, William   M934
Price, Elizabeth   M1000, 1002
Nevitt, Richard B.   M892, 893
RCMP Orders in Council   M8380
Shurtliff, Albert   M1140
Steele, S.B.   M1171, 1172, 3462, 4317
Walker, James   M986, 1270, 1536, 2471,
                                  2828, 3165, 3292, 6898

Montana Historical Society Archives
Baker, I.G.   SC 293
Brown, James W.   SC 482
Burlingame, Virginia A., Papers   A11:1–2
Healy, John J.: Interview   Microfilm 95
Hammond, John E.   SC 53
McNight, J.H.   MC 56
Power, T.C.   MC55

S.C. Ashby story   SC 283
Stocking, W.S.   SC 797

Public Archives of Manitoba
Adams, Archibald, Papers and Correspondence
                                MG 12, M1–M3
Morris, Alexander, Correspondence and Papers (Ketcheson
Collection)   MG 12, B2
Morris, Alexander, the Lieutenant-Governor's Collection
                                MG 12, B1
Walsh, James M.   Microfilm M 705

NEWSPAPERS

Calgary *Herald*
Fort Benton *Record*
Helena *Daily Herald*
Helena *Daily Independent*
Helena *Weekly Herald*
Helena *Weekly Independent*
Lethbridge *News*
New York *Herald*
Toronto *Globe*
Toronto *Mail*
Winnipeg *Free Press*

MAGAZINES

Alberta History
Beaver
Canadian Historical Review
Canadian Illustrated News
Glenbow Quarterly
Harper's New Monthly Magazine
Montana Historical Society Contributions Vols. 1–10
Montana: The Magazine of Western History
RCMP Quarterly
Scarlet and Gold

Notes

Glenbow Archives—GA
National Archives of Canada—NAC
Public Archives of Manitoba—PAM
Montana Historical Society Archives—MHSA
Minnesota Historical Society—MHS

Chapter 1

The Adventure Begins

Page 2 "In April, 1874, I was in Montreal": D'Artigue, p. 11.

Page 3 "If everyone knew as much": Based on D'Artigue, pp. 11–12.

Page 4 "On my way back": D'Artigue, p. 12.

Page 5 "I fancied I saw myself ": D'Artigue, p. 13.

Page 5 "Well Mr. C.": D'Artigue, pp. 13–14.

Page 6 "Seeing that I was in earnest": D'Artigue, p. 14.

Page 6 "My dearest mother": Willie Parker to his mother, April 5, 1874, GA.

Page 7 "Did he say he could ride": Based on "Thirty-Eight and a half Years' Service and Experiences in the Mounties," The reminiscences of William Parker. This slightly edited version is contained in *William Parker Mounted Policeman*, ed. Hugh Dempsey. Original in GA.

Page 8 "I have known William Parker": William Parker Reminiscences, p. 3. Historian Hugh Dempsey questions this version of the telegram, which comes from Parker's reminiscences written after he retired from the Mounted Police. The basis for Dempsey's doubts is his letter to his mother, dated April 5, in which he wrote: "...at last I thought of the Bishop and so away I runs about a mile & a half up town to find the bishop and luckily he was in his office at the chapter house or else I should have been scooped, his Lordship was very pleased to see me & gave me a bull character."

However, his mother was the wife of a reverend and the daughter-in-law of a professor of divinity. Willie's letters to her deal with pleasing topics like flowers and church parades, and how much he misses his family, not the realities of life in western Canada. For instance, in his personal diary entry, Jan. 28, 1875, he records, "Went to a Ball at Fawcetts and Bells, danced all night and had a big time, made love to a bitch half breed girl, got home at seven in the morning." Willie did not pass on that bit of news to his mother or the reverend.

Page 8 "Arrived at the Doctors": Parker to his mother, April 5, 1874, GA.

Page 9 "I had always been a close": Fred Bagley, '74 *Mounties, The Great March Across the Plains*, p. 3.

Page 9 "I, imbued with the romance": Bagley, '74 *Mounties*, p. 2.

Page 10 "How old are ye": Bagley, '74 *Mounties*, p. 2.

Page 11 "I had just been giving...break his nose." *Canadian Illustrated News*, July 1874.

The NWMP Goes to School

Page 13 "According to the Act": French to the minister of justice, January 13, 1874, PAC.

Page 13 "Make yourselves comfortable": Based on D'Artigue, p 16.

Page 14 "In the car, sitting opposite me": D'Artigue, pp. 14–15.

Page 14 "I don't think there is": D'Artigue, p. 15.

Page 14 "Hold, on old fellow": D'Artigue, pp. 16–17.

Page 15 "...and wishing to know": D'Artigue, pp 22–23.

Page 16 "Who the hell told you": Bagley, '74 *Mounties*, p. 6.

Page 17 "Blimey! Look at 'im": Bagley, '74 *Mounties*, p. 6.

Page 17 "That's right young fellow": Bagley, '74 *Mounties*, p. 6.

Page 17 "Even the officers": D'Artigue, p. 17.

Page 18 "My Dear Father": Willie Parker to his father, April 15, 1874, GA.

Page 19 "My friends who wanted me": *Scarlet and Gold*, Vol. 17, p. 17.

Page 19 "More suitable for aquatic": R.G. MacBeth cited in Stewart, p. 24.

Page 19 "We did have one good": *Scarlet and Gold*, Vol. 17, p. 17.

Page 20 "I'd as soon be in a penitentiary": Toronto *Globe*, January 2, 1874.

Page 21 "Show a leg": Stewart, p. 28.

Page 22 "Our work was unceasing": Steele, pp. 61–62.

Page 22 "Drill, drill, drill": Stewart, p. 26.

Page 23 "My Dearest Father": Willie Parker to his father, June 3, 1874, GA.

The Colonel

Page 26 "I would be quite willing": Hill, p. 58.

Page 26 "If the revolutionists": in Howard, p. 136.

Page 27 "Wild people": Sir John A. Macdonald to George Brown, October 14, 1869, Macdonald Papers, NAC.

Page 27 "Pure whites & British": Macdonald to William McDougall, December 12, 1869, Macdonald Papers, NAC.

Page 28 "Terrible deeds have been": Butler, p. 75.

Page 30 "What have you done": Alexander Morris to Macdonald, September 20, 1873, Morris Papers, PAM.

Page 30 "It would not be well": Macdonald to Lord Dufferin, September 24, 1873, Macdonald Papers, NAC.

Page 30 "I regret to have to state": French to Hewitt Bernard, French Letterbook, January, 17, 1874, NAC.

Page 31 "Constables who are in the habit": NWMP Daily Order Book, January 19, 1874, NAC.

Page 32 "Fur caps, mitts and moccasins": French to Hewitt Bernard, French Letterbook, December 18, 1873, NAC.

Page 33 "I send you today": French to Hewitt Bernard, Letterbook, January 17, 1874, NAC.

Page 34 "There are only two creatures": New York *Herald*, May 10, 1878.

Page 35 "There will be hot work": French to Hewitt Bernard, Letterbook, December 27, 1873, NAC

Page 37 "Mind your back": Based on '74 *Mounties*, p. 11; D'Artigue, pp. 19–20.

Chapter Two

Revenge
Most of this account of Jerry Potts and the death of his mother and half-brother is based on Hugh Dempsey, *Jerry Potts*.

The Confederacy
Page 44 The Blackfoot were the warriors: Hugh Dempsey, *Indian Tribes of Alberta*, p. 8.

Page 46 "I have killed, robbed": In Utley, p. 73.

Page 47 "But there is a Papal power": Missionary Notices, November 1854 in Nix, p. 12.

Page 47 "There are five priests": Missionary Notices, May 1870 in Nix, p. 12.

Page 49 "We were anxious to see": Tyrrell, p. 345.

Page 50 "The Indian has the gift": Jenness, p. 131.

Page 51 "Wildest chimera of": Goetzmann and Williams, p. 101.

Page 52 "Plyed the Blackfoot": Cited in Sharp, p. 31.

Page 52 "He was completely naked": Cited in Monaghan, ed., p. 35.

Page 53 "Bad medicine": Berry, p. 20.

Page 53 "We have this season": Cited in Dempsey, *A History of Rocky Mountain House*, p. 14.

Page 53 "One Rascal, the chief": Cited in Dempsey, p. 16.

Page 54 "Two men arrived": Edmonton House Journals, March 28, 1861, PAM.

Page 54 "I believe an American": Cited in Monaghan, ed., p. 40.

Page 55 "Old Paul came to me": Spry, pp. 216–217.

Page 56 "It is a work of peril": Butler, pp. 163–164.

Page 56 "Who and what": Butler, p. 265.

Page 56 "The Mountain House is perhaps": Butler, p. 260.

Destroyed from Within

Page 57 "About the only way": Cited in Newman, p. 202.

Page 58 "I have not a single one": Lamb, p. 424.

Page 58 "Connubial alliances are the best": Cited in Newman, p. 203.

Page 58 "Norton is one of": Hearne, p. 39n.

Page 58 "A girl of about fourteen": Harmon, pp. 118–19.

Page 59 "We have wept together": Harmon, p. 231.

Page 59 "Make them more English": Elaine Mitchell, "A Red River Gossip," *The Beaver* (Spring, 1961).

Page 60 "I never forgive or forget": Chittenden, p. 693.

Page 62 "Here lies a brave": Chittenden, p. 695.

Chapter Three

My Horse Is My Bride

Page 66 "I'm away, I'm away": James Finlayson Diary. This poem is the first page in his diary and he precedes it with "NWMP, Montana Territory, Stone Fort." But he likely meant Manitoba Territory. Stone Fort (Lower Fort Garry) is where they wintered in Manitoba in 1873–74.

Page 67 "Scarcely fit for": French to Hewitt Bernard, French Letterbook, December 27, 1873, NAC.

Page 68 "The only thing the Colonel": Joseph Carscadden Diary, p. 82.

Page 68 "The train being shunted": Commissioner's report to minister of justice, January 1875, NAC.

Page 69 "We proceeded about six": D'Artigue, p. 27.

Page 70 "My horse was a thorough bred": Henri Julien diary, August 5, 1874.

Page 71 "A repast on the prairies": D'Artigue, p 28. Fred Bagley in '74 *Mounties* identifies the Crimean War vet as Joseph Francis.

Page 72 "Sounded Reveille at 4 a.m.": Fred Bagley diary, June 15, 1874.

Page 72 "That day we travelled": D'Artigue, pp. 27–31.

Page 73 "The conduct of the men": Commissioner's report, January, 1875.

Page 73 "Well, if lucky you may": Commissioner's report, January 1875.

Page 75 "Get up, goddamn it": Based on Bagley diary, June 20, 1874.

The Bride's Revolt

Page 77 "At that moment we were": D'Artigue, pp. 33–34.

Page 78 "I was sleeping in a square": William Parker Reminiscences, p. 6.

Page 79 "I shall never forget that night": Steele, p. 62.

Page 80 "Turn your horses": Based on Steele, pp. 63–64.

Page 80 "Feel queer": *Scarlet and Gold*, vol. 2, p. 52.

Page 81 "Over the hills": Steele, p. 62, also Bagley diary, June 20, 1874.

Page 81 "Saddle up, Fred": Bagley diary, June 20, 1874.

Page 81 "Is he dead, sir": Based on William Parker Reminiscences, p. 6.

Page 82 "Not much Fenimore Cooper": Bagley diary, June 20, 1874.

They Hang Horse Thieves, Don't They?

Page 83 "Morning, sir": Based on Bagley diary plus numerous early accounts of his dealing with authority.

Page 85 "From my position": D'Artigue, pp. 35–36.

Page 86 "Looking in the direction": D'Artigue, p. 36.

Page 87 "Reveille at 5 a.m.": Bagley Diary, July 2, 1874.

Page 89 "He called me a murderer": Turner, p. 21.

Page 90 "What's that you've got": Based on Bagley's own account in his diary, in his unpublished memoirs and in several newspaper interviews in later years.

Page 90 "That boy Bagley": Bagley Diary, July 2, 1874.

Page 91 "Sioux Massacre": Winnipeg *Free Press*, July 6, 1874.

Page 91 "Reveille at 5 a.m.": Bagley Diary, July 6, 1874.

Page 92 "As we were going along": D'Artigue, pp. 38–39.

Chapter Four

The Territory

Page 97 "I never saw an Indian": W.S. Stocking Reminiscences, MHSA.

Page 97 "I abstained from giving": Cited in his Textual Commentary by Wayne R. Kime in his edited version of *The Plains of North America and Their Inhabitants*, by Richard Irving Dodge, p. 399.

Page 98 "An exterminating war": Haley, pp. 4–5.

Page 98 "Farmer Brown" and "wiped out": John William Morris, Old Fort Garry in the Seventies, unpublished manuscript, NAC.

Page 99 "We've caught the fella": Based on H.V.A. Ferguson, Fort Benton Memories, unpublished manuscript, MHSA. Also Helena *Weekly Herald*, August 27, 1868, *Montana Post*, August 28, 1868.

Page 101 "You are altogether different": Robert P. Higheagle Manuscript, cited in Utley, p. 182.

Page 101 "From the time we": "Story as told by Col. S.C. Ashby," unpublished manuscript, MHSA.

Page 102 "Let them kill, skin,": Cited in Brown, p. 254.

Whiskey

Page 106 "To brew this beer": Cited in Newman, pp. 162–163.

Page 107 "I never knowed what": Howard, p. 261.

Page 108 "I heard the missing man": John William Morris, op. cit.

Page 108 "Armed with their rattle": Ibid.

Page 109 "I suppose you know": Based on ibid.

Page 111 "Presently out at Whoop Up": Helena *Herald*, February 10, 1872.

Page 111 "There is no encouragement": Overholser, p. 226.

Page 111 "Well, Joe, I've got you": There are a number of versions of this story in memoirs and interviews located in both the Montana Historical Society and Glenbow Archives. One version is James Schultz, small collection, MHSA.

Page 113 "The fully developed bull-whacker": Fort Macleod *Gazette*,

July 29, 1882.

Page 113 "Godless wretches": "Red River and Beyond," *Harper's New Monthly Magazine*, XXI No. 112, August, 1870.

Page 113 "We were approaching Fort Whoop-Up": Calgary *Herald*, October 13, 1923.

The Traders

Page 115 There are many wonderful stories, some true, some obviously exaggerated, about Kamouse Taylor, but the wife-stealing incident is repeated many times in memoirs and interviews of other traders and settlers. See C.P.F. Conybeare, Recollections, in G.B. Coutts Collection, GA.

Page 117 "You don't want to get": J.J. Healy, unpublished manuscript, MHSA.

Page 118 "If we had only been allowed": Ibid.

Page 120 "Not bad for a six months": Helena *Herald*, June 15, 1870.

Page 123 "Come over yourself": Major Upham to J.H. McNight, McNight Papers, MHSA.

Page 124 "What a man has to work": Cited in Beverley A. Stacey, "D.W. Davis, From Whiskey Trader to Politician," *Alberta History*, vol. 38, no. 3 (Summer, 1990).

Page 124 "I do not hard work": Stacey, ibid.

Page 125 "Well, it's been tried": D.W. Davis Papers, GA.

Page 126 "These whiskey men would make it": "Story as told by S.C. Ashby," op. cit.

Page 127 "Hunting the buffalo and grizzly": Innis, p. 17.

Page 127 "We smoked several pipes with him": Milton and Cheadle, pp. 73–74.

Page 129 "Americans within two days Ride": Cited in Dempsey, *A History of Rocky Mountain House*, pp. 22–23.

Page 129 "Too many free Traders": Ibid., pp. 25–26.

Chapter Five

Warrior

Page 131 "There is no right and no wrong": Dodge, p. 235.

Page 135 "That night there was": Winfield S. Stocking Reminiscences, unpublished manuscript, MHSA.

Page 137 "Hold your noodle steady": O'Meara, p. 140.

Page 138 "Course, you take your chances": W.S. Stocking, ibid.

Page 138 "After supper Jerry sent": Ibid.

Page 138 "Then he begun to itemize": Ibid.

Page 138 "My friend, I forgot something": Ibid.

Page 139 "Go slow when you clear": Ibid.

Page 139 "At daybreak, the Indian": Ibid.

Baker's Massacre

Page 140 "I heard there is a war party about": Based on Missionary Notices, 1869, 1870.

Page 141 "The two brothers would pooh-pooh": Cited in "Introduction" by J. Ernest West, in McDougall, *Opening the Great West*, p. 10.

Page 141 "Fifty miles before dinner": McDougall, *In the Days of the Red River Rebellion*, p. 181.

Page 142 "There are three liars": Cited in "Introduction" by J. Ernest West, op. cit., p. 10.

Page 143 "I have heard a good deal": Butler, p. 384.

Page 143 "A few months later": Ibid., p. 305.

Page 146 "Cross the line": House Executive Documents, No. 269, 41st Congress, 2nd Session, p. 24.

Page 146 "For the present": Ibid., p. 28.

Page 146 "A sharp and severe blow upon": House Executive Documents, Ibid., p. 28.

Page 146 "The only good Indians": Brown, p. 166.

Page 147 "About the time of a good": House Executive Documents, Ibid., p. 7.

Page 147 "If the lives and property": Ibid., p. 47.

Page 147 "We're goin' Injun huntin'": Based on House Executive Documents, pp. 2–50.

Page 147 "My hair!": based on Dodge, pp. 337–38.

Page 148 "We're going out there to teach": Howard, p. 255. There are several other versions of this story and the dialogue is fairly consistent throughout.

Page 148 "What do you mean?": Based on House Executive Documents, op. cit., Kinsey, pp. 254–55 and Butler, pp. 268–70.

Page 148 "Now boys, there's the devils": Ibid.

Page 149 "The first great lesson": Howard, p. 255. He cites this as coming from Montana's first historian but does not note the name or publication. However, there are other similar versions in various collections in MHSA, including McNight, Ashby and Stocking.

Page 150 "It is useless": Butler, pp. 269–70.

Page 150 "You have spoken": Ibid.

Page 150 "But what of all that": Ibid.

Page 150 "It is better to die": Ibid.

The Battle of Belly River

Page 152 "Wouldn't you be better off": Sanderson, p. 13.

Page 153 "My children, I had a dream": Cited in Johnston, ed., pp. 8–9.

Page 154 "We are here!": Ibid.

Page 155 "The greatest event of my life": Ibid.

Page 157 "You could shoot with your eyes": Lethbridge *News*, April 30, 1890. Based on an interview with Potts by C.A. Magrath, quote also recorded as, "You could fire with your eyes shut and would be sure to kill a Cree."

Page 157 "When we returned": Johnston, ed., Ibid.

Page 158 "After the defeat of the Crees," Cowie, pp. 414 and 441.

Wolfers and Woodhounds

Page 164 "I am going to sell": Healy, op. cit.

Page 164 "I fixed everything all up": Ibid.

Page 165 "What are you skunks": Based on Healy, Ibid.

Page 165 "Healy, there is a serious": Healy, Ibid.

Page 166 "If you move a hand": Based on Healy, Ibid.

Thirteen Kit Carsons

Page 169 "It's been horrible": Based on the Winnipeg Trial, June 19, 20 and 21, 1876. Full depositions are in PAM. See also Winnipeg *Free Press* for those dates and Helena *Weekly Herald*, July 29, August 15, 1875. Also Fort Benton *Record* in late June 1876 and Winnipeg *Standard*, June 24, 1876, have various accounts. Additional information in the Taylor Papers, MHS and in the Morris Papers, PAM, see file #1177. Later sources include "eyewitness" accounts in the Helena *Independent*, November 18, 1886, and *Montana Magazine of History*, Autumn, 1953.

Page 170 "Goddamn thieving bastards": Ibid.

Page 171 "We've started in" Testimony of Abe Farwell, Winnipeg Trial, op. cit.

Page 171 "I will die here": Morris Papers. File # 1177, December '75 contains the depositions given to A.G. Irvine relating to the massacre. There is some disagreement about who was decapitated and who was beaten to death. There is also considerable debate about how many were killed.

Page 171 "He grabbed me by the arm": Ibid.

Page 172 "Wiped out the forty lodges": Helena *Daily Herald*, June 11, 1873.

Chapter Six
Departure

Page 176 On two distinct occasions": French, Official Report to the Minister of Justice, January 1875.

Page 177 "chicken hearts": Ibid.

Page 177 "They have not the pluck": Ibid.

Page 177 "I anticipated the backing out": French, Official Report to the Minister of Justice, January 1875.

Page 178 "To get badly cooked food": Ibid.

Page 179 "Here I come": Based on Bagley Diary, July 8, 1874, and '74 *Mounties*.

Page 179 "We moved off in beautiful order": Carscadden Diary, pp. 1–6.

Page 180 "non-entities": Carscadden Diary, p. 6.

Page 182 "I would here like to describe": D'Artigue, p. 45.

Page 183 "Bloody hell, man": Based on Steele, p. 51; Carscadden Diary, July 7, 1874.

Page 183 "Why didn't you tell me": Based on French's reports of conversations with his guides.

Page 184 "I hardly know when the day": J.F. Macleod to Mary Drever, July 10, 1874. Macleod Papers, GA.

Page 185 "Get those wagons ready!": Based on D'Artigue, p. 41; McIllree Diary, p. 9; Macleod to Drever, op. cit.

Massacre at Duck Lake

Page 188 "I had some qualms": Julien Diary, July 19, 1874. Actually written after a subsequent duck massacre, but Julien is clearly referring to the previous occasion as well.

Page 188 "This must be stopped": Based on accounts of Bagley,

Carscadden, D'Artigue and McIllree about French's disciplinary actions.

Page 190 "circus": *Scarlet and Gold*, Vol. 1, p. 31.

Page 190 "Don't worry about those balky horses": Based on Carscadden Diary entries between July 8 and 12, 1874.

Page 192 "[Here] we first encountered the hostility of the mosquitoes": Julien Diary, July 10, 1874.

A Plague of...

Page 200 "Well Fred, it looks like God has paid us a visit": Based on accounts by Carscadden, McIllree, Gagnon, Steele, Bagley, Finlayson, Denny and French about the grasshoppers. The diary accounts are dated July 12, 1874. Bagley also mentions them in *'74 Mounties*.

Page 201 "Here now, boy, what's the problem": Ibid.

Page 201 "The air for a height of hundreds of yards": Steele, p. 68.

Chapter 7

The Death of Romance

Page 203 "Reveille at 3:30 a.m. on the march at 7 a.m.": Finlayson Diary, July 14, 1874.

Page 203 "imposition of the country": French, Official Report to the Minister of Justice, January 1875.

Page 204 "Oui, mon Colonel": Based on French's reports of conversations with his guides; Bagley Diary and *'74 Mounties*; D'Artigue also discusses French's relationship with the guides in various places during his account of the march.

Page 204 "The half-breeds and oxen could not be got to start": French Diary, July 15, 1874.

Page 205 "It is useless to mention how": D'Artigue, p. 44.

Page 205 "Many of the drivers are half-breeds": Carscadden Diary, pp. 10, 11.

Page 205 "My first experience of cart driving": Bagley, *'74 Mounties*, pp. 30, 31.

Page 206 "And yet, notwithstanding my disgust": D'Artigue, p. 44, July 16, 1874.

Page 207 "I've never heard such complaining": D'Artigue, p. 46.

Page 207 "Anyone with me?": D'Artigue, pp. 46, 48.

Page 208 "Increasing the pace of my oxen": D'Artigue, p. 47.

Page 209 "This was the most severe jolt": Bagley Diary, July 26, 1874; *'74 Mounties*, pp. 26, 32.

Rest

Page 210 "On the march at 7 a.m.": Finlayson Diary, July 15, 1874.

Page 210 "Reveille at 3:30 a.m.": Finlayson Diary, July 15, 1874.

Page 210 "Overshot the proper watering place": French Diary, July 17, 1874.

Page 211 "Government horses": Julien Diary, July 16, 1874.

Page 212 "What's going on here?": Based on McIllree Diary, July 18, 1874; Gagnon Diary, July 17, 21, 1874.

Page 212 "the Boundary Commission people may find them": French Diary, July 19 and 20, 1874.

Page 212 "To wind up all our sensations": Julien Diary, July 17, 1874. Though Julien records this as happening on the seventeenth, it is very clear from the other diary entries that the fire occurred on the eighteenth.

Page 213 "While we were getting dinner": Gagnon Diary, July 18, 1874.

Page 213 "Hunger and thirst is two of the worst": Finlayson Diary, July 18, 1874.

Page 214 "Enchanting": Gagnon Diary, July 18, 1874.

Page 214 "The usual run of men": Julien Diary, July 20, 1874.

Page 215 "The Souris is a clear rapid river": McIllree Diary, July 19, 1874.

Page 216 "carelessness": French Diary, July 18, 1874.

Page 217 "I left the team": Carscadden Diary, July 8 and September 9, 1874.

Page 217 "There's Sioux about!": Based on McIllree Diary, July 19, 1874; Bagley Diary, July 20, 1874; D'Artigue, pp. 49–50.

Page 217 "I don't believe his statement": French Diary, July 20, 1874.

Page 218 "What could he do?": D'Artigue, pp. 49, 50.

Diarrhea, Dust and Disobedience

Page 219 "Where are the rest": Based on Gagnon Diary, July 20 and 21, 1874; French Diary, July 21, 1874.

Page 219 "bring on those horses": French Diary, July 21, 1874.

Page 219 "I insisted on the men": French Diary, July 22, 1874.

Page 219 "Many of the men were not": Bagley Diary, July 22, 1874, '74 Mounties, p. 33.

Page 220 "I observed that Diarrhoea": Report of Surgeon John Kittson, December 19, 1875. In the North West Mounted Police Report for 1875.

Page 221 "We also suffered": Julien Diary, July 21, 1874.

Page 222 "It was about midnight": Gagnon Diary, July 22, 1874.

Page 222 "We had a very hard": Julien Diary, July 22, 1874.

Page 223 "[H]indermost wagons delayed": French Diary, July 22, 1874.

Page 223 "A, B, and C Troops had 12 horses": French Diary, July 23, 1874.

Page 224 "While employed in making hay": Julien Diary, July 22, 1874.

Page 224 "Started at 5:00 a.m. sharp": McIllree Diary, July 23, 1874.

Page 225 "Great Rivalry between the Troops": French Diary, July 24, 1874.

Page 226 "Started at 5 a.m.": McIllree Diary, July 24, 1874.

Sweet Sorrow

Page 226 "finally on Friday, the 24th": D'Artigue, p. 51.

Page 229 "Shurtliff came in about 11": French Diary, July 25, 1874.

Page 229 "right hand": French to Col. Hugh Richardson, August 12, 1874.

Page 230 "taking with the main body": French Diary, July 25, 1874.

Page 230 "My troop is changing": Gagnon Diary, July 24, 1874.

Page 231 "Hundreds of miles remained": Denny, p. 23.

Page 231 "Under these circumstances": D'Artigue, pp. 55, 56, 57.

Page 232 "The valley is just": Gagnon Diary, July 24, 1874.

Page 232 "Church parade a.m.": Bagley's Diary, July 26, 1874.

Page 232 "The service consisted as usual": Bagley, '74 Mounties, p. 35.

Page 233 "One shotgun had been issued": Bagley, '74 Mounties, p. 37.

Page 234 "Did nothing in particular": McIllree Diary, July 25, 1874.

Page 234 "Nearly had a stampede": McIllree Diary, July 26, 1874.

Page 234 "Still in camp": McIllree Diary, July 27, 1874.

Page 234 "This singular rock is a white": Julien Diary, July 25, 1874.

Page 235 "We had pemmican for the first time": Julien Diary, July 24, 1874.

Page 235 "first rate stuff": McIllree Diary, August 24, 1874.

Page 236 "At work dividing stores": French Diary, July 27, 1874.

Page 236 "Writing official reports and letters": French Diary, July 30, 1874.

Chapter 8

On the Road Again

Page 238 "My horses": Based on Gagnon Diary, August 1, 1874.

Page 238 "Almost every one is sick": Gagnon Diary, August 1, 1874.

Page 239 "I learned from some of": D'Artigue, pp. 59, 60.

Page 241 "Road making parties very busy": Bagley Diary, July 31, 1874.

Page 241 "Those troops who did not": French Diary, August 3, 1874.

Page 241 "Went down early in the": McIllree Diary, July 30, 1874.

Page 242 "Went to bed.": McIllree Diary, August 3, 1874.

Page 243 "My tent was blown completely away": Julien Diary, August 4, 1874. The storm actually started on the night of the third and extended into the morning of the fourth.

Page 244 "The deer had begun to": Julien Diary, August 4, 1874.

Page 244 "He [Denny] is to begin": Nevitt, pp. 22, 23.

Page 246 "Hello! I say, anyone!" Based on Denny, pp. 25–26.

Page 246 "Would I be right in assuming": Ibid.

Page 247 "The effect of this loneliness": Julien Diary, August 4, 1874.

Page 248 "Did dear Mother receive my": William Parker to his father, August 4, 1874.

Henri's Adventure

Page 249 "On Monday my sketch of": French Diary, July 31, 1874.

Page 249 "Had a long pow wow": French Diary, August 2, 1874.

Page 250 "After leaving the B.S.": French, Official Report to the Minister of Justice, January 1875.

Page 251 "I shall also remark that": Carscadden Diary, August 30, 1874.

Page 252 "I was bound to have": Julien Diary, August 5, 1874.

Page 254 "It was now far past sunset": Julien Diary, August 5, 1874.

Old Wives and Played-out Horses

Page 254 "Marched at 6 a.m.": Bagley Diary, August 6, 1874.

Page 255 "and it was the most delicious": Carscadden Diary, August 30, 1874.

Page 255 "I soon lost my prejudice": *Scarlet and Gold*, Diamond Jubilee Edition, p. 12.

Page 256 "Well, Paul, what do you": Based on French.

Page 257 "Please, what happened to": Based on Julien Diary, August 8, 1874; Bagley Diary, August 9, 1874.

Page 257 "This is barbarous, infamous, cruel": Julien Diary, August 8, 1874.

Page 257 "Damned right, Artist": Based on Julien Diary, August 8, 1874, August 9, 1874.

Page 257 "Got up at 6 a.m.": McIllree Diary, August 9, 1874.

Sooty Sons of the Plains

Page 260 "After leaving Roche Percée": D'Artigue, pp. 64, 65.

Page 262 "We at first met them": Julien Diary, August 13, 1874.

Page 263 "The great spirit gave the land": Julien Diary, August 13, 1874.

Page 264 "I will tell you. The White Mother": Julien Diary, August 13, 1874.

Page 264 "The White Mother has white children": Bagley Diary, August 13, 1874.

Page 265 "Well, it seems to me": Bagley Diary, August 13, 1874. The actual words quoted by Bagley are "Well, it seems to me that the Great White Mother must be a woman of very easy virtue." The somewhat prim Bagley admits he cleaned it up.

Page 265 "She sent these braves to": Julien Diary, August 13, 1874.

Pag 265 "The interpreter tells me that": French Diary, August 14, 1874.

Page 265 "The Indians came over and": McIllree Diary, August 13, 1874.

Page 266 "'Oh! Look out!' Carscadden warned": Carscadden Diary, August 13, 1874.

Page 267 "After breakfast took the gun": McIllree Diary, August 15, 1874.

Page 267 "The chief consulted their": Report of Surgeon John Kittson, December 19, 1875. In the *North West Mounted Police Report for 1875.*

Page 269 "What're they saying?": Based on Bagley Diary, Carscadden Diary, McIllree Diary, August 13–15, 1874.

Page 270 "For the fellow who had": Julien Diary, August 14, 1874.

Chapter 9

Interlude

Page 272 "Pemmican is first rate stuff": McIllree Diary, August 17, 1874.

Page 273 "I find he has purchased": French Diary, August 18, 1874.

Page 274 "Marched about 9 to a pond": French Diary, August 19, 1874.

Page 274 "I hope you were not": William Parker to his mother, August 19, 1874.

Page 275 "Marched 25 miles and halted": Carscadden Diary, August 22, 1874.

Page 276 "Raining all last night": Bagley Diary, August 22, 1874.

Page 276 "Stopped about 10:30 where there": McIllree Diary, August 20, 1874.

Page 277 "An' is it standin' there": Bagley Diary, August 25, 1874.

Page 277 "Did you fayed my": Bagley Diary, August 20, 1874.

Page 277 "Honest traders!": Julien Diary, August 21, 1874.

Page 278 "agreeable": Carscadden Diary, August 22, 1874.

Page 278 "His nineteen years on the frontier": Gagnon Diary, September 16, 1874.

Page 279 "A man named Morrow": Bagley Diary, August 16, 1874.

Page 280 "Doing nothing in particular": McIllree Diary, August 26, 1874.

Page 281 "did not fancy our coming": Julien Diary, August 15, 1874.

Page 281 "As these Cypress Hills are": Bagley Diary, August 28, 1874.

Page 282 "Looks like business": Finlayson Diary, August 23, 1874.

Romance Returns

Page 283 "Good morning, sir,": Based on French Diary, September 2, 1874.

Page 283 "I took a carbine from one": French Diary, September 2, 1874.

Page 284 "Buffalo steaks for dinner": Bagley Diary, September 2, 1874.

Page 284 "There were some more going": McIllree Diary, September 2, 1874.

Page 285 "My comrades fell back": Julien Diary, September 2, 1874.

Page 287 "We were crossed today": Carscadden Diary, September 7, 1874.

Into the Valley of Death

Page 290 "But the Indians were so effeminate": D'Artigue, pp. 66, 68.

Page 291 "to keep all horses tied up": French Diary, August 20, 1874.

Page 291 "Our half-breeds suggested": Bagley Diary, August 30, 1874.

Page 293 "We gave them some tea": French Diary, September 4, 1874.

Page 293 "Our guide knows the road": French Diary, September 5, 1874.

Page 294 "Started at 2:30 p.m. to get": French Diary, September 6, 1874.

Theirs Not To Reason Why

Page 296 "Attention": Based on Carscadden Diary, September 9, 1874. Also Defaulters Book in Record Group 18, NAC lists punishments for this incident.

Page 297 "Biscuits were stolen from the wagons": Based on Carscadden Diary, September 9, 1874.

Page 297 "I'm sorry, sir": Ibid.

Page 298 "right hand": French to Hugh Richardson, op. cit.

Page 300 "The country is a barren waste": McIllree Diary, September 11, 1874. He expresses similar sentiments on September 9.

Page 300 "Three of B Troop's boys": Finlayson Diary, September 9, 1874.

Page 300 "It looks very much like starvation": Carscadden Diary, September 9, 1874.

Page 301 "I had a blanket taken": French Diary, September 10, 1874.

Page 301 "I shall never forget": Carscadden Diary, September 9, 1874.

Page 302 "God Save the Queen": Bagley Diary, September 11, 1874.

Page 302 "Confound their politics": Bagley Diary, September 11, 1874.

Page 303 "This night when our sufferings": Finlayson Diary, September 10, 1874.

Page 303 "Reveille at 4:30 a.m.": Carscadden Diary, September 9, 1874.

Page 304 "I begin to feel very": French Diary, September 10, 1874.

Page 305 "The commissioner and his guides": Bagley Diary, September 10, 1874.

Page 306 "I believe that there is": Carscadden Diary, September 10, 1874.

Turning Tail

Page 306 "a prairie hero": Julien Diary, July 14, 1874.

Page 308 "What's he say?": Denny, p. 35.

Page 310 "Our guide Morreau says": French Diary, September 12, 1874.

Page 310 "We are lost on": Finlayson Diary, September 11, 1874.

Page 310 "The depression seems": Bagley Diary, September 12, 1874.

Page 311 "There is but one opinion": French Diary, September 12, 1874.

Page 312 "five forts between the Milk": French to Hewitt Bernard, Deputy Minister of Justice, December 29, 1873.

Page 312 "And on August 12": French to Hugh Richardson, Ministry of Justice, August 12, 1874.

Page 312 "The extermination of this den": Carscadden Diary, September 14, 1874.

Page 314 "Two men came in": French Diary, September 14, 1874.

Page 315 "Fancy bumping into you": based on McIllree Diary, September 14, 1874, Denny, p. 35.

Page 316 "They had been one hundred": Denny, p. 35.

Page 316 "They had been up the Bow": French, Official Report to the Minister of Justice, January 1875.

Page 317 "At last. At last": Carscadden Diary, September 12, 1874. (Carscadden has no September 12 notation, the quote appearing on September 11, but the events clearly happened on the twelfth.)

Page 317 "This march had all the": *Scarlet and Gold,* Diamond Jubilee Edition, p. 12.

Page 317 "Sub constable Thornton, who": Bagley Diary, September 16, 1874.

Page 318 "Commissioner's Lake.": French Diary, September 15, 1874.

Page 318 "Hurrah for Le Colonel!": French Diary, September 15, 1874; Bagley Diary, September 15, 1874.

Chapter 10

Benton

Page 322 "Greetings!": McDougall, *On Western Trails in the Early Seventies*, pp. 174–192.

Page 323 "'Cause I'm Fred Watcher": Ibid.

Page 323 "I'm afraid there is only myself": Ibid.

Page 324 "Oh, but Parson, we don't": Ibid.

Page 326 "John the Baptist": Ibid.

Best Wishes

Page 326 "Reveille at 6 a.m.": Bagley Diary, September 18, 1874.

Page 326 "Splendid camp.": Bagley Diary, September 19, 1874.

Page 328 "This evening an overgrown lout": Bagley Diary, September 20, 1874.

Page 329 "This is my sixteenth birthday": Bagley Diary, September 22, 1874.

Page 329 "He left here with the": Finlayson Diary, September 28, 1874. Though he makes this remark nearly a week after French departs, he is clearly referring to the day the commissioner left.

Page 332 "Sometimes we've hired": Based on Denny, pp. 39–45; Sharp, *Whoop-Up Country*, p. 88; J.P. Turner, *The North West Mounted Police*, Volume 1, pp. 159–66; Berry, *The Whoop-Up Trail*, p. 77; Nevitt, *A Winter at Fort Macleod*, p. 19; Dempsey, *Jerry Potts, Plainsman,* pp. 13, 14.

Page 332 "Got just the man": Ibid.

Page 332 "obtained the full particulars": French Diary, Sepember 25, 1874.

Page 333 "nailing all the ruffians": French to Colonel Hugh Richardson, September 25, 1874.

Page 333 "generally very low.": French Diary, September 25, 1874.

Page 333 "Started at noon, rather a": French Diary, September 26, 1874.

Page 333 "A good deal of trouble": French Diary, September 27, 1874.

Marching to Many Ghosts

Page 335 "Whiskey": Steele, p. 76.

Page 337 "Most of us washing": Finlayson Diary, September 27, 1874.

Page 337 "Reveille at 4 a.m.": Finlayson Diary, September 29, 1874.

Page 337 "Reveille at 6 a.m.": Finlayson Diary, September 30, 1874.

Page 338 "Reveille at 6 a.m.": Finlayson Diary, October 1, 1874.

Page 338 "Reveille at 6 a.m.": Finlayson Diary, October 2, 1874.

Page 338 "Being in a stationary camp": Finlayson Diary, October 3, 1874.

Page 339 "A party of men": Finlayson Diary, October 4, 1874.

Page 339 "Reveille at 6 a.m.": Finlayson Diary, October 5, 1874.

Page 340 "Reveille at 5:30 a.m.": Finlayson Diary, October 6, 1874.

Page 340 "Reveille at 5:30.": Finlayson Diary, October 7, 1874.

Page 340 "They don't look like": Based on Denny, pp. 39–45; Sharp, p. 88; Turner, Volume 1, pp. 159–66; Berry, p. 77; Nevitt, p. 19; Dempsey, *Jerry Potts, Plainsman*, op. cit.

Page 341 "Nudder hill": in Dempsey, op. cit., p. 7.

Page 342 "Bad medicine. Many ghosts": Based on Denny, op. cit.; Sharp, op. cit.; Turner, op. cit.; Berry, op. cit.; Nevitt, op. cit.; Dempsey, op. cit.

Page 343 "Where are we going?": Ibid.

Page 343 "That I am," he responded": Ibid.

Page 344 "So your story is that": Ibid.

Page 344 "Let this be fair warning": Ibid.

Page 344 "I've got the authority to": Macleod to W.F. Sanders, August 10, 1877, cited in Sharp, p. 110.

Epilogue

Page 346 "Three years ago when the Mounted": Horrall, p. 64.

Page 347 "Our progress was slow": Steele, p. 73.

Page 348 "To travel in such a": D'Artigue, p. 61.

Page 349 "[A] romantic scene took place": D'Artigue, p. 71.

Page 350 "Reveille at 6:30 a.m.": Bagley Diary, September 28, 1874.

Page 350 "We are pestered at night": Carscadden Diary, p. 59. (He cites no specific dates between September 14 and October 2. On the march back east, Carscadden is sparse with his dates.)

Page 350 "Colonel French arrived in camp": Bagley Diary, September 29.

Page 351 "The Comr brings with him": Carscadden Diary, p. 62.

Page 351 "As we expect to reach": Bagley Diary, October 14, 1874.

Page 352 "This march to Qu'Appelle": Carscadden Diary, p. 69.

Page 352 "One man from each tent": Bagley Diary, October 16, 1874.

Page 352 "This tedious march lasted ten": Carscadden Diary, p. 70.

Page 353 "[T]he Comr starts for Fort": Carscadden Diary, p. 74.

Page 354 "The column was a wonderful": William Parker's Reminiscences, p. 10. Also Parker to his brother Harry, November 28, 1874.

Page 355 "The uniform of Trumpeter Fred": Bagley Diary, November 14, 1874.

Page 355 "[W]e had to stand in": Carscadden Diary, p. 76.

Page 355 "After remaining in tents": Carscadden Diary, p. 80.

Page 356 "Stock taking all day": Bagley Diary, November 23, 1874.

Page 356 "I must say however that": Carscadden Diary, p. 76.

Page 357 "The Indians remain with us": Carscadden Diary, p. 81.

Page 357 "pretended furious attack": Bagley Diary, January 17, 1875.

Page 357 "After the Sergeant Major": Bagley Diary, January 17, 1875.

Page 358 "Acting Sergeant Crawford, and Sub": Bagley Diary, January 18, 1875.

Page 359 "Another matter I must refer": Carscadden Diary, pp. 86, 87.

Page 359 "I have managed so far": Bagley Diary, March 3, 1875.

Page 360 "McCarthy, the cook, received his": Bagley Diary, March 5, 1875.

Page 360 "Patches of earth are beginning": Bagley Diary, March 30, 1875.

Page 360 "We came here with 60": Carscadden Diary, p. 77.

Page 361 "not less than 10 lbs.": Report of Veterinary Surgeon, J.L. Poett, Swan Lake Barracks, November 12, 1875.

Page 361 "By this mail came news": Bagley Diary, April 2, 1875.

Page 361 "We now have bread": Bagley Diary, April 13, 1875.

Page 362 "Some amusement caused daily": Bagley Diary, May 13, 1875.

Page 362 "Queen's birthday was celebrated": Bagley Diary, May 24, 1875.

Page 362 "Our kit bags, which we": Bagley Diary, May 27, 1875.

Page 362 "This day, being the anniversary": Bagley Diary, June 6, 1875.

Page 362 "A Board of Officers inspected": Bagley Diary, June 15, 1875.

Page 363 "We look forward to his": Carscadden Diary, pp. 88, 89.

Page 363 "What is this, Captain": Bagley Diary, July 7, 1875.

The Rest Is History

Page 364 "for your complete disregard": Hewitt Bernard to Colonel French, January 12, 1875.

Page 364 "I have slaved night": Colonel French to Hewitt Bernard, February 9, 1875.

Page 365 "You white people": An interview with Harry Mills, quoted in Dempsey, *Jerry Potts, Plainsman*, p. 19.

Page 365 "A master of finesse": Steele, p. 277.

Page 365 "influence with the Blackfoot": Steele, p. 276.

Page 366 "Among the members": Bagley, '74 *Mounties*, p. 20.

Page 367 "Our mission was over": Julien Diary, final entry in October, no date given.

Page 367 "Have been laid up": McIllree Diary, September 26 and 29, 1874.

Page 370 "We companioned them": McDougall, *In the Days of the Red River Rebellion*, pp. 13–14.

Page 372 "Whiskey hunting is not": Donkin, p. 90.

Page 372 "Then pass the tea": written by Frank Carruthers, in Bagley, '74 *Mounties*, Appendix G.

Index